The Cavalry Horse

and his Pack

Col. John J. Boniface

Must Have Books
503 Deerfield Place
Victoria, BC
V9B 6G5
Canada
trava2911@gmail.com

ISBN: 978-1-77323-216-4

U. S. CAVALRY OFFICER ON CAMPAIGN.

"Formerly the unit was the regiment; it is now not the regiment, not even the troop or company; it is the individual soldier. In the circumstances of modern warfare the man must act far more on his own individual responsibility than ever before, and the high individual efficiency of the unit is of the utmost importance."

—*Theodore Roosevelt.*

CONTENTS.

v

ILLUSTRATIONS.

PREFACE.

To a large extent, any book on Cavalry is a compilation; it is very difficult, if not impossible, to write anything absolutely original on the subject, and, consequently, originality is not claimed for this work. Its object is to place in the hands of the young cavalry officer one volume embracing the duties and responsibilities which confront him from the moment he joins his troop, and to make clear to him how things are done in the cavalry service. The author has consulted all the professional works pertaining to the cavalry horse and his pack that were within reach, and to this has added the results of his own observations during ten years of cavalry service. To this he has added a vast amount of information obtained from those older cavalry officers who have made our cavalry service all that it is.

The desire has been to place in the hands of the new cavalryman a book in which he can find what recognized authorities have to say on the cavalry subjects treated of, as well as what our senior cavalry officers have found to be best under the varying conditions of garrison, march, and camp. No attempt has been made to touch upon tactical matters, it being intended to treat only of those practical daily duties which constantly confront us in field and post.

The clearest and most valuable information obtained has been that derived from personal experience and that given by our own senior officers of Cavalry.

There were many other interesting and valuable facts which came to hand in writing this book that it was desired to include in this volume, but to use them would have made the book unwieldy, and so they have been left out. However, as these omitted subjects are inseparably connected with those herein treated of, they will of necessity occur to the young officer as he studies the various chapters.

In placing this book before the service, the author bespeaks for it the generous consideration of his seniors, from whom we younger officers have learned whatever we may know of our own branch of the service, and who have given us such splendid past achievements that we must bestir ourselves mightily would we lead our own guidons as honorably. If the book has faults, the aim is lofty; and if it has not been reached, it is because the author's strength is not equal to his enthusiasm and love for our branch of the service. It is hoped that for many it will not be without charm, and for those new to the service, not without profit.

In cavalry knowledge, practice is worth more than theory, and each one has need of his own experience; that experience each one hastens to acquire for himself, and cares not to find it in books. Yet books are good, and this one is a record of facts; its truthfulness the author certifies, and offers this to the reader in compensation for whatever else may be found lacking. The older officers caution us: "Avoid the rocks on which we were once wrecked"; younger officers ever answer: "The sea on which you have sailed we, too, would brave in our turn, and we demand our right to be shipwrecked." But it pays to prepare ourselves as well as possible before we approach the water; getting wet through ignorance is disagreeable and unprofitable.

The writer desires especially to express his deepest appreciation to Colonel C. C. C. Carr, Fourth Cavalry, for his encouragement, advice, and revision of the proofs, and for placing at his disposal his forty-two years of splendid active cavalry experience; also to express sincere thanks to the War Department for the illustrations and professional papers placed at his disposal; to the Hon. F. D. Coburn, Secretary of the Board of Agriculture of the State of Kansas, not only for the excellent illustrations loaned, but for his generous help in every way; to Veterinarian Alexander Plummer, Fourth Cavalry, for his cordial advice and sound suggestions regarding diseases of cavalry horses and their treatment; to Assistant Chief Packer Mooney, of the Army, for his kindly assistance in helping him procure the excellent illustrations on packing and for much good advice and information on the subject of pack-mules and pack-trains generally; and to the Mehlback Saddle Company for the many fine illustrations freely loaned.

Jno. J. Boniface,

First Lieutenant, Fourth Cavalry.

School of Application for Cavalry and Field Artillery, Fort Riley, Kansas, May 25, 1903.

BOOKS CONSULTED.

The author desires to make a general acknowledgment of the assistance he has found in the preparation of this book in the many standard works in the Military Library of the Cavalry and Field Artillery School at Fort Riley, Kansas. Nearly all the works in that library and many others bearing upon the subjects treated of in this book have been carefully consulted and often freely quoted. A partial list of the works consulted appears below:

Facts for Horse-Owners, . . .	Magner
Journals of the United Service Institution, .	
Maxims for Training Remounts, . .	Blunt
How to Tell the Age of Domestic Animals, .	Liautard
Horses' Teeth, . . .	Clarke
Horses and Stables, . . .	Fitzwygram
Journals of the Cavalry Association,	
Kansas State Agricultural Reports, .	
United States Agricultural Reports,	
Breeders' Gazette, New South Wales.	
Horses, Saddles, and Bridles, .	Carter
Seats and Saddles, . .	Dwyer
U. S. Cavalry Drill Regulations, .	
Army Regulations, . . .	
The Soldiers' Pocket-Book	Wolseley
Scientific Horse-Shoeing, .	Russell
Cavalry Outpost Duties,	De Brack, trans. by Carr
The Horse, . .	Youatt
The Exterior Horse, . . .	Goubaux and Barrier
Reports of the Smithsonian Institute,	
The Horse in Art and Nature,	Brown
The Horse, ...	Stonehenge
History of Cavalry,	Denison
Modern Cavalry, . .	Denison
Achievements of Cavalry, .	Wood
Letters on Cavalry, . .	Hohenlohe
Organization and Tactics,	Wagner
Security and Information, . . .	Wagner
Manual of Military Field Engineering,	Beach
Remount Systems Abroad,	War Department
Hand-Books of Foreign Armies, . .	British War Office
Les Passages de Rivières par la Cavalerie, .	Géraud

The Cavalry Horse and His Pack

CHAPTER I.

Brief History of the Horse and Pack.

Earliest Historical Mention—Original Home—African Horse Forefather of the Arab—Historical Proof—History of Original Arabian Blood—The South African Horse—All Thoroughbred Lineage Traceable to Original African Horse—Necessity of Pack Appreciated from Earliest Times—Constant Effort Necessary to Reduce Pack to Lowest Efficient Limit.

In all the ages for which we have authentic history, the horse has been the sturdy and esteemed servant of man; equally in the vocations of peace and productive industry, subduing the wilderness and its savages, whether human or brute, the march of armies or the shock of battle, he has borne a part conspicuous and potent, adapted and adaptable to innumerable forms of men's service this long, as no other animal, the time for his displacement is not yet, although evil prophets may proclaim the horseless age as already ushered in.

No machine of steam and steel, of cog or cam, no vapor-fed motor, no craft propelled by batteries or boilers can successfully succeed the Percheron at the plough, the Hackney at the carriage, the Patchen in light harness, or the Denmarks or Thoroughbreds for all saddle purposes, lazily cantering to my lady's hand, or fiercely charging as at Balaklava, Winchester, and Mars-la-Tour.

The horse has been used for purposes of war from earliest time, and while there has gradually developed during latter years a tendency on the part of some military men to belittle the services that have been rendered

1

by cavalry in modern wars, and also to predict for that branch of the service a diminishing sphere of action in future conflicts, let not the young cavalry officer concern himself along these lines. In order to controvert such narrow statements, reference is only necessary to the operations of cavalry in our own great Civil War, in the war between France and Germany, the war between Turkey and Russia, the colonial campaigns of our own country in the Philippines, and those of Great Britain in South Africa; all of these campaigns are replete with important work performed by cavalry, and well illustrate the great necessity for a sufficient amount of cavalry in active service. The changes in modern methods of war have not and will not diminish the prestige and importance of the cavalry arm; but, on the contrary, will demand of it greater skill, greater endurance, greater preparedness, greater peril, and there will be greater need of superior, well-trained horses and men.

The first we hear of the horse seems to be in the Bible, where we are told that Pharaoh pursued the Israelites with several hundred chosen chariots pulled by horses, and that he also pursued them with men on horses, about fifteen hundred years before the birth of Christ. Although modern Europe, England, and America owe much to Arabia for the improvement of breed, it may well be doubted whether horses were found in Arabia in very early times at all. The author of the Book of Job, in describing the wealth of that patriarch, who was a native of Arabia and the richest man of his time, makes no mention of horses. Five hundred years later Solomon imported gold, silver, and spices from Arabia, but all the horses of his own cavalry he procured in Egypt. Among the articles exported from Egypt to Arabia in early times were horses. In the fourth century two hundred Cappadocian horses were sent by the Roman emperor as the most valuable present he could offer to a powerful prince of Arabia. So late as the seventh century the Arabs had few horses, for at the close of Mahomet's murderous campaign against the Koreish near Mecca, his captures contained thousands of camels and sheep, but no horses. These and many other circumstances sufficiently prove that however superior may be the present breed, it is comparatively lately that the present horse was naturalized in Arabia; indeed, the Arabs do not deny this, for until their horses began to be deservedly valuable, within the last century, they were content to limit their pedigree to one of five on which Mahomet and his four immediate successors fled from Mecca to Medina on the night of the Hegira.

At an early period in the history of war, as in the present day, strength, activity, endurance, and skill with weapons were the great qualifications for a soldier, and the skilled warrior who had the greatest endurance was likely to be successful; he, therefore, who, encumbered with defensive armor, had a long distance to march before coming to close quarters with his adversary was at a disadvantage by being out of breath and weary at the commencement of the conflict; this has, in all probability, been the cause of the first use of the horse in war. It was soon perceived that the soldier who could be carried without fatigue and placed fresh upon the spot where he would be obliged to exert every energy in deadly conflict would have a great advantage in a hand-to-hand struggle over one who had been obliged to march heavily laden for a long distance; this probably led to the invention of chariots of war. The earliest records prove clearly that these chariots were used to convey the warriors to the field of battle; on approaching the foe, the warrior, after throwing his projectile weapons, alighted from his chariot to engage in the inevitable hand-to-hand conflict, while the charioteer turned the horses' heads around towards camp and awaited nearby; the warrior, if wounded or hard pressed, could then conveniently retreat to his chariot, which was open to the rear and low to the ground, leap in, and be carried to the safety of his own camp. Homer gives many instances of the employment of these war chariots at the siege of Troy in his "Iliad"; in the fourth book, speaking of Agamemnon, he says: "He left his steeds indeed, and his brass variegated chariot, and these his servant Eurymedon, son of Ptolymeus, son of Pirais, held apart panting; him he strictly enjoined to keep them near him against the time when weariness should seize his limbs commanding over many."

This war chariot was used simply as a means of rapid conveyance, and there is no evidence in Homer of its being in itself used as an offensive weapon, nor is there any record of horses being mounted and made use of for the saddle. In the fifteenth book of the "Iliad," in a simile, Homer refers to a man mounting a horse in driving it to water, and vaulting on and off its back, and mentions it as a feat creating surprise, which leads to the inference that horsemanship as an art was almost unknown in his day. It is asserted by Père Amyot that chariots were in use in China as early as 2600 B. C., and that cavalry also were in use about the same time in that country. It is difficult to believe these statements, however, as the Chinese pride themselves upon their antiquity greatly, and one is apt to believe some of the Chinese history is like the Welsh gentleman's pedigree, which contained a note opposite the name of the tenth or twelfth member of his family, to the effect that about this time lived Adam in the Garden of Eden.

Chariots were used in India at a period more remote than the siege of Troy; in Egypt also chariots were in use in the eighteenth century before the Christian era, or more than five hundred years before the Trojan War. When Joseph was taken into favor by Pharaoh, he made him ride in the second chariot which he had, showing that chariots were in use for some purpose at that early date. This is the earliest mention of the *use* of the horse in history. The early term "horsemen" was at that time applied to the charioteers, and is often confounded with the present acceptation of the word, which means men *mounted* on horses. Horsemen are not represented on

Egyptian monuments, even upon those of a later date, while chariots are continually represented. If cavalry had existed, the artists of those days would certainly have represented them. In the Assyrian sculptures chariots appear first, and as horsemen come into use they also are represented. The first use of the chariot seems to be described in Genesis, forty-first chapter, forty-third verse, and this places the date at 1715 B. C.; and the first use of the chariot for war purposes is contained in Exodus, fourteenth chapter, ninth verse. History shows these chariots drawn by horses to have been used in the Trojan War, also used by Cyrus, also by the Britons against the Romans, and Herodotus mentions the Zaveces, a nation of Africa, as employing the chariots with their women as charioteers.

It is impossible to fix the period at which cavalry was first used; they were not known in Greece at the time of the Trojan War, or when Homer wrote. The Bible does not speak of cavalry until after the time of David; but when Herodotus wrote, cavalry was in general use in Asia, and had been for a long time. It is generally supposed that horsemen fighting as cavalry and riding on horseback came into use about one hundred and twenty years after the Trojan War. It is very likely, although there is no historical evidence of it, that the Scythians were the first people to use the horse to ride upon; once the custom was originated, it required but a very short time to make it universal. The Scythians were very skillful with horses, and continually in the habit of mounting them long before the Greeks had conceived the idea of men riding upon horses at all, for it is clear that the fable of the "Centaurs" was originated by the Greeks having seen or heard of the horsemen, whom they mistook for single animals, half man and half horse. About the year 885 B. C., Assyrian sculptures began to show mounted men, cavalry, and later on, in the years 722 to 705 B. C., the representations of the reigns of Sargon and Sennacherib show considerable cavalry. At first the horse of cavalry was peculiarly equipped; he wears a head-stall, a collar, and a string of beads; the trappings being almost the same as for the chariot horse of that time; the bit was a heavy species of snaffle; there appears no saddle; the seat of the earliest pictures is remarkable, showing the knees drawn up as high as the horse's back and pressed close against the neck and withers, the legs and feet being naked and hanging close to the shoulder. These cavalry representations in the early sculptures illustrate the very earliest ideas of mounted soldiers, and that the proper and natural way of sitting the horse was not then discovered.

Later, as the years roll by, many changes are observed. A pad or cloth, either square or of the shape of the modern saddle-cloth, is used in place of a saddle; it is usually fastened with a single girth, although sometimes a breast-strap and a species of crupper appear; all these are highly ornamented; there is a marked improvement in the seat; it is much more graceful and correct; the reins are now held in the left hand, the right being used for the spear; the collar disappears. Later, about 680 B. C., the saddle-cloth shows great enlargement and is made of thick hide or felt as a protection against missile weapons. The early Greeks had no cavalry; later on it came into use as a part of the army, and the horses were provided with defensive armor, while their riders wore boots and spurs, and their weapons were the lance, the long sword, and sometimes the javelin. The cavalry of the Greeks used neither saddles nor stirrups, nor were their horses shod; the troopers either mounted their horses bareback, or used a light rug or mat of skin upon which they sat. Alexander the Great was the first among the Greeks to employ cavalry to a great extent; he divided it into heavy (which used coats of mail, helmets, brazen greaves, swords, and short thrusting pikes), light (carrying only a sixteen-foot lance), and dragoons (intended to fight both on foot and on horseback). Alexander had one regiment of Thessalians and one of Macedonians in which the men and horses both were almost completely covered with armor. These two regiments were the flower of his cavalry. Alexander was the first to use the cavalryman and horse as a projectile weapon. In later years the Greek cavalryman was trained to sit well upright upon his thighs, and not as if in a chair, and was taught to cling to his seat with the thighs, letting the leg from the knee down hang loosely; the reins were carried in the left hand, and training in horsemanship was very popular. Xenophon, the earliest writer on the horse, tells how to choose with geat care the cavalry horse, and impresses upon the reader the necessity for caring for the feet, and advises standing the horses on smooth, round stones in order to harden the feet, as shoes were not then known. He advocates the occasional dismounting of the troopers to relieve the horses, when in field service.

If the early legends which form the basis of the first period of Roman history are entitled to any credence, it is clear that the mounted service was both understood and made use of to a certain extent from the very foundation of the state, although the persons whose names are mentioned in connection with it were probably mythical. Romulus had three troops of one hundred men each, as a sort of body-guard, made up of the patrician youths; these were armed with sword and javelin, and were trained to fight both mounted and dismounted. The social class from which the Roman Cavalry was drawn was the highest, both in rank and wealth, in the community. This seems to have been the custom in all the early nations, except some of the Greek States. The Romans were the first to use the curb-bit. They used neither saddles nor stirrups; a pad or covering was used to sit upon, and this was kept in place by a girth, a breast-leather, and a crupper. Their sole defense was a round shield, covered with ox-hide, and a helmet. They had lances, swords, and javelins. As they were lightly armed—in fact, almost destitute of protection—they incurred great risks. Later on armor came into Roman use. The Carthaginian Cavalry, under Hannibal, wore coats of mail, helmets, brazen greaves, and carried swords and a short thrusting-pike. The Numidian Cavalry was Hannibal's best mounted force; their horses were small, thin animals, and were ridden without saddles; the men were poorly equipped—in fact, almost naked—and the horses were managed with whips or thongs of leather. These Numidian troopers performed such enormous service that it is hard to realize they were so badly equipped. They used no reins nor bridles, for Polybius, in describing the battle of the Ticinus, speaks of the heavy cavalry *with reins* being placed in the center, and the Numidians, *without*, on the flanks. Strabo says that "the Numidian directed his horse with a small rod, and, without being led, the horses would follow their troopers like dogs." The corroborative testimony of Polybius, Strabo, Silius Italicus, Herodianus, and Virgil confirms the statement that the Numidian used no reins. Later, under Publius Scipio, the Roman Cavalry was modelled after the Greek, then considered the best. Great training of the individual trooper was given, and it is interesting to note that each trooper "was taught to make the right or left about face." The Romans, from earliest time, used both bridle and reins. There were no stirrups used until nearly two hundred years after the invention of the saddle, or about the end of the sixth century. There is some difference among early writers about the Roman shoeing; it is certain they did not use the iron shoe with nails. In Greece we know the iron shoe was not used, for Xenophon tells us how to harden the hoof. It is certain, however, that the Romans conceived the idea of an artificial covering as protection to the horse's foot, for it is a well-established fact that mules and beasts of burden were sometimes provided with a metal or wooden shoe, called "solea," which was held in place by thongs of leather crossed over the hoof. Suetonius tells how Nero went with two thousand mules to compete at the Olympic games, and all these mules were provided with shoes consisting of a plate of silver attached to the hoofs by thongs. The mules used by Poppæa are said, on the same authority, to have been shod with shoes of gold. All these statements prove the use of horseshoes of one kind or another during the Empire, and although there is no direct evidence that the cavalry horse was shod, it is fair to assume that the Romans would not have neglected them when they used shoes on mules and other beasts of burden. The earliest positive evidence of the use of horseshoes nailed to the hoof is that furnished by the skeleton of a horse found in the tomb of Childeric I. with shoes fastened in that way; this was found in 1653. Childeric I. reigned A. D. 458 to 481, so this fixes the date of horseshoes as far back at least as 480.

Cæsar employed thousands of Germans in his cavalry; they rode their horses without pad or saddle-cloth of any kind, and considered the use of pads as a gross luxury, so much so that they never hesitated to attack any cavalry that was found riding upon pads or cloths. The early Spanish Cavalry were trained to dismount, fasten their horses by pickets attached to their bridles, and then fight on foot. This is believed to be the first historical knowledge of picketing horses, and has come down to us as the lariat and picket-pin. Later on, we find the Parthian Cavalry mounted on fleet and active animals, using a headstall and single rein and the horses ridden with hardly any equipment. By the year 312 we find the Roman Cavalry completely covered in armor, horses as well as men, and both very heavy.

In the feudal ages the Saracen Cavalry occasionally wore breast-plates to protect the horses; they wore cuirasses, boots, gauntlets, and other defenses, and were much given to embellishing their bits with silver ornaments. They used the lance, battle-axe, and sword. The Greek Cavalry at this period, as given us by the Emperor Leon, wore gauntlets of iron, breast-plates and frontlets of iron or felt on the horses; the bits were strong and large, and the saddles, which by this time had come into general use, were roomy in the seat, had two stirrups, a valise and a saddle-bag in which could be carried three ·

or four days' provisions. Shoes of iron were in use also, fastened by nails to the hoof; the horse-trappings were ornamented with a tuft or plume upon the head, several

KNIGHT IN ARMOR.

on the saddle-cloth, as well as one hanging from the horse's jaw. Attached to the saddle was a sheath containing a battle-axe with a blade on one side and a point on the other.

During the age of chivalry every knight or member
of the order of chivalry was beyond everything a cavalier,
and his title to his rank was primarily based upon his reputation as a cavalry soldier. No brief history of the cavalry service would be complete without a reference to the
time when the cavalry service contained within its ranks
all the warriors, the statesmen, the nobles, and the gen-
erals of the age. The highest ambition during this time
was to be able as a skillful cavalier to enter the order of
knighthood. There were many distinctions maintained
between the squires and the knights of this time, both in
dress and equipment. The squires were allowed only
ornaments of silver, gold being reserved for the exclusive use of the knights. The armors on horse and man
were superb and very heavy; many armors of the man
alone weighed two hundred pounds. So very heavy were
they, in fact, that at the battle of Zagonari, in 1423, the
only men who were killed were three knights, who, having
fallen from their horses, were unable to get up from the
mud, and were ridden over and miserably suffocated.
What must the weight have been on the horses at this
time? The knight was accompanied by two or more
squires. After getting on his horse, these men armed
him, and he then had to stay there. With the invention
of gunpowder these armors were at first thickened and
then gradually disappeared, leaving only small plates,
which may be likened to the present cuirass worn in some
of the foreign services for dress. Saddles, which are said
to have first been used by the Visigoths, and are thus
first mentioned by Sidonius Apollinaris in connection
with these people, were also enormous affairs for the
knights, having large projections added to them in front
and rear to support the heavy-armed man and to make the
seat more comfortable and more secure. The knight was
armed with an enormous lance and also carried a sword,
generally straight; some of these swords were seven and
eight feet in length. These swords were used by the knights
only after they had gotten off their horses. A small dagger

was attached to the pommel of the saddle at times, while
the heavy sword was worn usually on a belt on the left
side, and thus we keep the custom up, though, fortu-
nately, we have reduced its length and weight. Battle-
hammers and various other huge instruments were also
used. The noble knight charged down upon the enemy at
a dignified walk. The immense influence, socially, of chivalry, the great protection of the armor, the neglect of the
infantry service, and the contempt into which that service naturally fell when composed of only the lowest
classes, all tended to give the knights an exalted idea of
the cavalry service and a contempt for anything outside
of it. The tournaments, which were the only military
exercises of the knights during the Middle Ages, were the
great occasions for these huge, over-weighted cavalrymen
to display their mettle and skill. The introduction of
gunpowder changed all this armament, and although
the barbarian hordes of many wild districts had been
employing themselves as light, quick cavalry for hundreds of years, it was only after the armor on horse and
man was found to be useless against the projectiles from
firearms that it passed away gradually and light cavalry
service came into prominence the world over. The
advance of rapidity and penetration in firearms has
ever gone onwards, at times making sweeping strides,
and the rôle of cavalry, once that of merely walking up
to the enemy and engaging him, has become one of the
most complicated and brilliant rôles of any branch in the
world.

The changes caused by this invention, however,
were very gradual, for it took many years for the invention of gunpowder to be so utilized, and the weapons
adapted to it to be so improved as to render its use
more effective than the old projectile weapons, which had
been brought to perfection; consequently we find for a
very long period both types of missile weapons used con-
temporaneously in most armies. Heavy cannon are first
mentioned in the year 1301, when the town of Amberg,

in Germany, had constructed a large gun; Ghent had them in 1313; Florence in 1325; the Germans in 1328; Edward III. used them at the siege of Cambrai in 1339 and at Crécy in 1346; cannon were introduced into Russia in 1389, and the Taborites used howitzers in 1434. Portable firearms were invented somewhat later, and are first mentioned among the Flemings about the middle of the fourteenth century; they were adopted at Perugia in 1364; at Padua in 1386; in Switzerland in 1392; they were continually being improved upon until in 1420, at the seige of Bonifacio in Corsica, leaden bullets, fired from a small hand-cannon, penetrated even the solid armor. Gradually came the later improvements, giving us the carbine and rifle, and the pistol came in 1521. Cartridges were first used in Spain in 1569, but in France not until 1644. Breech-loading firearms date from the beginning of the sixteenth century; they were all of German invention. Revolvers were of little use until the Colt's pistol was made, which is now the best of all and more used than any other.

During the sixteenth century the cavalry underwent many changes. Carabineers were instituted first in France under Henry II.; they were composed of light men, used a short arquebus, a pistol, and probably a sword; they formed a light cavalry. Dragoons also came into use about this time; according to Père Daniel, the creation of this arm is due to Marshal de Brissac, who is said to have first used them in Piedmont; the credit is given to Pierre Strozzi by Duparcq, however, and he states that in 1543—that is to say, seven years before the wars which De Brissac carried on in Piedmont—Pierre Strozzi placed five hundred arquebusiers on horseback, in order to save them from fatigue, with the idea of fighting on foot in case of need. Cuirassiers were another type of cavalry of about this time, and were first organized by Prince Maurice of Nassau in the wars in the Netherlands. These forces of cavalry were called "Cuirassiers" from the cuirass of steel worn on the person of the rider as a defense.

In Hungary we now see the Hussars, a light cavalry of a very formidable character. These troops were called "Hussars" from the Hungarian *huss*, which means the twentieth, and *ar*, pay. Their saddles were of very light wood and placed upon blankets folded; over the saddles were worn skins with the fleece outward, which covered the pistols and housings. The horses were ridden with bridoons instead of bits, so that they could pasture at the shortest halt without unbridling. These troops were light and well suited for foraging, reconnoitering, and outpost service. The Turkish Cavalry at this time had attained a high reputation; they were essentially light cavalry; they relied mainly on the curved sabre or cimeter; their horses were small, but spirited and well-trained and bitted. With the exception of the saddle, they were lightly equipped. They did not wear any armor at all; it was this ability to be quick that made them such excellent light cavalry. In the Thirty Years' War under Gustavus Adolphus, the light cavalry wore no armor at all, and it was trained to charge at full speed. Even in the time of Napoleon, cavalry charges were often made at no faster gait than the trot, so this charging by Adolphus' cavalry at full speed was remarkable at this early time. About the end of the fifteenth century we begin to hear of the cavalry in Russia, known as the Cossacks. It is said that there were Cossacks in the army of Ghengis Khan in 1224. The Cossacks are mentioned in the year 1444, when the Moscow militia fought against the Tartar sultan Mustapha. We hear of them also in Poland in 1516, and before 1579 the Cossacks had fought against the Turks with the armies of Emperor Rodolph II. They were light cavalry in every sense of the word; they were armed in the same manner as the other Russian troops—that is, with sabers, lances, bows and arrows, and afterwards with pistols and carbines. These irregular horsemen were most valuable auxiliaries, and from this period they always formed a very important portion of the Russian Army.

The French Cavalry of Louis XIV. was magnificently equipped, and the most expensive body of soldiery maintained in Europe. The Dragoons were armed with long, straight swords and with muskets and bayonets; they at first carried no carbine; attached to the saddle each trooper carried an axe or intrenching tool fastened to the pommel. The German general Montecuculi, in 1664, armed his Cuirassiers with casques, breast-plates, back-plates and iron gauntlets reaching to the elbow; they carried the long sword, pistols, and carbines. The light cavalry were maintained in but small numbers, and were armed with sword and carbine. This general was especially partial to the lance; he used Dragoons and understood their use thoroughly.

The cavalry service from the earliest times, when the horse was used, as has been shown, simply to carry the warrior to the battle-field, down to the present time, has been distinguished by certain characteristics. The speed of the horse and the impetuous spirit that constant hard riding only can give, have distinguished the cavalryman for his dashing and chivalrous temperament, and his boldness and vigor have never been surpassed. No matter what changes have been made in the art of modern war, the great value of cavalry, on account of its mobility and speed, has always kept up its reputation and rendered necessary the maintenance of large bodies in all armies. The cavalry has always been pre-eminently qualified, no matter how mounted, armed, or equipped, to cope successfully with whatever enemies it has had against it. The light horse of the Persians, the Greeks, the Romans, and the later nations has been of incalculable service down to the present time. It has a reputation second to none other on earth, a prestige that makes its officers and troopers strong, self-reliant, capable, brave, and efficient. The young officer entering this service, then, should learn his work thoroughly and become, in spirit, in ability, in feeling, a part of it.

Nothing very definite is known of the original African horse. Those in Southern and Western Africa were introduced there by the Dutch, being imported from Ba-

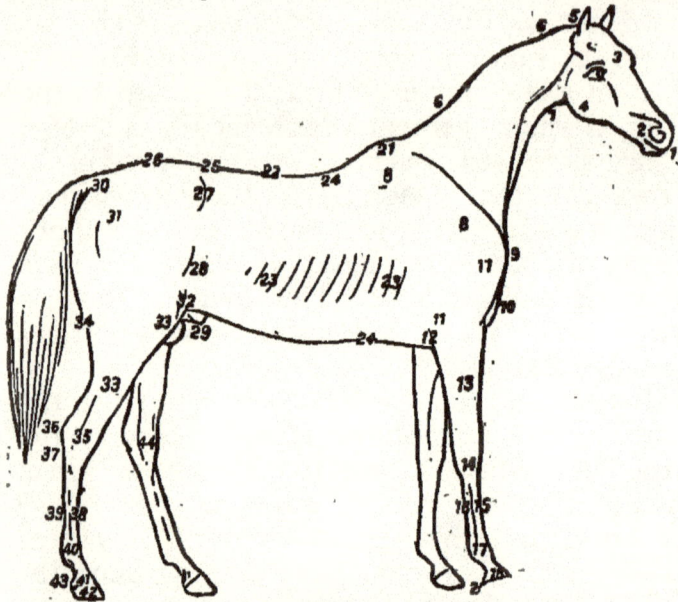

POINTS OF THE HORSE, WITH NAMES.

HEAD.

1, Muzzle.
2, Noatril.
3. Forehead.
4, Jrw.
5, Poll.

NECK.

6, 6, Crest.
7, Throttle or windpipe.

FORE QUARTER.

8, 8, Shoulder blade.
9, Point of shoulder.
10. Bosom or breast.
11, 11, True arm.
12, Elbow.
13, Forearm (arm).
14, Knee.
15, Cannon bone.
16, Back sinew.

17, Fetlock or pastern joint.
18, Coronet.
19, Hoof or foot.
20, Heel.

BODY OR MIDDLE PIECE.

21, Withers.
22, Back.
23, 23, Ribs (forming together the barrel or chest).
24, 24, The circumference of the chest at this point, called the girth.
25, The loins.
26, The croup.
27, The hip.
28, The flank.
29, Sheath.

30, The root of the dock or tail.

HIND QUARTER.

31, The hip joint, round, or whirlbone.
32. The stifle joint.
33, 33, Lower thigh or gaskin.
34, The quarters.
35, The hock.
36, The point of the hock.
37, The curb-place.
38, The cannon bone.
39, The back sinew.
40, Pastern or fetlock joint.
41, Coronet.
42, Hoof or foot.
43, Heel.
44, Spavin-place.
45, Chesnut.

tavia, Java, South America, and Persia. The gradual development of the skeleton and conformation into the modern horse must have been a slow one of thousands of years of breeding and feeding and use. The early North African horse of the Barbary States gradually became known as the "Barb," possessing pure Morocco blood, and it is probably from him that our modern well-bred horse has sprung.

The horse and his near allies, the ass and zebra, constitute the genus *Equus*, a small group of animals of the class *Mammalia* (an animal which suckles its young), so distinct in their organization from all other existing members of the class that in many of the older zoölogical systems they were placed in an order apart under the name of *Solidungula* (hard-hoofed animals). Investigations in comparative anatomy have demonstrated that their structure is but a modification of the same general plan upon which the tapirs and rhinoceroses are formed, and the discovery of the characters of extinct species by Cuvier during his searches into the fauna of the Paris Basin, continued in various European localities by Kaup, Gervais, Gaudry, Huxley, and others, and recently conducted on a more ample scale in the prolific fossiliferous strata of North America by Leidy, Marsh, and Cope, have revealed numerous intermediate stages through which the existing horses appear to have passed in their modification from a very different ancestral form.

We have as yet no cognizance of the history of any mammals of the group to which the horse belongs before the dawn of the Eocene Period; of where they lived and what they were like, from what earlier forms and by what stages of modifications descended, our actual knowledge is an absolute blank. We have, however, certain knowledge that when the land which formed the bottom of the great Cretaceous ocean which flowed over a considable portion of the present continents of Europe and North America was lifted above the level of the water and became fitted for the habitation of terrestrial animals, it was very soon the abode of vast numbers of herbivorous mammals belonging to the group now called *Ungulata* (hoofed animals). These various classes of animals be-

came soon separated widely, the chief distinction being
in the structure of the feet. These classes of "hoofed
animals" are now best known in the forms of the horse,
the tapirs, and the rhinoceroses, from which the other

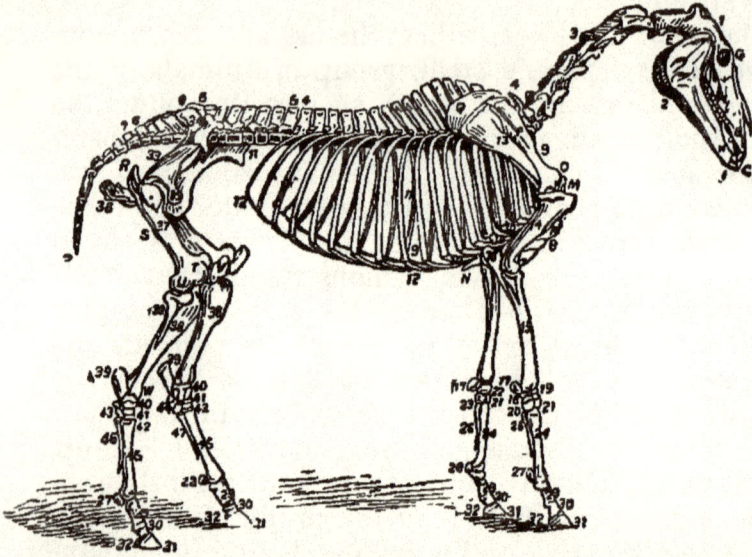

SKELETON OF MODERN HORSE, WITH NAMES OF PARTS.

A, Molar teeth.
B H, Canine or tusk.
C I, Incisors.
E, Atlas.
G, Orbit.
M, Cariniform cartilage.
N, Ensiform cartilage.
O, Coracoid process of scapula.
P, Spine.
Q, Cartilage.
R, Trochanter major.
S, Subtrochanterian crest.
T, Trochlea.
U, External condyle.
V, Patella.
W, Hock joint.
1, Cranium.
2, Lower jaw.
3, Cervical vertebræ.
4, 4, Dorsal vertebræ.

5, 5, Lumbar vertebræ.
6, 6, Sacrum.
7, 7, Coccygeal vertebræ.
8, Sternum.
9, 9, True ribs.
10, 10, Cartilages of true ribs.
11, 11, False ribs.
12, 12, Cartilages of false ribs.
13, Scapula.
14, Humerus.
15, Radius.
16, Elbow.
17, Os pisiforme.
18, 19, 20, 21, 22, 23, Carpal bones.
24, Large metacarpal bone.
25, Outer small metacarpal bone.

26, Inner small metacarpal bone.
27, 28, Sesamoid bones.
29, Pastern bone.
30, Small pastern bone.
31, Coffin bone.
32, Wing of the pedal bone.
33, 34, 35, 36, Os innominatum.
37, Femur.
38, Tibia.
39, Os calcis.
40, Astragalus.
41, 42, 43, 44, Tarsal bones.
45, Large metatarsal bone.
46, Outer small metatarsal bone.
47, Inner small metatarsal bone.

classes are but offshoots. Great as may be the present
difference between these animals, we can trace their history step by step, as revealed by the fragments preserved
from former ages, further and further back in time, their

differences continually becoming less marked and ulti-
mately blending together, if not into one common ances-
tor, at all events into forms so closely alike in all essen-
tials that no reasonable doubt can be held as to their common origin.

The remains of the earliest known animals to which it
is possible to trace back the modern horse by a series of
sucessive modifications are found in the lowest strata of
the great lacustrine formations assigned to the Eocene

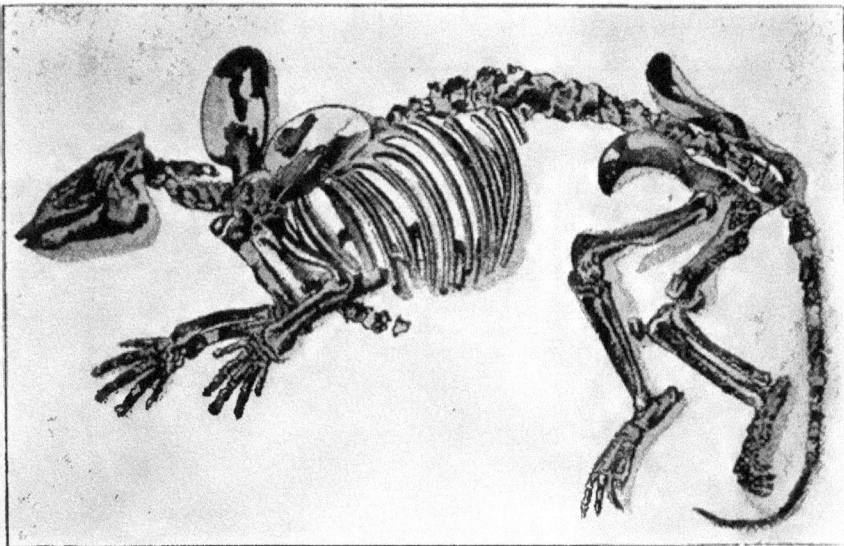

FOSSIL SKELETON OF THE HORSE WITH FIVE TOES.

Period, spread over considerable portions of the present
Territories and States of New Mexico, Wyoming, and
Utah. That similar animals may have existed in other
parts of the world is extremely probable. It is only
within recent years that these fossils have been discovered and brought to light. A little animal, scarcely
larger than a fox, presented the most generalized form as
yet discovered; besides the four well-formed toes of the
fore foot, it had at least a rudimentary fifth toe. The
transition from this horse-like animal of the early period

to the horses of modern times has been accompanied by a gradual increase in size. The diminutive Eocene animal above was succeeded by an animal about the size of the sheep in the Miocene Period; this again, in the Pliocene Period, was succeeded by an animal about the size of the donkey; and it is only in the Pleistocene Period that animals appeared which approach in size the present horse. Important structural changes have also taken place, owing to the changes in the life of these animals and the changed conditions of their work and surroundings. The neck has become elongated, the skull altered in form,

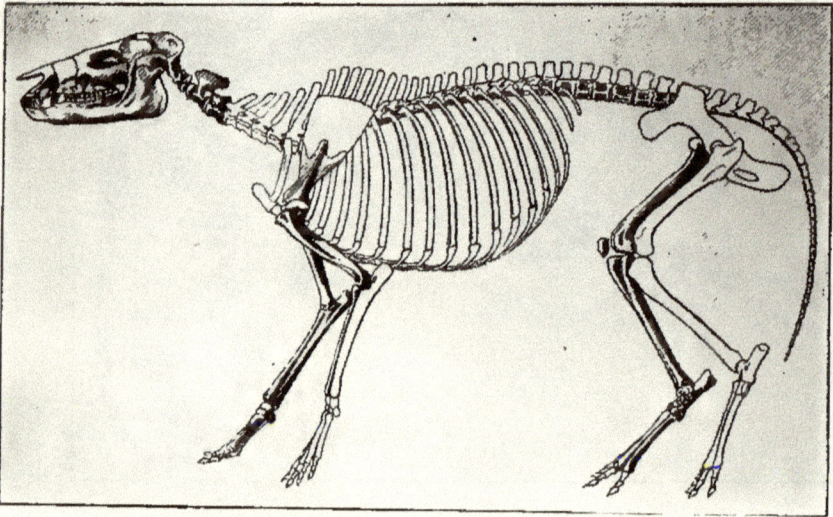

FOSSIL SKELETON OF THE HORSE WITH FOUR TOES.

the teeth greatly modified, the limbs lengthened, and the toes reduced in number to one.

The small horse-like animals of the Eocene Period with four, or rudiments at least of five, toes on the fore foot have already been mentioned. In the early Miocene Period the animal most like the existing horse was one the remains of which have been found both in Europe and America in a fossil state. In these fossils there were three well-developed toes, reaching the ground, on each foot. In later times the lateral toes were much reduced in size and did not reach the ground, though containing the full number of bones. Horses, or rather horse-like creatures, were later met with in the Pleistocene Period, whose feet, for the first time, showed the true horse exactly or nearly as we know it now, with but one toe. The outer toes were reduced to rudiments of the metacarpals or metatarsals only, the so-called "splint bones" being entirely concealed beneath the skin, and the middle toe, greatly elongated and broadened, forming the present hoof. Fossil remains of true horses, differing but very slightly from the smaller and inferior breeds of those own existing, have

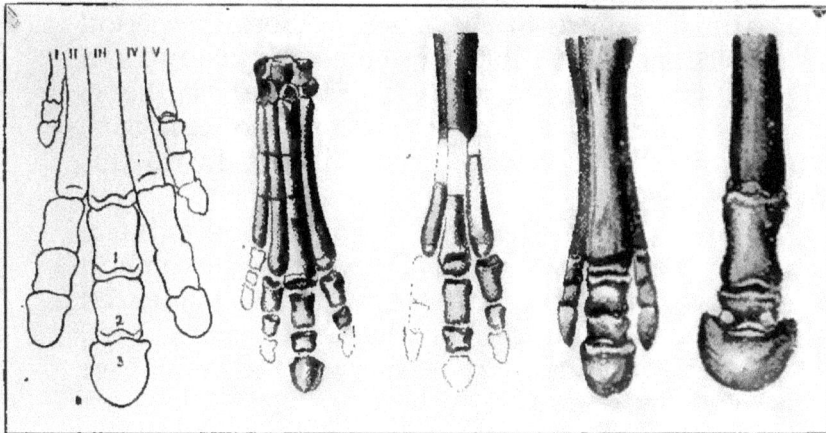

EVOLUTION AS SHOWN BY THE SKELETON OF THE FOOT.

been found abundantly in deposits of the most recent geological age in almost every part of America, from Escholtz Bay in the north to Patagonia in the south. In the southern continent, however, they became quite extinct, and no horses, either wild or domesticated, existed in either of the Americas at the time of the Spanish Conquest, which is the more remarkable, as, when introduced from Europe, horses proved, by their rapid multiplication into countless wild herds, that the climate, food, and other circumstances were highly favorable to their existence. The former great abundance of horses in

America, as revealed by fossil remains, and their later complete extinction, and their perfect acclimatization when reintroduced by the Spaniards, form curious but as yet unsolved problems in geographical distribution.

There are at present six distinct modifications of the horse type in existence, sufficiently distinct to be reckoned as species by zoölogists, and yet so closely allied the one with the other that they will, at least when in captivity or domesticated, breed with perfect freedom with any of the others. These are the horse, the common ass, the zebra, the quagga, the dauw, and the Asiatic wild ass.

From the evidence of philology, it is plain that the horse was already known to the Aryans before the period of their dispersion. The Bible is replete with instances of his early use, as has been shown. To say that the horse originated in Africa or in early Persia and Armenia is to conjecture only, and each cavalryman is left to do this for himself.

As our own American horse of good blood is but a descendant of the English horse of good blood, which in turn comes down from the Arabian, which, as evidenced above, is a descendant of the North African horse, etc., the above facts enable us to know more of the animal we ride in our cavalry to-day.

Ever since the horse has been known to man, use has been made of him for saddle purposes both in peace and war; without him military history would be barren of those stirring events with which we are all so familiar, and which make us look forward to the achievements of our cavalry in all future wars. From the very beginning, no doubt, riders in all lands devised ways and means of carrying with them on horseback the simple necessities of camp and field. Every cavalry service has found it absolutely imperative to carry equipment, clothing, ammunition, and rations upon the individual horse, and it is an interesting study to read of the many experiments tried in all armies for the improvement of the cavalry horse and the packing and carrying of necessities on his back. No tribe or nation has ever ridden long without devising some simple means of carrying on horseback those indispensable articles necessary to the welfare and protection of both horse and rider. In early times the pack consisted of a rude affair in which necessary articles were tied together and hung in front and behind the rider over crude saddles made of the skins of wild animals sewn roughly to sticks or arches, and it has only been with the knowledge and experience which come with time and study and skill and usage that these barbaric contrivances gradually assumed modern forms, until to-day the pack is a wonderful and scientific arrangement, upon which improvement would be difficult.

It was quickly realized that the less the pack and the more carefully it was adjusted the more service would the horse render; that it should be hung low to help the horse preserve his natural equilibrium; that it should not chafe the horse nor interfere with his free action at all gaits; finally, that the horse himself should be well trained, well bred, well cared-for, and his rider fearless and skillful and considerate. These were the cardinal principles governing the handling of the cavalry horse and his pack ages ago, and they apply equally well to-day.

There is a limit quickly reached in the breeding of cavalry horses and in the reduction of the cavalry pack; the first depending upon the horse supply of the country in which the cavalry is raised, the average price paid by the Government, the climate, the method of purchase, and especially the demand; the second depending upon the country in which the cavalry is to operate and the importance of independence and efficiency in all the various duties cavalry is called upon to perform, for the pack is lighter or heavier according to season, service, resources, and climate.

CHAPTER II.

CLASSES OF CAVALRY.

Heavy Cavalry—Medium—Light—Different Classes of Each—Interchangeability of Designations—Arms—Equipment—Weight of Men and Horses in Each Class—Height of Horses in Different Classes—Austrian Cavalry—English—Russian—Belgian—German—French—American.

Cavalry is not merely good men mounted on good horses and armed with modern weapons and a good supply of ammunition. The history of the first two years of the Cavalry in the Civil War amply demonstrated this, at an enormous expense to the Government. Volunteer cavalry regiments, hastily organized, mounted, and armed, lasted but a comparatively brief time, owing to ignorance and carelessness in the care of horses and the lack of time to train them in cavalry work. As a result these regiments were constantly having to be supplied with remounts, until finally the Cavalry Bureau was organized in 1863 to take charge of everything pertaining to the Cavalry. It was not until these regiments had learned cavalry life by nearly three years of active war service that results were commensurate with the expense of keeping them in creditable condition.

In no branch of an army is ignorance or carelessness so costly as in its cavalry arm. Horses are not merely machines of speed. Endurance for arduous service can be expected and acquired only when the horses are guarded jealously against all unnecessary harsh treatment, and when feeding, watering, saddling, packing, grooming, marching, and camping are well understood and systematic methods employed.

In the cavalry arms of nearly all foreign services, the cavalry is divided into two and sometimes into three

24

classes, known as light, medium, and heavy cavalry
In the American and Austrian Cavalry services no such
distinctions are made. Where these distinctions are
made, the chief difference among the classes is in the
weight of men and horses; the name of the class itself
indicating whether the horses and men are light weight,
heavy weight, or medium weight. However, there is
considerable distinction between the rôle of heavy cavalry and the other; to use an old quotation, "No carpenter would use his mallet as a hammer, or his chisel as a
saw"; and it would be the grossest folly to employ heavy
cavalry on reconnoitering duty, on raiding, patrols, or
screening duty, if either light or medium cavalry form
part of the cavalry with the army. Medium cavalry
exists only in one or two of the European armies, and the
line of distinction between it and the light cavalry is not
always clearly defined, and for this reason the division of
cavalry into heavy and light seems the more reasonable.
In mounted shock-action heavy cavalry finds its proper
field, while in all the arduous varying duties of patrolling,
screening, reconnoitering, raiding, escorting, and scouting light cavalry stands pre-eminent. No better definition of light cavalry can be imagined than that given by
that splendid light-cavalryman, De Brack, himself a pupil
of La Salle, Montbrun, Colbert, and Pajol: "Light cavalry is to precede our column, scouting our flanks, surrounding them and concealing them with a bold and vig-
ilant curtain, following the enemy step by step, haras-
sing and annoying him, discovering his designs, exhausting his forces in detail, destroying his magazines, captur-
ing his convoys, and finally forcing him to expend in
defensive operations the strength from which he might
otherwise have reaped the greatest advantage."

The British Cavalry is divided into Dragoon Guards,
Dragoons, Hussars, and Lancers. The Dragoon Guards are
heavy, its most illustrious regiments being the Household Cavalry; the Dragoons are medium, and the Hussars and Lancers are light. The horses of the British

Cavalry are about the same, averaging 15½ hands high and 1090 pounds in each class. The men in the light cavalry are from 5 feet 4½ inches to 5 feet 6 inches; in the medium,

BRITISH CAVALRYMAN ON HORSE.

5 feet 6 inches to 5 feet 8 inches; and in the heavy, 5 feet 8 inches to 5 feet 10 inches. Thus, very light men under 5 feet 4½ inches are excluded from light cavalry,

and large, powerful men over 5 feet 10 inches are excluded from the heavy. A distinction is made in the horses as well as in the men, the light cavalry getting the lightest horses to go with their light men, and the heaviest horses to go with the heaviest men. All British Cavalry are armed

BRITISH INDIAN LANCER AND HORSE.

with carbine and saber, and officers and non-commissioned officers carry pistols, and the Lancers in addition carry the lance. Equipment and accessories composing the pack vary according to the service; and the pack, owing to the vast difference in service in England's many colonies, varies greatly in weight.

The German Cavalry is divided into Cuirassiers, Uhlans, Dragoons, and Hussars. The Cuirassiers and

GERMAN UHLAN MOUNTED.

Uhlans are heavy, and the Dragoons and Hussars are light. In the heavy cavalry the average weight of horses is 1083 pounds, and the average weight of the trooper is

187 pounds.   In the light cavalry the horses average about 950 pounds in weight and the troopers 143 pounds. All the German cavalry regiments are armed with the

RUSSIAN CAVALRY SOLDIER MOUNTED.

lance, saber, and carbine, and officers and non-commissioned officers carry revolvers.

The Russian Cavalry is divided into Cuirassiers, Uhlans, Dragoons, and Hussars, largely similar in weight

COSSACK OFFICER MOUNTED.

and size to the German.   The Cuirassiers and Uhlans are heavy, and the Dragoons and Hussars are light.   All the cavalry regiments are armed with saber and rifle with bayonet, and the officers and non-commissioned officers carry pistols.

The Belgian Cavalry is divided into Chasseurs, Lancers, and Guides. The Guides are heavy, and the Chasseurs and Lancers are light. The Chasseurs and Guides

RUSSIAN HUSSAR OFFICER MOUNTED.

are armed with carbine and saber; the Lancers carry the lance, the carbine, and revolver.

The Austrian Cavalry is not divided into light and heavy. Its Cavalry is known as Dragoons, Hussars, and Lancers, but all are considered light cavalry; all are sim-

AUSTRIAN HUSSARS IN FIELD UNIFORM.

ilarly armed and equipped, carrying the saber and magazine carbine, and the officers revolvers.

The French Cavalry is divided into Cuirassiers, Dragoons, Chasseurs-à-Cheval, Hussars, Chasseurs d'Afrique, Spahis, volunteer scouts, and remount companies. The

Cuirassiers are heavy cavalry, the Dragoons are known as Cavalry of the Line, and all the others are light cavalry. The Dragoons and light cavalry are armed with a magazine carbine of small caliber and sabers; the officers and sub-officers being armed with revolvers in place of

AUSTRIAN DRAGOONS IN FIELD UNIFORM.

the carbine. Each man in the cavalry also has a dynamite cartridge weighing about 3½ ounces attached to the saddle.

The American Cavalry before the Civil War was composed of mounted regiments as shown in the following table.

FRENCH HUSSAR SOLDIER MOUNTED

FRENCH CUIRASSIER MOUNTED.

First Dragoons, organized by Act of Congres March 2, 1833;

Second Dragoons, organized by Act of Congress, May 23, 1836; converted into a regiment of Riflemen by Act of August 23, 1842; reconverted into Second Dragoons again by Act of April 4, 1844;

. Mounted Rifles, organized by Act of Congress, May 19, 1846;

First Cavalry, organized by Act of Congress, March 3, 1855;

Second Cavalry, organized by Act of Congress, March 3, 1855.

On May 4, 1861, one new cavalry regiment was organized by direction of the President and designated the Sixth Cavalry; this action of the President was confirmed by an Act of Congress on July 29, 1861.

On August 3, 1861, the designations of these regiments were changed by an Act of Congress, as follows:

The First Dragoons became the First Cavalry;

The Second Dragoons became the Second Cavalry;

The Mounted Rifles became the Third Cavalry;

The First Cavalry became the Fourth Cavalry;

The Second Cavalry became the Fifth Cavalry;

The Sixth Cavalry remained the Sixth Cavalry.

After the Civil War four new cavalry regiments were organized, as follows:

Seventh Cavalry, by Act of Congress, July 28, 1866;

Eighth Cavalry, by Act of Congress, July 28, 1866;

Ninth Cavalry (colored), by Act of Congress, July 28, 1866;

Tenth Cavalry (colored), by Act of Congress, July 28, 1866.

The colored regiments were composed of colored enlisted men, the officers being white.

At the outbreak of the Spanish-American War in 1898, therefore, the American Cavalry was composed of the above ten regular regiments, all designated simply "Cavalry," each regiment possessing approximately 1,000 officers and men. Various volunteer cavalry organizations were mustered into the United States service for this war, in a somewhat similar manner to that adopted during the Civil War. Also similarly, these volunteer regiments were later mustered out of service when no longer needed.

On February 2, 1901, five new cavalry regiments were added to the Regular Establishment, as follows:

Eleventh Cavalry, by Act of Congress, February, 2, 1901;

Twelfth Cavalry, by Act of Congress, February 2, 1901;

Thirteenth Cavalry, by Act of Congress, February 2, 1901;

Fourteenth Cavalry, by Act of Congress, February 2, 1901;

Fifteenth Cavalry, by Act of Congress, February 2, 1901.

And the above is the present approximate strength and the present designations of the American Cavalry.

From 1861 all regiments have been designated simply "Cavalry," and are practically light cavalry, as American Cavalry has ever been. The cavalry work in our early wars, in the Civil War, in our Western campaigns, and in our more recent colonial campaigns, has distinctly been light cavalry work, although designated under the common head of "Cavalry." Judging by the size and weight of our men and horses, American Cavalry might better be termed Dragoons, but its work has always been that defined by De Brack as light cavalry work, and such we really are, and such our work and training have always made us. Indeed, the Dragoon is generally a light cavalry man. In the British Cavalry Dragoons are medium, but in the other services Dragoons

are classified generally as light. The classifying of the
Cavalry as medium is surperfluous. There is no well-
defined set of duties for medium cavalry, and it being
in no sense a heavy cavalry, it is wiser to call it light
and obviate a meaningless designation. Under Sheri-
dan, Wilson, Merritt, Minty, Buford, Bayard, "Grimes"
Davis, Farnsworth, Ulrich Dahlgren, Pleasanton, Stone-
man, and others on the Union side, Morgan, Stuart, For-
rest, and others on the Confederate, American Cavalry did
all that De Brack's definition implied.

Referring again to the quotation used in the early
part of this chapter, that "No carpenter would use his
mallet as a hammer, or his chisel as a saw," it cannot be
impressed upon the cavalryman too forcibly that this
cavalry maxim is the deduction of all great cavalry leaders from their own experience in handling the different
classes of cavalry. In cavalry work, to obtain satisfactory results, the two classes must be used in their proper
field. While it often becomes necessary in campaigns to
utilize the available cavalry at hand in work for which it
was not intended, such work should be demanded only in
emergencies; better still, the cavalry should be husbanded
according to its character, and not frittered away in unnecessary details on courier, orderly, and headquarters work.
When its opportunity comes, its work will demand all its
strength and endurance, and there is no more speedy way
of ruining it than by utilizing it recklessly for the thous-
and minor duties occurring in war and field service,
duties which could far more economically and wisely be
performed by mere mounted orderlies from infantry
organizations. To husband the strength of horses and
men always is a lesson that we cannot learn too well.
We should not imagine, in our zeal to do well, that every
note must be carried at a mad gallop, every march made
a forced one, every camp a hardship, every bit of grooming a useless waste of time, or every man and horse
equally intelligent, enduring, and capable

CHAPTER III.

THE HORSE SUPPLY.

Definition of Term—Remounts—Horse Supply of England—Its
Remounts—Average Cost—Training—Horse Supply of Ger-
many—Its Remounts—Average Cost—Training—Of Russia—
Of France—Of Austria—Of America.

The term "horse supply" defined means simply the
horse population of the country of which mention is
made. Upon it depends the ability to raise and maintain
a cavalry force, to a large extent. Russia leads the world,
having the greatest horse supply of any country; next
to which comes America (the United States); then the
others: Austria, Germany, France, and England about
even, and the lesser countries proportionately smaller.

By the term "remount" is meant the horse purchased to fill up the vacancy caused in a cavalry service
by the loss of one of its horses. In time of peace the procuring of proper remounts is not a very difficult matter,
some countries supporting government breeding-farms
for this purpose, others supporting or partly supporting
studs only, while others procure their remounts by purchase. In time of war the subject of remounts becomes
one of the most important as well as one of the most
difficult to handle.

Germany possesses a horse supply of over 4,000,000,
nearly 3,000,000 of which are found in Prussia alone.
These enormous resources give Germany ample horse-
flesh from which to select its yearly remount of about
9,000 horses, the average price of which is $180, not
including the additional expenses of travel, etc. The
class of horses principally used for light cavalry purposes
comes from Prussia, Eastern Prussia, and is a mixture of
about 50 per cent pure English blood and 25 per cent

39

of Lithuanian or Oriental blood. Both in nature and looks the Eastern Prussian horse largely resembles the horse in Southern France known as the "Tarbeen." The minimum height for the different classes of cavalry is as follows: heavy cavalry, 16 hands; light cavalry, including its various classes, 15½ to 16 hands. The average weight carried by the light cavalry man is 250 pounds, and as an average a light cavalry horse lasts about ten years.

To the system of obtaining remounts for the German Cavalry and their splendid course of training before the animals are permitted to take part in drills is, in a great measure, due that wonderful precision of movement which marks all their mounted evolutions. The remount service of the German Government is considered of such importance that it is under a special department of the War Ministry, at the head of which there is an inspector-general of remounts with the rank of major-general. A brief description of this remount system will serve to show the great pains taken in Europe to produce superior cavalry horses, and it may be taken as the best system in existence.

In the first place, the entire country is divided geographically into six great circles, and to a certain number of the remount dépôts are assigned these territorial divisions for their sources of supply. Horses are, in times of peace, purchased at from three to four years old by commissions consisting of cavalry officers and veterinarians under the orders of the Remount Department of the War Ministry. This commission begins its work in May of each year and continues until September. The date at which purchases will be made is announced beforehand, so that sellers may have an opportunity to prepare. The number purchased is always 5 per cent over and above the number required, in order to make allowances for losses and those proving unfit for service. In the Bavarian and Saxony systems the remounts are sent directly to the regiments after purchase, but in the Prussian system they are distributed to four remount dépôts, where they are kept for a year, during which time they have an opportunity to develop. At the end of this time all remounts not unfit for the cavalry service are sent to their regiments. At the head of each remount dépôt is a civil official, the administrator, who is selected for his good judgment in regard to horses, his own good horsemanship, and his ability as an agriculturist. Under him is an accountant, with an inspector over each of the farms, from one to four under the administrator's charge. There are from one to three veterinary surgeons at each dépôt, and one forage-master for each farm. The grooms are hired civilians, and the remainder of the employees are old soldiers. The stables on these remount farms are mere closed sheds, in which the horses are never tied up, but are allowed free access at all times to the paddocks adjoining their stables. They are neither marked in any way except by a numbered ticket, nor shod, and receive only ten minutes' grooming a day. Their daily allowance of forage is 12 pounds of hay, 7½ pounds of oats, and 15 pounds of straw, with green food several months in the year. The cost of maintaining these animals is in some degree reduced by agricultural sales and by cattle-breeding, but it is stated that the annual cost of maintaining one animal averages $65.

Each regiment annually receives a certain number of horses and has an equal number condemned. Each regiment has in addition a remount fund, out of which it is at liberty to purchase young horses on its own account, the regiment having a right to sell at once any young horse which appears worthless as a cavalry animal during his first two years' service, and also of ridding themselves at once of an animal accidentally disabled. Thus the remount fund, before mentioned, accumulates from sales of this character, and also from the sales of the forage which has accumulated, due to the loss of such horses from the regiment. Once a year each regiment sends a detachment under charge of an officer to the dépôts to receive its authorized quota of remounts.

The training of the remounts at the remount dépôts receives the greatest attention. The greatest care is taken from the very beginning not to spoil their dispositions and to gradually accustom them to military duties. The first few weeks they are merely ridden around among the old horses to make them feel at home in their new surroundings and to accustom them to having the weight of a rider on their back. They are then gradually taught to allow their teachers to handle them on all parts of their bodies, and the greatest patience is exercised to give them confidence in their riders. Later on much attention is paid to jumping, and the remounts are taught first to go over the obstacle led alongside an old horse, and afterwards by themselves. Much importance is also attached to teaching the remounts the gaits and to proficiency in passing easily and promptly from one gait to another.

In order to be ready for the immense number of remounts which would be required in the event of war, a muster of all the horses in the empire is made every ten years. Every horse-owner is bound to produce for the committee who make the census in each department all his horses, excepting stallions, horses under four years of age, horses blind in both eyes, mares with foal, and horses worked underground in the mines. Out of this number submitted are picked riding and draft animals. On mobilization, each province must furnish the number of horses required, a fixed price being paid for them by the State. As a partial recompense for this obligation forced upon the people, the Government provides thoroughbred stallions for the service of mares throughout the country.

The war strength of the German Cavalry consists of 3,203 officers and 106,993 men, of which number 6,498 are non-combatants. As it is accurately determined that Germany has within her bounds 215,709 trained cavalrymen, there is, in case of war, an excess of 115,000 to draw on for train and artillery work.

As it is not possible to give in detail in this book the remount system of each country discussed, what is believed to be a typical remount system is placed before the reader in the above, to enable him to appreciate the great care and attention given in Europe to the cavalry arm.

Austria, often mentioned as possessing the finest cavalry in Europe, has a horse supply of nearly 4,000,000, but these horses are nearly all raised in a haphazard, indifferent way. These horses of Austria are very similar to the native horse of Russia, probably owing to the fact that great numbers of Russian horses are introduced into Austria annually. As the Government owns its own government studs, imperial studs, and local studs distributed thoughout the empire, the Austrian cavalry horse is carefully bred and reared and vastly superior to the general run of horses. As a remount is required yearly of over 6,000, the large breeding and training dépôts are at all times scenes of great activity and experiment. The Austrian Regulations require that the cavalry horse be between five and seven years of age, of a minimum height of 15¼ hands. At this height a horse can be accepted only when especially well developed. As the entire cavalry service of the Austrian Empire is considered light cavalry, its horses would seem to be somewhat large. However, as the Austrian cavalryman carries 297 pounds, including himself, a smaller horse seems to have been found undesirable. The average service of the cavalry horse in Austria is about seven years; the average price paid by Austria is $101.32, whenever they need to purchase outside mounts. This price is low, considering the very fine class of animals Austria uses in her cavalry. But it must be considered that Austria buys young remounts when her government supply is not sufficient, buying three-and-a-half and four-year-old horses, and training them over a year before assigning them to a regiment.

Russia has a large horse supply of over 25,000,000 in European and Siberian Russia. Southern Siberia furnishes a small 14½-hand horse of hardy build, and Southern Russia a somewhat larger horse, though probably a mixture of Siberian and Southern Russian blood. These southern horses are principally utilized for the light regular cavalry, although several Cossack regiments are mounted wholly on the South Siberian horse of 14½ hands, and are said to be ideal light cavalry. The Government buys horses very young, and subjects all but those destined for the Cossack regiments to severe training. The Cossack horse is sent direct to his regiment, the Cossack being an acknowledged horse-trainer and rough-rider and generally on duty at remote frontier garrisons, where the time for training green horses is plenty. The light cavalry horse of Russia must be from 15 to 15¼ hands high, from three and one-half to seven years old, and the average price paid is about $150. After twelve years' service, all cavalry horses are arbitrarily condemned, good or bad. These condemned horses are allowed to be sold to officers, generally bringing from $12 to $20.

France, in the campaign of 1870–71, was obliged to purchase horses abroad for the remount of her troops, despite its horse population of over three million. Its annual remount, even in time of peace, is nearly 15,000. The foreign purchases, made mostly in America, gave little satisfaction; it being claimed that the remounts secured were irritable, badly formed, and unable to stand hard service. It would seem France must have gotten mongrel Western horses, and that the fault rested principally with its own purchasing commissions. The "Tarbeen" horse of Southern France is an especially fine light cavalry animal of more or less Oriental style and blood, but the supply is limited, though regular and even. Many Algerian horses are also purchased yearly, cavalry commissions regularly visiting Algiers for this purpose.

The Algerian horse is a descendant of the Barb, and possesses in consequence Moorish blood. The French light cavalry regulation horse is from 14½ to 15⅛ hands high, flowing tail and mane, four years old, and either geldings or mares. The "Tarbeen" horse and the Algerian horse are both light 14½-hand horses as an average, and every year the commission goes throughout Southern France and Algeria for the purpose of getting these horses for light cavalry remounts. The French cavalry horse is specially trained under special instructors at Saumur, at St. Cyr, at the War School at Paris, and at several other large cavalry remount dépôts. The horses are usually bought at three and one-half years, trained one year, and put in their regiment at four and one-half years. The average purchase price is $160, and the average length of service eight years.

Belgium's horse population, about 300,000, belongs apparently to one well-known type, the Flemish, which formed a distinct race, and was often mentioned in ancient history as the horse of the time, and still shows strong qualities and fair proportions. In occidental Flanders he is very tall, strong, and enduring, but principally purchased for artillery and draft purposes. The best subdivision of this class is procured for the light cavalry in and around Bruges. This horse is more evenly gaited, more active, and of better shape and small. Belgium only requiring a yearly remount of about 1,000 cavalry horses, she has no difficulty in procuring desirable ones. The Government purchases either geldings or mares, from five to six years of age; horses with prominent noses as well as mixed colors, piebald, gray or white faces are not purchased. For Chasseurs the height is 15 to 15¼ hands, and for the Lancers 15¼ to 15½ hands. The purchase price is an average of about $75. The average service of the light cavalry horse is about seven years.

England has been called upon many times in the breeding of horses in our own country to furnish us some of her thoroughbred or half-bred blood, and the use by us of the English blood in breeding has been to improve the quality of American horses very greatly. As the quality of cavalry of every nation must ever depend mainly upon the quality of horse the country produces, this use in America of thoroughbred English stallions has given us a finer standard of horses from which to make purchases to mount our own cavalry. Let us see what the English Thoroughbred horse is, and thereby better understand our own.

Before the days of the Stuarts there was no reason to consider the English horse in any way superior to the horse of Europe; in fact, at that time the Asiatic horse was held to be superior to any other, and it remained for James I. and Charles I. to introduce Arab blood into England; but Charles II. may be said to have laid the foundation of the present English breed by the importation of four mares, from which may be traced many of the most celebrated horses of the last century. However, the main stock of the very best English blood of·to-day lies in the three following Eastern horses: first, the Byerly Turk, introduced into Ireland in 1689; and second, the Darley Arabian, imported early in the eighteenth century; and third, perhaps the most important, the Godolphin Arab, which seems more properly to have been a Barb, and was first used as a sire in 1731. The blood of the latter predominates to a greater extent than that of any other in the English Thoroughbred of to-day. We have every reason to believe that the well-bred horse of that time was diminutive in size as compared to those of the present. Babraham, a son of Godolphin, was the only well-known horse of his time that measured 16 hands, and we find it chronicled that out of 130 famous thoroughbred English horses in the middle of the eighteenth century, only 18 reached 15 hands, 11 of which sprang from the Godolphin, 3 from the Darley Arabian, and 2 from the Byerly Turk. We may thus fairly look upon the Godolphin as having first generated size in the English Thoroughbred horse, although feeding, care, and attention to crossing have aided. The growth of racing in England gradually led to cross-breeding for one purpose alone—speed, and as a result of this the "Thoroughbred," as he is called erroneously, gradually developed an elongated frame, as beautiful as his predecessors or more so, but to the eye of the cavalryman displaying diminished muscles and less prominent sinews and sharper and less powerful withers. As we find, especially in Kentucky and Tennessee, many Thoroughbreds out of stallions descended from the Godolphin Arab, the Byerly Turk, and the Darley Arabian, and as English Thoroughbred stallions are so extensively used in cross-breeding in America, it is well to know something of what we mean when we speak of good blooded horses.

The latest census of the horse supply of Great Britain shows a total of about 3,000,000, 2,000,000 of which are employed in breeding and agriculture and 1,000,000 privately or in trade. After obvious deductions for age, size, and unsoundness, about 70,000 horses are considered likely to be found fitted for military purposes. On reference to the estimates laid before Parliament annually, it is found that the total number of army horses of all classes belonging to mounted troops in Great Britain, Ireland, and the Colonies, exclusive of the regiments in India and of officers' horses, is nearly 16,000. From the same source it is found that the annual remount of these troops is about 2,000. The 31 regiments of British Cavalry make an average of about 24,000 of all classes, and when it is stated that the British Cavalry has but 16,000 horses and requires an annual remount of about 2,000, it must be explained that England does not mount full regiments in its Cavalry. For instance, the Household Cavalry contains 27 officers, 2 warrant officers, and 404 men, but only 275 riding-horses and 10 supernumerary horses per regiment. This rule applies to all its Cavalry of the Line as well. The British Army Book explains this by saying: "There is a constant flow of recruits passing into the ranks and temporarily unfit, men in hospital, others employed as regimental cooks or in other necessary dismounted capacity, men on guard and men employed as officers' servants, and it will not be hard to understand that the commanding officer's difficulty lies in finding effective men to mount his horses, rather than the horses for mounting his men.   If one of our 31 regiments were to take the field, it would be complete as an administrative body, with leaders, staff and regimental machinery, and there would remain only the need of supplying the additional horses." Such a departure from our own ideas seems to us to be radically at fault and a departure from well-understood cavalry principles, although recently the American Cavalry has begun to do this to a small extent.

The horses for the British Cavalry are purchased by an inspector-general of remounts, assisted by a staff of cavalry officers and veterinary surgeons.   Ordinary remounts are purchased from five to six years of age, between 15½ and 16 hands in height, and are sent either direct to regiments or to the remount dépôts.   The average price for the light cavalry horse is very high, being found to be about $245; the average length of service is about eight years.   When, from any cause, a regiment requires remounts, the regimental commander makes application to the inspector-general of remounts, who supplies the horses required.

To facilitate meeting the military demands for remounts in time of war, a system of registration throughout England and Ireland is arranged, being voluntary on the part of the owners.   Owners having large numbers of horses are invited to register them; those which on inspection by an officer of the Remount Establishment are found suitable are registered, the owners signing an agreement and receiving ten shillings annually for each horse so inspected and registered.   The register of the horses is kept on file in the War Office, and each horse is inspected annually by one of the officers of the Remount

Establishment, and the price at which they are to be purchased by the Government, if needed, is agreed upon. By the terms of the agreement, owners are bound, on the proclamation of the National Defense Act, to furnish, after forty-eight hours' notice, horses serviceable, sound, and of age, height, and class agreed upon at the previous annual inspection. If the owner fails to furnish the number and class of horses registered, a penalty of $200 per horse is inflicted. The agreement can be terminated by either party on six months' notice. There are about 14,000 horses so registered at present, 10,500 for draft or artillery use, and about 3,500 for cavalry purposes, which is sufficient for England's home defense and for small forces embarking for foreign service. To further meet the demands of war-time, the resources of England's colonies and also of foreign countries have been in the past and would probably be again largely utilized. Officers of the Remount Department have often visited the horse districts of Canada and of our own Western ranches and purchased remounts, and during the Crimean War the countries of the Mediterranean contributed largely. In the Abyssinian War, Syria and other countries sold horses to the British Cavalry.

The British cavalry horses are sent upon purchase to the remount dépôts usually, and are placed immediately under the instruction of riding masters and rough-riders, who train not only the young horses, but also all recruits, either officers or soldiers, and this initial training naturally greatly affects the entire future equitation of the British Cavalry.

CHAPTER IV.

AMERICAN HORSE SUPPLY AND REMOUNT.

Horse Population—Area—Variation in Size, Quality, and Price—
Remounts—Experiments—Average Cost—Length of Service
—System of Purchase—The Regulation Cavalry Horse.

In the United States the horse population is a little
over 16,000,000, and is scattered from the Atlantic to
the Pacific and from Mexico to Canada, representing
many different sizes, qualities, and classes and varying
greatly in value. Attention is called to the detailed
statement given by States in Appendix I.

It is believed that no horses, as we of to-day understand the modern horse, were in America prior to 1529,
and a careful study of various histories on this point
furnishes no data whatever antedating this year. In the
year mentioned a band of horses were introduced into
America by the Spaniards in Texas, and, as was the custom
in the early colonial days, they were turned out to make
their own living. The horses at that time were kept entire
(stallions). These horses were sold, as far as possible,
for domestic use, others roaming at will towards the north
and west, and no doubt from them originated our numerous herds of wild horses.

In 1539 De Soto, the Spanish explorer, landed in
Florida with 500 men and 237 horses. His course was
northward and westward. He reached the Mississippi
River, as we all know, and there died. His party continued across the great "Father of Waters," and traveled northward and westward still, crossing the Mississippi with 150 horses and 250 men. Later they became
discouraged, and reached the Gulf of Mexico in Texas,
built boats, and left on their return to Spain. When
they sailed away, they left their remaining horses, which

were few, on the Texas shores. These few horses and those which had become disabled and left on the way through the wilderness, many of them being stallions and mares, furnished the foundation for the great herds of wild horses which have existed in the Southwest and Texas for centuries in this country.

The settlers of Jamestown, in 1607, brought from England many horses for use in the "New World." In 1611 there was another large importation of horses at the same place, and quite a number of importations of English horses into Virginia followed all the way up to the year 1620. The colonies of North and South Carolina secured their horses from Virginia.

Henry Hudson, an Englishman, discovered the harbor of New York in 1609. In the following few years many horses were brought to this part of America by the English.

In 1629 six vessels arrived at Boston from England, bringing people and their horses. In these six vessels there were 25 mares and stallions.

Salem, Massachusetts, was founded in 1626, and in 1629 received a large importation of Dutch horses, and from then on for several years there was quite a number of importations of Dutch, Swedish, Danish, and French horses into the colonies of New York, Connecticut, Maryland, and New Jersey.

Port Royal, Canada, known as New France, was settled by the French some time prior to the settlements in Virginia, and many French pacing horses were imported. Quite a number of importations of Dutch and English horses followed, and the breeding of horses became quite a business in the Colonies as early as 1640. Breeding horses in Rhode Island became quite common as early as 1650. Two-thirds of the horses imported into the Colonies in early times seem to have been pacers. They made excellent saddle-horses, which seemed to be in great demand in the early days before the country had carriage-roads, traveling being nearly all performed in the saddle.

Along about 1700 wild horses became quite plentiful in Virginia, and they were hunted for sport, as everyone caught not having a brand belonged to its captor.

Thus, from these historical proofs of the early horses in America, it can be seen that the horse was bred in this country for over one hundred years, laying a very great foundation for the horse of to-day. There was thus introduced into America in the earliest colonial days the horse with English blood, the horse with Dutch blood, with French, with Spanish, with Swedish, and with Danish blood. Last, but not least, came the blood of the English race-horse, which has been imported into America from very early colonial times. These importations of the English thoroughbred racing-horses commenced about 1750, and have continued almost every year since then, largely influencing the style, disposition, size, shape, and quality of our best animals.

The remount system used in the United States Cavalry is one that is regulated by Acts of Congress. It is known as the contract system. All purchases are made by officers of the Quartermaster's Department, assisted by veterinarians, and all horses are sent direct to regiments. Contractors under this system agree to furnish to the Government, at an agreed-upon contract price, a specified number of horses conforming to the Army standard. Occasionally contractors are required to present the horses at some designated point for inspection and purchase by the Government, while at other times agreement is made between the Government and the contractor under which officers of the Quartermaster's Department or Cavalry, accompanied by veterinary surgeons and the contractors, visit particular sections of the United States and inspect and purchase therein the horses presented by the contractors.

There is no distinction made in the American cavalry service between light and heavy cavalry, and the regulation cavalry horse is the same for all regiments, but in each regiment (composed of twelve troops each),

each troop is mounted upon horses of the same color, so far as possible. The cavalry horse in our service must be sound and well bred, gentle under the saddle, free from vicious habits, with free and prompt action at the walk, trot, and gallop, without blemish or defect, of a kind disposition, with easy mouth and gait, and otherwise to conform to the following description: A gelding of uniform and hardy color, in good condition, from 15¼ to 16 hands high, weight not less than 950 nor more than 1150 pounds, from four to eight years old, head and ears small, forehead broad, eyes large and prominent, vision perfect in every respect, shoulders long and sloping well back, chest full, broad and deep, fore legs straight and standing well under, barrel large and increasing from girth toward flank, withers elevated, back short and straight, loins and haunches broad and muscular, hocks well bent and under the horse, pasterns slanting, and feet small and sound. A horse under five years old is not accepted unless a specially fine, well-developed animal.

As soon as cavalry horses are purchased in our service, the letters "U. S." are branded on the left shoulder; and as soon as the horses are assigned to troops, they are branded on the front of the hoof of the near fore foot with the number of the regiment and the letter of the troop. As soon as horses are assigned to the troop, they are assigned to individual riders, who exclusively train and use them.

Many experiments have been made in the American Cavalry with the various different classes of horses found in the United States. In Texas from 1865 to 1875 we used what might be called a mongrel, with the exception of a few well-bred horses that came from Tennessee and Kentucky. After a few long and hard Indian campaigns, these well-bred horses were the only ones remaining of the original mount. We experimented with the Texas cow pony, but one scout rendered them unfit for immediate future service. The average weight of a cavalryman fully armed and equipped is about 225 pounds as a minimum, and as the cow pony weighs only 700 to 850 pounds, the proportion of dead weight is too much for the frame. A good proportion is 4 to 1. Thus a 225-pound load takes a 900-pound horse. From 1875 to 1888 we got our cavalry horses principally from Kansas City and St. Louis, Mo. While many of these horses were good, still a large percentage of them were of Clydesdale blood, which stock is fit only for draft-horses. Later an attempt was made to supply us with ranch-bred horses from California and Nevada, one or two regiments being so mounted. It was considerably a success, these chosen horses being about three-quarters American and one-quarter Spanish blood and possessing remarkable endurance and stamina for long service over most difficult country, and were as hard as steel. They were small, average 14½ to 15 hands, and from 900 to 950 pounds in weight, and were very great "rustlers." Many of these horses were seen and recognized in the service years afterward, still performing the roughest kind of cavalry field work and apparently good for plenty more service, but the supply was very small.

At one time we mounted part of our cavalry upon Oregon horses bred out of native mares by ordinary stallions of Clydesdale blood, and the result was most unsatisfactory—no nerve, no agility, no intelligence, and heavy in hand. Troop H, Fourth Cavalry, at that time one of the troops that were using these horses, had two Thoroughbred horses given to it by General Stanley. Sergeants were assigned as riders, and these two horses were in excellent condition even after H Troop had been twice newly mounted. Our experiments in the past have shown that many advantages are derived by purchasing none but horses which are at least *fairly* well bred. Most men appreciate the good qualities of a horse they are obliged to ride, and it is a well-known fact among cavalrymen that when a man is mounted upon a fine, well-bred, intelligent horse, he will give it far more attention than if he were mounted upon a mongrel, heavy, lumbering one. The success of the Cavalry Bureau during the Civil War was remarkable in fitting for further service thousands of temporarily incapacitated horses that had become broken down through inexperience and careless abuse by hastily enlisted men. Civilian experts for a time were used by the Quartermaster's Department to choose and purchase the horses for our cavalry regiments in conjunction with officers from that department. In the past, boards of cavalry officers have been used for the purchase of our cavalry remounts, but "it has frequently happened that officers of other arms of the service have been employed on this duty. Purchase in open market in the past has also been tried, by boards of officers appointed from the organizations requiring horses. These boards were permitted to go into the districts where horses could be procured and purchase such horses as were found to be acceptable, the only restriction being as to a certain average price for all the horses purchased. This method gave great satisfaction to the Cavalry, but was objected to by the Quartermaster's Department, and, having no warrant of law to sanction it, had necessarily to be abandoned."

The purchase of our remounts under the present system does now meet with the entire satisfaction of cavalry officers, it being held by many cavalrymen that we are better qualified to do the purchasing, because of greater familiarity with the qualities, conformation, training, and use of our cavalry horses. About $600,000 is expended annually for our remount in time of peace of about 8,000 animals for all purposes. This makes an average of $75 a head, a sum too small to procure well-bred horses; but a species of scale exists, making it practicable to pay as high as $125 for cavalry horses, for which price very satisfactory animals can be procured. This can be readily seen by a perusal of Appendix I.

Judging by the idea which prevails in European cavalry services, it would seem that the horses purchased for the American Cavalry are too old when first bought; if

purchased at four years old, they would not be too young
for at least a year of careful training before being placed
in regiments, owing to the great care our horses receive;
but at seven and eight years old horses have certainly
passed the best period for training. Physically,
the regulation horse of the American Cavalry service,
as actually seen in our troops, is a powerful, fine, and
tolerably well-bred animal, possessing sufficient bone and
sinew, intelligence and courage, energy, lightness, and
endurance for all light cavalry work. A horse of the
minimum regulation height and weight is the most satisfactory. Occasionally a few horses creep into the cavalry possessing the maximum height and weight allowed,
but these are undesirable, for they have been found too
unwieldy, cumbersome, and slow of gait and action for
our light cavalry work. As the regulations governing
our cavalry recruiting service require that the cavalry
recruit shall weigh not more than 160 pounds, and as the
men enlisted for the cavalry generally average 15 or 20
pounds less than that, which is the weight usually assigned
to light cavalry regiments, the light horse described as the
minimum regulation animal allowed is the one procured
as far as practicable.

The horses of Kentucky and Tennessee are pre-
eminently the best fitted for the saddle and light cavalry
work. The neck is long, withers prominent, chest deep,
and girth well developed. They make, in spite of often
deficient loins and lack of croup, the best of saddle animals. In the States of New York, Pennsylvania, Ohio,
Michigan, Indiana, Illinois, Wisconsin, Iowa, Missouri, and
Kansas the production of horses is very great, especially
of draft animals. The introduction of English blood
some years ago seems to have produced some improvement, especially in spirit and intelligence. On the other
hand, horses are so abundant in America, either native
born or possessing some Spanish extraction, that many
excellent, beautiful, hardy, and small animals can be

found. Texas produces a considerable number of horses, but in the cavalry trials which have been had with them they were objected to as lacking in roundness of sides and thighs and having weak limbs and defective hocks. A few years ago, however, Texans introduced a cross-breed of American and full- or half-blood English stallions, which has also tended to improve the standard of horse in the Southwest. In California, and other parts of the West also, the introduction of English stallions of full blood during the past twenty-five years has largely improved the breed. The Kentucky and Tennessee Thoroughbreds are all the outcome of cross-breeds from full-blood English stallions. They are all admirably muscled, low, and add to these qualities symmetry of curve and length of forearm.

The question of whether a thoroughbred horse is desirable for cavalry purposes is a much-mooted one. While the real Thoroughbred horse may not be wholly desirable for cavalry work, yet the other extreme, as represented in Clydesdale, Percheron, and Norman horses, is vastly worse, and a horse half-bred midway between these two mentioned classes, small, hardy, agile, and quick, probably typifies the light cavalry horse of to-day.

CHAPTER V.

CLASSES OF HORSES.

Percheron—Clydesdale—English Shire—Cleveland Bay—Hackney —French Coach—German Coach—Thoroughbred—Saddler— Trotter—Pacer—Kind Required for Cavalry.

There are a great many breeds of horses throughout the world, caused by cross-breeding of various standard types. As an outcome of this haphazard cross-breeding, Western America is overrun with a small hardy horse of Spanish extraction. Southern Russia is overrun with a somewhat similar class of horse, the outcome of cross-breeding between South Siberian and Southern Russian native horses. Mexico possesses a native breed of horses with almost pure Spanish blood, the first horses there having been introduced by the Spanish explorers of centuries ago. South Africa, in like manner, has a native breed of horses of small, hardy build and great endurance, which were introduced there by the Dutch centuries ago. In like manner most of the countries of the world have certain breeds of horses which may be said to be native to the country. These various breeds of horses swell into a thousand classes when their lineage is traced and pains taken to establish the history of any particular class.

However, among the various breeds of horses there are certain well-known breeds in modern use in Europe, Great Britain, and the United States and elsewhere that have become deservedly famous for the size, style, disposition, and qualities possessed. From these several well-known types there also spring a hundred classes created by cross-breeding and careless breeding. This has produced thousands of horses possessing generally more or less standard blood, but often little if any likeness to their parent strain, yet amply qualified for cavalry purposes.

These cross-bred horses are probably better adapted to the hardships of cavalry life than a pure-blooded horse, and are accustomed to inferior forage, inferior care, and privations which would soon ruin thoroughbred animals.

As every cavalry officer is sooner or later called upon to examine and inspect horses for the cavalry service, it is well to recognize the standard type of each of the well-known classes that exist in Europe and America to-day, and to have the ability to recognize suitability or unsuitability of each for cavalry service. Those most commonly known are the Percheron, the Clydesdale, the English Shire or Cart Horse, the Cleveland Bay, the Hackney, the French Coach, the German Coach, the Thoroughbred Trotter or Pacer, the Thoroughbred Saddler, and perhaps one or two others. It will be sufficient to the cavalry officer to be reasonably familiar with the classes of horses mentioned above. Other classes are not so well known, the lineage is not so well traced, and much is guess-work.

The Percheron breed of horses was brought to a high state of excellence in the district which was once known as La Perche, in Northern France, south of Normandy, corresponding in the main to the present departments of Eure-et-Loir and Orne, which, along with the other departments of Eure, Loir-et-Cher, and Sarthe, comprise the chief breeding-ground or original home of the Percheron, and nowhere else are they found more purely bred or so nearly allied to the original type.

Horses from this region have been largely imported into the United States, where they are now bred and reared extensively; the first importation to attract wide attention being made nearly fifty years ago into Ohio, where they were commonly known as French horses, but since, upon closer study of their origin and history, they have been designated as Percherons. From time to time other importations were made, and the appellation of Percheron has been firmly fixed upon these horses throughout the United States. All together, however, there has

Missing Page

been much disagreement in this country as to the proper name of these horses, arising principally from the fact that earlier importations of French horses had been called Normans, and these French horses have been variously known here as Percherons, Percheron-Normans, Norman-Percherons, Normans, and French Horses—a superfluity of names excedingly confusing and unsatisfactory. The publication of the Percheron Stud-book in France in 1883 simplified the matter, and the breed is now called simply Percheron.

The lineage of a large percentage of the most noted of the modern Percherons seems to have been satisfactorily and definitely traced to the sire Gray Arabian, Gallipoli, imported into France about 1820, and to the Arab blood is generally attributed the more general gray color; the form, disposition, and general characteristics also being strong evidence of their being of Arabian descent, while their original size is believed to be derived from the large black horses of Flanders.

In that part of Normandy contiguous to the coast, especially north of the river Seine, the Flemish element seems to have made its influence more strongly felt, and there the horses possess more of the Flemish and less of the Percheron characteristics than those bred farther south in the heart of La Perche, which will account for the diversity in the character of the horses brought to America. Those procured near the coast or north of the river Seine have usually leaned strongly toward the Flemish type; they are larger, coarser, and more sluggish, with less energy, endurance, and action than those bred in Eure-et-Loir and the adjacent departments, and are better adapted to heavy draft purposes than their lighter but more hardy, active, and stylish relatives of the interior, frequently weighing from 1700 to 2000 pounds in high flesh, and producing larger horses when crossed upon our common stock.

In France the original color of gray is the most popular, while in this country black is perhaps the favorite.

According to high authority, the French breeders develop the blacks not especially for quality, but to suit the fancy of Americans; and if the quality feature is in the smallest degree lost sight of, there is great likelihood of not only producing an inferior animal, but at the same time one altogether too large. Probably the most desirable horses of this breed at the present time will weigh between 1650 and 2000. The Percheron horse, no doubt, stands among the first of the draft breeds of the world. He has excellent conformation, attractive style, activity, and endurance, considerable speed, united with power, amazing strength for his weight, and a kind and docile disposition. He is especially adapted to the moving of immense loads at a rapid rate, and in the early days of France was largely used in drawing heavy diligences and post-coaches.

CLYDESDALE.—The Clydesdales seem to have had origin in South Central Scotland, in the rich valley of the river Clyde, from which they take the name. Scottish authorities almost unanimously designate the Upper Ward of Lanarkshire as the place where they were first brought to any considerable degree of perfection and prominence.

According to records, and the views of various prominent writers on this subject, the breed undoubtedly has in its veins the blood of the great Black horse of Flanders, and it is reasonably certain that the Clydesdale is the product of native mares of Lanarkshire bred to imported Flemish sires, about the close of the seventeenth or beginning of the eighteenth centuries. The Clydesdale, no doubt, largely owes its present distinctive character to these native mares of Lanarkshire, known as the Lochlyoch stock, mostly of brown and black color, with white faces and some white on their legs, gray hairs in their tails and occasionally scattering over the body, and invariably a white spot on their bellies, the recognized mark of purity of blood. Their progenitors were likely of English origin and of a somewhat mixed character. There

is, however, reason to believe that Flemish stallions had been introduced into Scotland long before this, and previous records show that Scotland was recognized as an excellent district for horse stock-breeding even during the early Stuart reigns. The earliest positive recorded mention of great horses in Scotland is July 1, 1352, when William, Earl of Douglas, obtained a special edict of "safe conduct" from King Edward I. to take "ten grooms and ten large horses from certain places in Scotland to certain places in Teviotdale in the King's dominion."

Available data and information fail to indicate when or where the Clydesdale was first introduced into this country, but as the Clydesdale Society of America was organized in 1877, it is not altogether improbable that they were quite numerously imported from some time prior to that year, at least to such an extent that a Clydesdale society and stud-book were very desirable and valuable, not to say well-nigh indispensable; and, with the exception of the Percherons, there has been no other breed of draft-horses so extensively imported into the United States as these. Their popularity is, no doubt, well merited, and they have exercised a potent influence in the horse stock of America. With our breeders the color has always been an especially strong point in favor of the Clydesdale, the prevailing colors being dark, with usually more or less white markings on face, feet, and legs. Bays and browns predominate, although there are now and then blacks, grays, and chestnuts.

The approved modern Clydesdales have large, round, open feet, with particularly wide coronets, heels wide and clearly defined, and the presence of a heavy growth of long, silky hair from the knee and hock to fetlock is generally accepted as an indication of quality and good breeding. Pasterns long and set back at an angle, tail set well up, and the quarters and thighs should not be too sharply marked off; bones wide, flat, thin, and dense. They should have wide chests and low counters, with limbs planted well under them; oblique shoulders lying well back on high withers, and arching high necks, are also quite characteristic and very attractive. The head should be of medium length, and broad between the eyes and at the muzzle. An open, level countenance, vigorous eye, and large ear are also greatly valued.

Clydesdales are, as a rule, for such heavy horses, both fair walkers and trotters.

ENGLISH SHIRE OR CART HORSE.—From time to time centuries ago heavy horses from Germany, Holland, and Flanders were imported into England, and the mingling of their blood with that of the horse stock found there, and breeding from the best of successive generations, resulted in a type of sturdy, slow-going animal favorably known there as the English Shire or Cart horse. With this draft-breed, as with the others, the famous Black horse of Flanders seems to have been a dominating influence in their formation, and they so nearly resemble the Clydesdale in some ways that many intelligent breeders of both England and Scotland have argued that the two breeds should be classed as one. For many years the Shire has been extensively bred and reared in England.

As the various draft-breeds of the world apparently have for their ancestry the great Black horses of Flanders, the following from "The Breeds of Live Stock" should be of interest:

"No point in equine history is better established than is the fact that to the regions bordering on the western coast of Europe, once known as Normandy and Flanders, the world is indebted for the basis of its various breeds of draft-horses. Flanders especially was famed, away back in the Middle Ages, for its famous breed of Black horses, and this race appears to have been the prevailing one throughout the north of ancient Gaul and of Germany from the mouth of the Rhine eastward, and Professor Low thinks inhabited in the wild state the vast region of marsh and forest which stretched all through Europe eastward to the Euxine Sea. It was from this source that the rulers of Great Britain drew in large num-

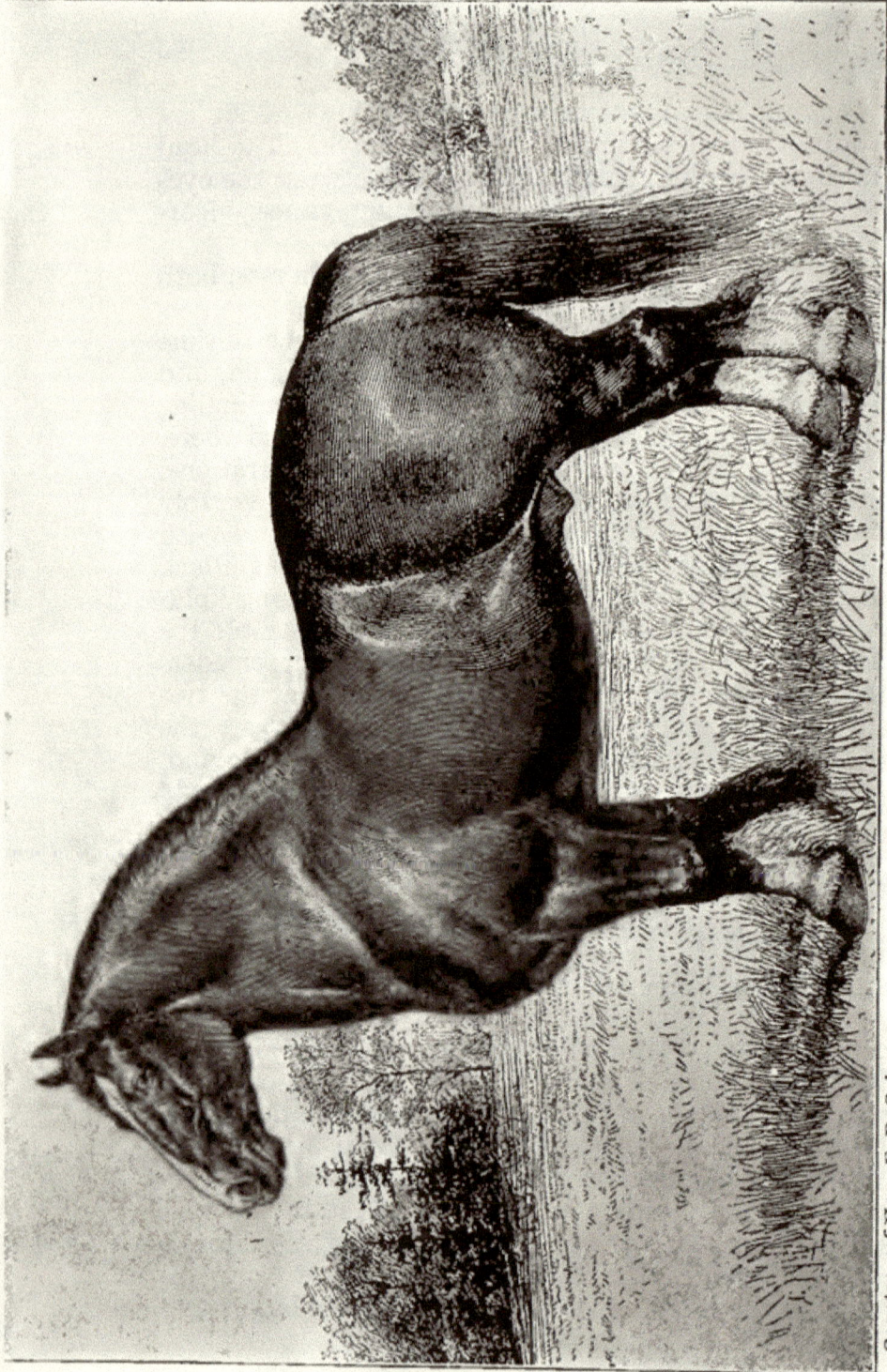

IMPORTED ENGLISH SHIRE STALLION "HOLLAND MAJOR."

bers for the purpose of increasing the size of the horses of the island. How or when this breed originated is a subject upon which history throws no light. But as early as the eleventh century they were largely imported into England, and royal edicts and regulations were repeatedly issued for the purpose of encouraging the use of large stallions of this breed."

While some are grays and roans, blacks, bays, and browns are the prevailing colors of the Shires, often marked with more or less white in the face and on the feet and legs, and, as with the Clydesdales, an abundance of fine silky hair from the knee or hock to fetlock is considered an indication of pure breeding. The Shire stallion should stand 17 hands high or over; legs big and massive; hair plentiful at all seasons without tendency to woolliness. Their action should be straight, level, and true, and the walk be forward and free. Hocks should at all times be kept together and in position; feet wide and open at the heel, with wall of sufficient depth to avoid giving the foot a flat appearance; the pasterns should slope sufficiently all around to enable smooth work. The head is of special importance, and should always be thoroughly masculine in character, while the bones should be as wide and massive as can possibly be had; the depth of both the heart and short ribs should be conspicuously present, and the walk true and level, without any symptoms of rolling.

These horses weigh from 1800 to 2000 pounds, and make no pretensions to gayety of carriage or dash, but are slow of motion and very powerful, and their extreme weight admirably fits them for the labors of the field, heavy truck and wagon use, as well as for transporting enormous loads.

In recent years these heavy horses have been imported into the United States, although not in large numbers, especially to the agricultural States of the Mississippi Valley.

CLEVELAND BAY.—One of the oldest and most popular of the English Coach breeds is that called Cleveland Bay, on account of the uniformly bright golden-bay color of the horses bred in the vale of Cleveland, Yorkshire, England.

The exact origin of the breed is a matter of some speculation. One authority states that they were a cross between Thoroughbred stallions and the large, active, and stylish native bay mares of Yorkshire, and were bred to fill the demand for fast, powerful, and stylish horses, useful for moderate farm and town work. Another theory, considered by many the most reasonable, is that it has been produced by a system of natural selection from the original breed of horses found in the southern part of the island of Great Britain, with the possible introduction of Eastern blood, probably the Barb, at a very early age.

It is an established fact that the existence of a breed of clean-legged, active, powerful horses was acknowledged more than two hundred years ago. Unfortunately, no written record of their early history was kept, and our chief source of information concerning it is tradition. In the early written record of the breed there appears the following description: "Yorkshire has long been famed for its breed of horses, and particularly this, the East Riding, in almost every part of which numbers are still bred, the prevailing species being those adapted for the coach or saddle. In the north part of the vale of York the breed has got too light in bone for the use of farmers, by the introduction of too much racing blood; but the most valuable horses for the saddle and some coach-horses are there bred. In Cleveland the horses are fuller of bone than those last described; they are clean, well made, very strong and active, and are extremely well adapted to the coach and plow."

Up to the earlier years of the eighteenth century the Cleveland Bays, previous to that time also called Coach

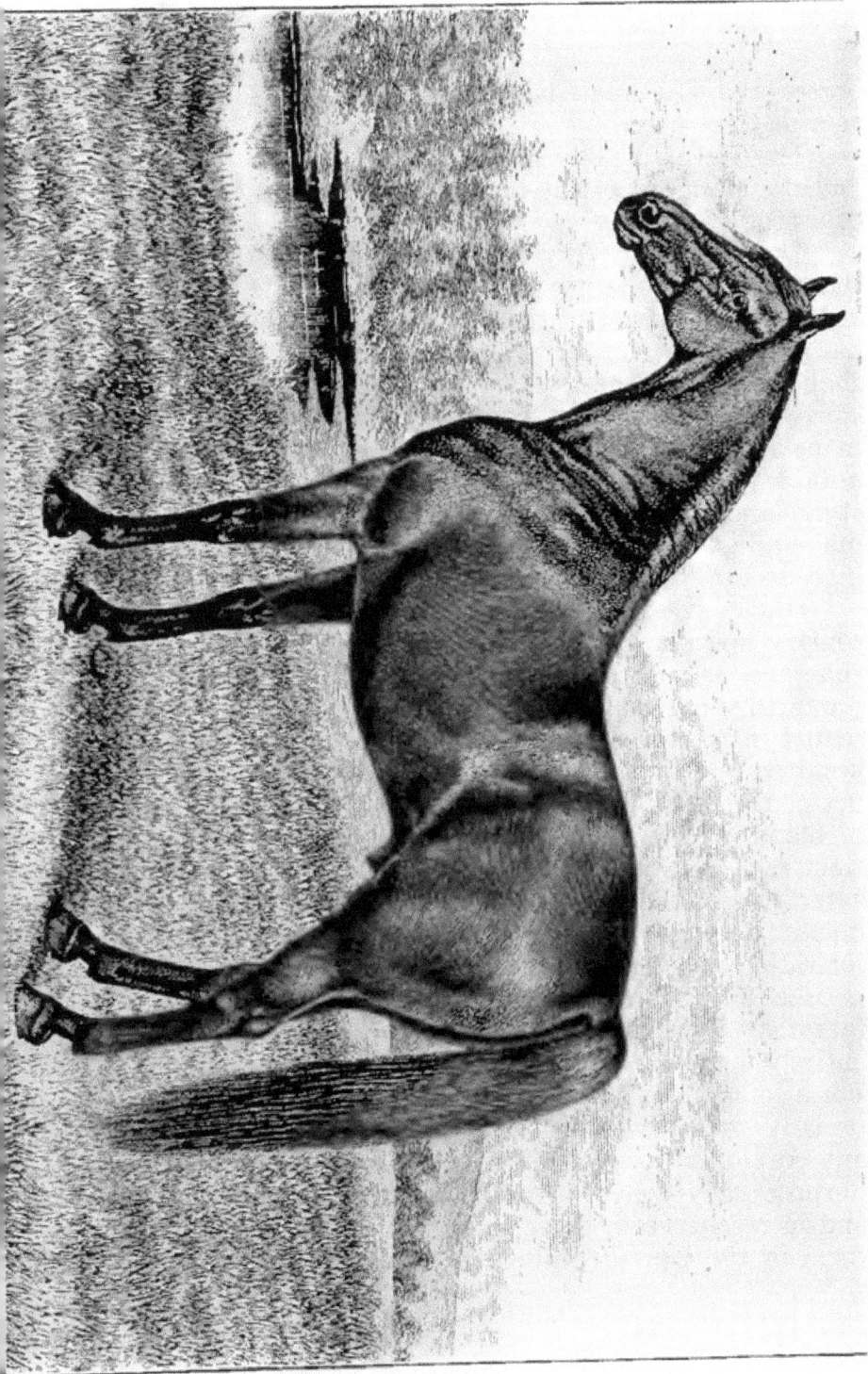

horses and Chapman horses, were probably not known as a distinct breed.

The Cleveland Bay Horse Society was formed in 1884, and the standard of the breed was raised by the creation of a stud-book.

The Cleveland Bay is the embodiment of combined substance and quality. His usual height is from 16 to 16¾ hands; his weight, from 1250 to 1500 pounds. He has a fine head, full bright eye, long arched neck, oblique shoulders, deep chest, short back, long quarters, strong cordy legs, and perfect feet. His color bay, full flowing mane and tail, and black legs, usually clear of white. His notable hardiness of constitution and staying powers, style, and elegant conformation are well calculated to make him a favorite with those who seek an animal seemingly so appropriately named "the general utility horse."

HACKNEY.—While there is more or less of the customary speculation as to the antiquity, origin, etc., of this race, as with others, it seems that all authorities are practically agreed that the Hackney has been bred and reared in Northern England counties for more than one hundred and fifty years, and is most probably the product of the Thoroughbred and the Norfolk County strains of blood, so blended and cultivated that an almost distinct race is established, combining all the desired characteristics of the two families. In the earlier days these horses were particularly adapted to and distinguished for riding and driving purposes, and as evidence of their peculiar fitness for either it might be well to mention the fact that the Hackney scarcely ever gallops, but relies entirely upon the trot and walk as methods of locomotion. For a long time, however, they have been bred more especially with a view to developing horses that can draw any sort of a rig at a rapid pace on the road, for which purpose they are pre-eminently and practically useful, and in recent years there has been an active demand for them in the United States.

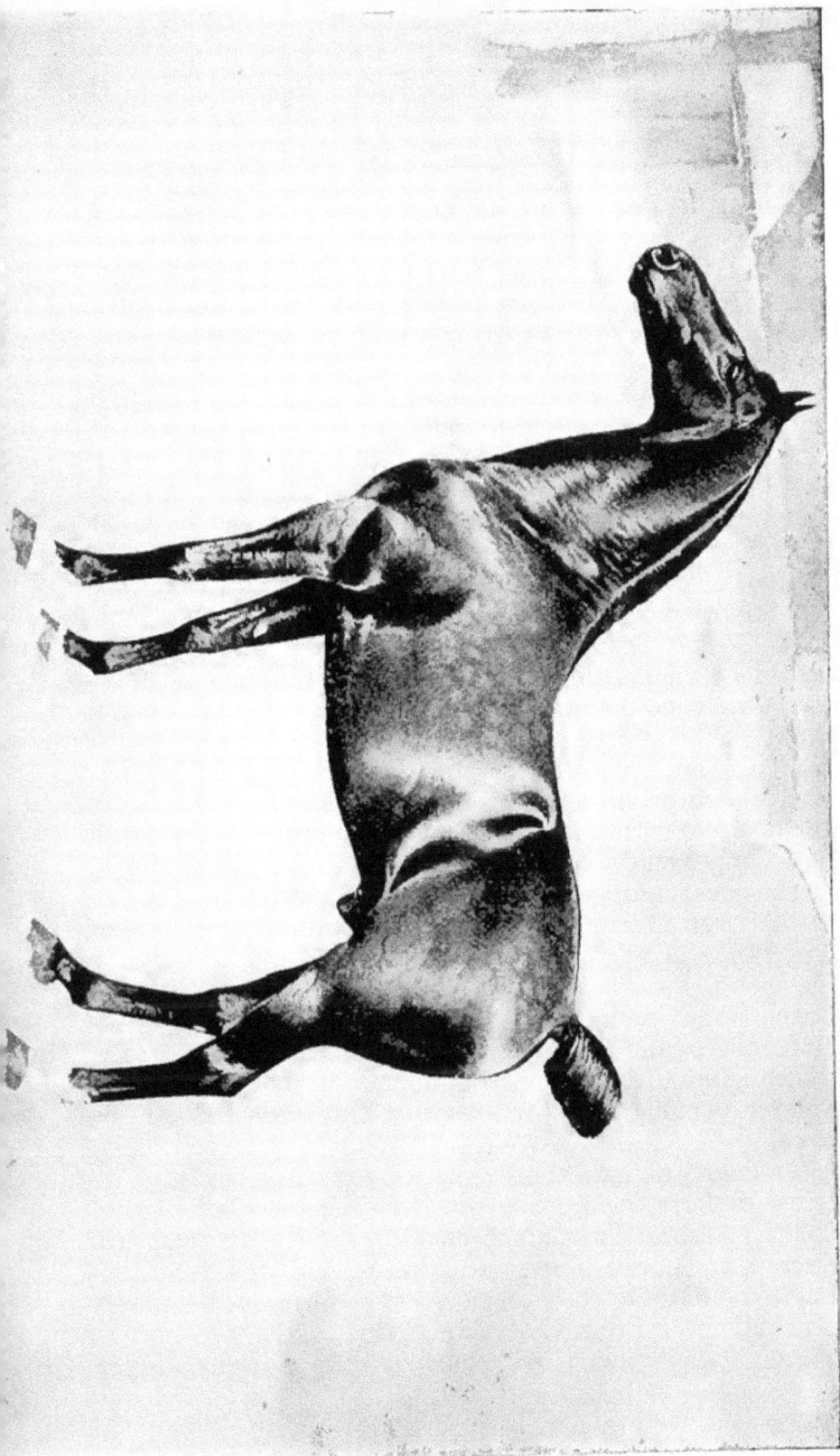

While Hackneys of all colors may be seen, those predominating are chesnuts, bays, and browns. The approved stallions should not be over 15¾ hands high. The conformation of the head should be symmetrical, wide at the jowl and tapering gently to the muzzle, and the eyes of good size, ears small and pointed; neck of fair length, nicely bent and rather thick at the base, though free from coarseness; chest wide and let down behind the forearms, giving plenty of space for the heart and lungs. Shoulders must be deep and lie well back; the leg bone short, flat, and largely supported with sinew, large at girth and closely ribbed up; fetlock short and strong; the foot circular and tending to the upright, and the frog well hollowed out and pliable. The thigh must be muscle itself; hocks clean and accurately jointed. The step should be short and quick, and good knee action is also essential; consequently plenty of freedom and liberty about the shoulders is necessary.

The Hackneys possess the elegance of a Thoroughbred, much of the sturdiness and substance of the Cart horse, along with a robust and vigorous constitution, and their appearance conveys the impression of strength, intelligence, courage, and quality combined.

FRENCH COACH.—The Coach horse of France resembles quite closely in size, action, and appearance the Cleveland Bay, which is the highest type of English Coach horse, and owes its existence to very similar circumstances and lines of breeding. The blood of the Thoroughbred largely predominates in both, the only difference being in the mares that have constituted the basis.

As early as 1780 the French Government began a systematic effort to improve the native horse stock of that country, especially for the cavalry service, by the introduction of Thoroughbred and Hunting stallions from England, and offering their services to the farmers at a merely nominal fee. From that time down to the present the French Government has continued its paternal super-

vision of the horse-breeding interests of that country, introducing from year to year Thoroughbred stallions in considerable numbers, and selecting the best of the male produce resulting from the union of the imported stallions and the French mares for use in the stud. Some of these imported stallions left a marked impress upon the stock of the country, notably among those being the horse Young Rattler, imported about 1820, whose produce were especially remarkable for their stylish, high-headed appearance and high, proud-stepping action. The get of this horse were selected by the government agents for breeding purposes, and to him more than to any other of these imported sires is ascribed the origin of the present so-called Coach horses of France. The foundation had been previously laid by crossing and re-crossing with the Thoroughbred, but Young Rattler and the stallions of his get gave the qualities which the French people especially fancied for coaching uses. Since that period this Coach-horse type has received, more largely than any other, perhaps, the fostering care and patronage of the Government, and certainly very marked improvement has been effected and a considerable degree of uniformity secured.

The departments of Orne, Calvados, Manche, Seine-Inferieure, and a portion of Eure in Western Normandy comprise the principal Coach-horse district of France.

Until comparatively recent years, French Coach horses had attracted little attention at the hands of American importers and breeders, but later the growing demand for large, stylish, high-stepping carriage teams and single drivers has led to their importation in considerable numbers. The stallions crossed with trotting-bred mares produce horses of substance, style, intelligence, conformation, and true road-action, coupled with fine courage. Many of these also possess a remarkable sweetness of disposition, entitling them to be loved as well as to be admired. The prevailing color is bay, but there are many chestnuts and occasionally a black. These horses are of good disposition, of uniform type, large, handsome,

high-headed, resolute, high-acting, capable of drawing
the coach, break, landau, brougham, mail phaeton, or kindred vehicle at a good rate of speed.

GERMAN COACH.—The northwestern portion of the
German Empire, largely composed of the provinces of
Hanover, Mecklenburg, that western part of Schleswig-
Holstein between the rivers Elbe and Eider, and the grand
duchy of Oldenburg, has for more than two centuries been
famed for its highly developed type of trotters and coaching horses. Carefully selected for generations and en-
hanced by a strain of Thoroughbred blood, they now
form a breed of good constitution, style, and action, much
in demand for carriage use and general purposes.

Early in the seventeenth century Hanoverian stock
was exported for the purpose of improving the breeds of
other countries, principally Great Britain, which country
afterwards furnished in return many Thoroughbreds, the
infusion of this blood proving of great benefit to the Hanoverian type by moderating their massiveness without
loss of strength. These horses are chiefly distinguished
by their elegance and stateliness of movement, and are
much used as state coach-horses. We are told that ever
since their introduction into England in 1820 these horses
have drawn the royal carriages, and it is said the King's
stables now contain more than one hundred specimens of
the breed. A bay of this breed, 16½ hands high, was ridden by the Emperor of Germany at the Queen's jubilee
celebration.

The German Coachers owe much of their rapid development to the fostering care and patronage of the Government, which lent encouragement to the breeding interests
as early as 1735 and established a government stud. Spe-
cifically for coach purposes, its paternal supervision date
back for more than a century. Formerly the privilege
of standing the stallions was reserved to the rulers, but
later was granted to farmers under certain imposed conditions and restrictions intended to maintain the character of the breed brought to such a high standard under

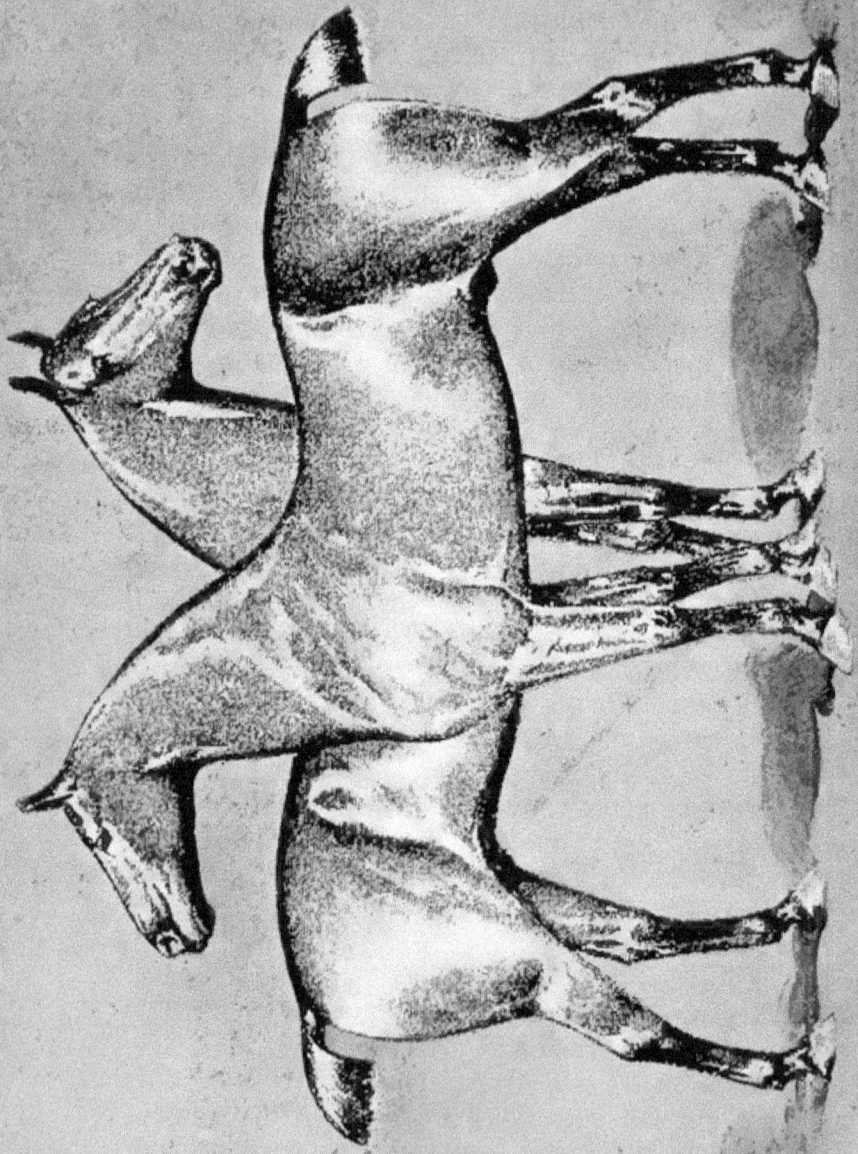

PAIR OF CHAMPION OLDENBURG "GERMAN COACH" STALLIONS.

government regulations. Regularity of movement and adroitness in walk and trot have been the aim of good breeders. The introduction of fresh blood apparently meets with no opposition if it promises improvement in either endurance or style. Possessed of large, strong bones, they are also suitable for agricultural purposes.

There are comparatively few German Coachers in the United States, but the importations, which have only been made in recent years, have produced an unusually favorable impression. They mature very early, being fit for work at two years and for breeding purposes at three, and are always spirited and hardy. Besides being exceptionally fine coach- and carriage-horses, they are not excelled for general purposes. They have proved themselves able to transmit their qualities to their offspring with great certainty.

The horses are nearly all solid colors—bay, brown, or black, stand 15¾ to 16¼ hands in height, and weigh from 1300 to 1600 pounds. The typical Coacher should trot very regularly, with free knee and hock action, be stylish and handsome, have short or medium back and good quarters. His shoulders should slope gracefully back, carrying a lengthy, well-arched neck and cleanly chiseled head free from meat. He should have a clear, full, expressive dark eye, and the visage of a Thoroughbred. His limbs and feet should be absolutely sound, with clean, flat bone, and his action should be high, bold, and square, with sufficient speed to roll off eight to twelve miles an hour with ease and grace; his disposition spirited and intelligent.

THOROUGHBRED.—Probably the oldest and best established of all breeds of horses of Europe and America is the Thoroughbred, a distinctly British production, especially noted and prominent throughout the world for endurance and running speed on the race-course.

At a very early period attention was directed toward the improvement of the native horse stock of Great Britain, and, as these horses were especially deficient in size, efforts were first put forth to remedy this defect by the

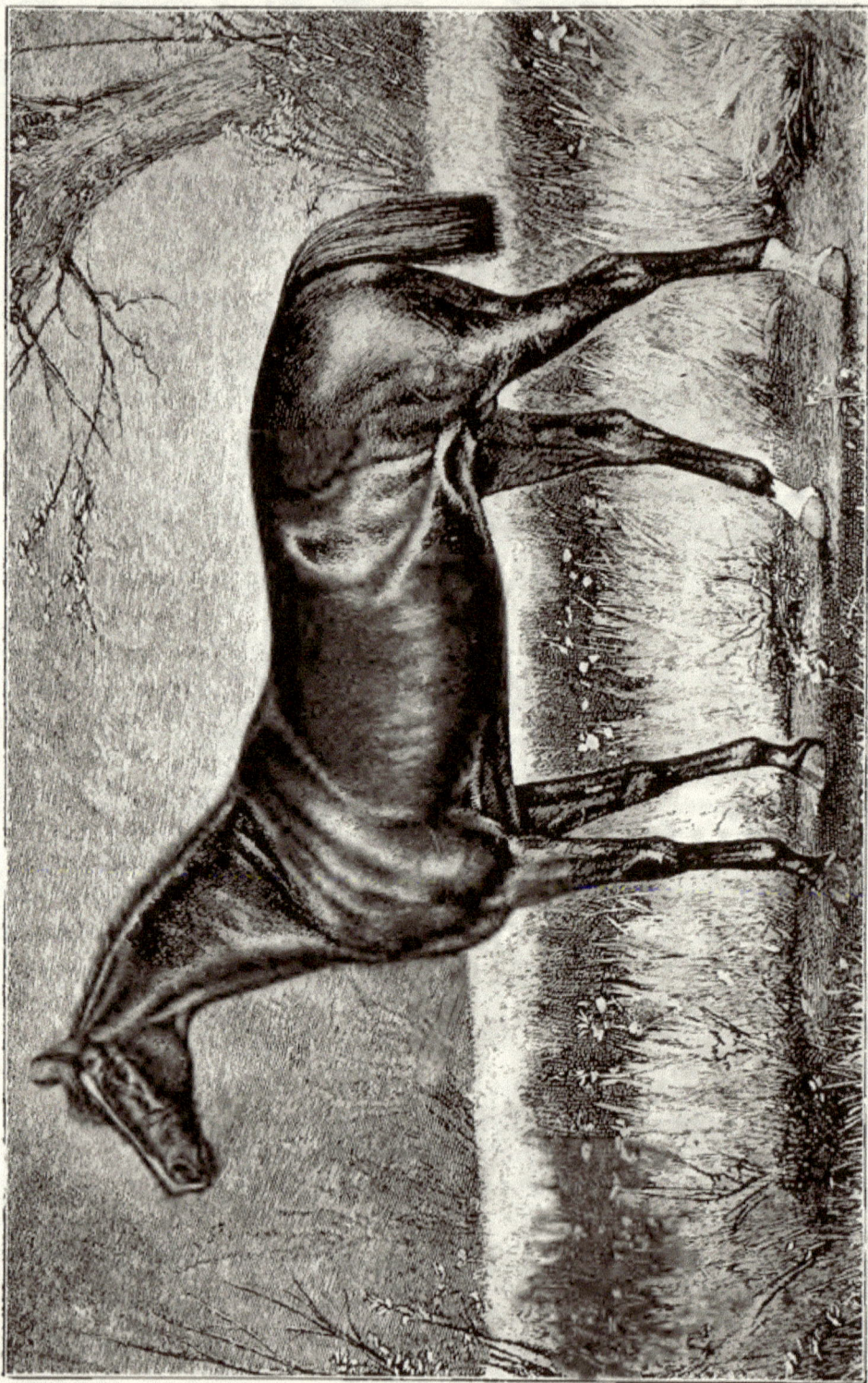

Courtesy of Hon. F. D. Coburn.

CHAMPION ENGLISH THOROUGHBRED STALLION "LEONATUS."

importation of the large, heavy horses from Normandy, Flanders, and Germany, but apparently there was no well-defined or settled purpose in view. At one time the object sought seemed to be increased size, and at another speed, grace, and beauty, for which Oriental blood was introduced, but not until the last half of the seventeenth century was the breeding for speed and endurance begun to be systematically conducted.

According to excellent authority, it seems that the foundation upon which the Thoroughbred was built was the promiscuous blending of the blood of native horses of England primarily with the larger animals from Normandy, Flanders, and Germany, and later with the lighter and more active horses of Spain, which were themselves practically identical with the Barbs. Numerous importations were also made from Egypt, Morocco, and Tunis, and likewise from Arabia and Turkey, until there was more or less of this Oriental blood in all the horse stock of Great Britain, except those bred especially for agricultural purposes. While the mingling of the blood of the Orient with the old races of England furnished the foundation from which was eventually evolved the now well-established Thoroughbred, much credit should also be given the English breeders, who, in their wisdom and care of selection and mating for successive generations, have probably been a more powerful factor in the formation of the breed as it exists to-day than the Oriental blood to which its superiority is so widely attributed.

For more than two hundred years horse-racing has been a chief amusement and recreation among English people, and to this fact and the constant growth and popularity of the sport is largely due the careful breeding and consequent purity of lineage of the English Thoroughbred horse. The term "Thoroughbred," when applied to horses, is used most frequently to designate one particular breed, and that is the running horse, and, as both the name and breed are derived from Great Britain, all our American Thoroughbreds are necessarily imported English animals or their descendants.

Most of these horses are altogether too light, too nervous, and too excitable for everyday business uses, and of course are ill adapted for slow, heavy draft; but in speed, courage, and endurance their superiors do not exist. Many of the best stallions and mares of England have been imported to the United States, and their influence on our horse stock has been most potent. As a means of improving other types, such as cavalry, hack, harness, and road horses, and as it is especially important and essential to have such horses of sound feet and legs, considerable speed, and medium weight, together with a capacity to bear a continuation of severe work, a cross with the Thoroughbred is likely to give the desired results. It is doubtful that there ever was a road-horse or trotter of prominence that did not possess in large measure this superior blood.

"Breeds of Live Stock" says: "The Thoroughbred having been for so many generations bred with especial reference to his capacity as a race-horse, it is not surprising that he should have acquired peculiarities of form and temper that render him undesirable for the more sober and steady uses of everyday life. He has been bred to run, and the form best adapted to speed and the mental qualities that most certainly insure the pluck and energy and determination so essential to success in a hard-fought race have been the qualities aimed at by breeders and the standard by which selections have been made. Such a course of breeding has made the Thoroughbred as a racer rather too lithe and light in form and too nervous and excitable in temper for ordinary business uses; but in speed, endurance, and resolution they surpass all other breeds, and there is scarcely a race-horse in existence but may be improved by a cross with them."

Thoroughbreds are usually divided into three classes: Trotters, Pacers, and Saddlers.

The trotting horse, like his immediate fellow, the pacer, is distinctively an American production of modern times, and is the outgrowth of the commercial tendencies

of Americans, coupled with their ardent love for tests of
speed and the possession of speedy, level-headed road-
sters for light business or private pleasure-driving, either
singly or in pairs.

Courtesy of Hon. F. D. Coburn.

"CRESCEUS."

Champion trotting stallion of the world; winner of the $20,000 purse in the stallion
race of 1900.

While breeders and trainers in the United States
have done most to develop trotting horses, their earliest
history goes back to England, where the trotting instinct
was first recognized and encouraged by tests of speed and

endurance. However, no records of note have ever been established across the Atlantic, and the development of the breed has been principally accomplished by enterprising Americans. In the earlier days of this century the improvement of the highways and the manufacture of lighter vehicles created a demand for light harness horses of beauty, style, and speed, capable of drawing a wagon and driver at a moderate speed for several hours at a time. Previous to this nearly all traveling was done on horseback, as the rough and well-nigh impassable roads of the period rendered journeying by means of the heavy wagons both slow and tedious.

The trotting gait was originally a natural inclination of some certain individual horses, and has been built up by cross-breeding of these horses. Our American horses are largely permeated with the blood of the English Thoroughbred. Many of the best stallions and mares in England have been imported to this country, and their influence is seen on every hand. It enters largely into the groundwork of all our trotting strains, and it is doubtful that a single great road-horse or trotter has been produced in this country that did not possess a large share of this superior blood as a foundation upon which the trotting superstructure has been built. In no department of stock-breeding is the influence of heredity and of patient selection with a view to transmission and improvement of a desired quality more apparent than in the breeding of the trotter. Fifty years ago the American trotting horse, as a breed, was unthought of, and one that could trot a mile in less than 3 minutes was a wonderful animal; but the ability to trot fast was a desirable quality, and breeders sought to perpetuate it. Animals that excelled the average as trotters were selected to breed from, with a view to perpetuating and intensifying this quality; but as its possession was at that time an accident—a spontaneous variation—it was found that but few of the immediate descendants of the animal first chosen with a view to breeding fast trotters could trot faster than their

remote ancestors; but when such of them as did show improvement in this direction were again selected for breeding purposes and coupled, it was found that, while there were still many failures, the proportion of the descendants that showed improvement in the trotting gait beyond the average of their ancestors was materially increased; and so, by selecting from generation to generation from such families as have shown a tendency to improvement in this quality, we have made considerable progress toward founding a breed of trotting horses.

The trotting horse now appears as, a permanently established type. In order that a horse may trot or pace, he must have the proper physical conformation, adaptation to the gait, and a favorable condition of mental and nervous organization. Unless possessed of mental or nervous habits, impelling him to trot or pace, he will not choose and tenaciously hold to these gaits. Speed depends upon similar conditions, and the horse lacking the quick temperament and highly organized nervous composition will not go fast at any gait. All these tendencies are, to a greater or less degree, capable of acquirement, and, once acquired by education, growth, practice, or blood, are easily transmitted or inherited.

The best trotters of to-day possess the inherited qualities of conformation, style of action, speed, and endurance well suited to render them valuable on the track or road and the means of much pleasure to their owners or drivers. Most of the fastest pacers came from the best lines of trotting breeding, and the pacing gait is acquired by them after their training begins. The greatest mistake made by breeders of trotters has been in mating for speed alone, to the neglect of size, style, and soundness, and the result is that a vast percentage of so-called trotting stock, which lacks in speed, is too small in size and too ordinary in conformation for much value in any direction.

Regarding pacers, in his book, "Horse Breeding," Mr. J. H. Sanders discusses the changeability in some

horses from a trotting to a pacing gait, and *vice versa*, as follows:

"Experience has most thoroughly demonstrated the fact that the trot and pace are, to a very considerable degree, interchangeable, and that most horses can be taught to adopt either the one gait or the other, at the pleasure of the rider or driver, as an intermediate manner of progression between the walk and the gallop. Instances where horses that have shown unusual speed as pacers have been changed into speedy trotters, mainly by increasing the weight of the shoes on the fore feet, are of everyday occurrence; and trotters may with equal facility be taught the pacing gait by the use of hobbles so adjusted as to compel the animal to move both legs on the same side together instead of moving the fore leg in unison with the hind leg on the opposite side, which constitutes the difference between the pace and the trot."

The success which has attended these and other methods of changing horses from one gait to the other, and the further fact that horses which show great speed as pacers so frequently descend from the well-established trotting families, has led to the generally established belief among horse-breeders that the trotting and pacing gaits are essentially the same; or, rather, that the taking of the one gait or the other is more a matter of accident or training than of inheritance. This theory, however, may be accepted no further than to admit that the form which is usually found in the fast pacer (a rather steep rump, with high, thin withers and well-bent hock) is one which appears to be well adapted to great speed in trotting when once the gait has been changed by any process of training. It is undeniable, however, that the form which is usually seen in our fast trotters is not that of the natural pacer, for with the former we frequently find that the animal is higher at the hips than at the withers; and while horses are frequently seen possessing this conformation trained to the pacing gait, yet they never take kindly to it, neither do they ever become fast pacers.

The trotter or pacer should have size and weight—
16 hands, 1200 pounds; but this does not imply that a
trotting-bred animal of less size is worthless.   Indeed, the
ideal size for a fast or even useful roadster or a harness race-horse is 15½ hands high, possessing quality and
substance, and weighing a little the rise of 1000 pounds.
True many horsemen prefer larger ones, but practical
horsemen and experienced road drivers stick very close
to these latter specifications.

Trotting-bred coach-horses come in another class,
and should have more size.   But in road- and race-
horses, breeding, substance, and quality, with medium
size, should not be sacrificed for height and pounds.

The American gaited saddle-horse is purely and distinctly American, and was formerly produced almost
exclusively south of the Mason and Dixon Line, before
that line was erased from the map of the United States.
He is older, however, than the Mason and Dixon Line, or
even the Stars and Stripes.   He is often referred to as the
Kentucky saddle-horse, but we must give Virginia, Tennessee, Georgia, Missouri, and other States due credit for
what they have done in developing and improving the
gaited saddler as we now see him—educated and accomplished, refined and polished, noble and good-mannered,
majestic and beautiful; perfect in symmetry and conformation; high-headed, high-tailed, arch-necked, fiery-
eyed; dignified and royal; armed with muscle, bone, and
sinew; endowed with substance, stamina, and endurance;
lithe-limbed, nimble-jointed, and sure-footed—the pride
of his owner and the admiration of all who see and know
him.

This saddler is also a roadster, safe and speedy, and
an all-purpose horse. Although new to many in the
North and West, he is of remote origin.   He has served
his country for more than a century. He went with Colonel Castleman and his Kentucky regiment to the Porto
Rican War.   He carried the chivalry of the South in the
Civil War.   Morgan's Raiders were mounted on him when

that daring chieftain made his bold dash northward. He served his country before his country had a name. He carried "Light-Horse Harry" Lee, and Marion, the

esy of Hon. F. D. Coburn.

CHAMPION GAITED SADDLE MARE "LADY GLENN."

"Swamp Fox," when these famous men of the Revolution had neither home nor country. We trace him back to the plain-gaited saddle-horse of 1730. After that date we find him developing into the five-gaited saddler or gaited saddle-horse.

There are at least four distinct classes of saddlers—viz., the plain-gaited or walk-trot-gallop horse, the hunter or cross-country horse, the gaited saddle-horse, and the high-school horse.

The plain-gaited horse is required to only walk, trot, and canter, but he must be an artist in these three gaits or he is of but little value as a saddler. In general make-up he is a fine animal and is the English style of a saddle-horse. He is usually a harness-horse, too, and a good roadster.

The hunter is a short-tailed, stately animal, trained to jump hurdles and fences and go over the bars without endangering life and limb of horse or rider. He also goes the walk, trot, and canter gaits, and is quite similar to the plain-gaited saddler in general make-up. Both have docked tails and plucked manes, and are sometimes called "park hacks."

The gaited saddler goes all the gaits of the hunter and the walk-trotter. In addition to the walk, trot, and canter, he goes at least two more distinct gaits and he often goes four more, making in all seven distinct, clear, clean, unmixed gaits. The gaits required to entitle him to recognition as a gaited saddle-horse are walk, trot, canter, rack, and running walk, fox-trot, or slow pace. He has his choice of either of the last three named for his fifth gait, but he must go the first four, and he must have the proper breeding. The slow pace, or amble, as it is sometimes called, is the least desirable of the seven gaits, and, except as a ladies' saddler, is seldom chosen as the fifth gait. The running-walk and fox-trot are business gaits, and are highly appreciated for road work and long-distance rides. The walk (flat-footed) should be regular, spirited, and quite rapid, except when the horse is allowed to loaf for a rest after a brisk brush along the road. If a horse walks 4½ or 5 miles an hour, he is good enough at this gait.

The running-walk is faster and easier than the flat-footed walk, and is quite similar in speed and ease to the fox-trot, but not quite so fast. It is a delightful all-day gait, and is performed with four beåts, like the rack, but not so fast or lofty. In going this gait the horse's reins are rather loose and he takes some of the arch out of his neck, and, if in full sympathy with his work, keeps time with his step by the nodding of his head. A horse of good endurance and clever at this gait will make from 6 to 7 miles an hour, and travel from 60 to 75 miles a day without great fatigue to himself or rider.

The fox-trot is quite similar to the running-walk, yet it has a distinct "loose-jointed" motion and "jog" not observed in any other gait. This, too, is an all-day gait, and good up hill and down, and this is where a fox-trotter and running-walker make time in an all-day journey.

The gaited saddler goes from a flat-footed walk into all his other gaits direct, but he should return to the walk from the canter and rack through the trot, and he should make all his short turns and sharp curves on the trot if going faster than a walk.

The rack is probably the most fascinating gait, and, if well done, is the hardest on the horse. He must go at a tension and rack against the bit, and he must get action from his hocks and shoulders as well as from his knees. If he goes in form, he will carry a high head and a high tail, arch his neck, and hold a vertical face. He must be pulled together, and remain collected from start to finish. If he goes in a pure, clear, bold rack, his feet make four-beat music, the rhythm of which cannot be mistaken for that of any other gait. The rack was formerly called a "single-foot" gait, and this term describes the action of the feet exactly, as only a single foot strikes the ground at one time.

Now comes the canter, which is the most graceful of all gaits and one that is quite easy for both horse and rider. There is a vast difference, however, between the canter of a gaited saddler and the gallop of an unrestrained horse or the lope of a bronco.   Any horse will lope or gallop when pushed beyond his trotting or pacing speed, but the gaited saddler goes from a walk, or even from a standstill, into a graceful, enjoyable, hammock-like motion, which we call a canter; his legs are never so well under him as when in the canter, and his neck is never so beautifully arched.

The high-school horse is simply the gaited saddler, finished in education, polished in manners, and taught other gaits, steps, and movements. When thus educated, when thus finished, he is a paragon of grace, ease, and beauty, and when in motion he is poetry set to music.

CHAPTER VI.

THE CAVALRY HORSE.

The American Cavalry Horse Compared to Others—General Characteristics—Stallions—Geldings—Mares—Age—Bones—Teeth—Neck—Knees—Hocks—Back—Tail—Croup—Proportions.

It has been seen from the preceding chapter that certain well-known types of horses exist from which have sprung all the various styles of horses in modern use. Each of these classes is especially adapted to the performance of certain work, as heretofore explained. To attempt to use a Percheron as a gaited saddle-horse, or a Thoroughbred trotter at the plow, would be manifestly demanding of an animal work for which Nature never intended him, and in like manner the experience of the different cavalry services of the world has gradually developed a distinct and separate class of horse for cavalry work. This horse might be said to embrace the disposition, spirit, agility, and intelligence of the Thoroughbred gaited saddle-animal and the large bone and strong sinew short back, stout forehand, strength, and hardihood of a Hackney, Clydesdale, or Percheron.

The horse generally found best suited for cavalry work is one which possesses the necessary strength of bone and sinew, fair proportions, steady gaits, normal mouth, good health, good intelligence, and good blood. Many experiments made by the American Cavalry with many styles of horses and the various experiments in cross-breeding for cavalry purposes that have been made in Europe and Great Britain in the past have led to the adoption of certain fixed rules in accepting cavalry horses. In a preceding chapter it has been shown what is held to constitute the light cavalry horse and the heavy cavalry horse in several of

the best cavalry services.   The regulation cavalry horse
in our own service has already been given in detail.

It will be seen that certain general qualifications are
deemed by all cavalry services to be indispensable.
These points among the various services are generally
the height, weight, age, and sex.   Let us see what they
usually are in the best services:

German light cavalry, 15–2 to 16 hands in height;
Russian light cavalry, 15 to 15–1 hands in height;
French light cavalry, 14½ to 15⅛ hands in height;
English light cavalry, 15–1 hands in height.

The weight in all these services for the light cavalry
horse is from 900 or 950 as a minimum to 1050 pounds
as an extreme maximum.   As Austria and the United
States are not divided into light and heavy cavalry, but
are both practically light cavalry, let us see what they
have:

Austrian cavalry, 15–1 to 16–1 hands, 950 to 1100
    pounds;
American cavalry, 15–1 to 16 hands, 950 to 1150
    pounds;

It will be noticed that the Germans, the Americans,
and the Austrians all use large horses, even for their light
cavalry.   Let us see what the heavy cavalry is in some of
these countries:

German heavy cavalry, 16 to 17 hands in height;
Russian heavy cavalry, 15–1 to 16 hands in height;
French heavy cavalry, 15¼ to 16⅛ hands in height;
English heavy cavalry, 16 hands in height.

It will be seen from the above that the French and
Russian and English heavy cavalry horses are all about
equal in size to the American and Austrian cavalry horse.
The weight of these horses of the heavy cavalry in Germany is about 1080 pounds; of the Russian, about the
same; and of the others, approximately the same also,
some of them running as high as 1150 pounds, but rarely
beyond that.   In some of these countries there exists
the central class of cavalry known as the medium.   Let

us see what the specifications are regarding height and
weight:

> French medium cavalry, 15 to 15–1 hands, 1080
> pounds;
> English medium cavalry, 15–2 hands, 1050
> pounds;

From the above tables it will be readily seen how
some countries use the horse as a medium cavalry animal
which other services desire as their light or even heavy
horse; in fact, the general average of them all will best
show what the size of the cavalry horse for the light cavalry service is, and this may be roughly set down as about
15¼ hands in height and about 1000 pounds in weight.
This horse is amply big enough for all light cavalry work.
The Russian Cossack uses a still smaller animal, often not
above 14½ hands, and does the hardest sort of field service.
Now let us examine as to the age of the horses used in
the various services:

Germany procures its cavalry horses between three
and four years of age, but does not put them into regimental or field service until over four and usually over
five years of age.

Austria-Hungary procures its cavalry horses between
five and seven years of age, taking younger animals, however, very frequently—often as young as three and a half
to four years old, if especially good.

Russia procures its cavalry horses between three and
a half and seven years of age, but does not use the younger
horses for a year or more, during which time they are
being trained at the dépôts.

France procures its cavalry horses between three and
eight years of age, also training the new horse for over a
year before sending him to the regiment.

England procures its cavalry horses between five and
six years of age, and the United States procures its animals for cavalry service between four and eight, horses
under five years being bought only when especially well
developed.

It would seem from the above, that experience has warned us not to use the horse when he is too young, for active field service; that the horse six years old and upwards can stand it, but the younger horse needs careful handling and training while his bones and form are maturing; also that the purchase of these horses under four years of age is advisable, wherever the horse is first subjected to long, careful training, as he learns more quickly than when older, and consequently can be moulded into a better troop-horse.

It now remains to be seen what these great cavalry services do as regards the sex of the horse:

Germany procures either geldings or mares;
Austria procures either geldings or mares;
Russia procures either stallions, geldings or mares;
France procures either geldings or mares;
England procures either stallions, geldings or mares;
United States procures only geldings.

A gelding is a castrated horse; the castration is usually performed when the horse is about one year of age, after he has gotten past the age when to castrate him might injure his form and strength. The castration of the cavalry horse is necessary as a means of control. The American Cavalry service has never used mares; the use of them is always attended with more or less danger of becoming in foal, especially if herded where there are other horses. They require more care and attention in this respect than they they would be worth in service. As to the physical strength, mares are frequently found fully equal to the geldings. The objections to the stallions are that they are inclined to be vicious and are often unmanageable to such an extent as to render them a nuisance anywhere near a troop. It would be impossible to herd them together loosely, as they would seriously injure themselves by desperate fighting. The gelding has been found to possess all the strength of bone and sinew and all the intelligence and spirit one could wish for, provided castration has not been performed too early in life. The period of gestation is eleven months, and after the colt is born he should not be castrated for at least a year. A horse castrated too late, say two years or upwards, generally possesses unusual strength and development, but is inclined to retain some of the viciousness of the stallion and be a bother in a troop. On the other hand, castrating too early often produces ewe necks, narrow frames, or other weaknesses.

The American Cavalry service is light cavalry in all its work and training, in the weight of its men, and its armament and pack, and therefore requires light, strong, agile horses. Large 1100-pound, 16-hand horses are generally less agile, slower, and more lumbering than the 950-pound, 14½- or 15-hand horse of light, hardy build and quick action. The use of a very large horse in such cavalry as the American Cavalry is not only an abomination to the man that has to ride him and a severe trial both to his patience and endurance, but a serious handicap to the troop in which the man is riding; and as a further illustration of the suitability of small horses for light cavalry work, it might be remarked that an 800-pound pack-mule frequently carries 250 pounds on his back in an awkward, elevated, balance-destroying manner and accompanies cavalry over all country; then surely a 900- or 950-pound horse ought to be able to carry the same load carefully distributed, hung low to help preserve his equilibrium, and frequently relieved by the dismounting of his rider.

At different times in the past the American Cavalry commands on the frontier have experimented with Western ponies for cavalry service, usually with unsatisfactory results. This is not strange, for while we all know of particular ponies of 750 or 800 pounds exhibiting great endurance, the average Western pony is not sufficiently well bred to possess or produce standard qualities. In many parts of the West the writer has known many ponies to exhibit remarkable stamina, endurance, and intelligence in all the work required in the cattle country, and there is no doubt that such animals can be found throughout the United States in large numbers and at comparatively small cost.

It has generally been held by our cavalry officers of years of experience in Western field service that the large horse used by the American cavalryman is necessary, but the advantage in having a smaller horse is in the greater ease to the trooper (and this wonderfully affects the horse, especially in the field with heavy pack-saddles) and the increasing of the efficiency standard by the smaller, lighter, more agile horse being far more in hand; and, furthermore, if the horse weighs but 900 or 950 pounds, he should be smaller in height, in proportion, and not weigh less at the expense of strength and symmetry.

During two years' service in the Philippines with the Fourth Cavalry the writer used a 14½-hand horse, weighing only a trifle over 900 pounds. He carried exactly the same weight in equipment and kit as the horses of the troopers, and was subjected for weeks and months at a time to the same exposure, work, forage, weight, and duty; he was one of the best animals in the troop at all times—hardy, strong, and in good condition. This horse was not especially cared for because he belonged to an officer, but underwent equal hardship, and held his own fully among hundreds of cavalry horses of more or less correct regulation type. It may be added that this horse was condemned by the Government as being too small for service in 1899, and it was afterward that he underwent the campaign and field service mentioned above. The horse mentioned was simply a plains-bred Nevada horse. Occasionally the writer observed here and there among the cavalry commands in the Philippines horses which had crept into the service despite the fact that they were smaller than the regulation horse, and in every instance that he can recall these small horses were giving most satisfactory service. Troop I of the Fourth Cavalry, at first mounted on native Filipino ponies of exceedingly small build, were afterwards mounted for the balance of its field service on American horses averaging about 14¾ hands and 950 pounds, and these horses were found most desirable. A large horse spreads the light cavalryman out absurdly, forcing him to curve his legs inward at a most unnatural angle to grip at all, and there is nothing easy about the seat or the gait or the management of the horse. The immediate bad result of this is a tendency on the part of the average rider to lounge in the saddle, and it would take a most exceptionally patient trooper not to lounge on a large, heavy horse, and this lounging in the saddle on field service is disastrous to a cavalry command.

A mixture of Thoroughbred and Percheron or Thoroughbred and Clydesdale or Thoroughbred and Hackney produces a fine light cavalry horse; he is small, between 14½ and 15 hands, weighing between 900 and 950 pounds, strongly knit, hardy, and agile. No cavalry has ever attempted to mount its men exclusively on Thoroughbred horses. The cavalry is the most expensive branch of an army, and to procure the Thoroughbred animals required would be too enormously expensive an experiment to try. Experience has taught that the care of the Thoroughbred horse is more than can be given him in field service. Experience has also taught that good horses suitable in every way for cavalry can be procured in sufficient numbers, while Thoroughbred animals could not. Most countries possess animals in large numbers possessing standard qualities, which, by care in selection and training, amply fulfill requirements.

The American regulation cavalry horse seems to cover all good points in an ideal light cavalry animal, except perhaps a little too much height and weight, as a maximum, if the light cavalry horse in use in most European cavalry and the light horse used so extensively in all parts of the West can be taken as the result of experience and experiment.

There are some apparent defects in horses which at once render them unfit for cavalry service; among these are lack of fair proportion in the relative parts of the frame, evident to the eye: cow-hocks, knock-knees, long

backs, tall withers, goose-rumps, bad teeth, defective eyes
narrow chests, knee-sprung, ewe-necks, sway backs, buck-
knees, roach backs, straight pasterns, short straight shoulders, narrow flanks, and many others; but those named

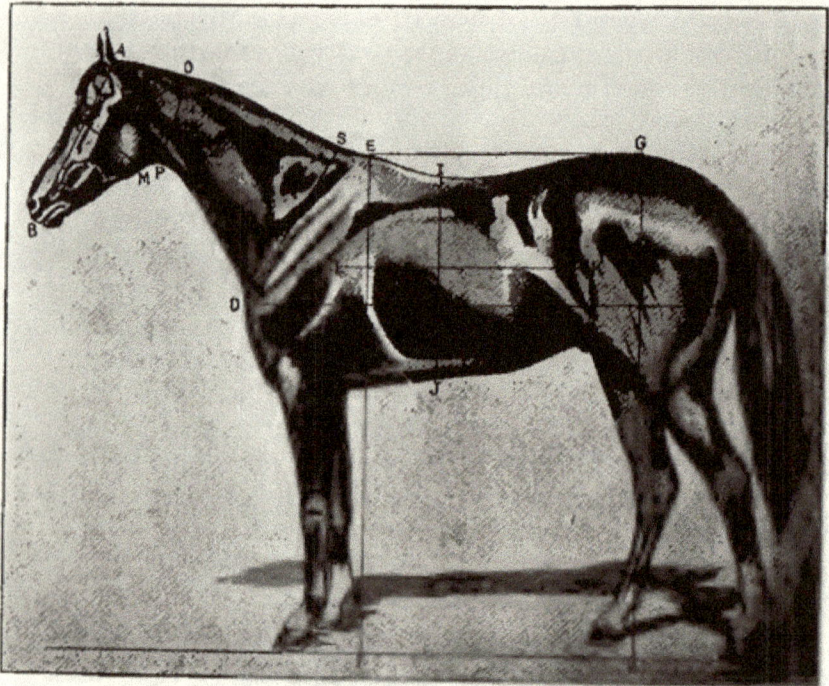

PROPORTIONS COMMON AMONG HORSES. (HAYES.)

1. Length of body (C D) = 2½ times length of head.
2. Height at withers (E F) = height at croup (G H).
3. Length of head (A B) = depth of body at lowest part of back (I J).
4. Length of head (A B) = distance of "swell" of muscle at posterior angle of shoulder-blade to point of hips (L K).
5. Width of head (M N) = ½ length of head (A B).
6. Length of head (A B) = distance of point of shoulder to top of withers (D S).
7. Width of head (M N) = width of upper part of neck (O P).
8. Height of withers (E F) = length of body (C D), about.

can readily be observed after some experience, and rejec-
tion of horses possessing them is imperative. Contractors will often present horses for purchase by the Government possessing these defects, and while some of them

may not be signs of actual unsoundness, such animals should be rejected if being purchased for cavalry work.

Let us consider these separately; many of them may be seen among the animals of a large command, as some poor horses will always creep in among the good ones.

Fair Proportion.—As the horse stands at ease, he should be viewed from all directions—from both sides, from the right and left front and rear, from the direct front and direct rear, etc. By taking the size of the head as the unit of measurement, the various proportions of the horse may be quickly obtained, approximately, by reference to the figure. It is seen that, with fair proportion—

1. Length of head equals length of shoulder from withers to point of shoulder; and

2. Equals length of barrel from immediately behind the shoulder-blade to immediately in front of the hip-joint; and

3. Equals the depth of the barrel from the center of the back to the belly, taken perpendicularly; and

4. Equals distance from stifle to point of hock; and

5. Equals distance from point of hock to the ground, along the leg; and

6. Two and one-half times the length of the head equals the height of the withers above the ground; and

7. Equals height of top of croup above the ground; and

8. Equals the length of the horse, taken from the point of the shoulder to the rear of the buttocks, horizontally.

All these measurements must be taken as a shoemaker measures the length of the foot, and they are approximate only. Some horses will, of course, vary somewhat, and still the general appearance of correct proportion will be good, while others will fall far short of any reasonable proportion by being long-headed, long-backed, low-withered, short-shouldered, etc. After experience, these points will be quickly caught by the eye, but it will pay the new cavalryman to actually do some measuring, and if he does so, he will learn much regarding relative proportion of the parts of the horse.

IDEAL HEAD.

The Head.—It should be reasonably small and neatly cut; the eyes should be large, clear, and intelligent and the vision perfect. This may be fairly ascertained by waving the hand before the eyes, and observing whether or not the horse blinks or moves away the head; if not, suspect defective vision. The forehead between the eyes should be flat and broad; the distance from the eye to the point of the jaw should be large; the width between the lower jaws should be great; the nostrils should be large, open, healthy, and free from coarse, bristly hairs, as these indicate inferior blood; the teeth should be sound and all present; the tongue and bars should be free from bruises, sores, or calloused places; the ears should be small and well carried; the lips should be thin, healthy, and firm; the chin-groove should be smooth, with no rough

THE "EWE-NECKED" HORSE.

prominences on the edges of the jaws at this place; the head should be carried well up, in a spirited manner. The horse should have what is known as a good face—if the line of the face, when viewed from the side, is straight, it is considered good; if this line curves inward, as though scooped out, the face is called "dish-faced," and is some-what unsightly; if, on the contrary, the face curves out-ward, it is known as "Roman-nosed"; it is unsightly in proportion to the amount of curvature outward; the more the curve the more ugly becomes the face, and this "Roman nose" is also apt to be accompanied by small nostrils. The head should be well set on the neck, and wholly lack stiffness in movement.

The Neck.—The neck should be moderately long, full, reasonably arched, with a good, neat crest, and gradually grow larger as it approaches the shoulders; the muscles on the sides should be strong, well developed, and prominent; the under side, or "throttle," should be full and well outlined; the neck should not bulge out at the upper end on the under side, as this is apt to interfere with the hollow between the jaws, and instead of the neck entering this hollow as the head is drawn in, the lower jaw-bones come against this thick part of the neck and cause the rider to have to exert unusual pressure on the reins to manage the animal. Occasionally the neck grows smaller as it approaches the shoulders, and seems to sink in on the top near the withers; this is known as "ewe neck," and is unsightly, and may be an indication of lack of strength; at any rate, it is unsightly. When the neck is straight, it is probably more satisfactory; when the neck curves upward, it is known as an "arched neck," and is usually the result of training the horse to carry his head in this manner, though it may be natural to some horses This arched neck is frequently seen in animals that have not been castrated until quite old, and in stallions this curved, powerful neck is one of the most striking marks. The mane should be full all along the "crest" of the neck. As the length of the neck and the position of the head upon it materially affect the management of the horse and his gaits, a careful study of the mechanical principles involved here will prove interesting.

The Withers.—The withers are the bony ridge which is the forward combination of the back. Its posterior limit is, as a rule, ill-defined, for the curve made by the withers usually runs into that of the back in a gradual manner. Its anterior termination can often be felt by the hand, as the bony ridge ends abruptly in the crest. The withers materially affect the fit of the saddle, and as they cover large, strong muscles, demanding free action, it is important that they be well formed. If too high, the saddle is apt to pinch them; if too low, the saddle is apt to slide forward and chafe them; if too narrow, the saddle is apt to pinch them; and if too broad, the saddle will be held up too high and consequently press into the back at the

THE "HIGH-WITHERED" HORSE.

cantle. The withers should be moderately elevated, and just what this means will have to be learned by experience and observation; suffice it to say that they require careful attention when saddling, as they are easily made sore, especially if badly formed.

The Back.—The back must be short and straight in the cavalry horse; it must be built to sustain weight; it must be broad enough to let the side-bars rest snugly; if too narrow, the side-bars are apt to pinch the spine and press on the ribs below in a perpendicular manner and cause sore back; if the back is too wide, the saddle will be lifted too high off the back and part of the under surface of the saddle will not rest as it should; if too short, the saddle will bruise the withers; if too long, the entire back will probably be weak and the saddle apt to slip. A long

CHUNKY HORSE AND SHORT BACK.

back is the result of cross-breeding for trotting purposes, and is worthless for the cavalry horse. If the back curves downward, it is called a "sway back," and is liable to be weak, besides which, the saddle cannot be made to fit properly; both ends of the side-bars will press into the withers and back under the cantle, and an uneven bearing surface being thus obtained, the back will soon be chafed sore. If the back curves upward, it is termed a "roach back," and the saddle cannot be made to fit this either; as it touches only near and at the center, the saddle rocks and the back again becomes sore. The cavalry horse must have a straight back and a short one. The sway back is weak, and the roach back is worthless for cavalry, though strong.

The Croup.—This is the region from the end of the back to the tail; it should have a moderate curve, be broad and strong, as it contains the propelling muscles and important joints; the tail should be carried up on it fairly well, for if hung low down, it indicates coarse blood; if the croup inclines very rapidly to the rear and the tail is set on low down, the croup is called ''goose-rumped''; it is unsightly, shows coarseness, and is more or less of an indication of weak, undeveloped hind muscles; it is undesirable, in any event, in the cavalry horse.

The Shoulders.—These should be long and sloping well back, and have free action. Short, straight shoulders are indicative of hard gait, and the pounding on the horse's front feet will be considerable, to say nothing of the jar which such shoulders will communicate to the rider. The shoulder muscles should be well developed and healthy.

The Fore Legs.—These should be straight, as viewed both from in front and from the side. The knee should especially be straight; if it inclines to the rear, it is known as ''buck'' or ''calf'' knee, and is a sign of weakness generally, and a sign of too much strain on the back sinews of the legs always; if the knees bend to the front, the horse is known as ''knee-sprung.'' This faulty position comes from too much hard riding on hard roads, from founder, from old age, etc., and is a sign of worthlessness, so far as the cavalry is concerned. Such legs are unsafe at all times, and danger of the horse going down is very great. The upper bone of the fore leg cannot well be too long, and the lower part of the leg cannot well be too short; the leg must not be ''tied in'' below the knees—that is, must not suddenly become very small immediately below the knees, but should be of good, fair size all the way down, and as

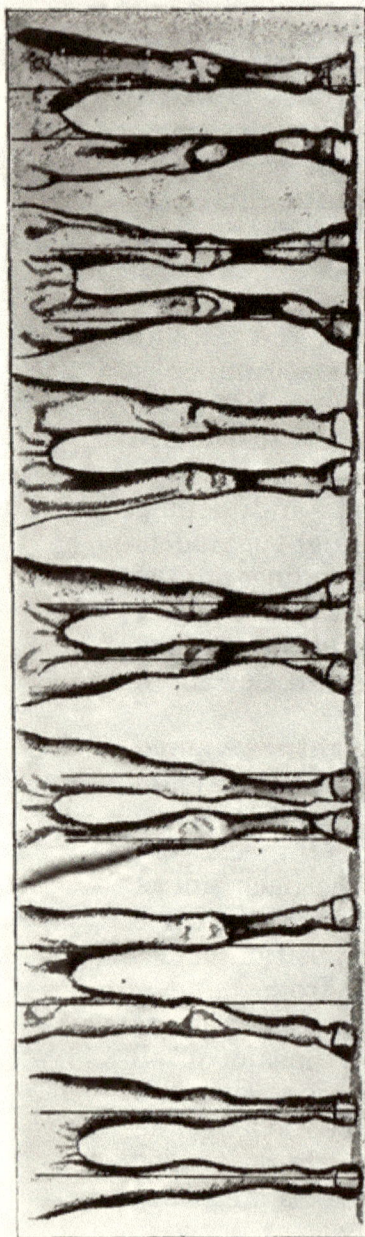

Standing straight and true. Too wide. Too close in front. Duck-footed and twisted cannons outwards. Twisted cannons inwards and pin-toed. Calf knees. Knees too open.

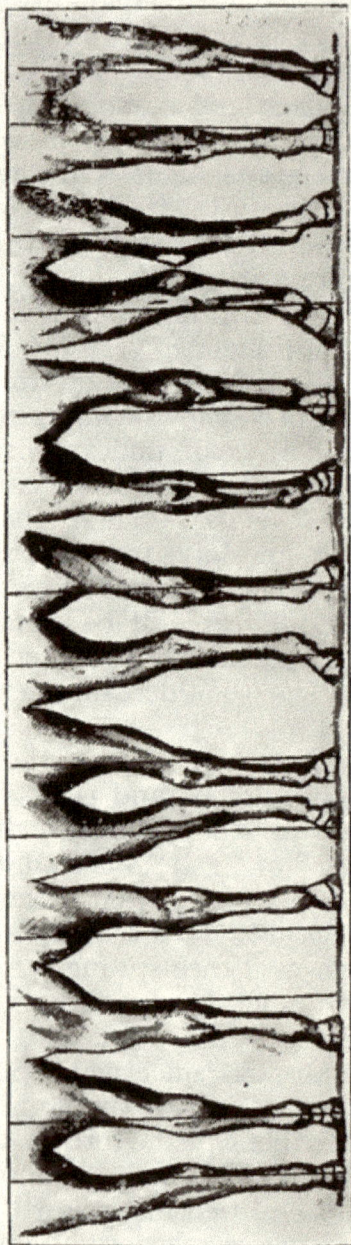

Standing straight and correctly. Too wide. Too close. Duck foot behind. Bow-legged and pin-toed. Cow-hocked. Too open.

FORE AND HIND LEGS.

large below the knee as farther down. The action at both the knee and elbow must be free and easy and wholly lack constraint.

The Pasterns.—These must be reasonably long and well slanting; if they slant too much, it is apt to be a weakness more than a sign of strength, and at any rate indicates that undue strain is thrown on the tendons; if

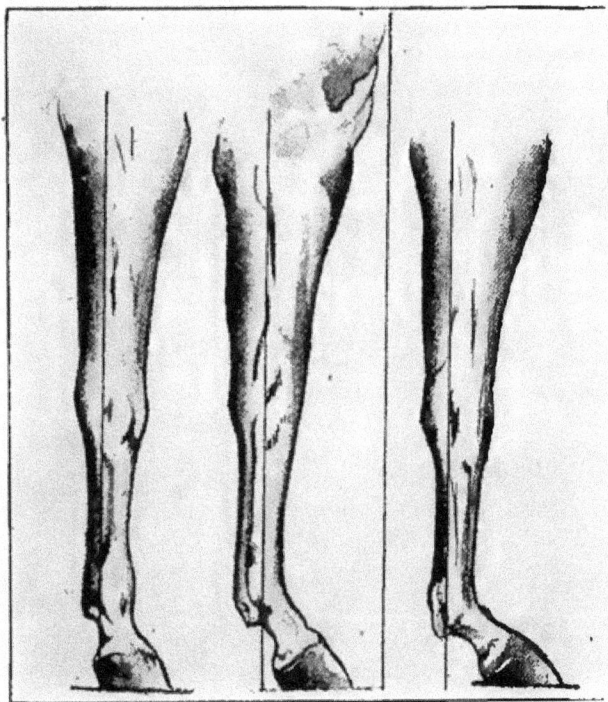

| Ankle short and too straight. | Leg straight and well balanced. | Ankle too long and straight. |

PASTERNS, THREE SIDE VIEWS.

too short, the gait of the animal will be rough and the jar both on the horse and on his rider will be considerable. A long, sloping pastern generally means an easy gait, but may also indicate weakness.

The Feet.—These should be small and sound; the sole, bars, frog, and walls should all be healthy, firm, and present a general appearance of durability and entire lack of bad odors or excretions of filthy smell; the ordinary hoof smell is easily distinguished from such indications of disease. The feet should be even in size and shape, and not too long from the coronet down to the ground at the toe; too long feet are an indication of navicular disease or past founder. There should be no flinching by the

GREYHOUND BARREL.

horse when the foot is tapped lightly with a hammer on the bars, sole, and walls; there should be no unusual heat about the feet; there should be no flinching by the horse when the frog is pressed firmly by the fingers; there should be no separation at any point between the sole and the walls. The horse should be stood on level ground when viewing the feet, as standing the fore feet on high ground throws the weight very much on the hind feet, and even if the horse has something painful the matter with the fore feet, he will probably stand easily in this position; the reverse is also true. The feet and legs should be carried well under the body, and not pushed out to the front or rear.

The Barrel.—This should increase slightly from the shoulders towards the rear—that is, towards the flanks;

. A GOOD ALL-ROUND WEIGHT-CARRIER.

if the contrary is the case, the saddle will not be able to stay in place without the use of breast-straps, as the cincha will keep slipping backward. The space between the last (rear) floating rib and the point of the hip should be as short as possible in the cavalry horse; the increasing of the circumference of the barrel towards the rear also may be considered a good sign as regards field service, as the horse will have more to lose in the way of flesh; a horse thin and narrowing toward the rear in the barrel can lose very little flesh in the field without injury.

The Chest.—This should be broad, full, and deep; if narrow, it is a sign of weakness and unfitness generally for cavalry service. Too broad a chest, however, is not necessary or desirable in the cavalry horse, but the chest, as viewed from the front, should appear reasonably wide, full, and deep. Narrow-chested horses rarely stand cavalry work for any length of time, although desirable to ride, owing to the ease with which the rider's legs can straddle and clinch the animal.

The Hind Quarters.—These should be full, well developed, carried lightly, and be plentifully supplied with strong muscles, as they are the propelling power. The stifle should be well set on and free from any stiffness or peculiarity of motion; the hocks must be broad and deep and free from any signs of enlargements, either hard or soft; if present, these may be signs of many diseases, especially spavin; the hocks should be well bent and under the horse; if they come together so as to touch each other, or nearly so, the horse is called "cow-hocked," and this is considered a sign of more or less weakness.

In viewing cavalry horses, it is always best to choose one of very good proportions and keep him near at hand, in order to compare each horse as he is brought up with this model. It will greatly aid in quickly discerning the lack of fair proportion, etc., in the other horses.

Many horses of excellent size and shape and appearing sound and suitable possess stable vices, and are as undesirable in a cavalry troop as horses actually unsound. Stable vices are rarely cured. The most common stable vices are weaving, wind-sucking, biting, kicking, cribbing, pulling back, continual pawing, and defective lying down. Horses possessing any of the above vices are a nuisance in a troop, and usually after very brief service are condemned and sold; if not, they tend largely to produce dissatisfaction among the troopers that have to ride them, and have to be specially cared for in stables, in camp, on the march, and elsewhere, and demand much attention, which they are rarely worth.

These stable vices are common among horses, and the name of the vice generally describes it; however, there are some in which this is not the case.

Weaving.—This is a side-to-side swaying motion, similar to that seen in animals caged. The writer has never seen a case of weaving during ten years of cavalry service; however, it does exist among the horses, and, if watched for, would probably be seen. The motion is wearing on the legs, more or less annoying to the other horse occupying the stall, and should be considered a defect.

Wind-Sucking.—This vice consists in the horse taking hold of the manger or halter-strap, pulling back somewhat on it, and sucking in his breath with a loud noise. It may be somewhat cured by coating the halter-strap and wood-work of the manger with some harmless, bitter medicine, such as aloes; tar will do.

Cribbing.—This consists in the horse's gnawing the wood-work of his manger and stall. As it wears away the teeth and thus interferes with mastication and consequently impairs the digestive system, it is a particularly bad vice; it also ruins the manger and stall; it will prevent the horse from doing it, somewhat, to coat the wood-work as before, or to cover the wood-work of the manger with tin.

Pulling Back.—This consists in the horse suddenly moving backwards to the full length of his halter-strap, and generally breaking it. Some horses do this persistently, despite all efforts to break them. A method that will work well on one animal apparently has little effect on another horse. A good way to stop the breaking of the straps and the getting loose of the horse in consequence is to pass a heavy rope through the halter-ring, then around over the animal's back and under the tail and back again through the halter-ring, then tie the two ends of the rope to the manger, so that when the horse springs backward the halter-strap will still be loose and the weight and tug will come on the rope; as this lacerates the under part of the root of the tail, the horse, after a few efforts to break the rope, will frequently desist. The writer has known some horses to be cured for months by this method.

As has been said, the stable vices are rarely cured; they may be checked or corrected for several months, but sooner or later the horse will go back to them. Biting, kicking, continual pawing, and defective lying down are themselves self-explanatory

In addition to the above defects and stable vices are several other equally bad ones, noticeable only when the horse is observed under the saddle. Those most commonly noticed are habitual bolting, rearing back, habitual stumbling, habitual shying, interfering, paddling, inability to trot, inability to walk, forging, general stubbornness, known in the service as "bull-headedness," and hard-mouthed horses.

These names generally themselves also describe the defects quite plainly, but we will look at them a moment.

Habitual Bolting.—This is the habitual running away of the horse when being ridden; it may come from bad bitting, bad riding, ill-temper of the trooper as manifested by his severe use of the spurs or reins, or as ill-temper in the horse. If an animal is found with this vice, it may be corrected very much by careful bitting and careful riding; the use of a milder or stronger bit, a lighter or heavier hand, as the case may be, may accomplish an entire cure, but sometimes the horse is too confirmed in it to be corrected. He should not be accepted for the cavalry if he is discovered to have this vice, and should be gotten rid of by transfer to the Artillery or to the Quartermaster's Department, if possible, if he is in the troop.

Rearing Back.—This is the rearing up of the horse on his hind legs when being ridden; it may be so bad as often to throw the horse entirely over backwards, and is about the meanest, most treacherous, and dangerous vice the troop-horse can have. The use of a martingale will do much to correct this vice; tying the halter-shank to the cincha between the horse's fore legs will keep his head down. The vice is sometimes caused by bad bitting and a heavy hand on the reins.

Habitual Stumbling —This explains itself. The stumbling is generally in the fore feet, and may be caused by a diseased or ruined foot or natural clumsiness; bad shoeing will cause it. This vice is much more apparent after a march has been long enough continued to weary the animal; it is dangerous at all times, and the horse, especially at the rapid gaits, is not to be relied on. A horse that habitually stumbles when fresh will do much more of it in field service. There is no real cure.

Habitual Shying.—This may be so bad that the least noise or simplest sight causes the horse to leap aside. The horse must be trained to pass blowing paper, etc., and the ordinary sights in garrison and field, in an easy manner, and to take unusual sounds quietly. Training and gentle handling will do much, and abuse nothing. Defective vision often is a cause of habitual shying, and if the shying continues daily, the eyes should be examined, and, if found diseased, the horse condemned.

Interfering.—This consists in the toe of one fore foot striking the other fore foot in moving forward; it may exist only on one side or on both; bad shoeing will cause it. If the horse interferes while fresh, he will be sure to do more of it when more or less tired from marching; it may be so bad at such times as to injure the feet or legs. Careful shoeing may correct it.

Forging.—This consists in the toe of the hind foot striking the shoe of the fore foot on the same side, the horse not getting this foot out of the way in time. This fault is apt to become much more pronounced as the horse tires. Careful shoeing will bring about much improvement.

Paddling.—The feet, in moving forward, do not go straight forward, but swing outward, horizontally, making small circular movements parallel to the ground as he walks; especially noticeable at the trot; fatiguing and unsightly. Careful shoeing may correct it.

Inability to Trot.—Some horses hardly ever trot, especially when in the troop. The horse breaks directly from the walk to a slow canter, and requires to be constantly held in to keep from treading upon the feet of the horses ahead; when out of ranks, may often be gotten to trot, but the excitement of drill, etc., makes the horse nervous, and the canter is stubbornly taken Training will do much to obviate this vice; heavy shoeing may correct it.

Inability to Walk.—Some horses in the troop will regularly and habitually take a jig-jog trot all day long while the other animals are walking. It is difficult to correct, is most tiresome to the rider, and results in sore backs. Heavy shoeing may do much good. Such animals, if placed in the lead, may sometimes be made to walk; but as their walk is generally slower than that of the other horses, the rate of marching at the walk is delayed, and the other troopers have to hold back their horses constantly to accommodate the gait to these ill-gaited horses. Training does much good, but some animals never seem able to walk as fast as the other horses, and keep this miserable trot up daily during even long marches.

Mouths.—The mouth may be either tender, normal, hard, or spoiled; the tender mouth requires a light hand, a carefully adjusted bit, and constant attention, else the horse will become nervous, irregular in the gaits, and a source of constant trouble in the troop. The normal mouth is the best, wherein the animal takes the properly adjusted bit easily and without fear and responds promptly to the reins. The hard mouth is where the horse bores on the bit, is callous to it, and requires constant good management of the reins to hold him. This mouth is sometimes cured by careful bitting. The use of a snaffle-bit on some hard-mouthed horses has made them easy to manage, but as a general thing such horses cause more hardship in a troop than they are worth. The spoiled mouth is one which has usually been ruined by early neglect or indifference in bitting him. Such a horse pays little or no attention to the bit or reins; at times suffers from the bit and at other times seems to be able to stand the most painful style. Careful bitting will do much to correct such a mouth, but the horse's mouth, once so abused, is very hard to cure and get back into the normal condition.

While contractors are not to be expected to produce $200 horses when the contract price is about $100, nevertheless horses possessing apparent pronounced defects, stable vices, or any disease, should be promptly rejected by the cavalry officer making the purchase. A number of diseases which would justify the cavalry officer in rejecting the horse are not apparent unless the officer is very careful in his inspection, while other diseases may be readily noticed, but considered lightly, when in reality they may be the outward indications of serious defects. The more rigid the officer is in demanding proper horses within reason, the better will the cavalry be for his care. Horses having any of the following diseases or indications of them should be rejected: watery eyes, nasal discharge, spavins, curbs, poll evil, fistula of withers, severe sore backs, severe sprains, ringbone, side-bones, thrush, quittor, evidences of farcy or glanders, or surra, corns, seedy toes, splints, poor feet from any cause, lameness, run-down condition, mange, scratches, wind-galls, thoroughpin, navicular disease, founder or laminitis, hoof-cracks, contracted heels, coughs, etc. These are discussed in Chapter XVIII.

Horses having defective feet may be often made to appear entirely sound by means of special shoeing. Old horses may be made to appear comparatively young by means of rasping off the corners of the incisors and burning marks on the tops of the incisors (Bishoping). Weak horses may be made to appear in good condition at the time of inspection by the administering of strong tonics; horses

with diseased kidneys or spine may be made to appear
entirely sound by being stood on high ground and holding
up the horse's head; a horse with diseased feet may be
made to appear all right by throwing the reins over the
horse's head and holding it back with the curb while the
horse is touched under the belly with a long whip—this
puts the horse on his mettle and he places his feet on the
ground without thinking of the pain that it causes him,
as his whole mind is taken up by the whipping; groggy
horses may be excited just before the inspection to such
a point as to make them conduct themselves at the time
of the inspection with a good deal of life.

The above tricks of horse-dealers might be multiplied
many times; these few are given only for the purpose of
making it evident to the young cavalry officer how all-
important it is to know a good horse when he sees one, to
know whether it is fit for cavalry service, and to know
whether it is worth the price asked.

A few primary facts should be kept well in mind in
determining whether or not a horse is qualified to perform
cavalry service. He must be a weight-carrier, but not
more so than to the extent required. For instance, a
Clydesdale horse or a Percheron, with his massive size
and strength, could carry an enormous load, but would
be very slow and unsatisfactory. The cavalry horse
must be able to walk, trot, and gallop, taking in each gait
straight action, and all artificial gaits are not only undesirable, but are positive defects. This can be well illus-
trated to any young cavalry officer if he will mount a good
cavalry horse and ride at the rear of a troop going at the
walk, trot, and gallop, the troop having at its head a leader
mounted on a single-footer, a running-walker, a pacer, or
a horse with any of the artificial gaits. While it is very
easy for the officer in the lead to ride a horse with one
of the artificial gaits, it is absolute ruin to the tempers
and gaits of the horses following behind him, to say nothing of the exasperation and exhaustion that it causes the
men. The artificial gaits are absolutely undesirable in

cavalry horses. The cavalry horse must be intelligent, and young enough to be taught all that pertains to his service as a troop-horse. Intelligence in a horse is usually very apparent to a cavalry officer of some experience upon a very brief inspection of the animal. The cavalry horse should be in good condition when purchased, and not bought with the idea of afterwards fattening him up. As dealers usually put their horses in the best possible condition when offering them for sale to the Government, it is fair to assume that a horse in poor condition when offered will not improve sufficiently after purchase to justify buying him.

It has been seen that the age of the cavalry horse is of great importance. The very young animal may be too tender to stand the service, and the very old animal too aged to justify buying him. While it is good to buy the new cavalry horse between three and a half or four years of age to perhaps six or seven, in order that while still young he may be taught the cavalry work he must perform, yet horses under five are rarely sufficiently developed to stand what field service demands of him; on the other hand, horses over seven or eight are very hard to teach, and any irregularities of gait or disposition that they may have are very apt to be found permanent and not easily corrected. Thus, it becomes necessary to know *how* to tell the horse's age, and this is most easily and correctly done by observing his teeth. It must be remembered that some horses eat harder food than others; some do a large amount of grazing over sandy country, and thus wear away the teeth more rapidly than those fed on soft food, while some have naturally harder teeth than other horses. All these things may materially alter the appearance of the teeth, and must be appreciated when determining age in the horse. Let us see what his teeth are.

Teeth.—There are six incisors in the front of each jaw, six molars far back on each side in each jaw, and in addition to these there are two "tusks" in the lower jaw, one on each side, about an inch or so in rear of the rear incisors, and two "tusks" in the upper jaw, one on each side, about an inch or so back of the rear incisors. These "tusks" do not touch (lower and upper), the upper ones being somewhat farther to the rear than the lower

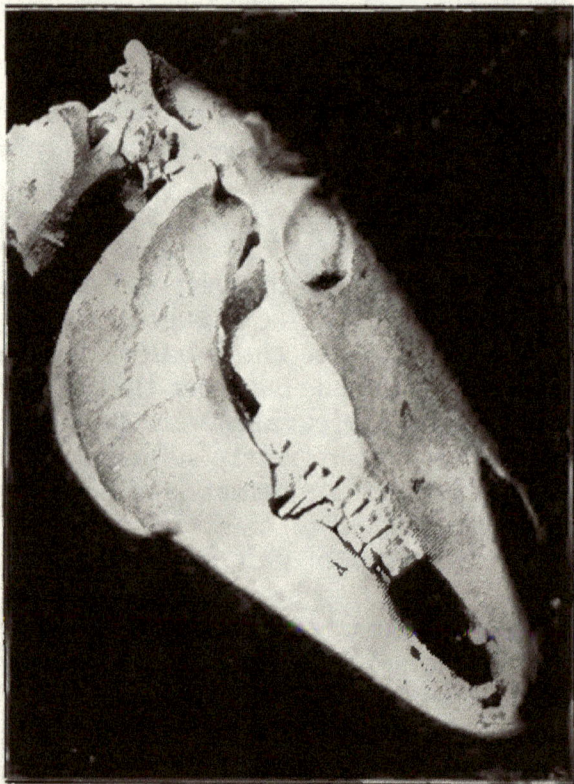

SKELETON OF HEAD.

Showing location of incisors, molars, etc., and showing probable cause of debility and final death of the famous trotting stallion "Ethan Allen."

ones. All told, then, the horse has thirty-six teeth and four "tusks," making forty in all. There may be one or more "wolf's teeth" present; these are small molars and come in front of the forward molars, usually in the lower jaw, and come up *against* the forward regular molars.

These are apt to cause trouble, and as they are easily removed by the pincers, this should be done. These "wolf's teeth" are rather uncommon among the horses, and the "tusks" are rarely found in the mare.

The Incisors.—Age is generally told by observing these twelve teeth. In the young horse, up to six or seven years, the angle form-ed by the upper and lower incisors as they come together is very obtuse, while in the old horse, from about nine years on, this an-gle becomes more and more acute until the upper and lower rows of incisors form so acute an angle as to appear to be in almost direct prolongation of the jaw in which they are. The incisors

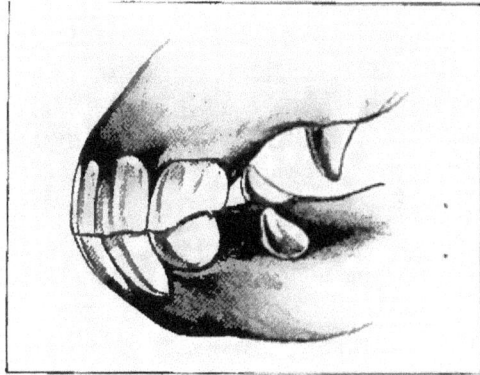

A six-year old mouth, showing the obtuse angle formed by the teeth in young horses.

are six in number in each jaw, and the two center ones in each jaw are called the "nippers," the next ones in each jaw are called the "dividers," and the last (rearmost) ones

welve year old mouth, showing the ngle of the teeth much more acute.

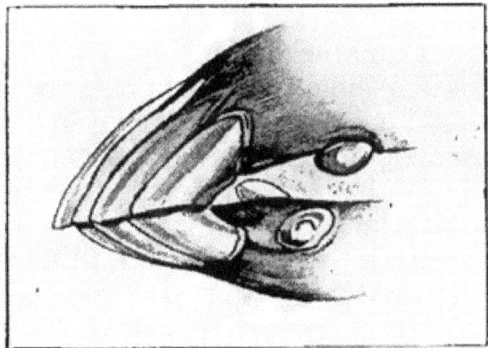

A twenty-year old mouth, showing the extremely acute angle of the teeth.

in each jaw are called the "corners." The figure shows one incisor tooth, and A is the *cul-de-sac* of the external dental cavity, surrounded by B, the central enamel; C. is the "dental star," and D is the whole surrounding enamel. The following figure shows this tooth again, giving the various shapes of the tooth in different parts of its length; first, flattened from forward backwards; then oval; then rounded; then triangular; then biangular, or flattened from side to side. These show important points in determining age The tooth of the young horse is first long in the direction of the jaw, then as the horse ages it becomes oval, then rounded, then triangular, then biangular, until in the very old horse the tooth is very long from front to rear and very narrow from side to side.

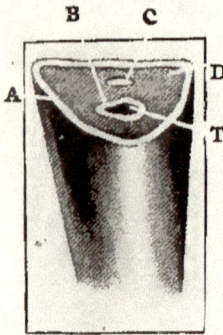

The Mark.

The "Dentinal Star," sometimes mistaken for the "Mark," and also the "Mark" itself.

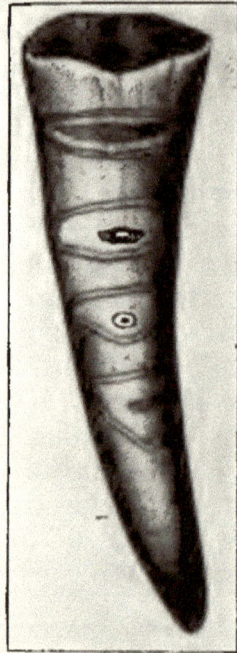

The forms successively assumed by the top of an incisor, in consequence of friction.

The Mark.—This is an almost circular hole in the center of the top of each incisor, as shown in a previous figure, extending down a considerable distance into the tooth. It is known as the "mark," and is conspicuous for its dark color, which is caused by the juices in the food getting into this hole and filling it up and thereby discoloring this part almost black. The surrounding edges of this "mark" are elevated enamel and white. As this hole or "mark" extends down into the tooth only a certain distance, it aids very much' in telling age, as it becomes obliterated as the crown wears away with the passage of years. After this "mark" has worn away, the top of the tooth consists only of the core of dentine surrounded by the external, hard, white enamel. There is a practice of "Bishoping," so called, by which is meant the burning of an artificial "mark" into the top of the tooth to make the horse appear younger, and this is often practiced by dishonest horse-dealers. This burned mark, however, being black and not surrounded with a circle of hard, high, white enamel, should be easily recognized. This "mark" in the natural tooth is often erroneously referred

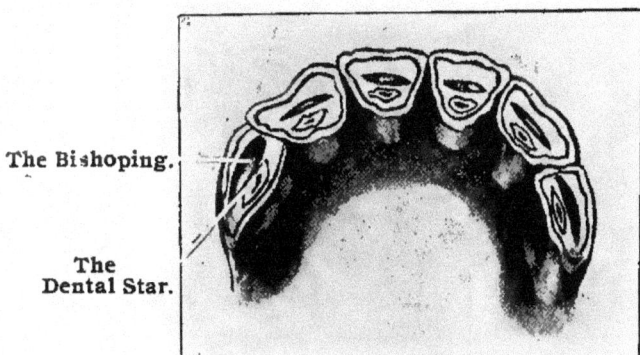

The Bishoping.

The
Dental Star.

A "Bishoped" mouth, easily recognized by the shape of the teeth
and the presence of the "Dental Star."

to as the "dental star." As the teeth all become much discolored after awhile by the juices in the food, it is not often easy to tell the "mark" without much practice and observation.

The Dental Star.—This is shown in a previous figure. It appears about the ninth year, and lasts from eight to ten years. The "star" may afford reliable data in determining age, but its presence is in itself evidence that the tooth has been worn to the original pulp cavity, and it becomes plainer until the bottom of the cavity is reached. It is sometimes called the "fang-hole" or "secondary mark."

As the incisors are in the front and consequently very accessible to look at, the molars, far back behind the cheeks, are rarely used to determine age.

Milk Teeth.—These are the first teeth of the young horse, and may be told from permanent teeth very readily, as they are usually smaller, rounder, whiter, and softer than the permanent teeth. The "corners" are sometimes hardly more than mere shells. These drop out by themselves as the permanent teeth come in. Colts are generally born in the spring with no incisors present; the first and second molars are present, and at the end of

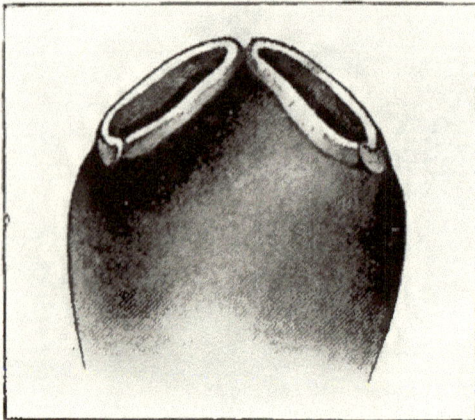

The one-month old mouth.   The mouth at about two months.

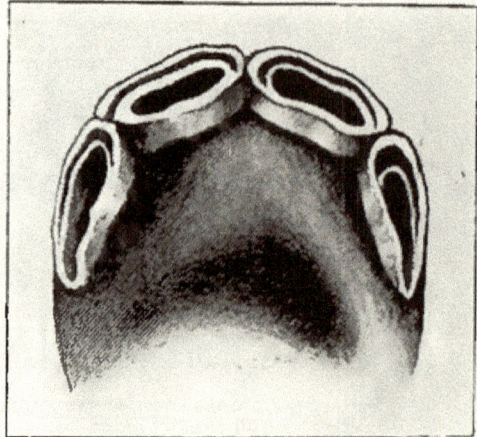

the first month the third molar comes up; the incisors, however, will make their appearance in from twenty-four hours to a few days; the "nippers" then come out, and at about one month the rear borders of these have grown up level with the front walls. About this time the "dividers" begin to show up, and for some time the colt remains with eight incisors only, the growth taking place between thirty and forty days. The "corners" vary in their growth from the sixth to the tenth month. In all these teeth the front walls first come up, and the rear walls come up later. This also occurs in the permanent teeth,

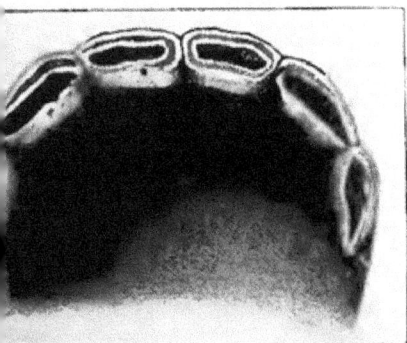

mouth at about eight to ten months.
out two years a full mouth of worn
teeth is found.

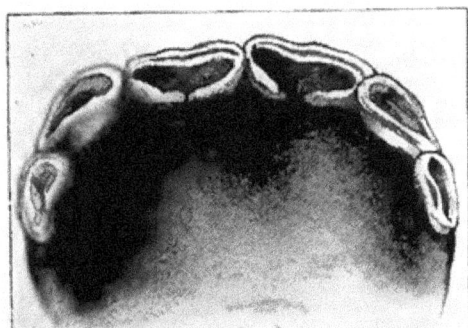

The mouth between two and a half and
three and a half years of age. The "nippers" are the first permanent teeth, the
"dividers" and "corners" are still worn
milk teeth.

and must be noticed, as this furnishes very valuable
knowledge in telling the age.   All the milk teeth are in
the mouth by the end of the first year, the upper teeth
appearing somewhat earlier than the lower ones.   Wear
and tear on the upper teeth is not quite as great as on the
lower ones, and for this reason, as well as because of the
greater ease with which the lower incisors may be seen,
the lower ones are usually used in determining age.

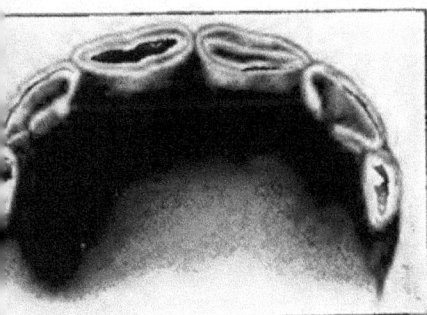

three and a half to four years.   "Nip-
and "dividers" permanent. The "cor-
are still worn milk teeth.

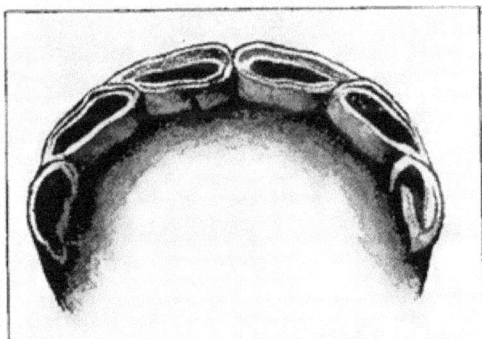

At five years. "Nippers" slightly worn.
"Dividers" fully up. Permanent "corners"
coming up as shown.

Permanent Teeth.—Incisors: At about two and a half
to three years the first incisors appear; these are the
"nippers," in both upper and lower jaws; at from three
and a half to four years the second incisors appear; these
are the "dividers"; finally, at about five years, the remaining incisors come up; these are the "corners"; at
about six years the inner walls of the "corners" have
grown up level with the front walls of these teeth, and
the mouth is complete in its twelve incisors. It must be
remembered that the front walls come up before the rear
walls in all of these incisors.

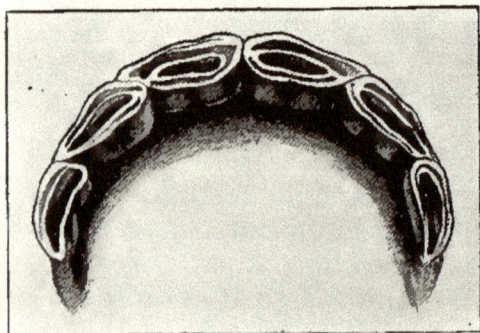

At six years. "Nippers" worn, "dividers"
becoming worn, "corners" fully up and
mouth complete.

The Tusks.—These
begin to appear at
about four and a half
years of age, and are
completely up at about
five and a half to six.
It is sufficient regard-
ing these to state that
in old horses the tops
of these "tusks" are
generally much worn
away, and consequent-
ly rounded or blunt,
while in the young animal the "tusks" are sharp and
come to a round point.

Molars.—The first molar appears a little after the
end of the first year, and is the first one of the permanent
teeth to come in; the same teeth come up in both upper
and lower jaws at the same time; the second molar comes
up a little before the end of the second year; at about
two and a half years the next molar comes up; at three
years the next three molars have appeared. The molars
are now all up.

Changes in the Permanent Teeth.—Up to the age of six
years, therefore, the age of the horse can be clearly determined from his teeth; for some years longer indications
may be obtained from the wear of the incisor teeth,

though this depends to a certain extent upon the food or other accidental circumstances. As a general rule, the depression caused by the infolding of the surface of the incisor, known as the "mark," is obliterated in the "nippers" at about six and a half years, in the "dividers" at about seven or a little after, and in the "corners" at a little after eight years. In the upper teeth, as these depressions are deeper, this obliteration does not take place until about two years later; after this age, eight years, it becomes difficult to tell the age from the teeth; at about seven and a half years the upper "corners" have become a little worn into the form of an angle, the rear ends of the

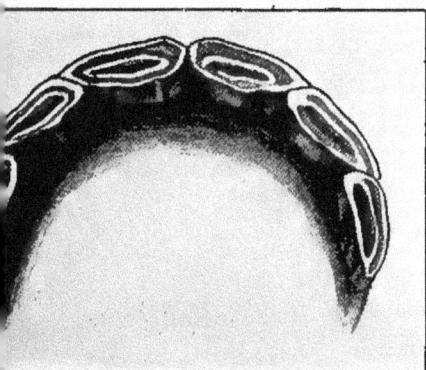

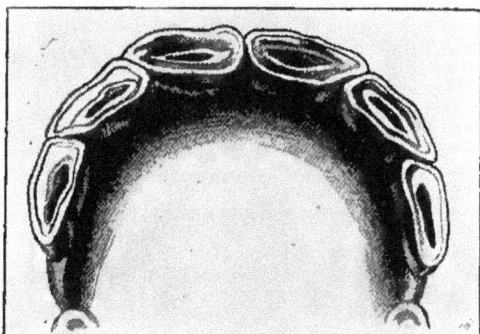

The mouth at about seven years.

The mouth at about eight years.

tops of these teeth inclining downward over the rear ends of the tops of the lower "corners," and as age increases this angle in the upper "corners" becomes more and more pronounced. Horse-dealers sometimes rasp off these angles for the purpose of making the horse appear younger. A horse said to be "rising five" is a horse that is approaching the age of five years; a horse said to be "five" is at that age; and when he is said to be "past five," he is beyond that age, etc. After a horse has passed the age of eight years, it requires an expert to tell his age unless he is *very* old, as shown by the poor worn teeth, the great groove in the tops of the upper "corners," and

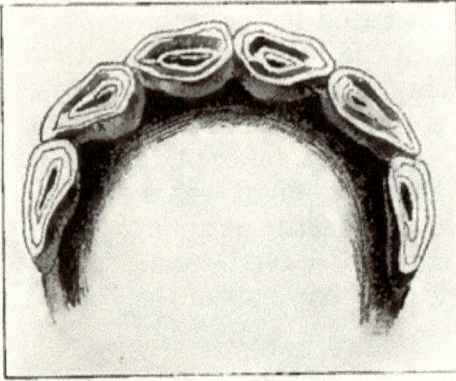

The mouth at about nine years.

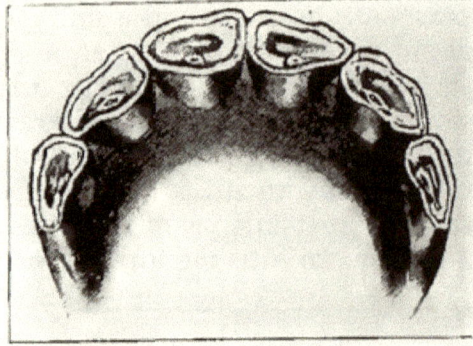

The mouth at about twelve years.

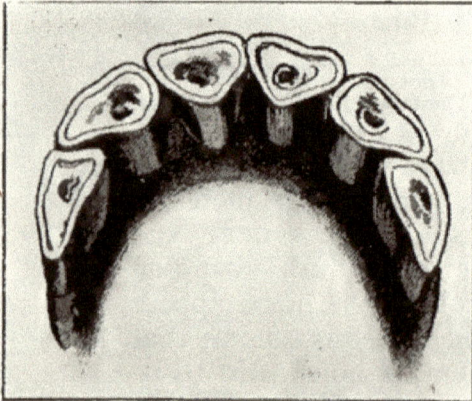

The mouth at about fourteen years.

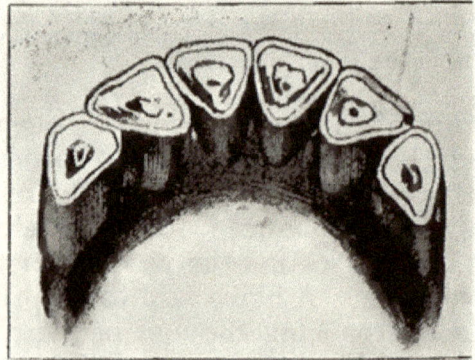

The mouth at about seventeen years.

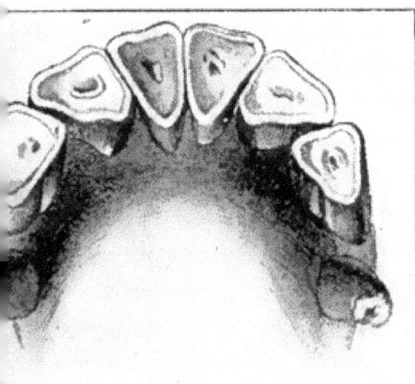

The mouth at about eighteen years.

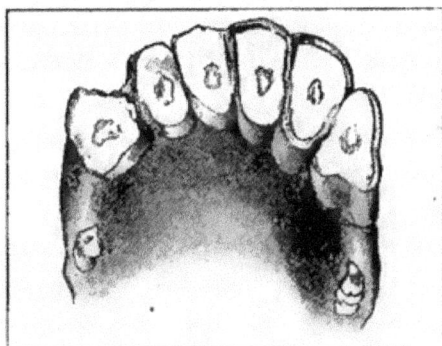

The mouth at about twenty-two years.

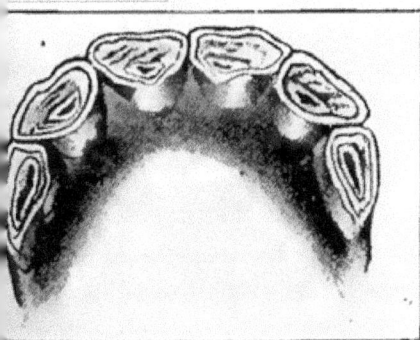

ctive jaw of an old horse, in which the ternal dental cavity is yet remaining.

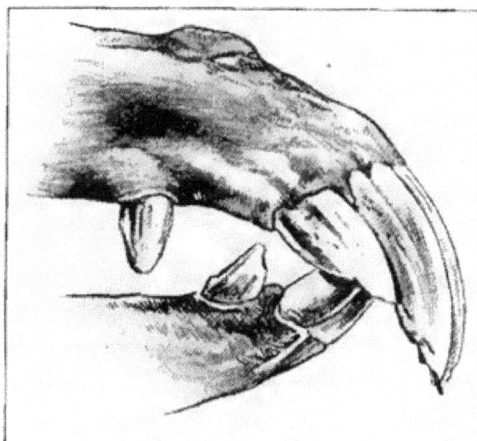

The "parrot" mouth.

the incisors forming almost a straight angle with the jaw in which they are placed.

A careful daily study of the horses in the troop will do much good in teaching the care of public animals, and develops an appreciation of what the cavalry horse should be, what he has been, what he really is, and what his work is.

CHAPTER VII.

SHOEING.

To shoe or not to shoe the horse has been a question discussed and experimented with for ages. While the wild horse, running at large across the vast grassy plains and valleys, where food is most accessible and water near by, may go for years without any protection to the feet other than that which Nature has given him, nevertheless the domesticated animal must be furnished some durable artificial covering for the crust of the hoof where it comes in contact with the ground, if his rider would save him and get fair wear and tear out of him; and in the cavalry services of the world, it is safe to prophesy, shoeing will never cease to be practiced and cannot be dispensed with. The shoeless experiment has been tried over and over again, but always with the same result—a return to shoeing. In dry weather the hoof becomes very hard, and it is wonderful how much wear it will then stand on the hardest of roads; but in wet weather the hoof becomes soft, and then friction on hard roads or mountain trails soon prohibits work without shoes. If work is persisted in under such circumstances, the hoof rapidly wears away and lameness, perhaps permanent, results. The advocates of the unshod horse theory say: "Rest the horse when he becomes a little lame, until he recovers"; but the cavalryman can afford no such luxury; his horse must be always available, always ready, and always strong and sound.

Xenophon, our most ancient authority on the horse, tells us that "in respect to the horse's body we must first consider his feet." Let us, then, do so. We have the

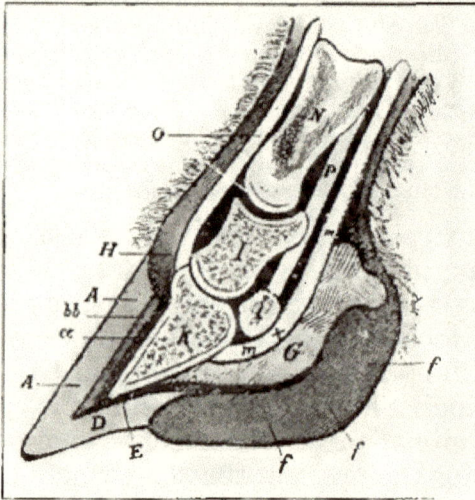

SECTION OF FOOT.

AA,	Crust or wall.	*k,*	Coffin bone or os pedis.
bb,	Insensitive laminæ.	*l,*	Navicular bone.
cc,	Sensitive laminæ.	*x,*	Seat of sprain of tendon passing
D,	Insensitive sole.		over navicular bone.
E,	Sensitive sole.	*mm,*	Flexor perforans tendon.
ff,	Insensitive frog.	*N,*	Great pastern bone.
G,	Sensitive frog.	*O,*	Extensor pedis tendon.
H,	Coronary band.	*P,*	Long inferior sesamoid liga-
I,	Small pastern bone.		ment.

hoof at the end of a system of levers, actuated by springs, and all working together to bear the horse's weight, to propel him forward or backward, to give such ease and lightness to his tread as will produce least fatigue and wear on him generally. The foot is perfect, generally, as Nature made it, but cavalry service has taught us that we cannot leave it so for the work he must perform, as work and soil rarely harmonize. It is said that on the sands of Arabia

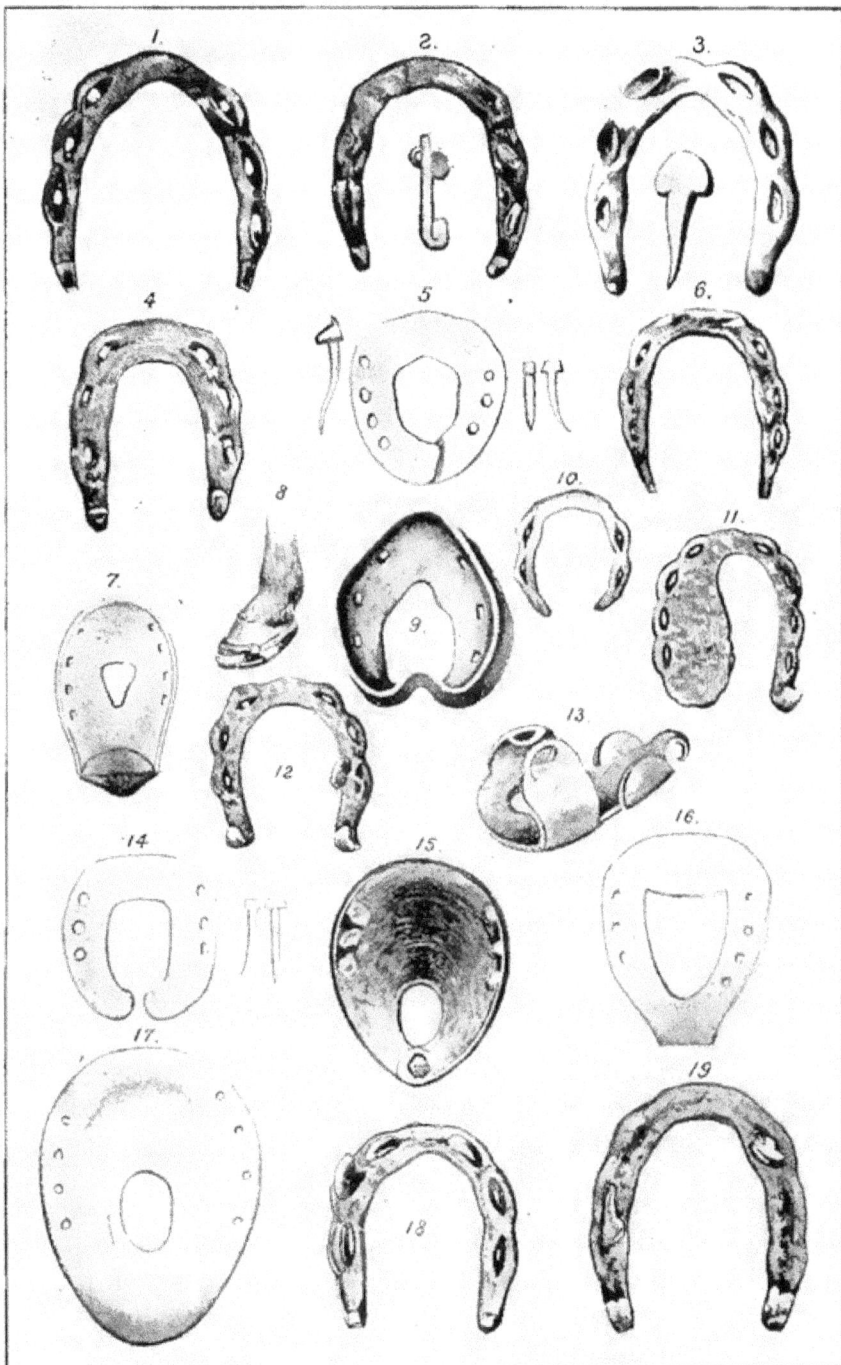

ANCIENT TYPES OF SHOES.

Nos. 1, 2, 3, 4, 6, 11, 12, 13, 18, and 19 are ancient Roman shoes.
No. 8, ancient Roman shoe, fastened on without nails
Nos. 14 and 16, African shoes.

Nos. 5 and 15 are Syrian shoes.
Nos. 7 an l 17 are Arabian shoes.
No. 9, French shoe of XIII. century.
No. 10, Tartar-Chinese shoe.

and Northern Egypt the horse is generally unshod, and that his feet are as Nature made them. The climate is hot and dry and the soil flinty, yet the horse's foot is said to be perfect, hard and dense, firm and small, and able to stand the wear and tear upon it; yet no cavalry has ever gone through either of these countries with unshod horses, if it could be avoided.

The hoof consists of three parts, distinct, which, though inseparably connected one with the other, may be readily separated after death by maceration for a few days in strong soda water. These three parts are known as the crust or wall, the sole, and the frog. The crust reaches from the hair to the ground, and averages about 3½ inches in depth. The front is known as the toe, the back as the heel, and the intermediate part on each side as the quarter. When the crust is looked at from one side, it should form an angle of about 45 degrees with the sole at the toe.

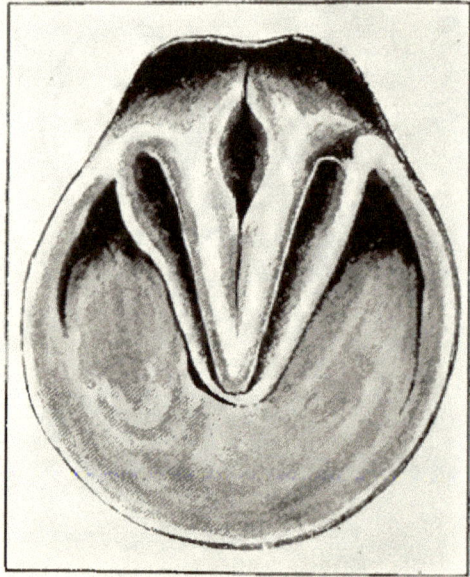

NATURAL HEALTHY SOLE.

The crust is often described as a section of a truncated cone. The back of the crust should join the sole, so as to leave a moderate substance at the heel. The front of the crust is rather more than ½ inch in thickness, while at the back the crust is barely more than ¼ inch thick. This proportion is, however, rather confined to the fore foot, for in the hind there is little difference between the toe and quarters in point of thickness. In examining the cut of the sole, it may be seen that the crust is bent inwards towards the frog at the heel on each side—these are the bars, which, in the natural foot, appear as sharpened prominences extending from the heel into the center of the foot, between the sole and the frog, and which are useful as buttresses supporting the crust from being crushed inwards by the superincumbent weight. The sole is the

b, Cleft of frog.

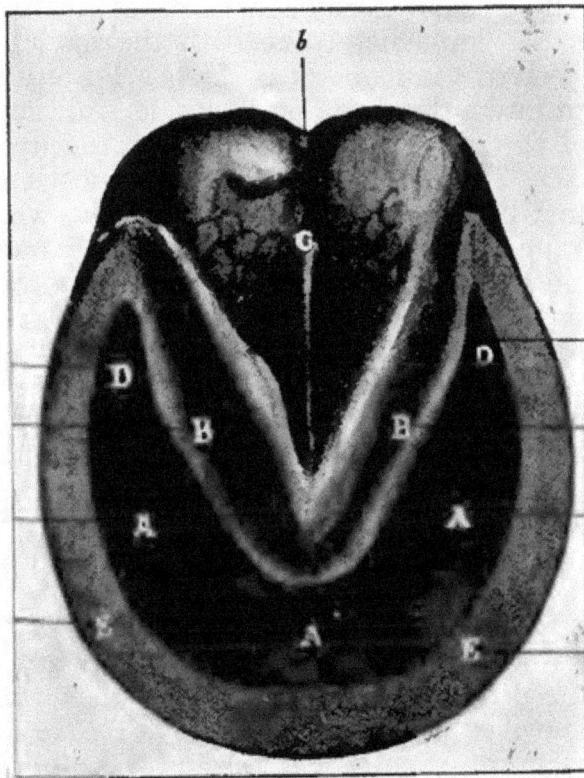

C, Frog.   D, Seat of corn   B, Bars.   A, Sole.   E, Crust or wall.

GROUND SURFACE OF FOOT, PROPERLY PREPARED FOR SHOE.

plate at the bottom of the foot, and is slightly concave on the lower surface, and is fixed to the inner edge of the crust and the outer sides of the bars, and not to their lower surfaces. Its usual thickness is about $\frac{1}{8}$ of an inch, but it will vary greatly in different horses, and it is thicker where it runs back between the bars and the crust. The frog is the prominent triangular and elastic substance which fills up the space between the heels posteriorly, the bars on each side, and the sole in front. In the middle is a longitudinal fissure, called the cleft, the sides of which should form an angle of about 45 degrees. In front of this cleft is a solid wedge of the elastic horny substance constituting the frog, which lies immediately beneath the navicular bone and has received the name of cushion. Posteriorly this is spread out into a thin band on each side, which covers the bulbs of the heels and passes around the upper part of the crust. The foot of the horse is a most complicated structure, both externally and internally, which is liable to derangement whenever the hoof (or horny case) is interfered with. Perhaps in no other organ does an injury so soon produce a return at compound interest, for the inevitable first result is a malformation of the hoof, and this again only adds to the original mischief. Hence it is that in the foot, more than in any other part even, prevention is better than cure, for in many of its diseases it happens that a cure cannot be obtained without rest, and yet it is also a fact that the secretion of horn will not go on perfectly without the stimulus of necessity afforded by exercise.

Shoeing is an almost unavoidable consequence of the horse's domestication, and an artificial protection for the foot is one of the penalties which civilization inexorably demands, and nowhere more than in cavalry service. That the ordinary iron shoe is the best and least hurtful means that can be devised, must be admitted, for, even with American ingenuity to help us, nothing yet has been discovered that will take its place. That the systems of horse-shoeing, as they now obtain, are pregnant with mischief to the foot, no one who is conversant with the facts will venture to deny. As a matter of physiological fitness, the shoe and its mode of attachment are utterly indefensible. Each time a horse is shod, each time a nail is driven, means so much injury to the foot. The better the job the less that injury is, but there is no such thing as absolute immunity from this evil. If we impose upon our horses work of a nature which entails upon their feet more waste of horn than Nature can replace during the ordinary intervals of rest, we are obliged to adopt a defense of some kind. It would be futile to inveigh against the form of protection in almost universal use—the iron shoe—unless we are prepared with a substitute not open to the same or equally serious objections.

"In preparing the foot for the shoe, do not touch with the knife the frog, sole, or bars; in removing surplus growth of that part of the foot which is the 'seat of the shoe,' use the cutting pincers and rasp, and never the knife. The shoeing-knife may be used, if necessary, in fitting the toe-clip. 'Opening the heels,' or making a cut into the angle of the wall at the heel, must never be done; the rasp may be used on this part of the foot when necessary, and the same applies to the pegs. No cutting with a knife should be permitted; the rasp alone when necessary. Flat-footed horses should be treated as the necessity of each particular case may require. In forging the shoe to fit the foot, be careful that the shoe is fitted to and follows the circumference of the foot clear round to the heels. The heels of the shoe should never be extended back straight and outside of the walls at the heels, as is frequently done. Care must be taken that the shoe is not fitted too small, the outer surface of the walls being then rasped down to make the foot short to suit the shoe, as often happens. Heat may be used in preparing and shaping the shoe, but the hot shoe must never be applied to the horse's foot under any circumstances. Make the upper or foot surface of the shoe perfectly flat, so as to give a level bearing. A shoe with a concave ground surface should be used."

The above paragraph outlines the regulations governing horse-shoeing in the United States Cavalry, and is the outcome of many years of hard service and vast experi-

ence.   It gives the principles of American Cavalry shoeing very plainly, and differs more or less from the methods used in foreign services.   The practice of trimming
the frog and thinning out the sole till it visibly yields to
pressure. of the thumbs is brutal and ruinous.   The frog
is Nature's cushion and hoof-expander, placed there by an
all-wise Hand; by its elasticity it wards off concussion
from the less elastic portions of the structure, and by its
resilience assists in maintaining the natural expansion of
its horny surrounding; that is to say, it does so in its

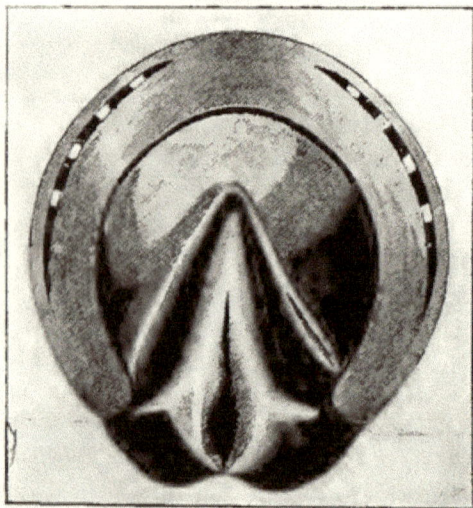

REGULATION AMERICAN CAVALRY
SHOE PROPERLY ON FOOT.

SIDE VIEW OF SAME.

natural state, but the knife's touch is fatal to it; once cut
and carved and deprived of pressure, those very acts cause
it to shrink, dry, and harden, and at once lose those very
attributes which constitute its usefulness to the foot.
By paring down the thickness of the sole until only a
thin film of soft, partially formed horn is left, protection
is taken away from the sensitive construction within, and
the sole itself, or what is left of it, dries and shrinks upon
exposure to the air, and thereby entails a further and still
more serious injury to the foot.   The practice of remov-

ing the bars, known as "opening the heels," is also brutal and injurious. It means nothing more than opening a road for them to close over. On a foot that has had its frog and sole "trimmed" in the above fashion and the bars removed, many an amateur shoer places a shoe, often too small, and the rasp is then called into use to reduce the hoof to fit the shoe for appearance's sake. It is sad that Art and Nature should so often be at variance. This rasping down of the hoof-wall weakens the entire structure of the hoof incalculably, yet this is a very common practice among new troop blacksmiths unless guarded against.

The shoe should be as light as the weight of the horse and the nature of his work will permit. Heavy shoes not only burden the animal that must wear them (for there is truth in the old saying that "An ounce at the toe means a pound at the withers"), but they also increase the concussion inseparable from progression. The legitimate mission of the shoe is to prevent undue wear of the walls, and a light shoe will do this quite as well as a heavy one. It is, moreover, entirely erroneous to suppose that a heavy shoe necessarily wears longer than a light one, as experience proves the contrary, in many instances, to be the case. Even among the mammoth draft-horses used in America by great express companies, whose shoes must of course be made with reference to the weight they have to bear and the inordinate strain to which they are subjected when the animal which wears them is at work, do not require great, heavy iron shoes, which but add unnecessary weight and consequently greater concussion to the feet. The shoe should stop before it reaches the frog on either side, as contraction is liable to result if the frog is clamped between the two ends of the shoe. If this has been done, however, the frog and foot can be often gotten back into shape by lowering the walls at the heels a little, so as to restore frog-pressure, when the latter will speedily recover its lost characteristics, and a healthy condition will gradually return.

In many countries what is known as hot-fitting—
that is to say, after the foot has been trimmed and leveled,
momentarily applying the shoe at a red heat to the foot—
is generally practiced to the almost entire exclusion of
any other method, and the system is not only found to
answer, but receives the endorsement of many acknowledged competent authorities. The advantage claimed
by the advocates of hot-fitting is that a more accurate
accommodation for the shoe is obtained by this method
more readily than by any other, and that the contact
between hoof and shoe is consequently made more inti-
mate and enduring. They also claim that in moist climates
it is the only way by which the shoe can be made to stay
on the foot for any length of time. In no part of the
United States is there a single place where this hot-fitting
need be done, nor is there any such spot outside of it. In
every cavalry garrison of the American service, both in
the United States and in the Philippine Islands, ordinary cold-shoeing has been found most efficacious, and no
other way has ever been used, least of all hot-fitting; and
in the shoeing of horses for the most severe field service,
both in hot and cold climates, it is doubted if any nation
in the world has had more opportunity to learn the most
beneficial way of doing it than has the American Cavalry.

The fewest nails, and these of the smallest size that
will properly hold the shoe, should be used. Three of the
commonest mistakes made in shoeing horses are using
too many nails and these of too large a size, and driving
them too high up into the walls. If a perfectly level bearing has been obtained, it is astonishing how few and how
small the nails need be to hold the shoe in place securely.
After the nails have all been driven in, the ends should
be twisted off and the stubs rasped down smooth, to avoid
the horse's cutting himself, and also to prevent any of the
nails from working loose. No shoe should be allowed to
remain on the horse for more than one month, or five weeks
at the outside in case of emergency. Some horses require
to be shod oftener. Climate, season, work, etc., all have

their influences as to shoeing the horse, but the above length of time is considered as long as the shoe can reasonably be expected to sit well on the foot, as the steady growth of the hoof will cause the crust to lap over the shoe at the edges, and thus the shoe will be doing more damage than good.

The shoe on the horse's foot during summer months is required only to prevent wear and tear upon the foot, but in winter the necessity for shoeing is made more imperative, as the ground is still harder than in summer, and the slippery condition of the roads and trails requires a special style of shoeing to prevent the animal from falling. Various patterns of shoes have, from time to time, been fashioned to meet this latter requirement, but the commonest of all the styles tried, fashioned with toe- and heel-calks, or calkins, is, though perhaps faulty, the one best suited to the requirements of winter traveling. The shorter, the sharper, and the smaller the calkins are, so much the better for the foot, so long as they answer their purpose. High calkins, while they confer no firmer foothold, may injure both the foot itself and the leg to which it is attached. Navicular disease is believed by some authorities to be one of the results of high calkins, besides a string of other ailments of more or less severity. In using calkins, care must be taken that the one at the toe is of the same height as the two at the heel; otherwise undue strain is thrown upon the part of the foot that is lowest, and consequently both foot and leg will be injured. Owing to the wearing down of the toe-calk, the shoes will require more looking after in winter than summer, in ordinary cavalry work. The calk often performs a slight twisting motion in the ground, as the foot is planted, if only the toe-calk is used, and this is liable to work the shoe loose. The practice in the American cavalry service has been to "rough shoe" the troop-horse only when absolutely necessary in winter, and is rarely done, except for a few mounted patrols in and about the garrison or camp; when "rough shoeing" is done in the troop, the horses having on the shoes with calkins should be kept sufficiently far apart from each other and the rest of the troop animals to prevent their injuring other horses by kicking. A kick from a "rough" shoe often results in broken bones.

Shoeing for gait has produced many styles of shoes, and some of these are marvels of ingenuity and many are successful. By intelligent use of special styles of shoes, the gait of the horse may be changed considerably or

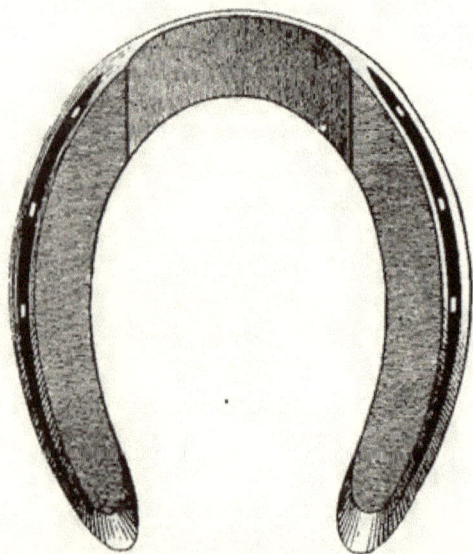

FRONT VIEW OF SCOOP-TOE ROLLING-
MOTION SHOE.

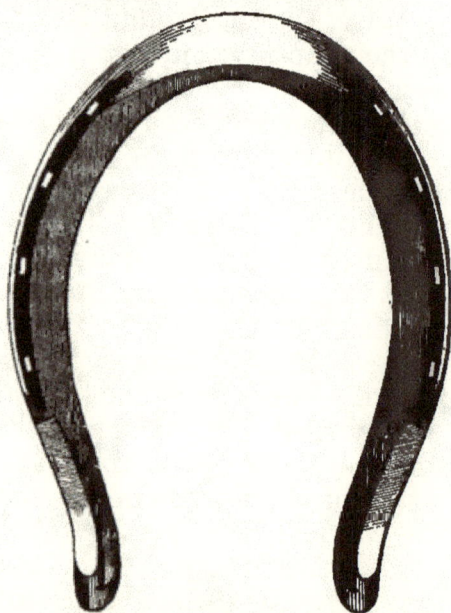

HIND-FOOT SHOE TO BALANCE
THE ACTION.

desirable gaits maintained. The number of these special styles of shoes for gaiting purposes is infinite, but as many are applicable only, or in large measure, to horses used solely for speed purposes, no detailed explanation of them need be given here. A few simple styles, easily made by the troop blacksmith, may be mentioned. Among these are the scoop-toe or rolling-motion shoe for the fore feet (see plate), and the shoe (see plate) for the hind feet, which, while they obviate "forging" or "clicking," a habit hurtful to the horse and disagreeable to the rider, do not in any way tend to inflict any injury on the feet or limbs. The scooped or rolled toe confers a mechanical advantage, enabling the horse to get over his toes more promptly, and thus remove the front foot from the stroke of the hind extremity, while the lengthening of the branches of the hind shoes, by increasing the ground surface, retards the flexion and extension of the hind limbs, and this is what is required in the prevention of the above faults. The common practice of increasing the weight of the outside web of the hind shoes, to open the action of the legs, is equally good and harmless when not carried to an extreme. (See page 144, figure 8.) The shoe shown on page 144, figure 1, is the most effective model of shoe to square and balance the gait of new horses, but the period of its use should be strictly limited and the weight of the toe gradually reduced as the desired gaits become established. An ingenious shoe to prevent "paddling" is shown on page 144, figure 10, but, as "paddling" is the result of a physical malformation, mechanical means can only overcome the habit, but never wholly cure the horse of it. For "founder," spavin, stiff knees, and some other diseased conditions of the feet, either front or hind, a very excellent "cushion" shoe is often used, possessing several rubber cushions along the sides of the shoe, sometimes made to reach entirely through the shoe and touch the ground, or only on the top of the shoe, in the shape of a pad, between the horse's foot and the shoe. These cushioned shoes are very good, but as they wear out rapidly, they should never be allowed to remain on the foot more than a few weeks at a time. The method of forging a bar across the heel of the shoe, thus connecting the two ends about $\frac{1}{2}$ inch from their extremities, or at the extremities themselves, has often been used to raise the foot higher off the ground in diseases of the frog or bars, when relief for a few days is necessary, and these bar shoes have been found very good, but should be used very carefully or permanent injury may result, either from the frog getting no

pressure and consequently no chance to expand, in the
natural way, or by the bar pressing down on the frog
and actually hurting it.　(See plate below, figure 4.)　The
above methods of shoeing for gait are rarely used in the
service; they are given but to illustrate that the gait is
affected by shoeing, and some of the styles that prevail.
As in field service it is often necessary to shoe horses on

TYPES OF MODERN SHOES.

1, Toe weight.
2, Front shoe, American Regular Cavalry.
3, Hind shoe, American Regular Cavalry.
4, Bar shoe, with ice-calks.
5, Russian screw ice-calks.
6, Mule shoe.
7, Spavin or stifle shoe.
8, One method of side-weighting.
9, British Cavalry shoe.
10, Shoe to prevent "paddling."
11, Charlier shoe.

the march and at difficult times, shoes should be fitted
to the fore and hind feet of every troop-horse and carried
in the saddle-bags of the trooper, together with sufficient
nails, six or eight, to put the shoe on with in case one is
lost off.　The shoe as issued to troops is not prepared for
the foot; it has to be fitted and the ends cut off the right
length and the toe-clip hammered in, and all this requires

the forge, which often is missing when in the field. While it is possible to leave some or all of the troop-horses un-shod while in garrison, provided the soil of the surrounding country is soft and free from sharp rocks, etc., in the field the animals must be shod all round. Very frequently in garrison the horses are left unshod on their hind feet, and this does good, if the soil and work harmonize; but it should never be allowed where roads or country are hard or rocky, or liability to sudden field service is to be expected.

Some years ago the question of shoeing was taken up by the American Cavalry to such an extent that the War Department convened a board of cavalry officers to go thoroughly over the question. This board procured the opinions of a large number of experienced cavalry officers. Nearly all the recommendations submitted to the board were in favor of a lighter shoe, or half shoes, or three-quarter shoes, or mere steel tips for the toes, and some of the recommendations were in favor of no shoes. The object, of course, was to permit the foot to remain as far as possible in its natural state, and reduce to a minimum the weakening of the hoof caused by rasping, cutting, and nails, to protect the sole and bars from mutilation, to allow natural frog-pressure and growth, and to avoid con-traction with its attendant evils. An experiment was tried in a number of American Cavalry garrisons of con-structing the "corrals" and picket-lines of stone and stand-ing the shod and unshod horses upon these, either tied or loose, and observing the effects on their feet. It was not long before many horses were lame and continued so, and as a result these tortures to the foot of the horse ceased to be built. As time passed, the stone flooring of these picket-lines became possessed of thousands of sharp points of rock, caused by the chipping of stones from the pounding of the horses' feet, and these sharp projections caused corns, bruises, etc., too much to believe the plan a safe one.

Experiments with aluminum shoes have been made at various times in cavalry services, the advantage of this

shoe being in its very light weight as compared to the regulation iron shoe. These aluminum shoes corresponded
in size nearly to the ordinary American No. 3 shoe; they
were about $\frac{1}{2}$ inch in thickness, and in the toe of each
front shoe was set a narrow piece of steel about $1\frac{1}{2}$
inches long, to prevent rapid wear. The front shoe,
weighed $7\frac{1}{2}$ ounces each and the hind shoes 6 ounces each,
making a total weight of 27 ounces. As the regulation
iron shoe No. 3 front weighs 17 ounces and the same size
hind shoe weighs $15\frac{1}{2}$ ounces, the saving in weight was
very great, a total of 65 ounces for the iron shoes
per set as against 27 ounces per set for the aluminum.
Subjected to field service, the aluminum shoe was found
easy on the horse because of its light weight, but it frequently broke, and for this reason was not considered
serviceable for rough field work. By adding more steel
to the shoe this defect was overcome, but the addition of
steel destroyed its one virtue—lightness.

In Germany the cavalry has experimented with paper
shoes. After severe tests on all service, it was found that
the lightness and elasticity of this shoe helped the horse
on the march, making it possible for him to travel faster
and farther without fatigue than the iron-shod horse,
and it was also found that the paper shoe was unaffected
by water or other liquid. In manufacturing the paper
shoe, the sheets of paper were pressed closely together,
one above the other, and rendered impervious to moisture
by the application of oil of turpentine; the sheets were
glued together by a sort of paste composed of turpentine, whiting, gum, and linseed oil, and then subjected
to enormous hydraulic pressure. Paper shoes were also
made by grinding the paper up into a mass, combining it
with turpentine, sand, gum, litharge, and certain other
substances, and then pressing it and afterwards drying
it; but these shoes were less stout and elastic than those
made by thin sheets of paper laid one upon the other.
The paper shoes were fastened to the horse's foot by
means of nails, or with a kind of glue made of coal tar

and caoutchouc. The general results obtained, however, were not altogether satisfactory, and the iron shoe still holds its own.

At one time it was claimed by American horse-shoers that a substance had been invented which, by painting the sole of the foot thickly, prevented wear and tear upon the hoof. Had this been successful, shoeing horses would have ceased to be a consideration; but the theory was quickly exploded by means of practical tests, and it is improbable that we shall ever discover a way of saving the horse's hoof and protecting it from wear and tear by any other means than that of shoeing. In early times horses first went unshod, and it was found that their hoofs quickly went to pieces when subjected to field service in campaign. The old American Indian and trapper method of saving the hoof by means of rawhide boots tied around the "ankle" by buckskin thongs is well known. The Filipinos and Japanese have constructed rude makeshifts made from the bamboo and grasses in the form of sandals. Rubber boots have been experimented with, in the United States and abroad, and if they could be made to last a reasonable time, would certainly be easy on the foot; but they quickly wear out and heat the foot too much. These rubber boots are largely used in civil life by racing men as temporary means of saving the foot from shoeing.

In the Austro-Hungarian cavalry service the horses at the remount dépôts are not shod. There being comparatively few hard roads in the empire, especially in Hungary, the horses of the army are not habitually shod. The metalled roads generally have paths of earth on the sides for riding, so that the horses are seldom ridden on hard ground. They have, as a rule, very fine feet. When shoes are used, they are made of iron, with a groove, and have holes for six nails. The foot is cut by the farrier the least possible. The condition of the ground has guided, somewhat, the location of the cavalry garrisons. Shoeing is placed under the direct charge of veterinarians, assisted each by nine farriers, and it is said that not more than 1200 horseshoes are used in a regiment in a year. The horses of the government breeding-stables are shod only exceptionally, even the service animals going unshod. Austrian experience has proved to their cavalry that leaving their horses unshod in their country has a salutary effect on the horn of the hoof, the quality of the foot becoming fixed in the breed, so that there are but few defective feet. What has been said, however, of the Austrian highways and the location of the cavalry garrisons must not be forgotten in considering Austrian methods.

Shoeing cavalry horses in France is somewhat similar to the method in the American service. Every horse is required to be reshod once a month. The hoof is prepared for shoeing about as is the American. Cutting away the sole or trimming the frog is prohibited. The frog is, however, cleaned, and loose parts removed. It is even prescribed that its point shall be brought to the center of the sole and superfluous parts of the bars removed. After the shoe is formed to fit the foot, it is set on *hot* and held firmly till the hoof is evenly burned on its whole bearing surface. The shoe is then removed, quenched, reset, nailed, and clinched. Orders regulate the dimensions of the shoes for the various units. In winter horses are shod frequently with shoes having holes for the reecption of ice-calks. Permanent rough-shoeing is almost never practiced. The calks are provided for the heels only, or two for the heel and two at each side of the toe. These calks are of steel, square in cross-section, about ½ inch high, and screw in place. A French method of shoeing of some years ago, known as the "Charlier" method, consisted in cutting a groove all round the sole, at the edge, for the shoe to lie in, so that it would be level with the bearing surface of the sole and allow the frog to project below both shoe and sole, which were one continuous surface. This method is used by many horsemen in civil life, but it was found that the sole and bars, after repeated using of the Charlier method, became dangerously thin, and in the Hippological Museum in Fort Riley, Kansas, there is a specimen of the foot after this style of shoeing had been used some time, wherein it is shown how the sole was finally so thin that the application of the hot shoe to the groove burned a hole completely through the sole near the toe.

In the German cavalry service the horses at the remount dépôts are left unshod. The feet are carefully watched by the veterinarian, and the farriers go over all the horses and fix their feet every month. The soil in the vicinity of these remount dépôts is generally sandy and dry. A squadron of German cavalry is allowed each month from $10 to $10.50 for shoeing its horses. On a peace footing, there are 139 horses in a squadron, and this monthly allowance not only proves sufficient for them, but often is not all expended, so that a reserve fund is constituted to provide for unexpected needs. The squadron commanders are entirely free to have or not have their horses shod in their squadrons. It is customary not to shoe the horses in the winter—that is, from the first of October to the first of April. During this period, which is devoted to the instruction of recruits, the horses work only in the riding-hall or on the exercising-grounds, which are prepared for the purpose and are soft. They can then, barring exceptions, as indicated by the veterinary surgeon, go without shoes. During the summer all depends upon the special conditions in the vicinity of the garrison. If, in going to drill, the squadron is obliged to habitually traverse a considerable part of a city, encountering hard roads, the front feet are kept shod. If, on the contrary, the ground in the neighborhood is not too hard, the horses are left entirely unshod until the fall maneuvers. For these maneuvers the horses are shod all round, as it is difficult to foresee what kind of ground may be encountered. But in exceptional cases, where it is known that they will be used only on soft ground during the maneuvers, economy is preserved by shoeing only the fore feet. In the cities the cavalry never furnishes mounted patrols or mounted orderlies. All this service is done by soldiers on foot. This permits doing without shoeing the greater part of the year, thereby incidentally saving a part of the fund allowed for shoeing. There is, nevertheless, always in the storehouse a large supply of shoes, enough not only for shoeing the squadron horses all around at the moment of mobilization, but also for a reserve supply to take along.

In the British cavalry service all the horses are shod. The kind of shoe used in all branches of the service is the concave shoe—that is, one which is concave on its ground surface and flat on its foot surface. (See page 144, figure 9.) This applies for both front and hind shoes. The number of nails to the shoe is from six to eight, according to size of shoe, and the nail-holes on each side are opposite the holes on the other side. One toe-clip is used on each fore shoe and two on each hind shoe. The calks may be used, when necessary, on light horses. Special shoes, as tips or half-shoes, or shoes turned up at the toe, may be used at the discretion of the veterinarian. The sole and foot are prepared for the shoe almost exactly as in the American service. The shoes made by farriers are not allowed to be fitted when too hot. The chief feature in the English cavalry shoeing is "cold shoeing"—that is, the cold fitting of shoes issued ready for immediate use, and nails requiring no preparation, both being provided already shaped so far as possible; but, as different horses have different feet, the shoes must be fitted when necessary. The number of shoes per year for each horse is limited to eighteen sets. Careful instruction is given by veterinary surgeons to the troopers in "cold shoeing." In winter frost-nails are issued for "roughing" the feet to prevent slipping. These are made of steel, with chisel-shaped heads, and are put on as follows: one is inserted in each heel of each fore shoe and one in the outer heel of each hind shoe; when necessary, these frost-nails are also placed in the toes of the shoes.

In Italy, as in France, the method known as "hot shoeing" is used in the Cavalry. The hot shoe is applied to the foot without being quenched. The Italian model of hand-forged shoe is used exclusively.

CHAPTER VIII.

BITTING.

Bits—Early Use of—General Classification—Principles of Each Class—Necessity for Good Bitting—Use of the Snaffle—The Bar-Bit—The Curb-Bit— Mechanical Principles—Leverage— Mouth-piece— Port— Upper Branches— Lower Branches— Rings—American Curb-Bit—Weight—The Horse's Mouth— Measurements Necessary in Fitting the Curb-Bit—How to Take Them—Adjustable Bits— Curb-Straps *versus* Curb-Chains— Double-reined Bridles— Single-reined Bridles— The Bit and Bridoon—Foreign Practice and Bits.

Nowhere in the world of riding is prompt response from the horse to his bit so absolutely indispensable as in cavalry. One stubborn or dull-brained animal in the troop during drill, marching, or elsewhere, can do more to aggravate both men and horses and destroy uniformity and cohesion in ranks than half a dozen ungainly animals who are, despite their lack of agility, bridlewise. To gain that perfect control over the cavalry horse so indispensable to efficiency and ease in riding, the bit gradually came into use centuries ago, and by modern improvement and a careful study of the mechanical principles involved, the good cavalry animal of to-day should respond instantaneously to the will of the rider. However, as the adjustment of the curb-bit can cause much or little pain, and consequently much or little success in the management of the horse, the most intelligent nicety of adjustment is imperative. In the early centuries bits were at first not known, the horses being managed by means of loops around the nostrils, as is still the custom in some isolated countries, and may be seen daily in the Philippine Islands even at this late date. The Romans. are the first people in history known to have employed the curb-bit, and since then it has been refined from a

heavy instrument causing much unnecessary torture to
the horse, to a most scientific appliance where pain is
reduced to a minimum and management of the horse per-
fected by careful training and adjustment.

The various styles of bits in modern use may be generally classified as "bar," "snaffle," and "curb" bits.
Each of these classes possesses many styles and variations
of manufacture, but the principles involved in each class
remain the same. The bar-bit consists of a straight or
slightly curved mouth-piece, with either rings at the ends
of the mouth-piece in which to attach the reins, or short,
equal upper and lower branches at the ends of the mouth-
piece to prevent the rings from being drawn into the
horse's mouth, and having the rein-rings attached at the
ends of the mouth-piece as before. In the bar-bit there
is no lever-action whatever, and the mouth-piece is one
continuous piece, whether straight, curved, or of rubber
or chain. The bar-bit with straight or curved mouth-
piece made of metal or rubber is an easy bit in the mouth,
if properly used, and is largely used on driving-horses.
The bar-bit with chain mouth-piece is about as brutal a
form as could be devised. By reference to plate on page
154, several styles of bar-bits may be seen. The bar-bit
is attached to the ordinary head-stall.

The snaffle-bit consists of a jointed mouth-piece having large rings at the outside ends for the reins. The
joint is placed in the middle of the mouth-piece, and may
be either single or double. On some snaffle-bits short
cheek-pieces are placed, for the same purpose as on the
bar-bit. The snaffle possesses no lever-action; it is the
mildest form of bit known, and in the training of the
cavalry horse is invariably used during the first stages.
By reference to plate on page 154, several styles of snaffles
may be seen. The snaffle is attached to either the ordinary head-stall, or, as is most frequently done, to the
halter head-stall, by means of snaps attached to the
rings of the bit.

Missing Page

The curb-bit consists of the mouth-piece, having generally the center of the mouth-piece curved more or less, and this curve is commonly known as the "port." There are two branches, one at each end of the mouth-piece, and their lower portions may be either curved, double curved, or straight. The portions of the branches above the mouth-piece are known as the upper branches and the portions below it are known as the lower branches. The upper branches bear a certain proportion in length to the lower branches, and this proportion, as will be seen later, is very important. At the upper end of each of the upper branches is a ring, made into the steel itself, to which the cheek-pieces of the bridle are buckled and into which the curb-strap or curb-chain is also fastened. At the end of each of the lower branches a swinging ring is placed, into which the reins are buckled. The curb-bit possesses lever-action, and this is made either very mild or very severe, according to the construction of the bit and the placing of the curb-strap.

While in the bar-bit the power is generally fully capable of giving sufficient control over the horse for all driving purposes, and on well-trained animals will be found to be all that is required for pleasure or individual riding, and while the snaffle-bit is the most efficacious bit known for the training of the new horse, still neither of these will be found sufficiently powerful to control the cavalry horse in ranks. The cavalryman must possess the means of such complete control over his horse that in-

SNAFFLE-BIT IN MOUTH.

stantaneously he can bring him down from the most rapid gaits to even a halt, wheel him to the right or left almost on his own ground, and perform various other equally important movements, and all this must be done easily with the left hand, as the right hand will be required for the wielding of the trooper's weapons. For these reasons the powerful curb-bit is indispensable, and so it is with

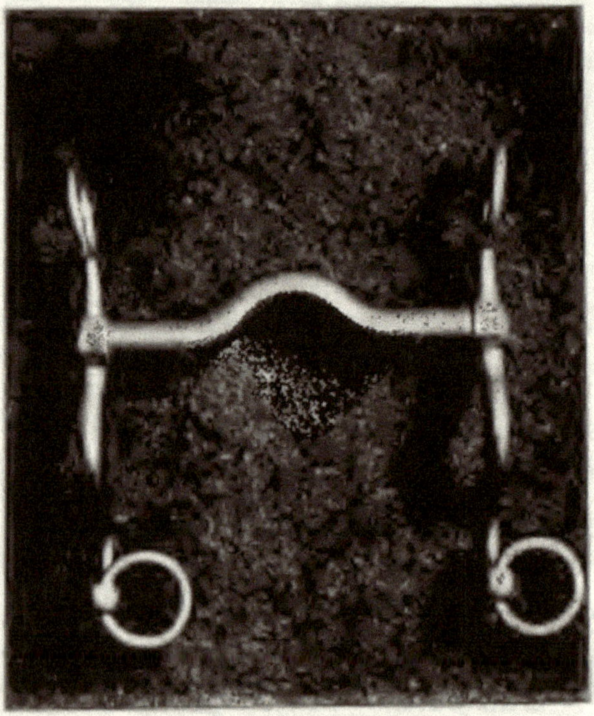

FIG. 62.

AMERICAN CAVALRY CURB-BIT, MODEL 1892—FIGS. 62 AND 63.

DIMENSIONS.

No.	Length of mouth-piece.	Diameter of mouth-piece.	Height of port.	Length of upper branches.	Length of lower branches.	Width between upper rings.	Width between lower rings.	Weight.	Diameter of branches at mouthpiece.	Diameter of branches at rings.	Diameter of rings.	Length of branches from center of upper ring to center of lower ring.
	In.	In.	In.	In.	In.	In.	In.	Oz.	In.	In.	In.	In.
1	4½	½	1¼	1¾	3½	5½	4½	13	⅜	¼	1	5¼
2	4¾	½	1¼	1¾	3½	5¾	4¾	13½	⅜	¼	1	5¼
3	5	½	1¼	1¾	3½	6	5	14¼	⅜	¼	1	5¼

this means of control that we must deal with especial care and understanding.

In the American cavalry service the snaffle-bit is issued to each trooper, and this is used for watering purposes when in the field and for the training of the horse in the elementary drills, etc. For regular cavalry work beyond this, the curb-bit is used. The weight of the American curb-bit now in use is given in the table below Fig. 62, and it is made in three sizes: No. 1, No. 2, and No. 3. These three sizes differ only in one measurement —the length of the mouth-piece, the length of this being $4\frac{1}{2}$ inches in the No. 1, $4\frac{3}{4}$ inches in the No. 2, and 5 inches in the No. 3. All the dimensions of this bit are given in detail below Fig. 62. From this plate it will be especially noticed that the height of port is $1\frac{1}{4}$ inches, or one-half the length of the port, which is $2\frac{1}{2}$ inches; also that the upper branches are $1\frac{3}{4}$ inches long, or one-half the length of the lower branches; it will also be noticed that the plane of the branches coincides with the plane of the port; it will also be noticed that the center of the upper ring, the center of the end of the mouth-piece, and the knob in the end of the lower branch through which the rein-ring passes form three points in the same straight line; it will also be noticed that

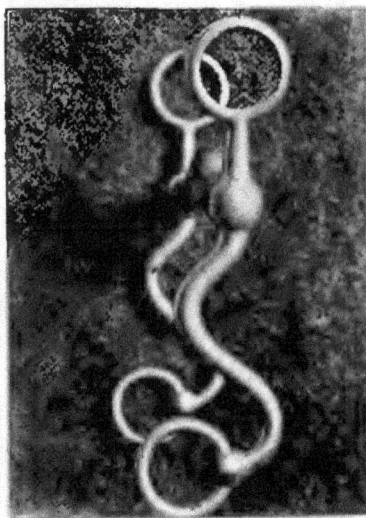

FIG. 68.

the upper ends of the upper branches slightly incline outward, away from each other; it will also be noticed that the mouth-piece is $\frac{1}{2}$ inch in diameter through its entire length. Let us consider the reasons which govern these dimensions, as they are all the result of careful study of the principles of bitting.

The Weight.—This must be no more than is absolutely necessary to sufficient strength. Additional pounds in the horse's mouth materially affect his management and his gaits. The discomfort caused by a bar of anything in the mouth is too apparent to need illustration, and additional weight only increases this discomfort. Experience has shown that ½ inch in diameter is all that it need be to possess the required strength, and thus weight may be limited here. Frequently a mouth-piece less than ½ inch may be used advantageously, and more weight saved. The lower branches are made tapering smaller toward the ends, thus saving additional weight. As a matter of weight, the single curb-bit is a great advantage over the bit and bridoon of the European cavalry services.

Length of Mouth-piece.—As horses' mouths differ in width, so must the length of mouth-piece, to enable us to fit them all properly. No pinching of the mouth at the sides can be permitted; not only is this clamping uncomfortable and even painful to the horse, but also chafing to the tender lips at the sides. Some years ago General Carter (then captain of the Sixth Cavalry) measured the mouths of the horses in the cavalry squadron at Fort Leavenworth, and found that one-third of the mouths measured less than 4 inches, and nearly all were between 3¾ and 4¼ inches. Only two horses measured as much as 5 inches. To have the bit too wide will allow the bit to come against the sides of the mouth as the reins are pulled, thus bruising it. As the horse waves his head slightly in traveling, the branches of the bit will swing against the sides of the mouth if the mouth-piece be too long, thus causing a succession of more or less painful blows on the lips at the sides. Too long a mouth-piece will also make the adjustment of the curb-strap bad, as it will be stretched out and thus rest on the tender bones above the curb-groove instead of setting snugly all around this groove. As these bones are sharp and narrow, this bad position of the curb-strap will cause much pain.

Height of Port.—This must be only sufficient to allow the tongue to lay comfortably in it; never high enough to touch the palate, which causes much pain and makes the horse bore away with his head from the rider's hand. The object of the port is to take just enough pressure off the tongue to throw the required weight on the bars of the horse's mouth, and no more. As these bars are sensitive, and the mouth-piece of the bit rests on them, or (with a low port) partly on them and partly on the tongue, great pain can be caused by having too high a port, and thus throwing enormous weight on the bars. This height of port must be carefully considered, and a bit used that will regulate the weight on the tongue and the weight on the bars of the mouth, as circumstances require. The use of the extremely high port often noticed in the cattle country among cow-boys is not only irrational, but destroys the very purpose of the port by crushing the palate, which was never intended to be touched, and thus losing that very pressure on the bars that is required. Such a high port causes acute pain in the wrong place, and nothing else.

Length of Port.—This must be just enough to allow the tongue to lie in the port without having its edges cut. If too narrow, the edges of the under side of the port rest on the edges of the tongue, and a sharp jerk may cut the tongue half in two; if too wide, the edges on the under side of the port will rest on the bars of the horse's mouth and bruise them badly. The edges of the port should never be too sharp, for even with the best bit and adjustment cutting of the tongue or bruising of the bars may result if the rider has a heavy hand.

Length of the Upper Branches.—The length of these upper branches is governed by the principle of leverage involved, which will be discussed later.

Length of the Lower Branches.—The length of these is also governed by the leverage action, and will be discussed later. Whether these lower branches are straight, curved, or double curved, makes little difference, as the *straight* length of the branches must be a continuation of the line of the upper branches.

Outward Inclination of the Upper Branches.—This in the No. 1 bit is, measuring from top of branch across to the top of the opposite branch, as can be seen in table below Fig. 62, 5½ inches; in the No. 2 it is 5¾ inches, and in the No. 3 bit it is 6 inches. Were these branches parallel to each other, their tops would, owing to the broadening of the horse's jaw as it goes higher, crush into his jaws above the mouth, and a fit could not be secured; the mouth-piece would be pushed too far down on the bars toward the incisor teeth, and the tops of the branches would bruise the jaws. To prevent this, they incline outward, and should not touch the horse's cheeks. As some horses are unusually large in the jaws above the upper ends of the mouth, a bit, otherwise fitting properly, may have the upper branches crowding into the cheeks, and must be slightly bent out more than usual to fit correctly. As both the cheek-pieces on the bridle head-stall and the curb-strap must be buckled into the rings on the tops of these upper branches, they must be bent outward far enough to prevent these straps from chafing the lips or cheeks, as frequently happens.

Plane of the Port Must Coincide with Plane of the Cheek-pieces.—If the plane of the port inclined backward, the port would continually dig into the back part of the tongue; if the plane of the port inclined forward, the port would dig into the roof of the mouth as the horse stood at rest, and would turn forward and downward and press backward on the tongue whenever the reins were pulled. This faulty position of the plane of the port would consequently take the pressure off the bars when the reins were pulled, and place the entire weight on the tongue, which would probably injure the tongue, and would also require more pressure on the reins to control the horse.

The Center of the Hole in the Upper Ring, the Center of the End of the Mouth-piece, and the Center of the Knob in the End of the Lower Branch Must Lie in the Same

Straight Line.—If the line formed an angle such that the lower branch inclined to the rear, pressure in the leverage action would be lost, and the action of the bit would partake more and more of the simple action of a bar-bit the farther to the rear the lower branch was inclined. If the lower branch inclined to the front, pressure would be against the mouth-piece instead of around it, and a pull on the reins would push the mouth-piece farther and farther up into the edges of the horse's mouth the greater the lower branches inclined forward.

Having considered the actual bit and its dimensions, we now come to the principle of leverage, the great consideration in the curb-bit. For an exhaustive consideration of the curb-bit from every standpoint, combined with great personal experience in cavalry bitting, as well as elucidating the results of the labors of other investigators in the same field, the writer would commend to the new cavalryman the work of the late Major Francis Dwyer, of the Imperial Austrian service, entitled "Seats and Saddles, Bits and Bitting." To those who will read this exhaustive treatise on bitting it will appear like a revelation, so startling and novel is its information, and it may be added that cavalrymen the world over have adopted this work as authoritative. In the use of the bit in the horse's mouth, one thing, and only one thing, is desired— to control the cavalry horse with the least possible pain. To do this, the curb-bit cannot be merely placed in the animal's mouth and allowed to stay there by buckling up the head-stall so that it cannot fall out, but it must be placed on the bars, in the proper position; must not touch either molars or tusks, and must be so adjusted that the curb-strap will rest snugly in the curb-groove under the bars. Before going into the principle of leverage itself, there are some dimensions of the horse's mouth which must be understood before the bit is placed in it. These measurements may be classified as the width of the mouth, the width of the tongue channel, and the height of the bars above the chin-groove. Let us see what these measurements are, and how to take them.

Width of the Mouth.—This is, as the words themselves explain, the width of the horse's mouth; but as this varies according to the point at which the mouth is considered, it must be taken at a particular place, and this place must be the place where it is determined the bit shall rest. The mouth grows wider and wider as it approaches the cheeks, obtaining its widest part at the upper termination of the lips. Inside of the mouth are the "bars"—these are the upper surfaces of the two lower jaws between the tusks and the first molars, where there are no teeth. Under the mouth, behind the chin, is the groove called the "chin-groove" or "curb-groove." The bits must rest somewhere on the bars, and as pain would be caused if the bit struck the teeth, it must be placed on the bars at such a point that this is impossible. As the curb-groove is to hold the curb-chain (or strap), this point on the "bars" must be chosen so that the curb-strap, when placed correctly, will lie snugly and neither mount up onto the tender, sharp under edges of the lower jaws or fall down onto the chin itself. This point, then, at which the width of the mouth must be taken, can be known, and is about 1½ inches above the tusks and 1 inch or 1½ inches below the first molars and directly above the curb-groove. The actual point known at which the width of the mouth is to be taken, insert a round, smooth stick (about 1 foot long and ½ inch in diameter) into the mouth, across the bars, at the selected place. This stick should have the inches and fractions of inches marked upon it, and must have a short stick attached to one end of it, firmly, perpendicularly to it. This short stick should not be over 3 or 4 inches long, and should be so fastened to the mouth-stick that not more than 1 inch of it is *above* it; if the upper part is too long, it may touch the jaws above the upper edges of the mouth, and if too short, may be drawn slightly into the mouth, enough to spoil the measurement. Adjust the stick on the bars at the right place mentioned, so that the short stick at the end just *lightly* touches the side of the mouth without pressing it in. Have the stick in the mouth *over* the tongue; then slide the thumb-nail along the other end of the stick in the mouth until the nail touches lightly the horse's mouth at the side; remove the stick and read the width on it carefully; this will give the width of the mouth at the correct place, and consequently a bit can be selected slightly wider, but *very little*, so that its mouth-piece and upper branches will set as they should when the mouth-piece of the bit is occupying the place on the bars where the stick rested. Care must be taken that the stick, when placed in the mouth, rests on each bar at the same place, and neither end higher nor lower on the bars than the other.

Width of the Tongue Channel.—This is the width of the space occupied in the mouth by the tongue as it lies quiet. The measurement is more difficult to take than the others, but, as it regulates the width of the port and consequently the amount of pressure on the tongue and the amount on the bars, it must be taken carefully. Open the horse's mouth and draw the tongue out with the hand to one side. Having removed the short perpendicular stick from the mouth-stick, place the mouth-stick in the horse's mouth at the same point as before, from one side, so that the end farthest in the mouth just touches the inside of the opposite bar near the top; slide the thumb along the other end of the stick as before, until the nail is at the inner edge of the near bar, at the top of it and at a point exactly opposite the other end of the stick, as was done in measuring the width of the mouth; withdraw the stick and read the measurement.

Height of Bars.—The "bars" in the horse's mouth have already been explained in the measurement of the width of mouth; they are the upper surfaces of the lower jaws between the tusks and the first molars. The height of the bars means their height above the bottom of the chin-groove, taken perpendicularly, and regulates the length of the curb-strap or chain, and the same considerations as regards choosing the place must be observed as before, and the place must be the same. Place the mouth-stick in the horse's mouth as before, over the tongue, until it is resting on both bars as in the measurement for width of mouth. Before doing so, the short stick should again be fastened on one end perpendicularly, and this short piece should have the inches and fractional parts marked on it. After the mouth-stick is correctly adjusted, place another straight stick parallel to it and tangent to the bottom of the chin-groove, but not *pressing* into the groove; move this stick sideways until one end of it touches the short stick depending from the mouth-stick, and then read the length on the short stick; this gives the height of the bars, and from this the length of the curb-chain or strap can be determined. The length of the curb-strap (or chain) has been found to be about 1½ times the length of the mouth-piece.

Knowing the various dimensions of the curb-bit and the reasons therefor, and knowing what measurements of the horse's mouth are necessary and how to take them, the fitted curb-bit is now placed in the animal's mouth and its leverage action studied after the curb-chain or strap is adjusted. Let us consider now this leverage action.

"With a plain, smooth snaffle, there is no question of lever-action; the amount of power applied to the reins is conveyed unaltered in quantity to the horse's mouth; to use a scientific expression, there is none of that mechanical advantage obtained which a mechanical power alone is capable of conferring. A still greater amount, however, of mechanical advantage may be obtained by means of a lever—a bit furnished with a curb of a proper length acts as such. There are, we know, several kinds of levers, and it will depend altogether on the manner in which the bit and curb are arranged whether we obtain a lever-action that is favorable to us or quite the contrary. It is therefore necessary to say a word or two on the principles of lever-action.

"In the first order of levers the power is applied at one end, the weight being placed at the other, and the ful-

rum (or prop) between the two, dividing thus the lever
into two arms, a longer and a shorter one; the mechanical advantage obtained is proportionate to the relative
length of these two arms. Thus, if PF (Figure 64) be
equal to twice WF, a power equal to 1 applied at P will
counterbalance a weight equal to 2 applied at W, but
as regards the curb-bit it is more necessary to observe
that the power and the weight move in *opposite* directions
or rotate around the fulcrum (or prop) as is shown by the
arrows. Applying this to a curb-bit, the cheeks of which
represent the lever, there can be no question as to where
the power is applied, being the lower ring to which the
rein is attached, nor as to the direction in which it is to
act, being towards the rider's hands; and if the bit acts as

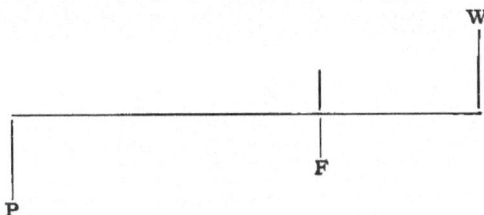

W

F

P

NOTE: PF = 2 FW.

FIG. 64. FIRST CLASS OF LEVER.

a lever of the first order, the fulcrum (or prop) must be
represented by the bars in the horse's mouth on which
the curb-bit rests, and the pressure of the curb-strap or
curb-chain on the chin would necessarily represent the
weight to be raised. But it has been shown that in levers of the first order the power and weight move in opposite directions in their rotation about the fulcrum; in
this case, therefore, the horse's chin, in consequence of
the pressure exercised by the curb-strap, should move
forward—that is to say, *away* from the rider's hand; and
the greater the lever power of the bit, and the stronger
the pull on the reins, so much the more would the horse
be induced to stick out his nose—a very frequent occurrence. Now, in actual fact, there is no weight to be
raised, in the purely mechanical sense of the expression;

it is a question of the infliction of a certain amount of pain from which the horse shrinks, and if the curb acts more painfully than the mouth-piece in conseqence of its construction or position, we obtain the action of a lever of this first order, which we never wish."

As the infliction of unnecessary pain is brutal, and much more so if by its infliction we are not getting what we want—that is, easy management and control of the horse—let us see what can be accomplished by using a lever of the second order. "In a lever of the second order the power and fulcrum act, or are placed, at the opposite extremities of the lever, the weight being between the two. The mechanical advantage is proportioned to the relative distances of the power and weight from the fulcrum. Thus, if PF (Figure 65) be equal to 3 and WF

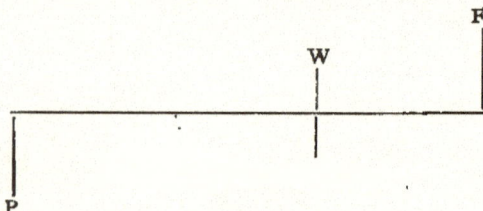

NOTE: PW = 2 WF.

FIG. 65.. SECOND CLASS OF LEVER.

be equal to 1, these numbers will express the relative amount of power gained; and it is to be *especially* observed that the power and the weight move in the same direction in rotation about the fulcrum. This is what we want for bitting. The weight in this case is represented by the pressure on the bars of the horse's mouth of the mouth-piece of the curb-bit, the curb acts merely as a fulcrum, the power is in the pull on the reins, and the horse's head follows immediately the pressure on the bars, in the direction of the rider's hand."

"It is very evident that, the direction in which the bit acts depending altogether on the relative amount of painful pressure exercised by the bit and curb, the horse's head will follow the rider's hand, even though the curb lacerate his chin, if only a greater amount of torture be applied to the bars of his mouth, the horse being left to deduce from the balance of pain what the rider's will may be. This is the system of bitting employed by the Arabs and other Orientals at the present day. Our Crusader forefathers borrowed it from them, and it is still more or less practiced among us."

By using the bit adjusted as a lever of the second order, better management of the horse and the least possible pain are the results. "It may be so adjusted as to render it perfectly painless, so that then the small amount of pressure exercised on the bars acting in the proper direction, and not being counteracted elsewhere, is the sum-total of pain inflicted, and even this may be reduced to a

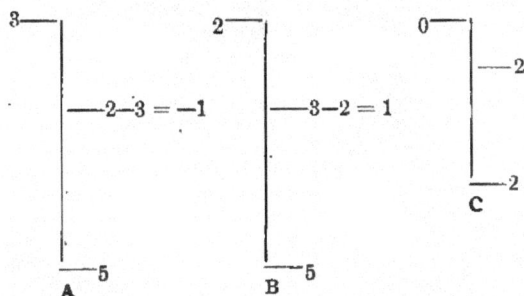

FIG. 66. SHOWING POWER APPLIED TO REINS.

minimum. Figure 66 shows that, supposing that a power equal to 5 be applied to the reins, it may, in consequence of various arrangements of the mouth-piece and curb, be made to exercise an amount of painful pressure as at A, where three parts act on the curb and only two on the mouth, which will make the horse bore into the rider's hand; or as at B, where three parts act on the mouth and only two on the curb; so that one really remains available; whereas, by reducing the painful action of the curb to 0, as at C, we find that the whole amount of action may be applied to the mouth, and therefore itself reduced to 2. Here we have the whole key to the entire theory and practice of bitting, and there is no difficulty in understanding that its immediate consequence will be to render bits of small dimensions equally efficient and much more certain and reliable in their action than the monstrous pieces of ironmongery often used can ever be.''

As we have seen that the American cavalry regulation curb-bit has the upper branches short and but one-half as long as the lower branches, let us see why this is:

FALLING THROUGH.

''The curb-bit may be likened to a pair of levers connected together by the mouth-piece.'' In the American cavalry bit the center of the rivet on each end of the mouth-piece is the point from which the length of the upper and lower branches is to be measured; in bits with curved mouth-pieces this is not so, the point then being a little higher up. The length of the upper branches is usually 1¾ inches, and this has been found to be the height of bars in the horse's mouth, which regulates the length of these upper branches. "If a bit is placed in the horse's mouth without attaching a curb-strap to it, when the reins are drawn the bit turns right around, and its branches come

STANDING STIFF.

to lie in the same direction as the reins; having no fulcrum, there can be no lever-action, and the bit is useless as a curb-bit, acting simply as a bar-bit, and is said to 'fall through.' Now, attach the curb-strap tightly and pull on the reins; it can hardly move the bit, causes the horse great pain with the slightest pull, and is said to

'stand stiff.' and the horse will poke his head against it.
Good bitting lies between these two extremes."

"The length of the upper branches will themselves
cause the bit to 'stand stiff' or 'fall through' if this length
exceeds or comes short of the height of the bars. This
can be seen from Figure 69, in which AB represents this

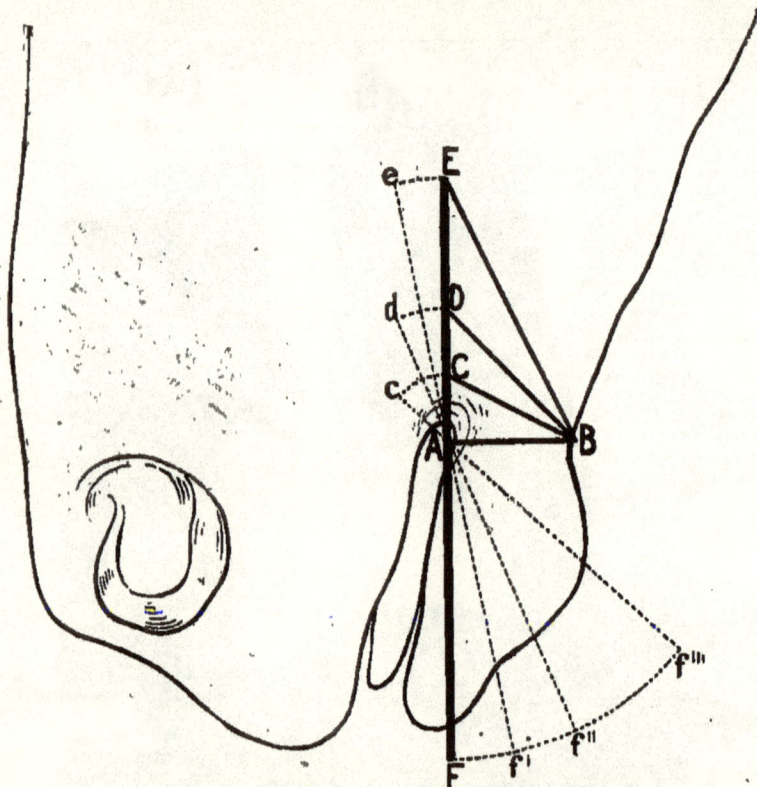

FIG. 69. MECHANICAL PRINCIPLES OF CURB-BIT.

latter dimension, AD an upper cheek precisely equal,
AC one of only half the same length, and AE one of
double the same. When a pull of the rein acts at F on
the lower bar, the curb will be drawn closer to the chin and
the mouth-piece to the interior of that organ; and supposing the amount of this 'closing-up' to be equal in the
three instances, the bit with a long upper cheek, AE,

will assume the position of *eAf'*; it will be stiff, and the curb, acting *upwards* in the direction of *e*B, will press on the sensitive part of the jaw. Moreover, there will be no lever action, the two arms of the lever being equal; the horse will therefore bore in the rider's hand. On the other hand, the bit with the short upper branch, AC, equal half AB, will assume the position *cAf'''*; that is, it will fall through. The curb will no doubt remain in the chin-groove and act forward in the direction of B*c*, but, forming a very acute angle with the branches of the

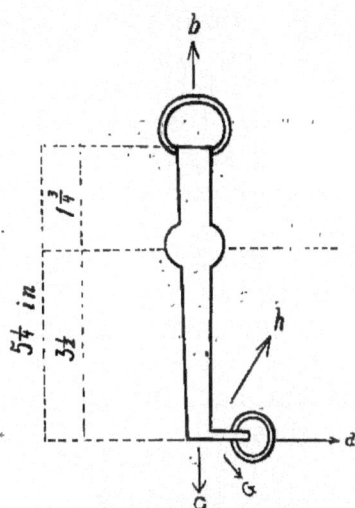

FIG. 69*a*. ANGLE FORMED BY REIN WITH BIT.

bit itself, will have scarcely any value as a *prop*. The lever action, however, will be very great, the lower branch, A*f'''*, being to the upper one, A*c*, in the proportion of 4 to 1; in fact, it will be too great, and therefore reduces the prop to a nullity. If the intermediate upper branch, AD, equal to AB, will assume the position *dAf''*, it will neither be stiff nor fall through. The curb will remain in the chin-groove, acting obliquely forward in the line B*d*, and will afford a sufficient prop or support; and the lower branch of the lever, A*f''*, being in the proportion of 2 to 1 to the upper branch, *d*A, there will be sufficient lever-action."

"Much depends on the *angle* at which the power is applied to a lever, and that a right angle is the most favorable one may be shown by pulling on the reins. In Figure 69*a*, if the bit were pulled in the direction *c*, it would have no other effect than to pull it out of the mouth did the head-stall not hold it in; if the pull were made in the direction *b*, it would only lift the bit up till the angles of the mouth stopped it; in neither case would there be the slightest lever-action; and the nearer any other direction, *g* or *h*, approached these perfectly inoperative ones, *b* or *c*, the less would be the value. It is therefore evident that the direction *a*, which is equally remote from both, must be most efficient. This is, however, precisely a right angle."

From the laws of mechanics and what has been said above regarding leverage, it will be remembered that if the power is distant from the fulcrum in a lever of the second order three times as far as the weight, which is between the two, then a power of 1 pound in the pull will be equal to 3 pounds in the weight; in other words, if the upper branches of the curb-bit are made 1¾ inches long, and the lower branches are made 3½ inches long, a pull on the reins of 1 pound will throw a 3-pound pressure on the bars of the horse's mouth, and this proportion is sufficient. Therefore, having decided as to the length of the upper branches, the lower branches are to be twice as long. This gives us the entire length of our American cavalry bit, which, as seen in Figure 62, is 5½ inches.

"Next in importance to the lengths of the upper and lower cheek-pieces comes the adjustment of the curb-chain or strap. The curb must lie in the chin-groove, without any tendency to mount upwards onto the sharp bones of the lower jaw; otherwise it ceases to be a painless fulcrum, and renders the best constructed bit uncertain in its actions." This position of the curb-chain or strap can only be obtained by placing the mouth-piece of the bit where it should be put—on the bars of the horse's mouth, just below the first molars, sufficiently low not to touch them and sufficiently high not to touch the lower teeth, or the tusks, and should be just high enough not to pull the angle of the horse's mouth upwards; a light touch is all that is required. The American Cavalry Drill Regulations (Par. 284) gives the following rough rule for placing the bit and curb-strap: "The position of the mouth-piece will be attained for the majority of horses by adjusting the cheek-straps so that the mouth-piece will be 1 inch above the tushes of the horse and 2 inches above the corner teeth of the mare. The curb-strap should be loose enough to admit one or two fingers when the branches of the bit are in line with the cheek-strap." The use of a chain curb is better than that of a strap, as the strap gets wet and afterwards drys stiff, and thus is apt to chafe the sides of the mouth and rub them raw; the chain never does this. However, the strap is easily made, easily repaired, and when broken or lost can easily be temporarily replaced by using one of the coat-straps from the saddle, which makes a very excellent substitute.

In the American service the bit is issued to the trooper, and, unless this is watched, bits are apt to be found badly fitting; for if a trooper becomes ill or is absent, and some other man rides his horse, this second trooper uses his own equipments, and the bit may not fit at all. It is believed that the most rational method is to issue the curb-bit to the horse, and never allow it to be changed without an inspection by one of the troop officers, as few of the troopers are familiar with the theory of bitting and are apt to let a fair fit go, without endeavoring to secure a correct one by trying many bits. There should be an improved "adjustable curb-bit" in every troop, on the plan of the practical instrument described above for measuring the mouth, and each trooper should know the dimensions of his horse's mouth and the size of curb-bit that fits him best. In some foreign services, especially the Austrian, adjustable bits are frequently used. The

very best way to fit the bit, however, is for an officer of
the troop to do the fitting himself, by trying many bits
until the right one is found, and then using it always on
the particular horse.

Some of the regulation cavalry bits have been made
with an extra pair of rings for double reins. These rings
were placed at each end of the mouth-piece and the extra
pair of reins attached to them. By using this bit and
the double rein, the lever-action of the curb-bit on well-
mannered animals can be dispensed with while riding ordinarily, the upper reins only being used, and thus the curb-

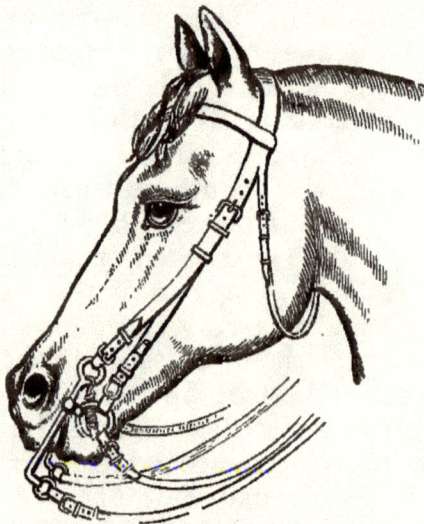

BIT AND BRIDOON.

bit becames for the time being simply a bar-bit. The
use of these extra rings and double reins will accomplish
much by easing the horse's mouth from all lever-action
whenever opportunity allows the trooper to dispense with
the stronger curb action. However, in actual cavalry
mounted work there *must* be the curb always present and
ready for instant use, as the bar action would not be
sufficient on the majority of troop-horses to control them
enough in times of accurate drilling, charges, etc. The
foreign services almost all use the double-reined bridle,

having with it a snaffle-bit with the second pair of reins attached to it. This arrangement is known as the "bit and bridoon," and has found favor almost universally abroad. The head-stall of the bridle possesses double cheek-pieces; into the rear ones the snaffle-bit is fastened, and the two bits are then adjusted so that when in the horse's mouth the snaffle will rest behind the curb-bit and somewhat higher up in the mouth. In this way the snaffle-bit may be used without disturbing the curb-bit at all, which would not be the case if the two bits were reversed in the mouth. In the American cavalry service the single rein has always been used; it is simpler than the double rein, simpler than the "bit and bridoon," and simpler to hold in one hand. After the trooper has been accustomed to riding, he can adjust the single rein with one hand, while it is not believed the double-reined bridle can be adjusted properly without the use of both hands. As the trooper must use one hand for other things, this is considered very much of a defect in the double-reined bridle. It is also that much more weight in the hand and on the horse, and that much more leather and metal to clean, of which the trooper already has a superabundance.

Foreign services all use the steel curb-chain in place of a strap. The American cavalry bit weighs but about 14 ounces as an average, while the British "bit and bridoon" weighs 2¾ pounds, the French "bit and bridoon" weighs 2 pounds, the German "bit and bridoon" weighs 1¾ pounds, the Russian "bit and bridoon" weighs 1¾ pounds, and the Austrian "bit and bridoon" weighs 2¼ pounds. These are the weights of the bits alone, excluding the double reins and head-stalls with the double cheek-pieces. It will be seen that the American bridle and curb-bit, weighing only 2 pounds 15 ounces all together, is hardly more than the weight of some of these double bits alone.

While theoretically proper bitting, as may be seen, becomes a very serious and somewhat complicated affair,

judgment, care, intelligence, and good common sense will
do much to procure satisfactory bitting. The bit now
in use in the American service
is believed to be the most hu-
mane bit used by any service
in the world, and the strength
and power of the bit is all-
sufficient. It is not desirable to
have too many sizes or classes
of bits for cavalry use; by care
in selection and fitting, the
three sizes in our service may
generally be made to fit all
horses.

After all the fitting, selection of the bit, and adjusting
are completed, some horses will
still be found that will not

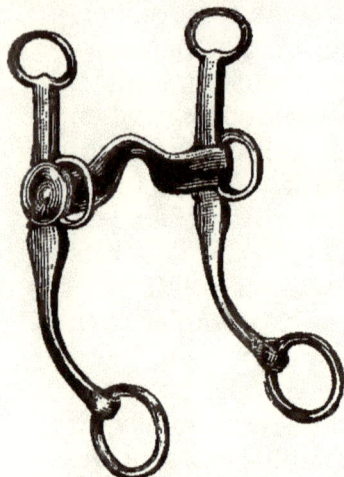

PRUSSIAN ARMY BIT.

take kindly to the curb-bit. These horses should be
fitted with extra care, and special training given them.
In the end it may be necessary to use the snaffle-bit on
the regular bridle head-stall; but as this at once destroys
uniformity of equipment in the troop, it is better to turn
the horse in to the quartermaster as soon as it can be
done, and get another in his place. After all has been
done to make the bit all that it should be in the way of
adjustment and size and fit, a light hand, good riding,
and occasional readjustment are essential to its working
well, and this should not be allowed to be neglected, but
the bits frequently inspected by an officer, when on the
horses. Many horses are pronounced vicious by their
riders because of bad bitting or failing to inspect the
adjustment occasionally and see that all is as it should be.

The bits issued abroad and in the American cavalry
service are now generally nickel-plated. After use, they
should be carefully washed and wiped thoroughly dry
before being put away. Much dirt and slime from the
horse's mouth remains on the bit after it is taken off, and

if left there, dries and becomes hard, and when next used will be apt to chafe the lips or tongue or bars. Cleaning and drying the bit after use will also preserve its appearance, which cuts a material figure in the appearance of the troop. Nothing looks more negligent than dirty, rusty bits, even if the danger to the horse's mouth be not considered at all. The horse is valuable to the troop in its skillful maneuvering just so far as he possesses agility and intelligence in answering the rider's will as communicated to him through the reins and bit; if these are han-

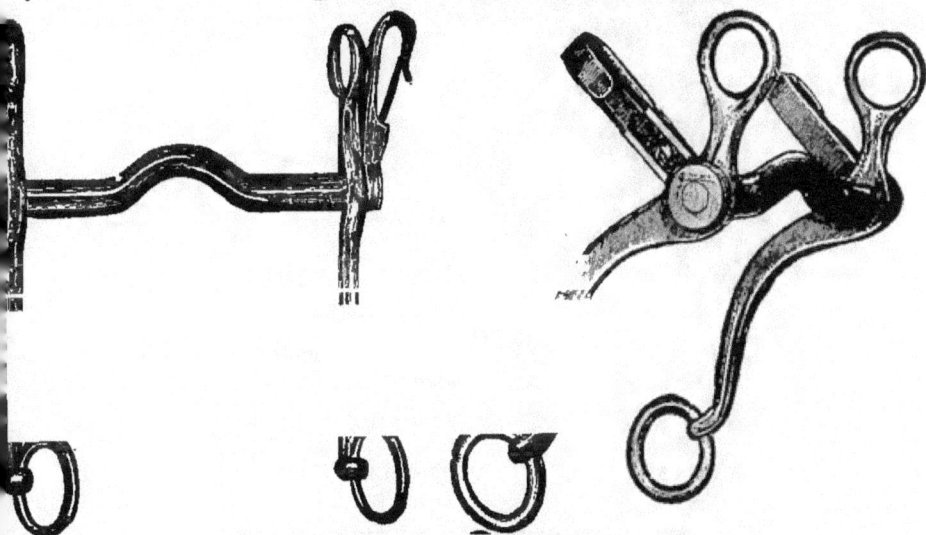

"WHITMAN" BIT—TWO VIEWS.

dled or adjusted roughly and negligently, the pain will destroy his gaits, his temper, and his lightness of movement; these in turn will react on the temper of the trooper, and the result will be a horse with a ruined mouth and one less efficient mount in the troop.

Of the many styles of bits manufactured in America, the "Whitman" curb-bit has found great favor among American cavalrymen, and is used by many officers. Two views are given above, of this bit. It possesses many excellent qualities. It is so constructed that by means of the snap-hook attachment and an ordinary pair of reins and curb-strap (or chain) a complete bridle is had by simply snapping the hooks into the halter-squares of the halter. The curb-chain (or strap) is fastened into the upper rings of the branches. It is very neat in appearance. Besides its very extensive use by officers in the

THE "WHITMAN" COMBINATION HALTER-BRIDLE.

American service, it is extensively used in our Western country and abroad. It can be used with the halter, but is *intended* to be used on the "Whitman" combination halter-bridle, as shown in accompanying illustration. When so used, this is one of the most satisfactory bridles in existence, for all-round cavalry work.

CHAPTER IX.

SADDLING THE CAVALRY HORSE.

A Fine Art—Horse's Back and Legs—Place for Saddle—Effects of Carelessness—Tendency to Saddle Too Far Forward—Saddling in Field Service—Adjustable Saddles—English "Wilkinson" —American "Wint"—Austrian Adjustable Saddles—Center of Motion—Equilibrium—Stirrups—Odd Forms of Horses— Spreading of the Saddle — The American "McClellan"—The American "Whitman"—The English Cavalry Saddle—The Russian—The German—The French—The Belgian—The Austrian—Use of Breast-Straps—Use of Cruppers—Single Cinchas —Double Cinchas.

Saddling in the Cavalry may be regarded as a fine art, to be learned partly from the text-books emanating from cavalry officers, and *largely* from one's own practical experience. Nothing is more destructive of the cavalry horse and his pack, when in field service, than ignorant, careless, or hasty saddling. Breaking camp too early in the morning, sounding the marching calls before the *impedimenta* have been packed and loaded and the horses' saddles and packs carefully put on, neglecting to examine the adjustment of the saddles and packs at frequent intervals while on the march, issuing saddles that do not fit the backs of the horses upon whose backs they are to go, overweighting pommel or cantle with the useless odds and ends that a trooper will gather together in the field unless constantly watched—all these and many more are causes, the effects of which in the field are amazingly far-reaching. There are very few horses that can carry a packed saddle and a trooper without the saddle needing readjustment and the pack straightening up every few hours when on the march; and at the occasional halts each saddle and pack should be inspected and corrected carefully. Watch the older cavalry officers and the old troopers in our cavalry troops on the march, and it will be observed that every one of them, at each halt, to rest or water, dismounts and readjusts the saddle and saddle - blanket carefully, straightens up his pack, and, if possible, removes the bridle, if only for a few moments.

The majority of cavalry horses become used up in front before they do behind. While there is a larger weight for the horse to carry on his front feet than on the hind ones, even without the saddle, still much of this destruction of the fore feet is believed to come from ignorant or careless saddling and a failure to place the saddle where the Cavalry Drill Regulations direct it to be put: "Place center of the saddle on the middle of the horse's back." Instead of this, men are often observed saddling up by placing the saddle well forward on the withers, and a popular idea seems to prevail, even among some old soldiers, that the saddle should be placed as far forward as the conformation of the

THE "McCLLELAN., SADDLE

horse will permit. The writer well remembers an old-time cavalry sergeant who always used to say to his men: "When you feel tired, place the saddle well forward on the withers and it will rest you." The writer recalls hearing a recruit tell the sergeant one day that he could not get the saddle any farther forward, and the old fellow growled out: "Well, put it on his neck." The horse, when subjected to the weight of the rider, saddle, and equipment, sustains about

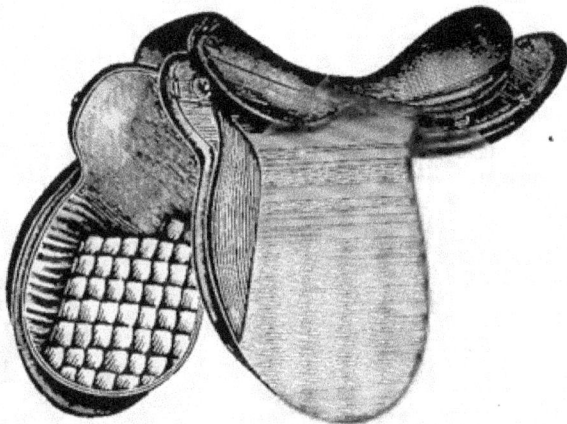

ENGLISH CAVALRY SADDLE FOR OFFICERS.

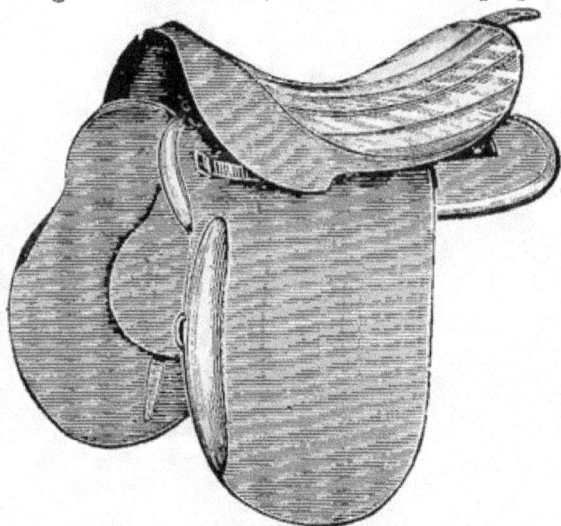

GERMAN CAVALRY OFFICER'S SADDLE.

two-thirds of the weight on the fore legs, if the saddle be too far forward, and the fore legs are no more qualified to carry this *excessive* preponderance of weight than the hind ones. True, the fore legs are weight-bearers and the hind ones propellers, but there is such a thing as overloading these same front legs, and a sure way to do it is to saddle up "well forward on the withers."

The further back the saddle is placed, after it passes the center of motion (which is the center of the horse's back), the rougher becomes the action of the horse on the rider, and consequently it is never placed there, and only gets there when it slides back accidentally. Many horses appear easier to the inexperienced rider when he puts the saddle far forward on the withers. When a trooper has assigned to him a roughly gaited animal, he soon discovers this, and begins to saddle up as far forward as pos-

SADDLING TOO FAR FORWARD.

sible. He quickly finds that by putting the saddle far forward it seems to make it easier on him, and at once it becomes a settled conviction in his mind that the saddle *should* be placed here, unconsciously believing that because he thinks it is easier on him it does not injure the horse.

The backbone of the horse is very similar to an arch, with the feet, fore and hind, for the abutments. To a certain extent this arch is a flexible one, and it has one characteristic especially true of this mechanical device, that of best supporting weight when it is applied equidistant from the abutments. The center of the back is also the "center of motion," and most authorities have agreed that this point lies over the fourteenth or fifteenth vertebra. This point is the preferable place for the center of the saddle to rest, because the supports here have less inertia to overcome than they have at any other point, and for this same reason the rider is subjected to less jar here from the motion of the horse, and because of the flexibility of the horse's back the rider's comfort is materially increased by the springy-motion obtained here. Most writers on this subject advocate this position of the saddle, and in the American service we have always so instructed our men; but because so few of them go into the reasoning of saddling, many of them get the saddle too far forward. Let the center of the saddle be placed over the center of the horse's back, draw the cincha moderately tight, and after an hour or two of marching, halt, dismount, readjust bridle, saddle, pack, and especially the saddle-blanket, and cinch-up reasonably tightly, and the result will be, at the end of the day's work, that both horse and rider will be found ready and willing for the coming service. There will be certain saddles which will require more attention, these having spread somewhat or the horse having lost much flesh. A very good way to avoid hurting the back of the horse in such cases is to place the bed-blanket over the saddle-blanket, and, if necessary, even turning in the front corners of this bed-blanket, to secure an even surface; but under no circumstances must any wrinkles be permitted to be in the two blankets anywhere, as they are sure causes of sore backs.

A cavalry saddle, in order to be as good as possible, should not warp or spread in several campaigns under all conditions of weather, nor break or bend when the saddled horse rolls on it, or when he falls or is thrown on it. It should further be so made that the lot of baggage a trooper is required to carry can be conveniently fastened to it with the weight evenly distributed. It should have as large a bearing surface as possible in conformity with the horse's back, without touching either withers or fore-part (top) of the croup; should leave the spine wholly uncovered, and it should be as light as it can possibly be made and still fulfill the other conditions. Each saddle in the troop should be carefully fitted to the individual horse's back, when the horse is in moderate flesh, and should then belong to that particular horse at all times, the same as the bit. A saddle, if adjusted so that the weight and fit are accommodated to the horse's physical conformation and physical strength, will give vastly greater satisfaction than one arbitrarily issued to the trooper for

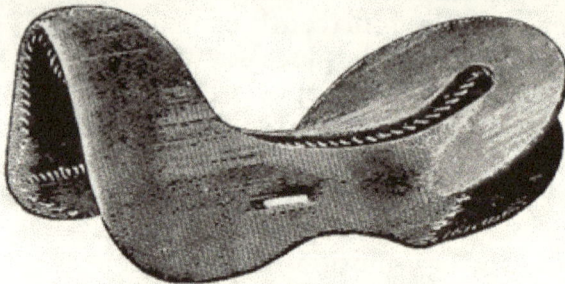

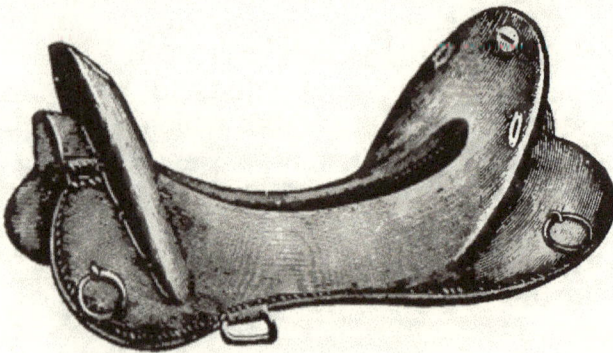

"MULEY" SADDLE-TREE.

"McCLELLAN" TREE.

use on any horse he may be given to ride. As it is occasionally necessary to change the troopers to other horses, owing to sickness among the animals, etc., issuing the saddle to the trooper instead of to the horse often results in saddles fitting very poorly. The effect of this bad fitting, especially in field service, will very frequently result in sore backs, and sore backs are the ruin of a cavalry command, temporarily at least.

In the British Cavalry each regiment is furnished with an adjustable saddle known as the "Wilkinson." This adjustable saddle is so arranged as to accurately measure each horse's back. It is a great advantage, and is the rational method of issuing saddles to fit each horse. The Austrian Cavalry also use adjustable saddles for issuing purposes, and that service has conducted many exhaustive experiments in this line, resulting in several very fine types of the adjustable saddle. Several other foreign cavalry services also use an

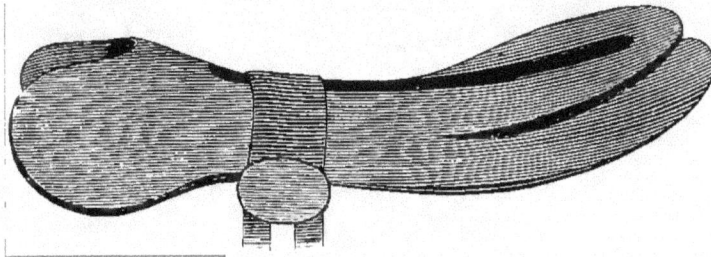

"WHITMAN-DWYER" SADDLE.

adjustable saddle for measuring the horse's back when issuing him his saddle.

In the American cavalry service many adjustable saddles have been experimented with, and one in particular, invented by Colonel Theodore Wint, of the Cavalry, is an exceptionally excellent one. This saddle is practically a "McClellan" saddle, and is divided into halves by a vertical cut through the middle of the pommel and cantle made in the direction of the saddle. The halves are held together by iron arches of equal curvature, two of which are fastened in front of the pommel near the top and two in rear of the cantle, the arches being perpendicular to the longitudinal axis of the saddle. These pommel and cantle arches are adjustable both in length and width, thus lengthening or shortening, broadening or narrowing

the entire saddle as required in fitting the horse. Once
the saddle is properly fitted, it is clamped by means of
thumb-screws, its measurement taken, and then a saddle chosen that corresponds. This saddle has been subjected to many tests and very hard service in the field,
and it seems was not considered wholly satisfactory for
actual field service, as the pommel and cantle arches easily

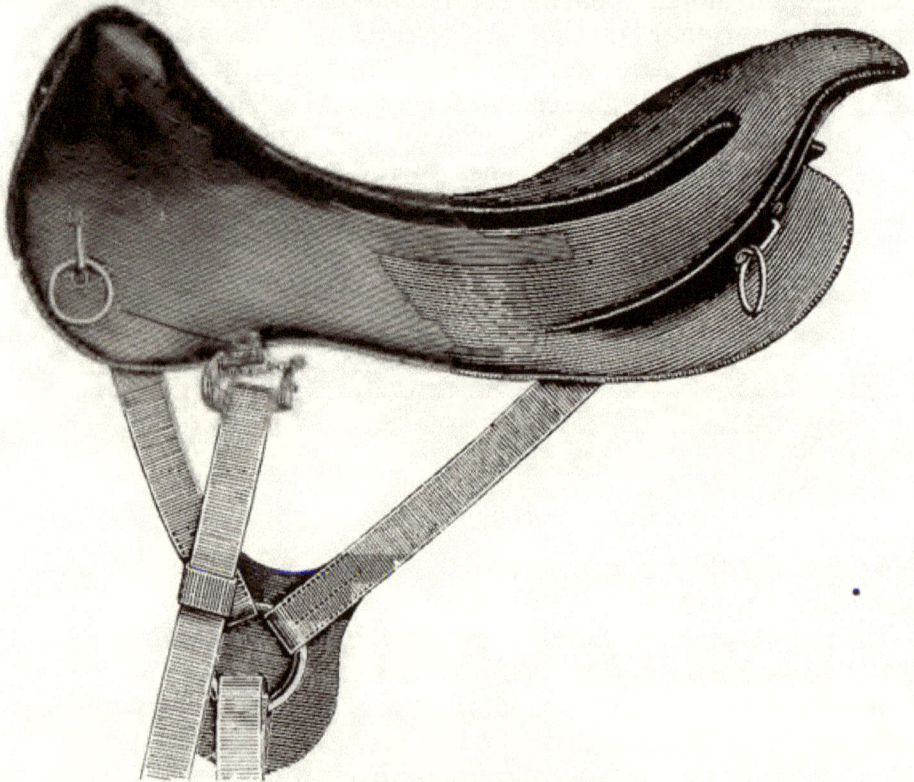

"WHITMAN" TREE.

broke, but this would appear to be a small defect that
could probably have been readily corrected; however,
no adjustable saddle is known that is sufficiently strong
to actually be used in field service, nor is this the province
of the adjustable saddle; it is intended only for the measurement of the horse's back, when a regular cavalry saddle is issued for general wear. As the horse rapidly loses

flesh while undergoing field service, an adjustable saddle strong enough for such service would enable the trooper to keep it always fitted to his horse's back; but so severe is the wear and tear on saddles in rough work that such a saddle has not yet been invented, and the adjustable saddle is reserved for measuring purposes, and in its place is invaluable in the troop.

There are four important points to be considered in saddling, after the saddle has been fitted and issued to the horse, and these are: first, that locomotion requires great freedom of motion at the shoulder-bone; second,

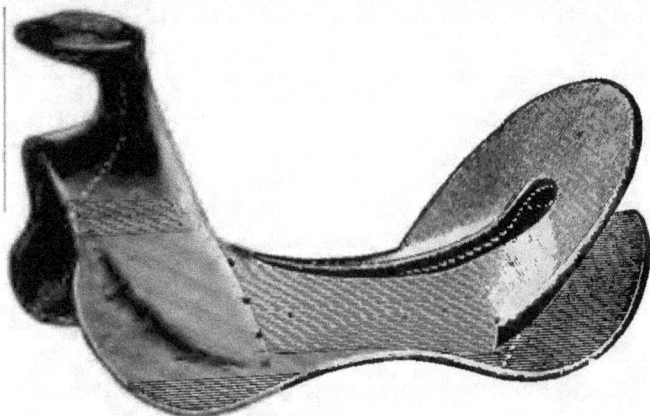

"TEXAS" TREE.

that any interference with its free movement must affect propulsion, owing to the angles of the shoulder-bones being unable to close or open to the required degree; third, that bad or careless saddling affects the safety of both horse and rider; fourth, that a saddle placed too far forward and tightly cinched causes excessive pain to the horse, restricts the free action of the lungs, and immediately results in sore back, exhausted forehand and legs, and stumbling. This latter quickly becomes noticeable on the march.

In addition to the above well-known points in saddling may be added several more borne out by experience: Never allow a single crease in the saddle-blanket; never permit the saddle-blanket to become hard and dry; never let it become filthy with hard dust or mud or sweat; occasionally refold it with a dry, soft, clean side next to the horse's back. In placing the saddle-blanket on the horse's back, put it on well forward, then gently smooth it backward until it reaches its proper place; this will smooth the hair in its natural direction; always have the saddle-blanket so placed that from 3 to 4 inches of it is forward of the saddle, to provide for the tendency of the blanket to work backward. This tendency comes from the fact that the hair leans to the rear, and, as the under side of the saddle is very smooth, the blanket gradually follows the direction of the hair backward until it may pass completely from under the saddle and fall off to the rear. This is not an uncommon sight, and as it will happen occasionally, even on well-formed animals, care must be taken that it is corrected before it has allowed the pommel to touch the back of the horse. Be careful in saddling that none of the coat-straps get caught under the saddle when cinching-up; these will often do this if the straps are left hanging loosely, and will cause sore backs.

As the horses loose much flesh in field service, many of the saddles will be too big after a few weeks' work, and it will be impossible to cinch-up tight enough to hold the saddle and blanket in place, even with the bed-blanket over the saddle-blanket; consequently some other method of securing the saddle in place, without injury to the horse, must be used, and a very easy method is by shortening the cincha itself; this may be done quickly in either one of two very practical ways, and as this is something every trooper will sooner or later have to do, it should be taught to every man in the troop. Take the cincha off the saddle entirely, and, holding it between the knees, grasp the first (outer) strand with the fingers of the right hand, twist this strand to the left, then twist the next strand to the right and pass it through the loop in the first strand, pull the second loop through and carry in towards the third strand, twist the third strand in the same way, pass it through the loop in the second strand, carry it towards the fourth strand, and so on entirely across the cincha; the last strand should be fastened with a string for a day or two, when it will hold by itself. In using this method of shortening the cincha, the center of the center division of the cincha should be worked across first; if the cincha is still too large, repeat the method across one of the ends of the cincha near the leather cinch-ring safes, and it may still again be repeated at the other

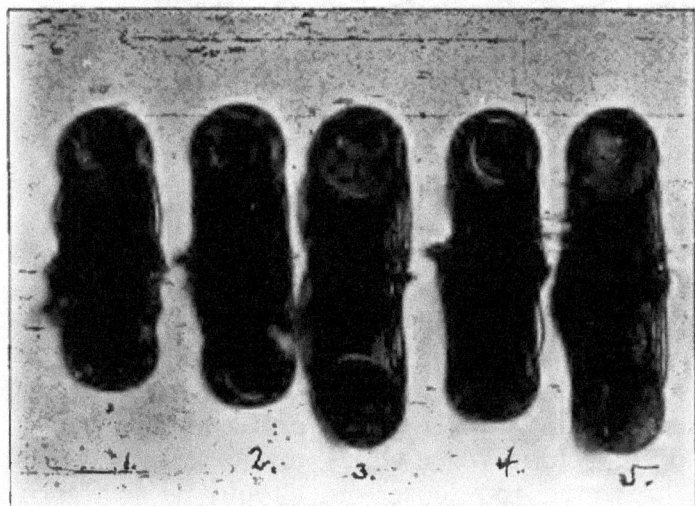

METHODS OF SHORTENING CINCHA.

1, Showing double lacing, with room for third lacing if required.
2 Shows shortening with stick, lower side.
3, Shows opposite side of No. 2, upper side.
4 Shows shortening by interlacing the strands, lower side.
5, Shows upper side of No. 4.

end if required, but this will rarely be necessary. The other method referred to is as follows: Cut a short stick about 12 inches long and 1 inch in diameter, taking care this stick is smooth and round its entire length; take the cincha entirely off the saddle, and, holding it as before, twist the first (outer) strand to the left, pass one end of the stick through this loop, twist the second loop to the right, pass the end of the stick through this loop, twist the third strand to the left, pass the stick through this loop, and so on entirely across the cincha; cut the ends of the stick off if they project beyond the edges of the cincha, cut notches in each end, pass a piece of twine from end to end of the stick, and tie tightly. In placing the cincha back on the saddle after shortening it by either of the above methods, the loops or loops and stick must be on the lower side, so as not to touch the horse's stomach. If these methods are properly done, it will be found that the side of the cincha next to the horse will be entirely smooth, and the cincha may be shortened sufficiently for almost any case.

Cinching the saddle on the horse is an important part of saddling; careless or improper cinching will quickly cause cincha sores in the vicinity of the girth-place, and these raw spots or boils are hard to cure, especially if the horse must be kept in use. Care should be exercised in cinching that the skin is not caught or pinched, or the hair pulled so as to stretch the soft skin and thus chafe it. The cincha should not be pulled *too* tight, but a *snug* fit is essential in keeping the saddle where it belongs, as well as for the safety of the rider. The cincha, when first fastened, should admit one finger between it and the belly; after exercising or marching for awhile—an hour or so—the cincha will be found too loose and should be tightened again. Two well-known methods of fastening the cincha-strap are plainly given in Par. 280 of the American Cavalry Drill Regulations, and need not be repeated here, except to say that the second method has been found more convenient by many cavalrymen, owing to the ease with which it can be untied, even when covered with icy mud or snow. This second method is largely used by cowboys, when using cinchas which do not buckle.

In cinching up, care must be taken that the leather "safes" under the quarter-strap rings and cincha-rings, do not touch or overlap; this is often caused by using too large a saddle or too long a cincha, and the overlapping will cause "cincha boils" and pinching of the horse's sides; this faulty cinching is shown on page 194, and the

illustration shown on page 193 shows about how these
"safes" *should* be placed when the saddle has been cinched
If a change to a smaller saddle or shorter cincha is not
possible, the cincha itself must be shortened by one of the
methods given above and as shown on page 189. In some
cases it may be best to have the troop saddler actually
shorten the quarter-straps on the saddle; but one objection to this is that such shortening of the quarter-straps
raises the quarter-strap ring and its "safe" to such a
point as to be uncomfortable to the rider's legs, and causes
this lump to press against the horse's ribs and cause pain.
Furthermore, shortening the quarter-straps would probably make the saddle a poor fit when used on any other
horse, and should rarely be permitted. The saddle should
always be cinched tightly enough to prevent it from moving or turning when the rider is in it.

Horses with low withers are very difficult to fit; the
downward inclination of the shoulders causes the saddle
to slip forward and bruise the withers. This may be recti-
fied by the use of the crupper, or sometimes by folding the
front corners of the blanket up smoothly under the pommel of the saddle. On the other hand, the conformation
of the horse in some cases is such as to cause just the opposite movement of the saddle—that is, slipping back. A
narrowing flank is a common cause of this, as it permits
the cincha to slide back from the girth-place onto the
stomach, and the farther back the cincha slides on such an
ill-formed animal the looser it gets. To prevent this, the
best means is the breast-strap.

The use of breast-straps and cruppers is to be discouraged. On the average form of horse they are never
necessary, and if used, add just so much to the weight for
the horse to carry, are just so much additional horse-
equipment to look after, and just so much extra leather
to keep clean. When the breast-strap is used, it should
be no heavier than is absolutely necessary; it should be
made in a "V" shape, having at the vertex of the angle
one single stout strap made with a loop at the end. There
should be buckles at both upper ends of the "V"; these

are buckled into the pommel-rings of the saddle, one on each side, and the under strap carried between the horse's front legs and the cincha passed through the loop. The breast-strap should not be buckled too tight, as it may chafe the horse on the shoulders or breast. When the crupper is used, it is attached by a buckle to the cantle of the saddle at the center, and, passing along the top of the horse's back to the tail, has a loop at the end through which the tail goes. As cruppers are not only unsightly, but very rarely necessary, they should not be used; better to trade the horse to the quartermaster for a better formed one. The crupper should not be buckled too tight, as it will chafe the root of the tail, on the under side, perfectly raw, especially if not carefully and frequently inspected. In some foreign armies both breast-straps and cruppers are used, but the crupper rarely; the breast-strap seems to be used more in the way of ornamentation than as a means of keeping the saddle in place. As whole troops use this breast-strap in some of the European services, the inference is that they use it wholly as ornamentation; otherwise they must possess enormous numbers of miserably formed animals, if entire organizations are compelled to use them to keep the saddles rightly placed. If the breast-straps are used as a means of ornamentation, it is an unwise idea surely—this making the horse carry the few additional pounds of leather merely for show. The cavalry horse has all that he can carry without loading him down with useless material.

Most cavalry services use the single cincha, except in the Russian Cavalry, where the double cincha is universally employed. The double cincha has many virtues, and on the Western plains of America it is seen on every cowboy saddle; but experience has shown that a sufficiently strong single cincha may be used satisfactorily, and the reduction of the weight on the horse's back must never be lost sight of. The double cincha increases the weight, and as it fits over the horse's stomach (a very undesirable place for cinching), it seems well not to use

t. The cowboy, riding bucking and wild horses, has
ound that the single cincha will not always keep the sad-
lle on the horse's back when the animal is "pitching,"
ut in a cavalry service of well-broken horses the single
incha is all that is required.

The cavalry saddle must be so made as to fit well
lown on the horse's back, to avoid making the animal

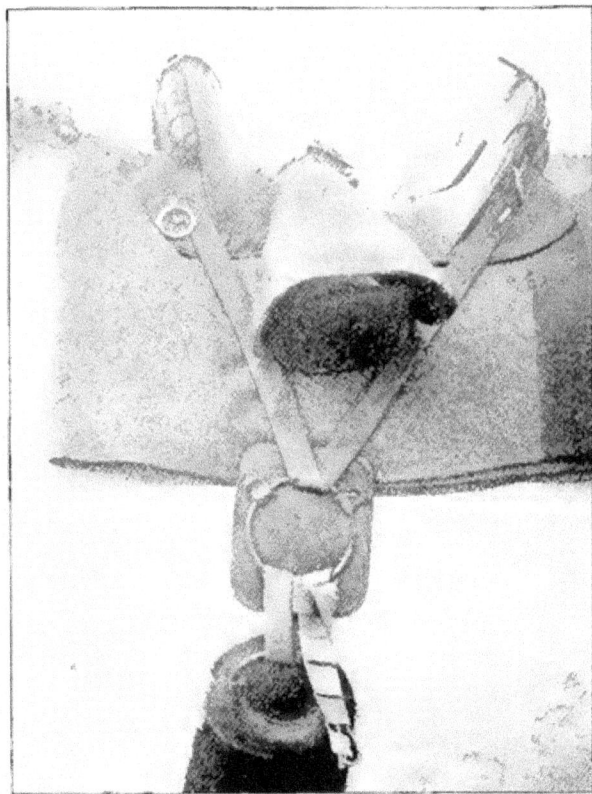

CORRECT CINCHING.

op-heavy when the saddle is packed. The equilibrium
f the horse must be maintained, else the base of support
ecomes too small for the height; at the same time, it must
ot touch the spine, and must be so constructed by means
f high pommel and cantle as to keep the pack off the

spine also. The side-bars must be as wide and long as possible, without either touching withers or point of the croup or pressing down on the ribs. There is no need of making the side-bars very deep, as this accomplishes no good and but adds to the weight of the saddle. The side-bars must be smooth on the bottom and slightly curved

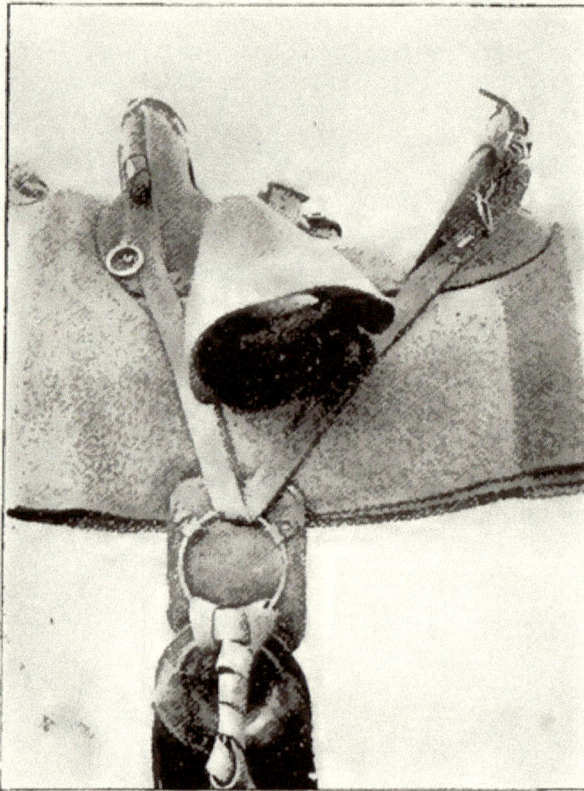

INCORRECT CINCHING.

upward at the fore and hind ends, to fit the conformation of the horse's back. The purpose of having the side-bars long and wide, smooth and slightly curved at the ends is simply the mechanical principle that the more surface covered the less will be the pressure at any one point. At no point should the saddle press into the horse's back with greater force than at any other point, else a sore back is the inevitable result.

It has been said that the saddle must be placed so that its center is over the middle of the horse's back, and that this middle of the back lies about the fifteenth vertebra. This seems plain enough, yet when the trooper actually comes to put the saddle on his horse, he is not quite sure. A good means of getting the saddle where it belongs is to follow one rule: The saddle should be so placed that three fingers of the hand can be placed between the withers and the front end of the pommel. By practicing this, it will soon become easy to properly place the saddle. As the pommel end of the side-bars is curved upward slightly, the fingers must be placed *against* the end of the side-bar, and not allowed to slide *under* the end, else the saddle will still be too far forward. When the trooper sits upright in his saddle, the fore limbs carry a little over one-half of the entire weight; when he leans back, the fore limbs carry a little less than one-half of the entire weight; and when he leans forward, the fore limbs carry probably two-thirds of the entire weight. What does this teach us? First, to let nothing touch the shoulder-blades; second, to carry no more weight than possible on the pommel; third, to make the trooper sit over the center of the horse's back, thereby saving the fore limbs from the unequal share of lameness, weight, and concussion which necessarily falls upon them.

It is necessary to remember that no two horses' backs are alike any more than men's feet are, and if our saddles are made according to regulations, horses' backs are not. Some are high in the withers, some low; some short and broad, others long and thin; some with backs like a billiard-table, others razor-shaped; some running high behind, others straight; some with a dip like a valley, others with an arch like a bow. All these forms are met with, and must be dealt with differently; but of all kinds of backs, be warned against the high-withered horse with hollows behind his shoulder-blades. This back cannot be made to stand active service for obvious reasons.

In fitting a saddle, it should be placed upon the *bare back*; the front of the side-board should rest 2 inches behind the shoulder-blade; it must be wide enough to admit the blanket without pinching the sides of the withers, with at least 2 inches to spare at the top, and follow the exact contour of the ribs.   At this part, remember, it must rest upon and against them in front, as the saddle must get a

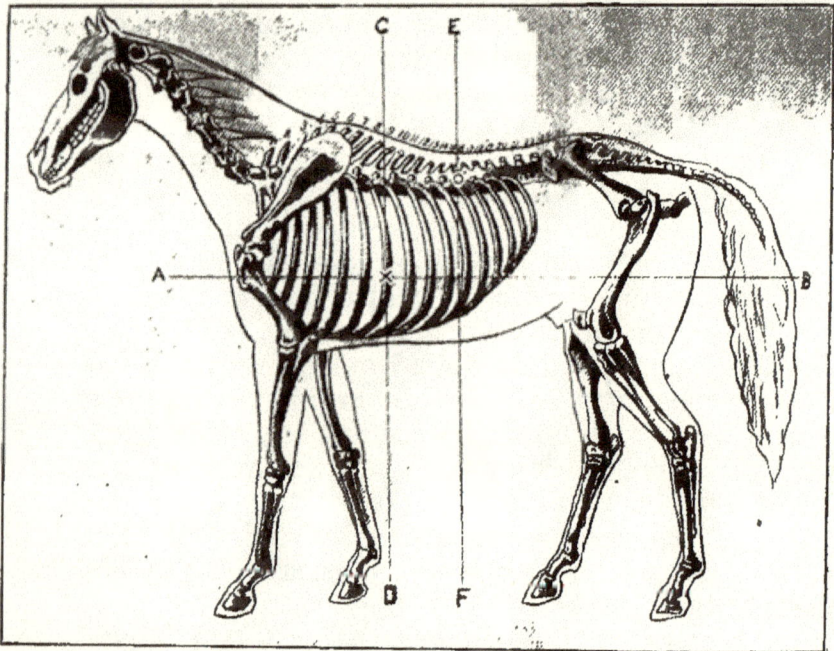

THE FRAMEWORK.

O = Center of motion.   X = Center of gravity.

hold there; the side-boards must fit exactly the shape of the back; if too oval or convex, the saddle will rock; if too concave, it rests only by its ends on the back, which will suffer; in front, the weight is transmitted downward and outward; behind, from above only.   The trooper is now placed in the saddle, and these points again considered, the fingers being passed under the front and rear of the side-boards to see that those parts are clear as well as the tops.

Sore backs are the immediate result of bad saddling; these may be divided into three classes:

1. Injuries to the summit of the spine.
2. Injuries to the sides of the withers.
3. Injuries to the weight-bearing surface of the back proper.

The first class (injuries to the top of the withers) are produced through the pommel touching these points, from being too wide or the tree spreading. This must be remedied by a narrower saddle or two blankets; there is no remedy for spreading—get another saddle.

The second class result from a narrow saddle, which rests vertically against these parts, instead of following their contour. The remedy is a wider tree.

The third class chiefly occur over the last rib, and are vulgarly known as "kidney sore"; they occur on the near side from extra weight of cantle pack on the off side, or the reverse. Their causes are various. When a saddle rests on the withers, it is higher in front, the posterior ends of the side-boards being driven into the back by the weight of the man gravitating to the rear end of the saddle. Leaning back, known as the "barber-chair seat," concentrates the man's weight behind, on the ends of the side-boards; the side-boards being posterior to the ribs and lying on the enormous propelling muscles of the loins— these, by their powerful contractions, create wounds by friction against the rear ends of the side-boards.

Loss of flesh, or "waste back," brings the weight nearer the bony column of the back; starvation or hard work produces loss of vitality of the skin, rendering it intolerant of pressure. This can be remedied only artificially by additional blankets. If the saddles are removed suddenly from hot, sweaty backs, the result is rapid evaporation, which produces tender skin, blisters, lumps, and swellings. The blanket should always be surcingled on the backs for half an hour or so after removing the saddles, especially when in the field.   In this matter we may learn much from experienced packers, who never remove the *aparejos* from their mules' backs for half an hour or so after getting into camp.

On the march troopers should be allowed at least twenty minutes to saddle their horses and make their blankets and saddles a comfortable fit, as it is no easy matter to fit a fully packed saddle against time, particularly on windy days, when the blanket will blow up into creases.   It is scarcely fair or just, either to trooper or horse, to saddle against time and then punish the troopers for sore backs; give them plenty of time to properly saddle first.

One frequent source of misery and injury to the horse's back is the continual chafing of the cinch-strap against the ribs.   This strap must not be clumsy, thick, too long, or stiff and hard through continual wetting; it should be kept smooth, clean, and soft with oil.   If too long, the trooper frequently will roll it through the quarter-strap-ring and cinch-ring, causing a protuberance, which injures the horse's ribs and interferes with the trooper's knee-grip.

As an excellent substitute for the breast-strap or crupper, or both, the use of the surcingle around the saddle is recommended.   It should have *no knots in it*, as are often seen.   If too long to buckle snugly, it should be shortened properly by the troop saddler.   It must be placed over the seat of the saddle, under the quarter-straps, and buckled so as not to chafe the horse or rider.

The illustrations on pages 180 and 184 give the American cavalry saddle, known as the "McClellan," in detail.   It is made in three sizes, No. 1, No. 2, and No. 3, according to the size of seat, the No. 1 having an 11-inch seat, the No. 2 an 11½-inch seat, and the No. 3 a 12-inch seat.   Some slight history of this saddle is given in Chapter X., and it may be added that many distinguished cavalry officers, both in the American service and abroad, testify in enthusiastic terms to its excellence.   It has been used

in the American service over forty years, on the severest
kind of service, in all seasons of the year, and has been
found remarkably satisfactory.   It is unquestionably
lighter and better made than any other military saddle
known.   It weighs 18 pounds, 2½ ounces, including hair
cinch, stirrups, stirrup-straps, quarter-straps, and coat-
straps.   It is very simple in construction.   The pommel
and cantle are of beech and the side-boards of poplar.

The two side-boards are each made in two pieces and
glued together; they are then glued to the pommel and
cantle and secured with screws.   The pommel has three
coat-straps and the cantle three; iron pommel and cantle
arches are riveted on for strength; the bare tree is
smoothed and painted with white lead, then the rawhide
cover is sewed on, and finally the entire saddle is securely
covered with fair leather.   The saddle is open throughout its entire extent over the horse's back, and thus
undoubtedly heats the back less than any other style.
The blanket sits well under this saddle, and experience
with hair and felt and woolen saddle-pads has demonstrated that the blanket is superior to any other method
of protecting the back from the saddle and weight.   It
may be refolded easily, and thus always present a clean,
soft, and dry surface for the horse's back, while the pads
frequently become hard and filthy and are difficult to
clean.   The blanket has the additional advantage of
being of use to cover the horse when necessary, or to cover
the trooper if the horse is not needing it.

It will be observed in the illustration on page 174 that
the stirrups are hung somewhat forward of the center of
the saddle.   This is to equalize the weight on the horse's
back when the saddle is packed and the trooper mounted.
If the saddle be hung up by a rope from its middle point,
it will balance quite accurately.   After the saddle is packed
while so hanging, it will be discovered that its balance
has been lost and that it requires from 23 to 25 pounds
more on the pommel to again balance it.   The more
pack that is put on the cantle in the way of extras,

the greater will this preponderance of weight at the cantle over the pommel be increased. To equalize this matter of weight, the stirrups are hung slightly forward, so that when the rider sits in the saddle with his feet in the stirrups the weight of his legs and his pressure on the stirrup-treads will tend to equalize the whole weight on the horse's back. In the large cowboy saddle this is not so. The pack carried is very small, and the weight of the cantle is not equal to the weight of the pommel, the pommel being high and having a pommel-plate or "horn" on top. In these saddles the stirrups are hung directly from the center of the saddle. This evens up the weight, and it also makes the cowboy ride with what is commonly known as the "fork" seat. It will be seen from this that the stirrups, the seat of the rider, the manner of cinching, the proper spreading of the saddle-blanket, and the general adjustment of the pack all enter into a consideration of good saddling. If any one of these is neglected, the result is unsatisfactory, and generally a horse with a sore back and a dismounted trooper.

The saddle known as the "Whitman," shown on page 186, was invented years ago, and has been used extensively in the service. It resembles the "McClellan" in many ways; its pommel and cantle are very low. This "Whitman" saddle has found great favor among cavalry officers for their personal riding, and is a strong all-round field service saddle, but has never been regularly used by the service as troop saddles, its use being only for officers.

The "Whitman-Dwyer" saddle, shown on page 185, has also won much commendation from cavalrymen. The peculiar feature in this saddle is the method of attaching the stirrup-straps to the saddle. These straps are made double, as usual, but instead of passing through stirrup-strap rings in the saddle, the straps pass entirely around the side-bars, as shown in the illustration. Greater security is thus claimed for it, as the stirrup-straps when so placed are subject to less wear than when passing through a metal ring, as in the "Whitman" and "McClellan" saddles. Some styles of cowboy saddles also have the stirrup-straps arranged in a manner similar to the "Whitman-Dwyer" method.

On page 187 is shown the tree of the powerful "Texas Cowboy" saddle. It is the saddle in almost universal use among the cow-men, scouts, packers, trappers, guides, and ranchmen of the frontier, and in its field has no equal. In the breaking of wild horses, roping cattle, etc., it stands pre-eminently *the* saddle for such work. Its weight is often as much as 40 pounds or more; it can be packed, has saddle-bags of leather, covered frequently with hair, which go behind the cantle. It has a double cincha, and generally possesses skirts permanently fastened to the saddle, with wool on their under side. The stirrups are usually hung centrally.

The English, German, Russian, Belgian, French, and Austrian cavalry saddles are all more or less on the order of the riding saddle known as the "English"; they possess open stirrups of steel, leather skirts on the sides, covered seats, low pommels and cantles as compared to the American, leather cinchas (and the Russians use a double one), and the weight of the various saddles is more. The English saddle weighs about 21 pounds, the German weighs 19.75 pounds, the Belgian weighs 34 pounds 6 ounces (including saddle with girth, straps, felt pads, and stirrups, complete), and the weights of the others are greater than that of the American saddle. The method of saddling is very similar, and it is given the most careful attention. The cinchas generally buckle instead of tie, as on the American saddle; the stirrups are placed somewhat forward of the center, as in the "McClellan" saddle. The English and German cavalryman uses a saddle-blanket, folded, while the Russian and Belgian uses felt pads attached to the under sides of the saddles, in addition to which the Belgian also uses the blanket; the Austrian uses the saddle-blanket, folded, and the saddle also possesses, attached to its side-bars, felt pads.

CHAPTER X.

The Pack.

The Cavalry Horse a Weight-Carrier —Variation of Pack — Old Packs—Early American Packs—Actual Weight Carried—American Pack—British—German—Russian—Austrian—Belgian—Evenly Distributed—Hung Low—Securely Fastened—Importance of Constant Care and Supervision.

The old cavalry saying, that a cavalry horse must be a weight-carrier brings us to the consideration of the weight he really does carry in actual practice. This weight varies greatly with climate, season, latitude, purpose, and resources. Service on the plains of North America in winter requires a much heavier pack than service in Cuba and the Philippine Islands, in which tropical countries we are enabled to reduce the pack in many ways. In a country where the resources are considerable in the way of houses, feed, etc., far less is necessary than in a country which has been devastated by war. With a cavalry force on an expedition where haste is all-important and the length of time to be consumed is short, it is generally possible to dispense with many articles of the regulation pack. Every circumstance that will enable the cavalryman to lighten his pack should be taken advantage of, but as many soldiers, if given much latitude in this respect, would abandon absolutely necessary parts of the pack for less important articles, careful supervision by cavalry officers is necessary before reduction is permitted. It is the careful, intelligent reduction of the pack to its *lowest efficient limit* that is always to be kept in view. Reducing the pack below this means serious injury to the welfare of the command, and permitting the pack to get above its lowest limit is a sure way of injuring the horses. Observation and daily care must teach the inexperienced officer what may be dispensed with and what may not.

The packs as now used in the American and British and European cavalry services are all the outcome of years of experiment and experience, and represent in most countries very perfect packs from the two important standpoints generally considered—the horse's capacity and endurance and the preparedness of the command. The packs of the different cavalry services differ considerably, so far as the articles carried are concerned, but all cavalry services observe these fundamental axioms. Many centuries ago the pack consisted of rude contrivances made of the skins of animals roughly sewn together and slung across the horse's back, from which the various articles constituting the pack were hung. Before the pack existed there had been used for centuries various devices in the form of metal plates, used to protect the horse from the hand-weapons of the ancients; but as methods of fighting improved it became necessary to carry on the horse additional arrows or spears, and from then on the pack took form, and has ever since been undergoing changes and improvements, and has resulted in the modern pack of to-day as represented in the several cavalry services. With time and study and experience, the number of articles has been greatly reduced, and the manner of carrying them improved, until the present American pack approaches more nearly to the ideal pack than ever before, and is believed to be superior to any cavalry pack in the world. Many years ago the American Cavalry used a high welted saddle, breast-strap, cruppers, shabrack, forage-nets, pistol-holsters attached to the saddle, wallets, and other articles now considered unnecessary and never used.

In this connection the student is referred to the old Cavalry Tactics of the United States Army for 1841, in which is given in detail the manner of packing the light cavalry saddle and also the heavy cavalry saddle, and an exhaustive manual of the lance, which appears to have been carried at that time. The saber was then carried attached to the waist-belt of the rider, and each soldier

had on his saddle in addition a valise for his extra clothing, etc.   To us in the cavalry to-day this old-style pack
seems to have contained many elements of positive disadvantage and especially to have had unnecessary weight and
bulk.   It simply illustrates in a slight way that in the reduction of these two elements to our present pack we have
displayed the result of the intervening years of experience.
Our saddle-bags and nose-bags have taken the place of
the wallet and forage-net; the saddle-blanket has taken
the place of the shabrack; the lance has long since disappeared; the pistol-holsters have been taken off the saddle and reduced to one, which is now carried on the person of the trooper; breast-straps and cruppers are used
only on a few ill-formed horses, upon whose backs the saddle will not properly rest; the saddle itself has been somewhat changed and lowered; and it is difficult for us to
realize what our old-time pack was unless the Drill Regulations of the early years are read.

The American cavalry pack differs very materially
from the European and British packs.   Many articles
which are considered unnecessary by us are regularly
carried by the foreign services; among these articles are
the telescopic canvas water-buckets, forage-nets, separate
pouches for horse-shoes and nails, hoof-picks, monkey
shoe-wrench, breast-straps, cruppers, blacking, grease,
etc.   However, on the other hand, the American service
carries some articles never used by foreign services; chief
among these appear the bed-blanket and the shelter tent.
The custom of foreign armies of billeting troops in the
houses of townspeople makes this possible in their districts so closely settled, but to the American cavalryman
of the great arid, unsettled plains of our enormous West
these two articles are especially indispensable.

In considering the cavalry pack, appearance and
style must play a very secondary part and efficiency alone
be aimed at.   It cannot be too frequently impressed upon
the reader that over-weighting of cavalry horses by using
heavy packs is a sure means of breaking down horses.

Lieutenant-General Sir Charles Napier, of the British Army, commenting on the British cavalry pack, said: "The British cavalry horse and pack are all right for parades and reviews, but in the field, half starved, if our cavalry have, at the end of a forced march, to charge the enemy, the biped, full of courage and fire, transformed by war-work into a wiry, muscular dragoon, is able and will-

REGULATION "McCLELLAN" SADDLE AND FULL PACK.

ing; but the quadruped, overloaded, cannot even gallop, but only stagger. Cavalry horses heavily loaded are expected to respond promptly to spur and hand while the riders wield their swords worthily, but they cannot—both man and animal appear inferior in the British Cavalry for this reason, to their Indian opponents. The vigor of the dark Eastern horseman, his impetuous speed, the sudden volts of his animal in seconding the cunning of the swordsman, is a sight to admire, but it is too much admired by men who look not to causes. The light-weighted horse of the dark swordsman carries him around his foe with elastic bounds, and the strong European, unable to deal the cleaving blows, falls under the light activity of an inferior adversary.''

The use of the pack on saddles is almost as ancient as the use of saddles themselves. Riding-saddles have been used for centuries, as history proves and as shown in a previous chapter. It is related that Constantine the younger was killed in the year 340 A. D. by falling from his saddle, and the Emperor Theodosius, in the year 385 A. D., forbade the use of saddles weighing over 60 pounds. Saddles may be classed under two types—Hungarian and Moorish. The original of the former consisted of wide, parallel bars joined at the ends by heavy bows, to which were secured parallel strips of hide. There were no stir-rups. The Hungarian saddle of the present closely resembles the primitive one, while the English saddle is the most highly developed form of the type in Europe, and the "McClellan" military saddle, named after General George B. McClellan, is the best of the type in the United States. These two saddles, though from the same source, are quite different in construction, as is well known. The tree of the English saddle is a skeleton on which the saddle is made; as completed, the seat and bearings are all padded, with scarcely anything of the original outline showing, except at the edges. Probably in point of style it is the most perfect saddle made, if one does not have to carry a pack; but, nevertheless, one who is in the saddle all day is glad to exchange the English saddle for something easier. The "McClellan" tree forms the saddle itself. The side-bars are shaped to fit the animal's back, and padding is dispensed with even for the seat, and among all the various military saddles known the "McClellan" holds its own as a pack-saddle. Many styles of saddles have been invented, all being modifications of the two classes given above. A late form is the pneumatic saddle, in which a rubber bag filled with air is placed under the leather covering of the seat. This saddle has been most successfully used in racing. The two objects of the saddle are to increase the comfort of the rider and lessen the concussion of his weight on the animal's back.

The so-called Moorish type probably originated in Persia. In the primitive form a number of skins were superimposed on the animal's back with a front and back wooden cantle, the whole confined by straps completely surrounding the animal. In the construction of its various forms the finest fabrics have been employed, and it has always been the most expensive saddle made. Mexican, Texas, and California saddles are derived from this type, retaining the main features of the original. The Moorish saddle has heavy, long bars, a high and broad arch, and a large knob or horn, which was originally in the shape of a box, in which to carry knives and other articles, the shape being much like the "muley" of the present time. The horn in its present shape is a Mexican addition, serving to hold a lariat or lasso. A characteristic feature of the Moorish saddle, even in the present time, is the hang of the stirrup leathers, which are suspended centrally under the body of the rider; whereas, in the Hungarian style, such as the present English saddle and the present "McClellan" saddle, the stirrup leathers are hung in front of the leg.

If we estimate the rider at 150 pounds and 10 pounds for his clothing, this makes the horse carry including arms, etc., approximately 200 pounds when in light marching order in our service; and estimating the rider at 150 pounds and his complete pack and equipments at 90 pounds makes the horse carry 240 pounds in our heavy marching order. This is a considerable load, but it is distributed very evenly and hung low to help the horse preserve his equilibrium, and is so arranged as not to chafe or bruise the animal at any gait. This largely tends to lessen the effect of the actual weight, and in addition to the

arrangement of the pack itself, the cavalry horse is frequently relieved of the weight of the rider for a few
moments at a time, during halts and over rugged country
when the rider dismounts.   The great advantage of requiring the men to dismount over rugged country for short
distances and lead their horses is amply shown by mere
reference to the above figures.

NEAR SIDE OF AMERICAN CAVALRY PACKED SADDLE,
ON THE HORSE.

In using light marching order, a few pounds more or
less are not very important.   This order is only used at
drills, parades, ceremonies, etc., where the horse is required to carry the weight for but a short time and then
is wholly relieved.   It is in the carrying of the heavy

packed saddle that caution must be observed. Used in the field on marches, escort duty, reconnoissance, courier service, outpost, etc., the heavy packed saddle is on the horse's back for long hours at a time, and every pound counts. The damage of a few additional pounds can hardly be over-estimated, for the horse already has a heavy load and is

OFF SIDE OF THE AMERICAN CAVALRY PACKED SADDLE, ON THE HORSE.

compelled to carry it over good and bad country for months at a time, and in addition frequently has an inferior, impatient, and unskillful rider, to say nothing of bad food, exposure, etc. It is important to carry only what is absolutely necessary, to hang it as low as possible, to help the horse keep his center of gravity where Nature and professional knowledge have found it easiest for him, and to have it all fit the particular animal and not chafe or bruise him or obstruct his free action at all gaits.

When it is considered that in addition to the weight of the trooper and his arms, the horse must carry saddle, saddle-blanket, saddle-bags, bridle, halter, lariat and picket-pin, curry-comb and horse-brush, side-lines, nose-bag, mess furniture, watering bridle, extra shoes, extra nails, rations, shelter tent with its pole and pins, extra ammunition, surcingle, bed-blanket, carbine scabbard, and extra clothing, we see that the individual horse becomes very much of a pack-animal and carries a very heavy weight. Each troop should have permanently a pack-train, either in civilized or savage warfare. To relieve the horse and yet carry what is believed to be necessary in the field, a pack-train seems to be about the only remedy. With one a cavalry command is footloose, independent of roads and wheels, and even of a base of supplies for a limited time. The pack-train could carry the rations, bedding, extra shoes, nails, etc., and as these are gradually reduced by use, the pack-animals could relieve the weakest horses by carrying most of their equipment. A good pack-train is rarely much behind the troop to which it is attached.

It is often possible to reduce the pack without lessening the efficiency of the command. The pack habitually carried in the Philippines illustrates this point. Except at drills, inspections, etc., this modified pack differs largely from the regulation pack. Much of the lightening of packs that was found practicable in the Philippine Islands was due to the permanently warm climate and the uselessness of carrying overcoats, hobbles, tent-pins and poles, sabers, and heavy clothing. The cavalry Philippine packed saddle, as weighed by the writer in the Philippine Islands and used by his troop when in the field, weighed approximately 75 pounds as a maximum and might have weighed a little less. This pack had sufcient to carry the trooper for weeks at a time in that climate at any season of the year, including four days' field rations in the saddle-bags, and it was found practicable, when necessary, to put five days' field rations in the saddle-bags, which, it may be added, lasted the troop six days each time on two different occasions, without complaint or suffering except on the part of three or four improvident troopers, who ate their rations up in about four days and borrowed from their more careful comrades the other two. This Philippine pack placed the bed-blanket over the saddle-blanket, leaving no cantle pack at all. The saddle-bags contained one pair of extra fitted horse-shoes, with ten nails, mess furniture, twenty extra rounds of pistol ammunition, twenty-five extra rounds of carbine ammunition, and the rations. The pommel pack consisted of one change of summer clothing, towel, soap, etc., enclosed in the shelter tent, rolled into a roll about 32 inches long and 4 inches in diameter; strapped to the middle strap of the pommel on top of the shelter roll was folded the poncho; the lariat was coiled and hung to the near cantle-ring; the carbine on the near side, as usual; the tin cup and canteen on the near side of the cantle; the surcingle around the saddle. The articles not carried consisted of the overcoat and cape, saber, saber-knot, saber-straps, poles and pins for shelter tent, heavy underwear, watering bridle, and hobbles. When there was room in the saddle-bags, the curry-comb and brush were carried in them; when these were full of rations, these two articles were tied in the nose-bag, which was hung from the off cantle-staple.

Of course, the above pack could be used in only a permanently warm climate. The intelligent reduction of the cavalry pack, however, in any country and in any field service, is always beneficial, and it was especially imperative in the Philippine Islands: first, because the horse was constantly in use and being called upon to traverse a country often over knee-deep in oozy mud and water, to ford and swim rivers repeatedly in the course of the day's work, and was often compelled to help himself across the worst places; second, because his troubles were increased very frequently by having to carry a recruit who had been trained but very little in equestrianism, if at all, and who had to be used at once because of the shortage of men and the continual moving of the troops; third, because the horse was fed on green rice grass in the rainy season, and scrubby *sacate* (a short, thin, curly, and somewhat wiry native grass of rather poor quality and none too abundant) and *palay* (sun-dried rice heads with six-inch stems) in the dry season. Oats and hay were for a long time entirely absent or so scarce as to be a luxury when received, and carefully issued to the weakest animals. The change from the regular forage to the native was an experiment requiring constant care upon the part of cavalry officers, else intestinal troubles and even laminitis appeared. It may be added that after the horses became accustomed to the *palay* and *sacate* forage, they thrived upon it and ate it readily; but while it was procured and used in about the same daily amount as the American forage, this daily allowance frequently had to be reduced by troop commanders when traversing different provinces, there being great difference in the weights of the various classes of the *palay*. The *palay* in Pangasinan Province, for stance, weighs about 26 pounds to the *menojo* (or bunch), while a *menojo* of *palay* in Zambales Province weighs from 32 to 36 pounds. As it was customary for troop commanders to purchase and feed *palay* by *menojos*, great care had to be exercised not to overfeed.

All these conditions and many others made the reduction of the cavalry pack in the Philippine Islands to its lowest efficient limit most imperative. When speaking of the cavalry Philippine pack, the writer does so for want of a better name; he does not mean that it was a recognized pack among all the cavalry troops. He used it in his troop (Troop M, Fourth Cavalry) and saw one or two other troops with somewhat similar packs. Doubtless each troop commander in the Philippines reduced the regulation pack considerably, each according to his experience and skill. The above serves only to indicate how important it is that the cavalryman, by thoughtfulness, attention, and the consideration of the condition of his horses, must guard them from being injured by the pack. Even where every possible care is taken, some horses will develop sore backs, lameness, etc., and many in field service will loose considerable flesh. All these inevitable occurrences demand that great care be exercised to keep cavalry horses in condition. Frequent inspections, to see that all the packs are always carefully adjusted, the saddle in the proper place on the horse's back and carefully cinched, neither too tight nor too loose, the saddle-blanket always smooth and even and soft and clean, are imperative. The pack will often slip after being put on, and immediate readjustment is necessary if the horse is to be kept up. Saddle-blankets sometimes slip forward and sometimes backward, depending largely on the conformation of the horse's back. Saddles that fit when a troop takes the field will be found in many cases to be too large after a few weeks' hard service, and these must be exchanged for others in the troop. Saddle-blankets taken off at the end of the day's work and thrown on top of the saddle gather dust and creases, and if placed upon the horse's back in this shape, will cause the pack to bore down, rub and chafe the horse's back, and soon make it impossible to use him. Often in a troop there are some careless men, who either do not notice such things or are lazy and do not care, and the result is inevitably an injured horse, perhaps temporarily and sometimes permanently.

There are three cardinal principles in packing the cavalry horse that never change. These have been referred to before in this book, but the only fear is that they have not been referred to often enough to impress upon the inexperienced reader how very important these three principles are. First, Carry only what is absolutely necessary; second, Hang it low to help the horse keep his equilibrium easily; third, Adjust it all to fit snugly and not interfere or bruise or chafe the horse, no matter what

his gait may be. Let us look carefully at these three
rules. In regard to the first, it is surprising how much the
new man in the cavalry finds necessary, and after a few
years of service it is also surprising to learn how much he

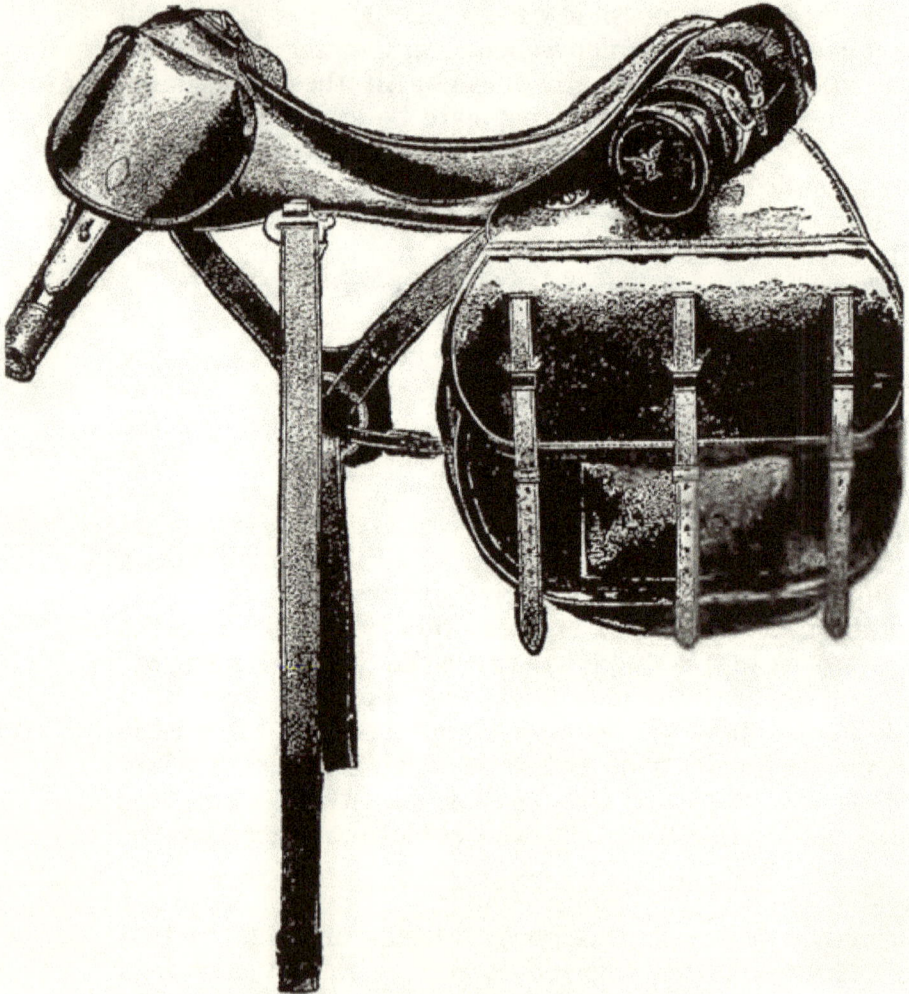

"WHITMAN" PACKED SADDLE, FOR OFFICERS.

dispenses with as the outcome of his experience. All
things considered, very little is required by experienced
cavalrymen when actually in the field on campaign. In
the campaigns in the Philippine Islands many cavalry

officers and men went along for months at a time with only what their saddle-bags would comfortably hold. "Somewhere in the rear" were their valises, but when they would arrive was too problematical for them to base any hopes upon, and in point of fact during the actual campaigning the "luxuries" contained in those valises were hardly missed.   On General Lawton's Northern Luzon campaign in 1899 most officers and men had for several months only what could be carried in their saddle-bags, and the men in the writer's troop did not see their barrack-bags or box-lockers from September 10, 1899, until they returned to the city of Manila *en route* for the United States in August, 1901.   In the meantime we all supplied ourselves by drawing from the Government new clothing as needed whenever opportunity occurred, and promptly discarded the old, reducing our effects always to a very few articles.   The second rule, "Hang the pack low," is simply the mechanical principle that the higher the load is carried, the base of support remaining the same, the less stable will the horse's equilibrium be.   As we cannot spread out the horse's legs to form a greater base, we must lower the pack.   For this reason the major portion of the pack is below the horse's back, rather than above it. However, the pack cannot be lowered beyond a certain point without interfering with the action of the legs and muscles; hence, we reach the third rule, "Adjust the pack so as not to bruise or chafe the horse at any gait."   Each article of the pack must be so strapped or hung as to leave muscles, legs, and spine free.

A brief comparison of our regulation pack with several foreign cavalry packs will show that we have the lightest pack of all.   Now that we have fair-leather equipments, we are abreast of Great Britain and Europe generally, where fair-leather equipments are almost exclusively used.   The consensus of opinion among American and foreign cavalry officers seems to show that fair-leather equipments are at least equally serviceable and satisfactory when compared with the black, and the fair-leather color much more so. Subjected to tests in all climates, in all weathers, to stains of dust and rain and mud and snow and sweat, the fair leather maintains its appearance, taking on a uniform and somewhat darker shade after some exposure and use. No dressing other than Castile soap is necessary, and there is an absence of stained clothing caused by the dressing on the black saddles rubbing off. Regarding the bridle complete, it may be said

FIG. 88*a*. AMERICAN CAVALRYMAN ON HORSE, NEAR SIDE.
(For description, see page 217.)

that curb-chains of steel, both for durability and comfort to the horse, have generally been found greatly superior to the curb-strap, whose only virtue is that it can be readily repaired. The leather curb-strap after a few wettings invariably curls up at both ends and chafes the horse's lips, making him fretful and nervous. Should the American Cavalry adopt the steel curb-chain, which is in use by most all foreign cavalry services, it would be

THE AMERICAN CAVALRY SADDLE, PACKED.

(See cut on page 208.)

NO.	EQUIPMENT ON HORSE.	LBS.	OZ.
1.	Bridle, complete with link-strap and curb-bit.	2	15
2.	Saddle, complete with 6 coat-straps, quarter-straps, hair cincha, 2 hooded stirrups, 2 stirrup-straps, 2 cincha-straps .18		2.5
3.	Saddle-bags	4	10
4.	Surcingle		12.5
5.	Lariat	2	1.5
6.	Picket-pin	1	6
7.	Canteen and strap		15
8.	Saddle-blanket	5	9
9.	Nose-bag	1	6
10.	Halter and strap	2	10
11.	Watering bridle with snaffle-bit	1	1.5
12.	Bed blanket	5	10
13.	Curry-comb		10.5
14.	Horse-brush		9.5
15.	Tin cup		7
16.	Meat can		14.5
17.	Knife		2.5
18.	Fork		2
19.	Spoon		1.5
20.	Lariat-strap		1.5
21.	Carbine boot, with straps,	2	2.5
22.	Shelter tent, half	2	15.5
23.	Poles and pins for shelter tent.		8
24.	Overcoat and cape	6	2
25.	Drawers, Canton flannel.		10.5
26.	Undershirt, woolen		14.5
27.	Socks, woolen		4
	Total	58	1.2

NO.	ON THE TROOPER.	LBS.	OZ.
1.	Cartridge-belt	1	5.5
2.	Pistol holster		8
3.	Spurs and straps		7
*4.	Carbine, magazine, cal. 30.	8	3.5
5.	Pistol, Colt's, cal. 38	2	1
†6.	Saber and scabbard, with straps	3	9

NO.	ON THE TROOPER.	LBS.	OZ.
7.	Carbine ammunition, 100 rounds	6	4
8.	Pistol ammunition, 20 rounds		10
9.	Campaign hat and cord		4.5
10.	Undershirt, woolen		14.5
11.	Drawers, Canton flannel.		10.5
12.	Socks, woolen		4
13.	Service blouse	2	4.5
14.	Service breeches	2	1
15.	Saber-knot		2
16.	Leggings, canvas		10
17.	Regulation shoes	2	
18.	Gloves, buckskin		1.5
19.	Woolen overshirt	1	0.5
	Total	33	5
	Grand total	91	6.2

NO.	‡ADDITIONAL.	LBS.	OZ.
1.	5 days' rations:		

		lbs.	oz.
(a)	Bacon	3	12
(b)	Coffee		6.4
(c)	Hardbread		5
(d)	Sugar		1
(e)	Salt		3.2
		10	5.6

NO.		LBS.	OZ.
2.	5 days' standard emergency rations	6	4
3.	Poncho	4	9
4.	Pair No. 1 regulation horseshoes	1	10.5
5.	Arctic overshoes	2	13
6.	Fur gauntlets		9
7.	Fur cap		5
8	Blanket-lined canvas overcoat	9	10.5
9.	Chambray overshirt		8
10.	Khaki trousers	1	11.5
11.	Khaki service blouse	1	7.5
12.	Cotton socks		2.5
13	Cotton undershirt		7
14.	Drawers, jean		7
15.	Toilet articles	1	3

*Carbine is carried in carbine boot, as shown in page 208.

†Saber is attached to saddle, as shown in page 209.

‡The following articles vary according to nature of service, climate, season, purpose, etc.

NOTE —The above weights were carefully taken by the author, using the trooper and horse shown in Fig. 86a. All of the equipments had been in use about one year. It was found that there was some slight variation in the weights of old and new equipments and in different equipments of approximately the same age.

a material improvement, and the American cavalry service would be still further ahead of the modern services of the world. The complete pack and equipments in the American Cavalry weigh about 90 pounds; and in comparison to this, the English packed saddle weighs 121 pounds; the German, 100 pounds, or more; the Russian, 120 pounds; the Belgian, over 102 pounds; and the Austrian appears to be the heaviest of all, weighing 137 pounds. It is difficult to understand why foreign cavalry services persist in carrying the trooper's arms as they do. In the Russian, Belgian, and Austrian Cavalry the carbine is carried on the trooper's back. The horse has to carry the weight in any case. The argument in favor of this method is that the trooper has his carbine always with him; but experience in our service has shown that carrying the carbine on the person of the trooper exhausts the man beyond endurance, especially on long marches at a trot, or where the horse is, as he undoubtedly would be in case of a remount in time of war, unbroken or nearly so. England's cavalry carries the carbine attached to the cantle of the saddle, on the off side, in a "bucket," the carbine hanging vertically, stock up, behind the trooper's right leg; the saber occupies a corresponding position on the *near* side of the saddle. Great Britain is, however, experimenting with a new method of carrying the carbine, which places the weight of the carbine behind the left thigh of the trooper, on the saddle, but the man must balance it, as the muzzle is upward and attached to his left shoulder by a strap. The German carbine, for a long time carried horizontally to the ground over the right leg of the rider and wedging him between it and the saddle, is now carried behind the right thigh, attached to the saddle in a manner somewhat similar to the old method used in the American service. The Russian, Austrian, and Belgian cavalry services go further still; not only is the carbine across the back of the rider, but the saber is attached to the waist-belt. Anyone who has tried this for any distance will acknowledge that it is a most exhausting way of carrying the saber, to say nothing of the nuisance that it is to the trooper when he dismounts to fight on foot.

In the American cavalry service the carbine is carried under the left leg, the stock inclining upward by the horse's neck, and in this position does not interfere with the rider or horse, and can be procured in an instant when the trooper dismounts; the pistol is attached to the waistbelt, and thus is always with the trooper; the saber is carried attached to the saddle on the off side in a position somewhat similar to that of the carbine. It is difficult to improve upon the method of carrying the trooper's arms as now adopted by us, it being admitted that there is no *entirely* satisfactory way of carrying the saber; while the troopers can draw and return either carbine or pistol at any gait, it is almost necessary to reduce the gait to a walk when about to return the saber. However, this is a small defect, and about the only one that can be found.

CHAPTER XI.

MARCHES.

How Generally Made—Gait—Average Daily March—Halts—Necessity of Care in Adjustment of Pack—The Horses' Feet—Watering—General Merritt's Experience—Ordinary Marches—Forced Marches—Instances.

When we talk of the light cavalry horse and his pack, our discussions must be based on what experience has shown us the light cavalry horse is required to do in active service. In the way of forced marches, etc., he will have to be prepared to perform the most difficult feats under most difficult conditions. To form an intelligent idea of what he will have to do in future service, we can do no better than to observe occasions in the past upon which the horse has been tested in cavalry field service to his utmost capacity, performing most remarkable feats of endurance, coupled with exposure, bad food, poor stables or no stables, unhygienic picket-lines, and the average rider on his back. If there be any truth in the wise saying that history repeats itself, such service will undoubtedly be called for in every bit of active field service in the future in which cavalry will be engaged.

Before bringing to the attention of the reader marches of cavalry which have been made in the past, illustrating the great strain which the horses of a cavalry command are subjected to in actual campaign work, there are some general rules which should first be considered in speaking of marches. In a previous chapter the artificial gaits taught to the trained saddle-animal have been considered, and these gaits are especially undesirable when on the march; while at drill and ordinary garrison duty the bad effect of artificial gaits may not be much noted, their presence in a cavalry command in the field is to be condemned. Horses with these artificial gaits travel very irregularly, and generally more rapidly at any gait than the regulation cavalry horse, accustomed to the three gaits, walk, trot, and gallop.

The result is, in a troop possessing some of these artificially gaited horses, that the other horses are continually having to hold back or close up, causing an irregular gait throughout the column, which is most trying to both men and horses. It is especially necessary that officers ride horses possessing only the three regulation gaits—the walk, trot, and gallop—and that their horses be trained to take each one of these gaits at the rate of speed required. The necessity for careful attention to proper gait, whether the command be moving at the walk, trot, or gallop, exists throughout the entire march, and the gait at which the troop is moving at any particular time should be the regulation gait and neither faster nor slower. By care in this, all the troop horses, with few exceptions, gradually learn the rate of speed generally adopted at each of these gaits, and the march is therefore uniform. Even in the best-gaited troops, there will generally be a few horses possessing irregular gaits. It is especially necessary that the gait at the head of the column be evenly maintained at all times; any irregularity of gait at the head of the column rapidly increases towards the rear until great discomfort is caused both for men and horses, and unnecessary fatigue is the result. During certain periods of the year horse exercise is held in all cavalry garrisons, and this exercise, together with drills, furnishes many opportunities of training all the troop horses to march together at the regulation gait. When the importance of steady gait is realized, the young officer leading the troop on horse exercise will appreciate the advantage of conducting this exercise at the regulation gaits, and not merely covering several miles at irregular rates of speed; horse exercise may be made to consist of something more than merely leading

the troop around the country for two or three hours, pay-
ing no attention to the gait.

On any march constant attention must be given to
the adjustment of the saddle and pack, to cinching, to
the position of the blanket, to the adjustment of the bit,
to the proper riding of the troopers, and that halts are
made at different times sufficiently long to enable men
and horses to relieve themselves and the packs to be readjusted if they have slipped, as some of them always
will. It is especially necessary that the officer leading
the troop on the march be careful to choose the best road,
avoiding all unnecessary detours and hills, and endeavor
to travel over as even country as possible, thus saving
unnecessary fatigue to the men and horses, and especially
preventing extra lounging of the men, which generally
comes from unnecessarily traveling over bad country or
holding to too slow a gait. Most cavalry officers of experience are strongly in favor of having the troopers dismount and lead their horses for short periods of time, or
when traveling over specially mountainous country. It
has been shown in a previous chapter how this dismounting of the rider relieves the horse of fully 150 pounds of
heavy weight, and it is not necessary to repeat it here.

Habitually the route march in the American Cavalry
is made in column of fours; when the roads are unsuitable
for this formation, or the command small, the column of
twos is used, and it may be added that the column of
twos is used almost invariably when the command consists of a squadron or less. In large columns the double
column of fours is sometimes used, and sometimes regiments or brigades are marched in parallel columns near
each other to shorten the column. When the road is
very rough or dusty, marching is made more comfortable
by permitting the troopers of the leading four or two to
increase the interval between themselves, the other troopers of corresponding positions in rear of them opening
out likewise. In the case of marching on a single road,
it is very important that the rear troopers or organiza-

tions be not checked by any irregularities of gait or momentary delays in front. In the case of two or more troops marching in column, the distance between troops should be somewhat increased, so that each troop may maintain a steady gait and escape the dust of the preceding troop. After passing over rough ground or through narrow defiles, the head of each troop in a column in march should always decrease the rate of march long enough to allow the rear men to close up to the normal interval without having to increase their gait. Distance thus lost by the troop is gained by the entire troop taking up an increased gait. If the above rule is not strictly adhered to, and the head of the column continues to move at the same gait it had before, the rear troopers must increase the gait, oftentimes being required to take up a gallop, to enable them to catch up and take their proper places. As these delays are repeatedly occurring on every march, it is easy to see that if the rear men are required to trot and gallop every little while to close up, the horses in rear will become much more quickly fatigued than those in front, and it will necessitate a slower gait to enable the tired horses in rear to keep up at all.

On starting from camp in the morning the first two miles or so is generally made at an easy walk, generally at a less rate than the regulation four miles an hour. At the end of this distance the command is halted for ten or fifteen minutes, to enable readjustment of the packs and to allow the men and horses to relieve themselves, and at these halts men should be required to attend to calls of Nature. Troopers are proverbially careless in this matter, and if this rule is not strictly adhered to, men will be continually requesting permission to fall out to relieve themselves. After the first hour of marching, there should be a halt of about five minutes every hour. At each halt the feet of the horses should be examined by their riders, to see that they have not lost a shoe or picked up gravel. Too slow a rate of march is to be avoided, as the time during which weight is on a horse's back is a severe trial to him, and the troopers, when the march is slow, are much more liable to lounge in their saddles, thus causing sore backs, than they are if the gait is brisk. The gait generally used in the American Cavalry when on the march is the walk and trot alternating, the most favorable ground being selected for the trot.

The rate to be taken on the march must be governed by circumstances, such as the condition of the animals and the state of the road, the object of the march, etc.; but it is the custom in the American cavalry service, under favorable conditions, that after the first halt the march will average a rate of five miles an hour, alternating the walk and trot as has been said, and occasionally dismounting and leading for short distances, especially in climbing and descending steep, rough hills. In dismounting and leading for short distances in summer, the horse is relieved of a great deal of weight and pounding, and some slight circulation of air passes along the horse's back under the saddle-blanket, and the men themselves are rested by the change; and in winter this dismounting of the rider enables him to keep his feet and legs warm, which become very cold and stiff when hanging idly from the horse's sides. The walk during the march should be at the rate of four miles, and the trot at not less than six and a half miles an hour. The last two miles or so before arriving in camp should be made at the walk. This permits the horses to cool off sufficiently to enable them to be watered almost as soon as they have reached camp, and brings them into camp quietly and without nervousness.

The average march in the American cavalry service, when a command is well broken to work, is about twenty-five miles a day. When starting on long-distance marches, the rate for the first few days is usually about twenty miles per day, the rate being gradually increased from day to day as the command hardens to its work. When a day's march is to be unusually prolonged, it is customary to make a halt of about one hour when about two-thirds of the entire distance to be marched has been covered. This halt should be made near water, if possible. Should the march be continued for a great number of days, it is generally the custom to wholly rest in camp about one day in every seven, to enable the entire command, men and horses, to recuperate, and the equipments and packs to be put in order, clothes mended, arms cleaned, etc.

It is best to change the order of marching so that the troops in rear of the column on one day march at the head of the column on the next, and so on. It is extremely fatiguing to march in the rear of a column of cavalry, where the dust is always thick and the gait more or less irregular, and the change from the rear to the head of a column should also be made within the troop itself by changing the platoons from day to day.

While actually on the march, no men should be permitted to leave the troop without permission from the officer in command of the troop. Generally a non-commissioned officer is left with any trooper who has to fall out during the march. The discipline and even the efficiency of a command is indicated to a great extent by the manner in which its ordinary marches are conducted.

In ordinary cases cavalry should not leave camp at a very early hour. If grazing is depended upon, this is especially desirable, for horses, as a rule, eat more freely during the early hours of the day. It is generally believed that horses, like human beings, obtain their best sleep between midnight and daylight, and if the march is taken up at an unreasonably early hour in the morning, the horses cannot be other than tired and sleepy, and the march made uncomfortable for the whole day. Ample time should be left, after a seasonable "reveille" for breakfast, for the horses to finish feeding and for the wagons and mules to be packed. The state of preparation for the march will advance more rapidly at some times than at others, owing to weather, etc., and no signal to begin the march should be given until all are ready. A hasty start in the morning and the sounding of calls too close together is a sure way of spoiling the day's march and starting the entire command off in a bad temper. The result of this will be innumerable delays during the day's march.

General Merritt's experience in active cavalry service leads him to say that cavalry in emergencies can march for from three to five days at a rate of 50 miles in 24 hours. A single march of not exceeding 100 miles can be accomplished in from 24 to 30 hours. The manner of marching depends on the total distance to be made. If the distance to be accomplished is more than 150 miles, the forced march should commence at a rate of not to exceed 50 miles for each day, and beyond 200 miles the daily marches should be reduced to 40 or even 30 miles. Without proper preparation a command will not be able to make such marches, either campaign or forced, and to accomplish such marches will be impossible unless the horses are in condition for it, and an attempt to do so would merely result in the destruction of a cavalry command through disabling or killing the horses. The marching of cavalry is so much affected by the immediately surrounding circumstances that no set rule can properly govern the length of marches and the manner of making them. The conduct of a regiment changing stations with its supplies furnished at designated points along the line of march or by accompanying trains is so unlike the march of a column scouting after hostile Indians or insurgents that a rule correct in one case would not apply in the other. In the former case a steady walk with the usual halt and increased distances would perhaps be the best manner of marching. Such a day's march would be from 20 to 25 miles, and would be little or no test of the endurance of men or horses, as both should improve under such conditions.

The proper manner of marching cavalry while scouting or on a trail is difficult to describe. If a commanding officer marches his column a long distance rapidly over a mountainous country, a percentage of his horses will undoubtedly become exhausted. If he does not march rapidly, he cannot expect to overtake an enemy, who oftentimes does not consider the suffering or loss of animals. It is probable, too, that when it has become too dark to travel the point reached is without water or grass or with but little of either. Hence it appears that no rule will apply to all cases. It is early enough if the cavalry starts from camp at about 7 o'clock in the morning on an ordinary march; including all halts, this will bring the troop to the end of the day's journey between 2 and 3 o'clock in the afternoon. This allows the horses to be turned out at once for grazing and to continue at it for several hours before it is time to bring them in to the picket-line and does away with the necessity for night grazing, which is one of the most arduous duties devolving upon cavalry in the field.

Before beginning the march, the horses should all be taken together and watered and allowed to drink freely. As most horses, however, will not drink very much early in the morning, advantage should be taken to water them again at the first opportunity and several times during the day as water is reached, care being taken that the horses are not watered until the gait has been reduced sufficiently long to cool them off. Whenever the horses are watered during the march, they should all be watered at the same time, as this enables the officer in command to judge of the condition of his horses in this regard. No men should be permitted to water their horses at odd times if they are within the control of the officer in charge.

Night marches may sometimes be necessitated by considerations regarding the enemy, or in the very hot season. They are always inseparable from the disadvantage of exhausting the powers of the troop. If they have to be adopted, special attention must be devoted to every arrangement that will secure the uninterrupted march in the right direction being maintained in the dark. Principal among these are to provide for close connection between all parts of the column, to avoid fatiguing delays by clearing away or moving around obstacles, and to follow the right road. In the vicinity of the enemy the strictest silence must be maintained, as there will be noise enough from clanking accouterments without the additional noise of conversation; conversation also tends to lessen vigilance.

The following is given as the method of a march of 32 miles in the German Army for a division of cavalry:

About 2   miles at a walk, half an hour.
About 2.33 miles at a trot, quarter of an hour.
About 2   miles at a walk, half an hour.
About 4.5   miles at a trot, half an hour.
About 2   miles at a walk, half an hour.
About 2.33 miles at a trot, quarter of an hour.
About 2   miles at a walk, half an hour.

---

17   miles in three and a half hours, with half an hour for short halts.
Grand halt for two or three hours.

About 2   miles at a walk, half an hour.
About 2.33 miles at a trot, quarter of an hour.
About 2   miles at a walk, half an hour.
About 2.33 miles at a trot, quarter of an hour.
About 2   miles at a walk, half an hour.
About 2.33 miles at a trot, quarter of an hour.
About 2   miles at a walk, half an hour.

---

15   miles in three and a quarter hours, with half an hour for short halts.

It will be seen from the above tabulation that the alternating walk and trot for cavalry on the march has been carefully studied in Europe as well as in America. The speed at all gaits must be uniform. The American Cavalry has had vast experience in marching over perhaps the roughest and wildest country in the world, and most cavalry officers adhere to the walk and trot alternating. It is now used by most armies of Europe as the marching gait, and is prescribed in most Drill Regulations of Europe as well as in our own.

There is much of interest to United States cavalrymen in reports that have come from South Africa of some
of the long, hard rides made there by the British mounted
troops. The accounts of some of these rapid forced marches
of cavalry are lacking in detail, but the specific statement
is made that a squadron of the Natal Mounted Rifles
recently rode 85 miles in 12 consecutive hours. The English reports give rides of 60 miles by detached cavalry
troops which were completed within the limit of the
daylight hours, and these achievements of the troopers
and their mounts are spoken of as though they were of
frequent occurrence. At first thought it may not appear that these rides are particularly remarkable, but the
fact must be taken into consideration that bodies of
troops, and not single individuals, are concerned, and
where this is the case the rapidity of the march must
necessarily be gauged by the rapidity and endurance of
the poorest horse in the outfit. Moreover, each animal
engaged had to carry weight of man and equipment to
an average amount of 250 pounds. Many of the horses
used by the English troopers were American-bred, and
this adds a natural interest to us with these rides, for it
gives us a chance to know the endurance of the American
animal under absolutely strange climatic conditions.

No army in the world, perhaps, has had the same
opportunities to test the endurance of cavalry horses as
has the small regular force of the United States. The
illimitable stretches of the plains, the almost impassable
mountain ranges, and the activity of the marauding
Indian mounted on his tireless bronco have been the
conditions which gave to the American cavalryman his
matchless chances for long, forced marches. It may be
interesting to compare some of the rides of American cavalrymen with the performances of the soldier horsemen
of other nations. The following instances are of record:

Captain Fountain, of the American Cavalry, in the
year 1891, with a detachment of his troop, rode 84 miles
in 8 hours This record is vouched for, and is better
than that of the Natal Mounted Rifles by about 4 hours,

the distance being within 1 mile of that made in South Africa. For actual speed this forced march stands, perhaps, at the head of the American Cavalry record, though other rides have been more remarkable.

In the year 1879, when the Utes succeeded in getting some United States troops into what was afterwards known as "Thornburg's Rathole," several mounted couriers succeded in slipping through the lines of savages. All of them reached Merritt's command, 170 miles distant, in less than 24 hours. The exact time was not taken, for "rescue was of more importance than record."

Captain Lawton, of the Cavalry, afterwards General Lawton, in the year 1876, rode from Red Cloud Agency, Nebraska, to Sidney, in the same State, a distance of 125 miles, in 26 hours. He was carrying important dispatches for General Crook, and, though the road was bad, his mount was in good condition when Lawton, looking five years older than he did the day before, handed over his bundle of papers to his general.

General Merritt has a forced-march record that has no parallel when the conditions of his journey are considered. He was ordered, in the fall of 1879, to the relief of Payne's command, which was surrounded by hostile Indians. Merritt's command consisted of four troops of cavalry, but at the last moment he was ordered to add to his force a battalion of infantry. The infantry were loaded into army wagons drawn by mules, and, with the cavalry at the flanks, the relief column started. The distance to be traversed was 170 miles, and it was made, notwithstanding the handicap of the wagons, over trails that were muddy and sandy by turns, in just 66 hours. At the end of the march the troopers went into the fight, and in the entire command not one horse showed a lame leg or a saddle-sore.

General P. St. George Cooke, with two troops of the Second Dragoons over 100 strong, marched from Lawrence, Kansas, to Fort Riley, Kansas, a distance of 98 miles, in less than 28 hours. The march made by the same officer with a regiment of cavalry, without a single feed of grain, of 22 miles a day for 99 days, may be mentioned.

Stuart's Chambersburg raid, consisting both of cavalry and artillery over 1800 strong, was made at a rate of 80 miles in 27 hours.

The march made by part of the Fifth Cavalry in the autumn of 1879 to Thornburg's relief, a distance of 170 miles, was made between 11 o'clock A. M., October 2d, and 5:30 A. M., October 5th; this was at a rate of 60 miles a day for 2¾ days. No horses were lost or disabled on the march; there were noticeably no sore backs among the horses after its completion, and men and horses were in condition for immediate service after the march.

It must be understood, of course, that all these American rides were made without changing horses. The steed of the start was the steed of the finish. The best rider, according to cavalry experts, is not the man who takes a five-barred gate or who can ride standing, but the man who, by instinct, feels the condition of his horse, and, though getting the most out of the animal, knows best how to conserve its strength.

To cite some foreign rides, it may be stated that a squadron of Dragoons of the Guard, during the battle of Colombey-Neuilly, August 14, 1870, pursued a body of French Chasseurs as far as Toul and summoned the town to surrender. On the next day the squadron was ordered to take part in the battle of Mars-La-Tour, distant 32 miles. It reached the latter place and participated in the early part of that battle, having marched all together in 2 days over 100 miles, and participated in a great battle. The same squadron sent some of its boldest cavalrymen to ride around the French on the 27th of August. Some officers' patrols made on that day nearly 85 miles.

After the engagements of Artenay and Orleans, two cavalry divisions pursued the enemy 34 miles, until stopped by the enemy's fresh infantry, covering the distance in about 6 hours.

In the advance on Chalôns in 1870 the advanced Prussian cavalry division made 85 miles in 2 days.

In 1884 two troops of Don Cossacks made 218 miles in 3 days under the worst conditions imaginable, as regards roads and weather. Upon arrival at its destination, the command was inspected by the commander-in-chief at a walk, trot, and gallop, and he expressed himself as fully satisfied with the appearance of the troopers and the condition of the horses.

Three troops of Ural Cossacks, marching over roads covered with several inches of snow and in some places knee-deep to the horses, made respectively 46, 50, and 56 miles in a single day.

In the Russian autumn maneuvers of 1883 detachments made 200 and even 300 miles in 5 days.

The above splendid forced marches in the American and foreign cavalry services might easily be added to by the dozen. Looking at the marches and peculiar duties of light cavalry in the past, and the work that is oftentimes demanded of it, as shown above, how all-important it is that we carry not one unnecessary ounce, have our horses and men well trained, well seasoned, and agile, our officers careful and painstaking on the march, in bivouac, camp, and garrison, and that every care be constantly exercised to improve remounts, field equipments, and packs, to enable us to perform such work!

Cavalry has lost nothing of its importance by the modern advancement of the other arms, and the work that it has had to do in the past will be required of it again. It is still and always will be an indispensable arm, but, to quote General Wilson: "It must be cavalry that can both ride and fight." To quote Kilpatrick: "It must be able to fight anywhere except at sea." And to quote my own colonel: "We must be cavalry that can ride down any mounted or dismounted force opposed to us, and be firm in the belief that no enemy can ride us down."

To live up to all this, the cavalry horse and his pack must be in perfect shape, and the man on his back must *know well how* "to both ride and fight."

CHAPTER XII.

PASSAGE OF RIVERS.

Necessity for Training—Methods in General—Bridges—Fords—
Swimming in Herd—Towing—Riding—Column Swimming—
Boats and Rafts—Logs—Austrian Experiments— Precaution-
ary Measures—Guiding the Horse.

In the last chapter the marching of cavalry in the field
has been discussed. As it is often necessary for cavalry
to cross streams in field service, the swimming of horses is
of the utmost importance, and in most cavalry services
of to-day occupies a most important place. In all field
service of cavalry it becomes necessary to make the passage of rivers, and whether these are broad and deep,
swift, shallow, treacherous, or narrow, must be carefully
determined before the passage is entered upon, but the
passage itself must be accomplished; the command must
go forward, and passage of defiles and bodies of water,
when encountered, must be effected. Nearly all cavalry
is carefully trained in this hazardous work in time of peace.
No war prevails but what reports of men and horses
drowned in arduous field service are sent in to headquarters with painful frequency. All men in the cavalry arm
should swim and swim well. Horses are rarely found
lacking in this quality; though all horses do not swim
equally well and coolly, it seems to be a provision of Nature to endow the horse with the knowledge and ability to
swim, and practicing in swimming rapidly overcomes
the temporary early fright.

To quote General Lloyd: "The passing of rivers is
justly considered as one of the most difficult and dangerous operations of war." The system of passing defiles
and rivers by cavalry, from a tactical standpoint, was
formerly very different from the system which should be

adopted now. In early times, before the cavalry had long-range firearms, on reaching a river or defile it was forced to go very slowly to be sure that no enemy with guns was on the other side. Nolan lays down the rule which mounted men should follow in the passage of defiles and rivers. He says: "Always pass a defile or river quickly." This, however, was not possible until the cavalry were given long-range firearms and enabled to cope with any enemy that might be opposed to them on the opposite bank of the river or at the opposite end of the defile. Bridges and fords may be considered a species of defile, shorter, generally, than defiles proper, but more difficult to force if ably defended. As this book does not pretend to deal with the tactical considerations involved in the passage of defiles and rivers by cavalry, let us go on at once to a consideration of the methods usually employed in the actual passage itself.

The different methods of effecting the passage of a river where there are no bridges or fords are many. In training cavalry in this work and in the passage of rivers in field service, every imaginable method has been tried —the *cinquenelle*, the pulley, the buoys, rafts of every kind, bags of skin filled up with air and hay and dry leaves, the flooring of wagons as rafts, swimming in herd and in column, using boats and towing the horses, etc., etc. The use of bags is very old, dating back some two thousand years to the time when they were using rafts of water grasses and little boats similar to those of the Indians, and bags of leather. We see Alexander in 336 B. C. using for the passage of the Danube bags of skin made out of the skins employed for the tents of the soldiers. Two years after, when he crossed the Don, he made bags of straw and built rafts—the cavalry crossed on the rafts, holding the horses by ropes, the horses swimming behind the stern of the rafts. The Greek army lost in that crossing part of its horses, but we must not forget the fact that the river was 1100 meters wide, and *we* do not care to cross such a river, even with our present means, except as a last resort.

Again, when Alexander crossed the Oxus in 327 B. C., he used bags of skins filled with hay and branches of the vine tree. These bags of skin were always made out of the skins used for the tents of his soldiers; they were sewed together, and then rafts were constructed by tying these bags in groups. The Egyptian warriors carried on their horses the skins of beasts which had been used as food, and with this leather made bags which were filled up with air or some light, dry material, and these they put together in the shape of rafts. Even to-day we cross rivers by the same means.

In the Jugurthine wars Marius gave to each century and squadron, for the crossing of the river Tana, a certain number of live animals (presumably oxen), the skins of which were to be used to make bags for the crossings, so that he was preparing the material for crossing rivers by supplying his troops with meat on the hoof. When the army arrived at the river, a great quantity of bags was thus already available. Thévenot, in his journey in 1659, said that the people living on the river Tigris and Euphrates kept in their traditions that their ancestors used the bags of skin, and he gives the following description of building the raft by them: "They tied together several bags of skin, and these were joined together at the four corners by several long sticks, very tight. They cover everything with branches, putting them crosswise, and tie these to the sticks on the exterior side; on the side of this platform they put branches of half a foot in diameter. They wet the under side of the bags every half-hour with water; every evening they blow up the bags again. One raft is able to carry 150 or 200 men at one time." Incidentally it would be very interesting to know just how these ancient people blew up these huge bags—Thévenot forgot to tell us.

In 1809 the English in the Peninsular War used bags of skin made out of the skins of animals killed on the spot, sewing the leather around the hoops of barrels. These bags were able to sustain a weight of 260 or 270 pounds, and the bags would remain entirely inflated for about five hours, and after twenty-four hours they were able to support about one-half of the weight mentioned above. The weight of the bag was about 40 pounds.

In 1810 the Ninth Corps of Napoleon's army in Portugal built rafts supported by bags of the skins of goats filled up with air, and these were put at the angles and sides of the flying bridges.

General Bourmont, in 1823, used for crossing the Tage small rafts constructed of wood and bags and skins, the horses swimming and held by a strap; but these rafts did not last very long, because several of the bags in them were smashed.

In the Civil War in America bags of gutta-percha took the place of boats in the armies of the West, but the troops on the Potomac rejected them on account of the facility with which they tore out. In 1845 the troops of the United States in the Mexican campaign built small bridges with bags of skins filled with air, three bags forming a raft able to transport three soldiers with their equipments. These bags were made of one coat of vulcanized rubber, one of cotton, then one of rubber again, and then one of cotton.

The Russian troops have also made many experiments with bags of many kinds. They use the skin of the oxen and blow the bag up through one of the legs by means of a tube. Four bags joined together by a stick and covered with the flooring are able to support ten men. With the same number of French bags, the French carried twenty men without either sticks or flooring. Each one of the Russian bags weighs about 24 pounds, that of the French about half. In 1832 Olivier Clisson, of the French Army, crossed the Lys with small boats made out of tubs and ropes; and while this was only for a comparatively small command, nevertheless the demonstration of ingenuity is a good one.

In the experiments made by the Russian Cossacks of the Danube, the idea was for the troops to cross the river with the help of their equipments.   One dozen lances were tied together and engaged in the handles of a dozen cooking-pots of metal, forming one part of a raft. Each bundle was made of 12 lances, and 12 of these bundles of lances formed one frame able to support 4 men with their equipments—that is, 96 lances and 48 pots of metal.   As each soldier has 1 lance and every 2 soldiers 1 metal mess-pot, one squadron can make only one raft. This raft is considered only as a last resort when other materials are wholly lacking.   The French troops in the Soudan crossed the Niger by using empty biscuit-boxes. In Germany, Russia, and Austria training is occasionally held during the winter months as well as in the summer.

Wherever the footing is good on both banks, cavalry can almost always, if necessary, swim across.   But swimming should be adopted only after a thorough preliminary search for bridges and fords has proven unsuccessful.

The most common kind of bridges which are used in armies are pontoon bridges, and for narrow rivers they serve a very good purpose.   Colonel Simcoe, in the American Revolution of 1776, had the bodies of his wagons so constructed that they could be used as pontoons as well as boats, and could hold six men, with their equipments, each.   This it would seem was a good plan, and must have saved the command from having to transport a regular pontoon-train.   Large rafts can be more easily made, and by crossing a cable they can be drawn backwards and forwards and a number of men and horses with their equipment crossed at each trip.   To officers who served in the active campaigns in the Philippine Islands this method is well known.

Instances have occurred in past active service where time has permitted the building of temporary bridges to cross the command.   Stonewall Jackson constructed a bridge over the ford of the South River, just before the battle of Port Republic, with wagons placed in the stream without their bodies, the axles forming beams to support the flooring, which was constructed of loose boards from a neighboring saw-mill.

AMERICAN PONTOON BRIDGE.

In "Modern Cavalry," by Colonel Denison, an account is given of a passage of the Rivanna River in June, 1781: "The water was fenced, as it were, with spars and canoes so as to make a lane, and the horses swam over between them; the men passed on the floats, which held with ease 130 men, and these continuous floats or bridges had been made in four hours."

It has a number of times happened in the past that word has been received by an invading column that certain well-known bridges had been destroyed by the enemy, and the troops have constructed bridges beforehand, hauled them forward as they marched, erected them upon arriving at the river, and rapidly crossed. This was done, as the reader will recall, by Cæsar when he crossed his invading army over the Rhine. Another noteworthy instance occurred at Alcantara in 1812, when Colonel Sturgeon invented secretly a network of strong ropes in such a way that it might be carried in parts. It was then transported to Alcantara, cables were stretched across the chasm from beams fixed up on each side, and a network was then drawn over and a bridge constructed on it, which took over the heaviest guns in safety. In the last war in Germany the Prussians, expecting that the bridge over the Riese would be destroyed, had, before the declaration of war, secretly measured it, and had caused a complete new bridge to be made ready to put up at once.

To cross a wide and unfordable river with a large army, or even with but one troop, is a tedious operation, requiring the greatest care and much hard work. It is almost needless to say that every exertion should be made to discover bridges or fords or to construct some form of rope ferry or temporary bridge if time, material, and the width of the river all combine to make this feasible. Of course much depends upon the breadth of the river. Where a small river flows into a large one, or islands are found in the main channel, the building of a bridge is very much simplified, these pieces of land themselves acting as piers. If a bridge is to be constructed, a point should be selected along the bank free from marshes, so that the horses can get down to the bridge, and, if possible, there should be deep water close to the bank; if not, arrangements must be made before attempting the construction of the bridge for laying out trestle piers to such a distance that the floors can be laid strongly or the pontoons can float and not ground when laden. It is wise, even after a bridge is found or constructed, not to ruin it by the passage of too many horses. If a hundred or more are taken over by the bridge and collected on the opposite bank, the others can frequently be driven into the water in herds, at a suitable place, and if no gap is allowed to break the lead, it is generally possible to induce the horses to enter the water and swim across to the others on the farther side. One-half or two-thirds of the men of each troop should previously cross in boats or by the bridge to receive the horses on the far side, each man carrying his arms with him. When there is a bridge, the horses, when swum over, should be passed near the bridge, but below it. When cavalry pass on a floating bridge, they should dismount and lead their horses. General Wolseley states that he once crossed a cavalry force over a rapid river in face of an enemy, there being no bridge and only a few canoes. Some 2,000 horses were swum across, as described above, with the loss of only an old one that could not stem the very rapid current. When the emergency or circumstance requires the attempt to be made, the men should undress and hold on by the manes or tails while crossing, never touching their horses' heads, and guiding them by splashing water at their heads on the side from which they wish them to turn.

On arriving at a river, the cavalry force should first make an earnest effort to find a ford. The use of a ford eliminates the great danger always present when swimming is resorted to, and also enables the force to pass the river more quickly than by swimming, and with less confusion. The continued use of a ford will, after a while, cause it to deepen to such an extent that swimming may in the end have to be resorted to; but this will happen only where the force crossing is very large. Previous to a force crossing a ford of any size, rows of stakes should be driven in, showing its exact limit. If the current is strong, ropes should be stretched from pole to pole and mounted men posted along its upper limit to break the force of the stream. When fording or swimming, torches or lanterns should be used at night to mark the line of crossing, or fires built on the opposite banks to mark the place of entrance into the water and the exit on the other side. When the current is rapid, boats or rafts should be always kept lying about near the dangerous places below the command, to pick up anyone who may be swept away. Strong swimmers, stripped and ready to plunge in at a second's notice, should be in these boats and on both shores below the point of crossing.

There are several well-known methods adopted by different cavalry services in teaching and performing the passage of rivers by swimming and rafts. When the stream is small and only fifteen or twenty feet wide in the deepest parts and the actual distance to be swum is short, a small command can generally effect a rapid crossing by going directly into the water in column of trooper and swimming across; but the river should be well known and inspected before this is attempted, and a few men sent across ahead at the most favorable point. The reconnaissance made for a ford should extend a mile or so up and down the banks before swimming is attempted in a large river; time consumed in this search is well spent if a ford is found, and if not, it will be much consolation, if accident occurs in swimming, to know that the method employed was unavoidable.

Whenever boats or rafts are available or can be made, all animals should be unsaddled and unbridled, the halters well buckled on the head and the halter-straps tied around the neck; the equipments and accouterments should be sent across on the boats or rafts together with a part of the men, especially those who cannot swim. These men, once across, remain under arms and ready to fight, while some of them remain on the bank and catch up the horses as they arrive, and tie them to trees, etc. The work of crossing any large river is very severe upon both men and horses, and every man must do the part assigned to him promptly. Now comes the swimming of the horses, the

SWIMMING IN HERD.

important part of the crossing. Several of the best swimmers among the men strip, and, selecting horses well known as steady swimmers, mount bare-back and ride them into the water and start across. All the horses should be allowed to drink freely before entering the water; if this is not done, many of them will stop and drink anyway, and the delay thus caused will place such a gap between the men who are on the lead horses and the balance of the herd that the herd will not follow.   As soon as the horses ridden by the men mentioned above have entered the water a few feet, the balance of the men lead or drive the herd toward the water and gradually force the horses into it, when, after some experience, the herd will strike out after the leaders and swim across.   The men on the near bank then cross by means of the boats or rafts, the horses are saddled up, and the command moves forward.   The writer has seen the above method employed many times by the American Cavalry in the Philippine Islands, and it rarely failed to work satisfactorily, even in bad weather, when the rain was pouring down in torrents during heavy thunder-storms.   In a large command several troops often cross at one time, each troop crossing at a point well away from the others. When General Lawton's cavalry command was crossing the Rio Pampanga, at Cabanatuan, in Northern Luzon, in the fall of 1899, during the rainy season, the horses of the entire command were crossed in this way, the majority of the men and the wagons and guns passing across either on boats found along the shore or on ferry rafts made on the spot.   The Rio Pampanga at the time was a wild, rushing torrent some 300 yards wide, and the crossing was one of the most difficult encountered by the troops on that arduous campaign.   A week before, this cavalry command crossed the same river at San Isidro, by means of the rope ferry.

At times, however, no ford can be found, no bridges, and no material is at hand to construct rafts or boats, and it becomes necessary to cross both men and horses by swimming.   In using this method the most painstaking care should be constantly exercised to prohibit haste and crowding.   The command, if small, should enter the water in column of trooper, with plenty of distance between individual men, the best swimming horses and men taking the lead.   When the space to be swum is short, it is often possible for it to be accomplished as described above, by simply entering the water and swimming across, and in small streams this is often done; but it is always a serious risk, and should rarely be attempted unless the distance to be passed over by swimming is very short—10 or 20 feet. In a large command the same strict precaution should be observed, and if other crossing-places can be located, several columns cross simultaneously. If only one crossing-place is available, it is still wise to make haste slowly and cross in column of trooper, though many crossings have been successfully made in column of twos. But the time lost and the danger incurred by the inevitable crowding and pushing in a heavy column is too great to justify the risk of attempting to cross a wide and deep or unknown river with the horses packed and the men on their backs once in a thousand times.

When it becomes *necessary* to have the men cross with their horses, experience has shown that it is best to leave the horse saddled and bridled, stirrups crossed, cartridge-belt and pistol strapped to the pommel of the saddle, reins knotted on the neck to prevent their entangling the horse's legs, and as the horse begins to swim the rider should gradually float off to the down-stream side, keeping hold of the pommel with one hand and the reins with the other, which should be used very gently and only to guide the horse, never to stop him. The landing-place should be a well-chosen one, somewhat farther down stream, to allow for drift. By splashing water in the horse's face if he attempts to turn or go wrong, much can be accomplished in making him swim in the right direction. Horses swim low, and, if allowed unrestrained action, will at once assume the natural swimming position. Attempts to make them hold their heads or forehands up tend only to confuse and frighten them. When rider and horse strike bottom at the point of landing, the rider should wade ashore and lead his horse out and not attempt to mount him in the water. Occasionally the violent swimming of the horse causes the rider to lose his grasp on the saddle.

Instead of pulling on the reins, and thus confusing the horse, the rider should grasp the tail and allow the horse to tow him ashore. The writer has seen horses so confused by the rough and ignorant actions of frightened riders that they have turned completely over backwards. This is not at all an unusual occurrence.

Another method frequently used in the field in crossing rivers is to place the men with their equipments in boats or on rafts, and then tow the horses one, two or three at a time across the stream. This takes considerable time, but has been found in actual service a very safe and satisfactory way. When no boats are available for this, use can frequently be made of a narrow foot-bridge; the men crossing on the foot-bridge, the horses swimming beside it, and the men leading the horses.

In almost every troop there will be some men who do not swim, and when neither bridges, fords, boats, nor rafts are available, these men men have frequently been crossed by requiring each man to enter the water naked and pushing a log or plank before him or lying upon it, and thus paddling himself across. The horses in this case swim across with their equipments on, as described, with a few good swimmers ahead.

How to discover a ford, prepare banks, rafts, boats, etc., is described so fully in the "Manual of Field Engineering," written by Major Beach, of the Cavalry, that no discussion of these points is necessary here.

The French Regimental System of Training.—The practice of the French Army in crossing rivers is carried on very extensively every year. A place is chosen wide and deep enough to permit swimming, and, if possible, near a bridge, and where shallow water can be found near by, so that the new horses may be trained in fording preparatory to their later lessons in swimming. Care is taken in choosing the place that no *débris* is allowed to remain on the bottom of the river, while depth and speed of the current are carefully measured and soundings are taken in several places crossing the river at the point to be used.

These facts are carefully gathered by the Engineers and to such an extent that any mile of any river has its plottings ready to be furnished to any regiment needing them. The first few horses are crossed by swimming and held on the other bank at the point of landing. The crossing places should be shady, as the sun striking on the water was found to have a permanently bad effect on the eyes of both horses and men. The bottom of the river-bed should be sloping to the point of exit and the point of entrance. The other general rules used by the French are similar, to a great extent, to our own.

THE FRENCH RAFT OF SACKS OR BAGS.

The Material Used.—This consists of small boats, rafts, boards, ropes, buoys, grappling-hooks; all of these are indispensable. The French stretch one or two ropes across the river, and build one or two rafts of great stability, but easy to be displaced. These rafts are built with twelve or eighteen barrels and sometimes two strong boats joined together and covered over on the top with flooring. These rafts are large enough to permit seven or eight men to embark on them easily. The edges of the rafts are built so as to be sufficiently high above the water to prevent the horses when in tow from getting their heads on top of the edges of the rafts. The edges of the rafts are provided with cleats or stringers to prevent the men from slipping off as they hold the horses by the halters.

Patrols.— Patrols are posted on both banks; the men chosen are good, strong swimmers, experienced in practical bridge-construction, and belong to a special detail in each regiment known as Sapeurs-Mariniers.

SOLDIERS CROSSING ON THE "SAC-CACHOU" WITH EQUIPMENT.

These men are trained in the spring to manage boats with horses in tow and to paddle the boat with one oar, and also to manage the boat with a long pole; to build every kind of raft and guide them with the hand, or rope, or pole; they are trained in constructing rope ferries, etc. They are taught cording and splicing of rope, how to use the pulley, the capstan, and the block and tackle. When the weather is warm enough, they are trained in swimming for long periods and distances, diving, rescuing men or horses in danger, throwing the buoy, the building of temporary break-waters, platforms for embarkment and disembarkment for horses, etc., etc.; so in the training of the passage of rivers they form an efficient body of men in each regiment. They are subdivided into chiefs of rafts, landing-men, conductors of life-boats, and life-saving divers. They are arranged on both sides of the river during a crossing; they are signal-men also, and possess a code of

CROSSING A CART ON THE BAG-RAFT.

signals pertaining to their own work. Each man in the detail has one particular duty assigned to him, and thus the men work systematically and together without confusion. Under this system, in the summer of 1897, about 1500 horses crossed one river several times, this river being 60 meters wide and 49 meters deep, making 10,000 passages all told, without the loss of a horse or man. A careful register of the operations is made at the time, showing the time, current, depth, weather, number of

men and horses, temperature of the water, tides, the limpidity of the water, the direction and intensity of the
wind, the influence of the rays of the sun, etc. No man
or horse is permitted to enter the water immediately after
eating. The exercises are usually very exhaustive for
both men and horses, and the condition of each man and
horse is carefully observed and a record kept. The
Sapeurs-Mariniers are often in the water for hours at a
time during a crossing, and need especially good care to
be kept in a healthy and efficient condition. As a reward for good work in the crossing maneuvers, furloughs
or money after the completion of' the work, for diving, for
guiding the boats, for the best horseman, etc., are given.
The French troops use to a large extent in their training
the Austrian position, which consists of the horseman floating on one side or the other of the horse, holding the saddle or mane, and thus being dragged by the horse. This
position is similar to the American.

The French in the above training use the *cinquenelle*,
the *sac-cachou*, etc. The two mentioned are used perhaps more largely than any other method; the former
(the *cinquenelle*) consisting of a wire rope stretched
across the river, to which the raft, is fastened, and thus
pulled across by the men on the raft—in other words,
a rope ferry, except that the wire rope has a tensile
strength far exceeding that of any other rope of reasonable diameter. The metal *cinquenelle* used by the French
Cavalry weighs approximately one-third of a pound per
meter, and the resistance to rupture of the rope is guaranteed by the manufacturer to be not less than 3600
pounds per meter. In using this rope the two ends are
made fast to tripods, trees, or "dead men" on both
banks, and tightened until the arc-formed by the rope
is the least possible, approaching the straight line. Tests
made by the French show that the *cinquenelle*, if subjected to a tensile stress of 1800 kilograms on 50 meters
length, will form a parabola which will measure 2 centimeters, approximately ½ inch. However, such a force

would stretch the rope to such a degree that a very small weight would serve to rupture the rope. The height of the *cinquenelle* above the water should be at least 6 inches, but it will often be found impossible to keep the rope from resting more or less in the water. The *cinquenelle* is carried rolled upon a wooden cylinder. When using the *cinquenelle*, the men and their equipments cross on the raft attached to the *cinquenelle*, and the horses are crossed by either swimming in herds, or towed a few

BUILDING THE FOOT-BRIDGE OF SUCCESSIVE RAFTS.

at a time behind the raft. The French found that a metal rope of ½ inch in diameter would sustain a tensile strain of about 12,500 pounds and weighed about 1 pound per meter. This is probably as large a *cinquenelle* as need ever be used. As the *cinquenelle* will take the shape of a corkscrew if not properly rolled when not in use, and as in this condition it will be impossible to stretch it straight again, it should be rolled loosely in the shape of an "8." If kept rolled upon the spools, it will also take the defective form mentioned above. The *sac-cachou,* mentioned above, is a rubber bag filled with air and cylindrical in shape. By the use of the *cinque-nelle* and sacks, the French have crossed a squadron of cavalry over a river 100 meters wide in an hour; the current being 1 meter per second. In 8 minutes they calculate to pass 17 horses by swimming, together with 17 men and their equipments by means of the raft and sack. They often use two or three *cinquenelles* at a time, and thus hasten the crossings.

Another method used by the French is known as the Dunop bridge, which is a narrow foot-bridge that can be taken apart and put together again very quickly, and does not weigh much. By tying the sacks to the *cinque-nelle* at 20-foot intervals and laying the Dunop bridge across the sacks, a very convenient form of foot-bridge is quickly secured, and the horses are crossed, each one swimming beside the foot-bridge, led by his trooper on the bridge. Temporary chutes are often constructed at the point on the near shore where the horses enter the water, like a passage-way, with flaring wings, to facilitate entrance into the water.

Cavalry should be able to cross all streams coming in its way. In case it comes across important rivers where the distance to be passed in swimming is long, it will be able to make the passage only with the aid of boats or rafts. A command in which *none* of the men can swim cannot undertake with any prospect of success to cross difficult rivers, either with or without boats. It is necessary, therefore, considering the importance of swimming for cavalry, that particular attention be given this subject. In most of our cavalry garrisons a large enough body of water to permit the swimming of horses and men for practice is to be found. If necessary, the place chosen can be deepened as desired. One of the best exercises to teach horses to cross rivers is to accustom them to going into deep water without being frightened. The fear which takes possession of most horses when they enter deep water will gradually disappear with practice. The best results are obtained by allowing swimming horses the greatest liberty; it is also the best way to avoid accidents. In order to make the horse swim, it will be sufficient in most cases to have him handled by a cool man possessing experience and ability to himself swim well. In a deep river a slight current is very useful, for experience proves that a horse ceases to struggle as soon as he feels the force of the current; experience has also demonstrated that it is easier to swim when there is a slight current. The horse, as soon as he loses touch of the bottom, swims in the direction in which his head points. All that is necessary, therefore, is to give the desired inclination to the head—that is, point it in the direction the horse is to go.

The swimming horse is most easily directed by means of the snaffle, knotting the reins on his neck that they may not catch his feet. When the horse starts to swim, the trooper leaves his back; to leave the back too soon before the horse has commenced to swim often causes the horse to stop as he is accustomed to do on land. Practice is necessary to teach the trooper the right moment at which to slide off. In the German cavalry service the trooper is taught to slide off towards the *up*-stream side of the horse. In the other services and in the American, the *down*-stream side is prescribed, and should be the way taught. While great liberty must be given the swimming horse that he may move freely, nevertheless it must be made apparent to him that he is still under control, and he must not be allowed to have his own way as regards direction. Stubborn horses should be taught swimming by the best swimmers. Often a change of riders will effect satisfactory results more quickly than keeping a timid man with a stubborn horse or an impatient man with a good one. Ordinarily the rider ought not to remain on the horse's back while swimming. The rider grasps the horse with his legs and brings his weight to bear on the hind quarters; the horse, being thus constrained in his movements, is liable to go over backwards or turn on his side. With some horses, especially those that swim low, it is advisable that the trooper sit *behind* the saddle, to allow the fore quarters to float high.

In the American cavalry service it is required that swimming be taught as follows:

1. Horse equipped with watering bridle only, the trooper floating beside him, on down-stream side, holding a lock of the mane in the up-stream hand.

2. Horse swimming and trooper swimming behind him, holding the tail, the horse thus towing him.

3. Horse swimming, trooper seated on the horse, with or without saddle.

4. The troopers will also be practiced in swimming the horses when fully armed and equipped.

5. Swimming the horses in herds.

6. Towing the swimming horse from a boat.

Many stubborn horses can be taught to swim by using the longe. The longe is to be held double, both ends in the hand, the horse led into the water, and the rider, holding the two ends of the longe and sitting in the end of a boat, which precedes the horse, should lead the horse into deep water and compel the horse to swim and swim straight. Just before the horse reaches foothold on the opposite bank, one end of the longe should be dropped and the longe pulled through the halter-ring and gathered in the boat, thus teaching the horse to continue swimming and leave the water unassisted. As the horse gradually improves the longe may be withdrawn further in stream, until finally nothing is necessary except to start the horse swimming, and he will go across. The longe should be neither too long nor too short, generally about 15 feet, and should have neither knots nor rings in it. Even after the best and most daring men have expended every method, there will occasionally be found some horse that will either not enter deep water or that will turn around persistently and start back. One or two such horses in a roop will often influence the entire herd, especially if they are among the leading horses, by going half across and then turning and swimming back. These horses soon become known in the troop, and when necessary to swim all the horses, these intractable ones should be withheld from taking the water until the herd is well started, and then driven in to follow. If boats or rafts are available, it will pay to tow these few stubborn horses over by leading

GERMAN LANCE-BOAT—FIRST STEP IN CONSTRUCTION

them after the boat, one man sitting in the stern and holding the halter-strap. It is rarely possible for a rider to remain on his swimming horse and lead another horse. It should never be attempted except for very short distances and with horses *known* to swim readily and coolly.

The saddle and pack should in field service be removed and sent across by artificial means whenever possible, as keeping it on the horse's back interferes very materially

with the horse's actions, and the risk of drowning is very
great. While on land the horse carries the packed saddle
steadily, it is a very different undertaking when swimming. The blanket and saddle-bags absorb water, and the
pack becomes very much heavier and topheavy. Without support for his feet, the horse burdened with a heavy
packed saddle frequently loses his equilibrium and turns
on his side, when drowning results. While it is generally
the force of the current that turns the horse on his side
when swimming with a rider or pack, even in still water
the danger is too great to risk if other means be at hand,
and except for very short distances, 10 or 20 feet, in well-
known streams, it should never be attempted unless the
passage is imperatively necessary at that point and no
other better way is possible.

In some European cavalry services, especially the
German, each cavalry regiment is furnished with two or
more portable folding boats and the necessary bridge
material.

The German Folding Boat.—This boat is formed of
three parts, each regiment carrying several of them complete. The boat is made pointed at both ends. The
body is made of wood and jointed by means of pivots;
the body is covered on the interior and exterior by canvas
varnished with Berton varnish. The space between the
two envelopes is filled up with air, which makes the boat
insubmergable. The bottom is all wood; the flooring and
the cross-beams keep the ribs from closing up; the stern
and the bow are joined to the boat by means of screw-
bolts and ropes. All together, the boat measures 6 meters
50 centimeters in length and 1 meter 50 centimeters in
width; the stern and the bow, joined together, form a
small boat of 3 meters 40 centimeters in length. Each
German cavalry regiment has two boats and the material
permitting it to construct a bridge 3 meters wide and 8
meters long, or a foot-bridge 1 meter wide and 20 meters
long. The material is composed of small beams with
hooks at the ends, so they can be joined together, and

cross-beams already prepared, and these beams have mortise holes to receive the ends of the aprons, so that it is supported securely; anchors, and ropes, and hooks, and oars complete the material.

At Aldershot, in England, a large pond has been constructed, in which the British Cavalry are now regularly trained in swimming, both man and horse, separately and together, under varying conditions, an effort being made to

GERMAN LANCE-BOAT—FINISHED FRAME OF LANCES READY FOR THE CLOTH.

have the practice resemble that which would be encountered in actual field service, so far as possible. The Austrian cavalry service, a few years ago, made exhaustive experiments in the swimming of cavalry commands, and these experiments are very instructive, as the experiments were carefully made and thoroughly carried out. These experiments were made by some Hungarian cavalry regiments at the river Thiess. The crossing was made near Zenta, where the river is over 300 yards wide and possesses considerable current. The command carried portable folding boats, air-tight inflatable bags, and water-proof sacks to be filled with hay, straw, or dry leaves. In 40 minutes after arrival on the river-bank the portable boats, each capable of carrying 12 men with their arms, saddlery, and accouterments, were ready, loaded, and in the water. These boats were put together and launched

GERMAN LANCE-BOAT—FINISHED AND READY FOR USE.

by 5 men, working leisurely, and they could have been launched in about 25 minutes in case of necessity. At the same time the balance of the command were unsaddling, good swimmers stripping, and several men with air-tight bags were sent across and located good landing-places for horses and boats. Air-tight bags were made up into rafts, each capable of carrying 8 men with their equipments, saddlery, etc. The rafts were of two kinds—water-proof, air-tight, inflated bags were made up into rafts, and water-proof sacks filled with something light, as straw, hay, or dry leaves, were also made up into rafts. The rafts of water-proof, straw-filled bags are an old idea. They are made by tying 9 bags together with rope, resting between double wooden frames. These rafts are slow and clumsy as compared to the comparatively new inflated, air-tight bag rafts, which are formed by tying 9 bags together, resting on single wooden frames, and which

EMBARKING ON THE GERMAN LANCE-BOAT.

move very handily and swiftly through the water. Both kinds, as well as the portable boats, are propelled by wooden hand-paddles, shovels and spades being often used for this purpose. The air-tight bag, 5 feet long and 3 feet broad and pointed at each end, is made of brown canvas with a mouth-piece at one end for inflating, and weighs under 2 pounds. Fifty bags were carried by each of the above regiments, strapped, folded, to the saddles. The average length of time in crossing the river and returning was 20 minutes. The horses were swum over in troop herds, led by naked riders on well-swimming horses, the men of each troop forming a semi-circle around their herd and driving it into the water after the leaders; the troops followed each other closely, to keep the lead. In crossing, some horses turned back and refused obstinately to take the water a second time.

TOWING HORSES FROM GERMAN LANCE-BOAT.

These were towed over after the rafts. The experiment was also made of towing a few horses behind the rafts, and forcing the herd to follow in the same way as described above, 25 horses at a time. Again, the men all stripped and mounted their barebacked horses and thus crossed; but this method was not much resorted to.

The method of swimming horses by droves, as described above, furnishes some very important lessons. First, it appears that this system could be adopted with any chance of success only at points of passage where the banks shelve gradually to the water's edge, as it is almost impossible to make horses go down steep banks and then take to deep water to swim. In this case towing would have to be used. Again, of the two drove systems the more successful is that where the men ride the leading horses into and across the river. This method, it may be added, was repeatedly used in the Philippine Island campaigns by the American Cavalry, with almost unvarying success. These riders should remain on the leading horses until they are wholly across; for if only one lead-horse turns back, in all probability the entire herd, or a large portion of it at any rate, will turn and follow him back. This was brought out repeatedly at Zenta, and in actual field service in which the writer had an opportunity of observing the various methods frequently resorted to. At Zenta whole droves of horses turned and followed a single leader back, and the fault could be traced to the fact that the riders on the lead-horses left their horses when nearly across, believing the horses would then continue across. There is no difficulty in catching up the horses as they arrive on the other side, as they are somewhat tired and generally make at once, of their own accord, for the nearest group of horses at the landing-place. At Zenta no horses were made to swim across with saddlery on and men riding; but it is well known that the Russian Cossacks practice this as an ordinary cavalry exercise, and it has often been done by the American Cavalry when scouting in the Western country and in the Philippines, and though sometimes resorted to and accomplished, it was never done if it could be avoided, owing to the danger. Whole squadrons of the Russian Cossacks, stationed near the Dnieper often enter that river in line, fully equipped, the rear rank at increased distances, and swim across, a width of some 250 yards of rapid water, without confusion or casualty; but it is inadvisable unless absolutely necessary.

At Zenta nearly 1500 cavalry crossed the Thiess in the above experiments, and, including the preliminary preparations and later saddling up, the time consumed to cross and form line was 2½ hours. By practice, it is fair to assume that it could be done under like conditions in less time. With every facility to effect a crossing, it will be seen that it takes time to pass a large river, even by a single troop, and additional time will be required if rafts are to be constructed out of whatever can be found, the river unknown and the weather bad. Another point to be considered in the crossing of rivers is their variability in swiftness of current, width, and depth; none can be depended upon to be always the same even in like seasons of the year. Two troops of the Fourth Cavalry crossed the Rio Pampanga at Cabanatuan, Philippine Islands, in November, 1899, in about 10 minutes by fording; moved forward, defeated insurgents at Aliaga, and returned in four days to find the Pampanga a wild, wide, roaring torrent 20 feet deep, and it took these two troops about 2 days of hard work to recross, which was done by means of native boats, rafts made from the woods near at hand, and swimming the horses with great diffi-culty, even though the horses had had much experience in swimming unknown rivers. The crossing of Lawton's Division of the Eighth Army Corps at the same time consumed over 11 days, during all of which time the rain came down in torrents.

The crossing of the Bystritza River by the Cossack Cavalry regiments in the Russian service some years ago will serve to illustrate the subject of crossing rivers by swimming still further. The experiments tried here were for the purpose of testing the use of canvas boats and rafts in conjunction with swimming the horses. For the purpose of solving this question, a regiment of Cossacks worked out several types of boats formed of lances covered with canvas. The best one, judging by the tests made, was formed of 16 lances covered with canvas in the shape of a truncated pyramid, and had a capacity of 1620 pounds. For crossing, a place was chosen on the river where the width was about 35 yards and from 7 to 14 feet deep.

The bottom was somewhat soft, and the banks in some places were steep, but not high. Three men dismounted, unsaddled their horses, took off their equipments, undressed, and, with Cossack swords held between the teeth, began to enter the water in mounted order, inducing the horses to jump into the river directly from the steep bank. In view of the small width of the river, to make the horses swim across a greater distance, the landing-place was fixed lower down stream, thus compelling the horses to cross a distance of about 100 yards. The crossing was made in full order; the horses willingly entered the water; each man, by holding the mane of his horse, swam on the side of the current. At the same time, the saddles and all the equipments, as well as the clothes of the men, were put into 2 boats made of lances and canvas, each of which contained about 25 saddles, the same number of carbines, and all the equipments and clothes of the same number of men. The crossing began at 5:30 P. M., and in 20 minutes the river was crossed, not only by the skirmishers and volunteers who crossed first, but the boats had also transported the saddles, carbines, etc., so that the men had time to dress themselves and to send off patrols for the purpose of reconnoitering the locality lying in front of them. This crossing in 20 minutes was by platoons. After the crossing was well under way, one small regiment crossed the river with 2 boats in 30 minutes. The boat itself is constructed very easily in 25 minutes, requiring only a supply of tarpaulins and lances, materials which can always be kept by commands and the transporting of which does not cause any difficulty. The buoyancy of the boat is sufficiently great, while at the same time it is very light, as only 4 men are required for its handling when loaded. The merits of the boat were so well demonstrated that the Cossack regiments were all supplied with a number of tarpaulins sufficient for 6 boats to the regiment, or 1 to each troop. It must be observed that the lances of which the boats are formed are

exposed to so great a strain that if they were made of pine
or light wood, they could not sustain it.   Not one of the
lances broke during the above experiment.   The lances
used were of beech, which is strong and at the same time
very elastic.

A most important demonstration of the practical use
of lance boats by cavalry was recently given in Germany,
during the maneuvers.   Each German cavalry regiment
is supplied with these new lance-boats.   They are very
simple of construction, being made of lances and sail-
cloth or tarpaulins, and by much drill and practice the
time consumed in putting these boats together is a
matter of moments rather than minutes.   In the recent
German experiments the squadrons came to the river at
a trot, dismounted, unsaddled their horses, unloaded the
lances and cloths, and constructed the lance-boats.   Each
horse can be loaded with sufficient outfit for a single boat,
and it is so arranged on the horse that he can take any
gait or clear any ordinary obstacle.   The men unloaded,
constructed the boats, and had them afloat in 8 minutes,
and it is claimed the boat can be taken apart and re-
packed in much less time.   These boats were found to be
very steady in the water.   Each boat has 24 air-tight
compartments, and should some of these be pierced by
shot, the boat could still be used.   These experiments of
the German cavalrymen were very successful.   The illustrations on pages 254, 256, 257, 258, and 259 will show
the type of the new lance-boat of the Kaiser's Cavalry.

One or two instances may be cited showing how
American Cavalry have crossed difficult rivers by utilizing
the means at hand.   In 1873 Colonel Sanford (then
Captain) arrived with Troop E of the First Cavalry on
the banks of the Malheur River.   The snow had begun
to melt during the day, but the men were most of the
time up to their waists in drifts, dragging their horses
after them.   The river was a raging torrent, of unknown
depth, and full of floating ice.   The only timber of any
size was pine or juniper on the mountain-side.   One exper-

iment in the way of a raft of this material proved that it
was impossible to utilize it. The command had to cross
or starve. A quantity of willow brush was found growing along the bank, and this was cut into dry lengths
of about 4 or 5 feet and from 1 to 2 inches in diameter. The packs were taken off the mules and the
canvas pack-covers were spread on the ground. These
pack-covers measure about 6 feet wide and 12 or 14 feet
long each. On these pieces of canvas the sticks were
laid in layers across the width. Heavier sticks were
placed lengthwise along the side to keep them in place,
and when the whole pile was about 4 feet high the
sides of the canvas were drawn over towards each other
and lashed backwards and forwards with lariats. The
sides, of course, did not cover the sticks, but that was
remedied by placing another canvas over the sticks before
the lashing took place. This gave the sides of the boat;
to make the ends, nothing was necessary but to bring up
the canvas from front to rear, and lash it securely. As
the sticks had been purposely laid so that the longest
came in the middle, the boat was shaped something like
a cigar, about 8 feet long and 4 feet wide, and, without a load, drew about 6 inches. A stout rope was placed
around each of what might be called the bow, waist, and
stern, and through this a line was carried. As the stream
was entirely too swift to admit of paddling the boat over,
a man swam across the river and towed the boat the first
time. Several lariats were knotted together, so that the
swimmer, after arriving on the opposite bank, could pull
the boat in to the bank. A similar line attached to the
stern enabled the command to pull the boat back to the
near shore, when it was found that the boat had taken in
a great deal of water through the pores of the canvas.
The bow was unlashed and the boat lifted up and allowed
to drain out. After that trip the canvas was so swollen
that it admitted no more water, and the boat carried an
average load of 3 troopers, with their arms and accouterments, saddles, bridles, etc., included. The horses and

mules swam the river under the guidance of a few men, but the material, equipage, and the bulk of the men were all carried across in about 3 hours from the time the command made the trial trip. This crossing was especially hazardous, owing to the swiftness of the current, which rendered paddling impracticable, and made it necessary to resort to the rope-ferry plan. One year later this same command crossed the Cœur d'Alêne River in Northern Idaho in the same way, using several of the boats mentioned above, and the crossing was made in about two hours. This river was much deeper and wider than the first river, but scarcely any current. The command at this time was considerably larger than it was before.

The boat used by Colonel Sanford, described above, was, more properly speaking, a raft. But out of the same material a very serviceable boat can be made. In the summer of 1880 Captain Parker, Fourth Cavalry, was camped with his troop on the banks of the Uncompahgre River in Colorado. The river was high, and the command set to work to make a boat out of means at hand, out of whatever they could find. Plenty of young cottonwood trees were growing around, and there was also a thicket of willows. For canvas a wagon-sheet was used, which had formerly served as a tent. The construction of the boat was begun by tracing on the ground the outline of a boat 11 feet long and 4 feet wide, sharp at both ends. At each end a strut-stick was driven; along each side 7 stakes were driven opposite to each other. A number of limber cottonwood poles and branches were then cut; 2 of the largest were lashed firmly to the stakes and the bow and stern, and were then bent over and lashed together in the middle, thus forming the keel. Smaller poles were lashed to the stakes driven along the sides, and then each pair was bent over and lashed together and also lashed to the keel, passing below the keel. These formed the ribs of the boat. The gunwale was formed by branches, which were bound to each rib and to the ends of the keel, the gunwale passing along the sides of the boat just above the tops of the stakes. Thus the framework of a boat lying bottom up had been constructed. To strengthen it, willows were cut, which were woven in and out among the ribs and keel. The lashings that held the boat to the stakes were cut. The basket-work boat was found to be remarkably stiff, except that the ends of the keel and of the principal ribs were inclined to spring outwards. This was effectually remedied by tying them down to the center of the keel with lariats. The protruding ends of the keel and ribs were then sawed off and the basket-boat covered with canvas. This boat, 11 feet long and 4 feet wide, weighed about 80 pounds. With 6 men on board, it drew but 3 or 4 inches of water and had but little tendency to upset. It was built by 4 men in from 2 to 3 hours. It was easily managed, and leaked but little.

There has been still another method employed in crossing rivers, of much use where there are a large number of men in the command who do not know how to swim. This method consists in placing the troop horses in single column, 7 or 8 at a time being crossed. The leading horse in each "column" is mounted by a good swimmer, and the horse especially chosen because of his known skill as a strong swimmer. The head of each horse in the column is then tied by the halter-strap to the tail of the preceding horse, and the small column enters the water with the non-swimming men on the horses' backs. The rider of the leading horse must have a cool head and a steady hand, and must guide his little column of swimming horses across to the opposite landing-place. While this method may have to be used at times, in order to cross the non-swimming troopers, it is always a risky way, and should only be used when other methods are of no avail.

When a river has a swift current and the water is above the horses' bellies, but still fordable, the subdivisions should cross with as wide a front as practical, to permit a freer flow and prevent damming the water, which might carry a horse off his feet; in crossing a *dangerous* ford, however, the column of twos is less objectionable than the column of fours. Cavalry should generally cross streams *below* a pontoon bridge, and when infantry is also crossing at the same time as cavalry, the cavalry should cross *above* the infantry or so far below that the water will not be dammed against them. Ice from $4\frac{1}{2}$ to $6\frac{1}{2}$ inches thick will bear cavalry marching in column of troopers or twos. Ice 10 inches thick has been found to sustain the heaviest loads. When a stream is frozen on both sides, but open in the middle, in consequence of the velocity of the current, a boom stretched across the open space will often check the velocity sufficiently to allow the water to freeze.

Cavalry will be forced to pass unknown rivers many times in every campaign and under all conditions of weather and season. The young cavalry officer leading a troop will be called upon to decide for himself as to the best means for effecting the crossing of his men and horses. In the troop will generally be found men who are more or less familiar with boat-building and others who are strong, fearless swimmers. The above methods and experiments illustrate what experience has taught in the past and how difficulties may be overcome, but the arduous nature of the work involved in the passage of rivers can probably only be learned in actual field service; but the cavalryman may prepare himself beforehand in many ways by knowing how such work is actually managed in the cavalry services of our own Army and those abroad.

CHAPTER XIII.

TRANSPORTING CAVALRY HORSES.

Two General Ways, by Rail and by Sea—Importance of Care and
Experience—By Rail—Methods Usually Employed—Capacity of Stock Cars—Ramps—Danger of Hasty or Careless Loading — Watering — Feeding — Unloading — Guards — By Sea—
Horse Transports –Methods in General—Portable Loading-Boxes
—Watering—Feeding—Stalls —Ventilation—Guards—Unloading—Importance of Policing—Methods on Board.

It frequently happens that cavalry troops are sent from
point to point, not by marching, but by railroad or steamship, and thus it very often falls to the lot of the cavalry
officer to superintend the loading and unloading of the
cavalry horse and his pack, and to care for both *en route*,
during long voyages by sea or long journeys by railroad,
at all seasons of the year. Upon the care, skill, and
intelligence with which this duty is performed will depend
the ability of at once being able to use the horse for cam-
paign-work at the end of the journey. It requires considerable practical skill and "horse sense" to perform
this duty efficiently, and it involves much hard work and
careful supervision by the officer in charge. Practical
good sense and an appreciation of the many injuries and
diseases to which the cavalry horse is exposed when being
transported in stock cars or steamships are indispensable,
that proper precautions may be taken to prevent the horse
from suffering, the Government from loss, and the expedition from failure.

While practical training in this important duty is
essential to its efficient performance, nevertheless a clear
idea beforehand of how to accomplish it best will be of
great value and save considerable confusion and delay
when the time comes

By Rail.—The troops being mounted with the saddle packed, march to the point of embarkation on the railroad and unsaddle. Each packed saddle with bridle is tied up in the saddle-blanket and marked with the trooper's name for ready identification later on; the bed-blankets, arms, and mess-kits the men usually keep with them, as they will be needed *en route.* In each troop the bundles of saddles are then carried by the troopers to the freight car designated for that troop and packed in. The trains of stock cars, freight cars, and passenger coaches are usually on the track waiting for the troops, and each troop has its proper share of cars assigned to it. This assignment of cars should be made promptly, that each troop may know its own stock cars, freight cars, and passenger coaches. If this is *not* done, much confusion always results, the annoying confusion increasing directly with the size of the command. As soon as the cars are assigned, each troop should place one or two troopers in charge of each car belonging to it, as a guard, and to indicate to the officers and men of the command, without delay, to which troop the cars belong. If facilities for loading the horses and baggage of more than one troop at a time are at hand, all the troops, or as many as possible, load simultaneously. If the loading facilities are limited, the troops load successively, according to the rank of the troop commanders present, or in such order as the commanding officer of the command may direct. Unless specially directed to do so by the commanding officer, a junior troop commander should never attempt to load his horses and baggage where the loading facilities require successive loading by troops, until those troop commanders senior to him have embarked their troops. A stock or baggage car should never be assigned for the use of different troops, if it can be avoided; each troop should have its own.

Details of troopers from each troop, under charge of an officer of the troop (or a non-commissioned officer if no officer be available), should load the troop baggage in the troop's baggage cars, while the remainder of the troopers then lead the troop horses, one at a time and quietly, into the cars, removing halters, etc., and never tying the horses in. It saves time to require each trooper to attach a leather card, bearing his name, to his horse's mane, before loading. This allows quick identification of the horses as they are being unloaded, day or night. The average American stock car holds 16 or 17 American cavalry horses. The horses are placed across the car, alternating head and tail, and placed sufficiently close together to prevent any horse from turning around, as shown in illustration below, in which the A's are loaded first, then the B's, etc. Each car is loaded at both ends

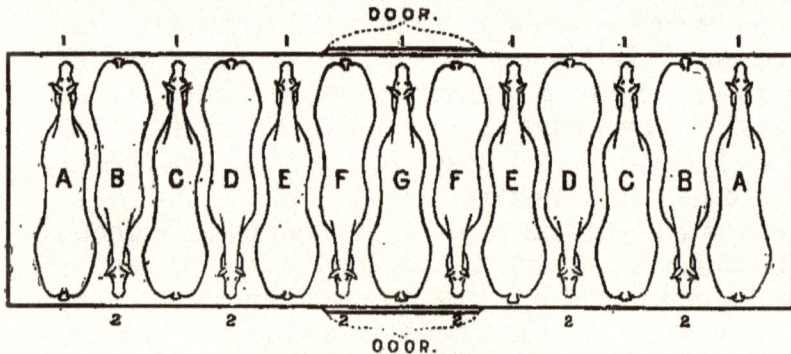

HORSES IN RAILROAD CAR.

first, each end working towards the middle; when the last horse is led in the remaining space, thus "wedging" the load, the doors on both sides are closed and locked, and so on with each car, until all the horses are aboard. Guards of one or two men are sometimes left on top of each car, but if the doors are securely locked and the train crew large enough, these guards can usually be dispensed with. All cars to be used for transportation of horses should have 3 or 4 inches of sand placed on their floors to prevent horses slipping. Before the horses are saddled to march to the railroad, they should have been fed, and immediately before loading should be allowed to drink freely. No blankets or straps should be left upon the horses in the car; these, if left on, frequently entangle the horses' feet and legs, cause nervousness and fright and many injuries, the result of kicking, etc.

It not infrequently happens that railroads fail to provide suitable means at the point of embarkation for loading the horses, and it will at such times fall to the officer in charge of the loading to display considerable ingenuity in overcoming these difficulties by utilizing means at hand. The usual height of the American stock-car door from the ground is about 4 feet, and there may be no platform level with the car door; even when there is such · a platform, there is generally an open space between the edge of the platform and the edge of the car door of a foot or two, and this space must be bridged over strongly before any attempt is made to load the horses. In loading horses, it pays to exercise great care. The horse will frequently step directly into the open space between the car and the platform if an attempt is made to load him by stepping him across this hole, and, falling heavily, almost always injures himself badly, and is frequently so seriously hurt that he has to be killed. Some horses will attempt to jump over this open space; as the top of the car door is in the way, the horse strikes his head violently against the door top, and is either thrown down between the car and the platform or passes into the car badly frightened and perhaps seriously injured.

Sometimes this open space is very wide, or there may be no platform at all, when it becomes necessary to construct some sort of bridge to reach from the car door to the point where the horse is on firm footing. This sort of bridge is known as a "ramp," and may be either permanently built to the platform or portable, as is generally the case. Several portable ramps have become well known by much use in our service, and are described below. Portable ramps are platforms usually about 3½ or 4 feet wide (average width, inside measurement, of stock-car door) and about 12 or 14 feet long, having side-rails about 3½ feet high on both sides and cross-cleats on the

floor about 1 foot apart to prevent the horse from slipping, and cross-cleats on the bottom to prevent the boards
of the floor from separating.   One end of the ramp rests
securely on the stock-car floor in the doorway, to which
the end is fastened by hooks or ropes to prevent the ramp
from slipping back when in use; the other end of the ramp
rests upon the ground or station platform.   As the floor
of the car door is usually about 4 feet high, the length of
the ramp must be about 12 or 14 feet, thus obtaining a
slope of about 1 on 3 for the horse to walk up.   If the
slope be too steep, the horse will rush up in excited jumps,
his head high, and injure himself by striking his head
against the top of the car door in entering, while a gentler
slope would require the ramp to be too long and heavy to
carry around.   The slope mentioned above is the one
generally used.   Only one horse is led up the ramp at a
time, and until he is wholly within the car and away from
the doorway no other horse should be allowed on the
ramp.   In wet or snowy weather the floor of the ramp
should be sprinkled lightly with ashes or dirt, to prevent
slipping.

The Fechet portable ramp (see page 273), one of the
best known in our service, was devised by Major E. G.
Fechet, of the Sixth Cavalry.   The ramp consists of seven
boards, 1.5 inches by 7 inches by 12 feet, joined together
in three sections (two for the outside, A A, and three for
the middle, B) by wooden strips (C) 1 inch thick and 2
inches wide, bolted to the upper surfaces, 1 foot between
centers.   These strips also serve as footholds.   Along the
middle of the outside boards extends a side-rail (D) 3
inches by 3 inches, held firmly by iron straps (E) $\frac{1}{2}$ inch
by $\frac{1}{2}$ inch.   On the outside of each side-rail are three
sockets (F) for the standards (G), which are 3 feet high,
along the tops of which are to be stretched ropes or chains,
from which are hung horse-blankets or canvas.   On the
under side of each section, 3 feet apart, are bolted iron
cleats (H), 0.5 inch by 2 inches, beginning at 18 inches
from the ends.   On the ends of each section are bolted

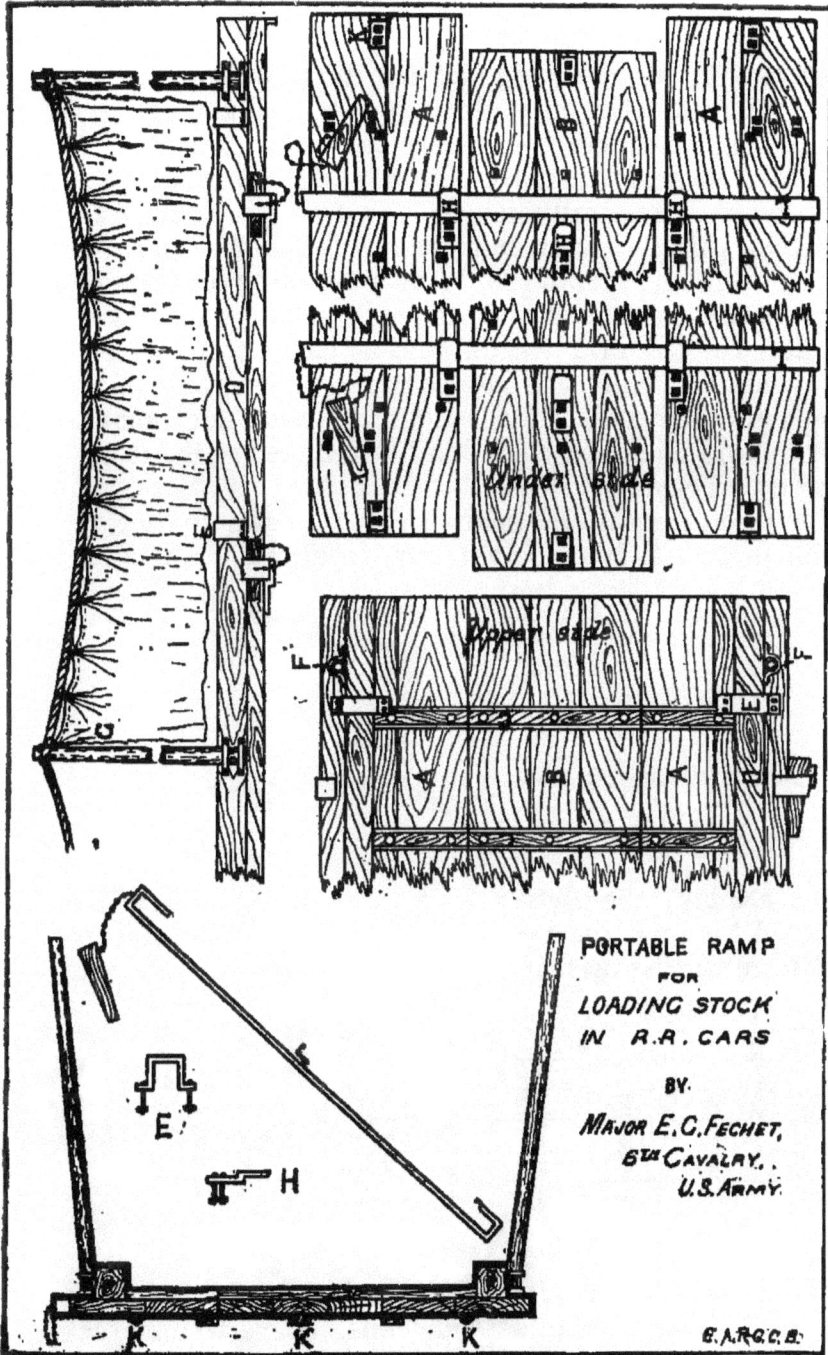

Under side

Upper side

PORTABLE RAMP
FOR
LOADING STOCK
IN R.R. CARS

BY

MAJOR E.C. FECHET,
6TH CAVALRY,
U.S. ARMY

E.A.R.Q.C.B.

FECHET'S PORTABLE RAMP.
(See page 272.)

iron claws (K) for catching the car floor or door-sill, to prevent slipping when in position for use. The three sections are held together for use by four iron tie-bars (L), ¼ inch by 2 inches, which are placed under the cleats (H), and the whole then firmly keyed. This form of ramp may be made longer or shorter, narrower or broader, as desired. By taking out the standards, it may be hung on the side of a car, between a door and an end. It is easily taken apart and carried in a wagon, and as easily put together again when needed. It is designed to combine both strength and lightness. Its weight is about 400 pounds complete, and could be considerably reduced without impairing its efficiency.

The two illustrations below show a common form of portable ramp, easily made and carried about. The illus-

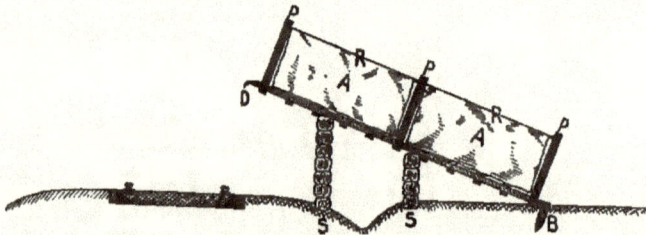

COMMON RAMP.

trations explain themselves; ordinary railroad ties (S S) are placed beneath the ramp when in use, to strengthen it, but need not be used if the boards are stout. A A are

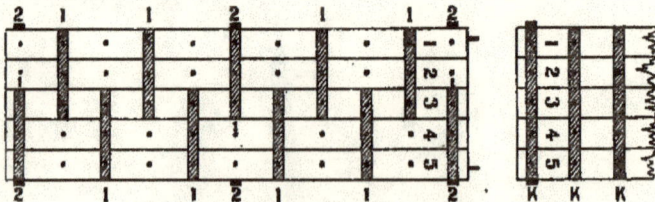

FLOOR VIEW OF SAME.

the horse-blankets, B the safety-posts, D the car-floor hooks, R R lariats used as side-rails, over which the blankets are hung. In the second illustration the No. 1's represent the upper cleats to prevent slipping, the No. 2's are the sockets for the uprights (PPP), and the left section is the lower side, showing cleats (K) extending wholly across to hold the boards together. All the cleats are riveted on, a lower cleat being beneath each upper one. Horse-shoes may be used as the floor-hooks (D), and with available lumber and nails this ramp can be quickly made.

Another excellent form of portable ramp which has been found of splendid use in actual service is very simple, and can be carried hung to the side of a car ready for unloading. It must always be remembered that horses once loaded have to be unloaded, and frequently at the worst places, as small, isolated way-stations or barren, level plains, devoid of timber or habitation. This portable ramp consists of six long timbers, 4 inches by 4 inches by 14 feet; six short timbers, 4 inches by 4 four inches by 6 feet, and twenty-four boards 1.5 inch by 12 inches by 6 feet, with footholds nailed lengthwise on one side. This is easily put together and very practical. To unload or load horses, rest the ends of three of the long timbers, equally spaced, on the car floor, the other ends resting against a short timber sunk in the ground and staked down. On these place the boards forming the floor; on each side of the ramp, on the boards, lay a long timber and fasten the ends to the timbers underneath. The boards should have cleats on the under side to prevent slipping sideways. If necessary, some of the remaining boards can be set edgewise between posts of the short timbers, as an intermediate support.

Another form of portable ramp is one devised by Lieutenant N. F. McClure, of the Fifth Cavalry, which is a sort of modification of one improvised by Lieutenant E. S. Avis, Eighteenth Infantry. The arrangement consists of eight good oak planks, each 12 feet by 1 foot by 2 inches, and two trestles; five planks for the roadway, the sixth plank serving as a reserve plank in case one should break, and the remaining two are for sides to the ramp. The roadway has seven cleats of hard wood on each side, making fourteen cleats on the floor, half on one side and half on the other. Those on the right side are slightly higher in position than those on the left side of the floor. Each cleat is of hard wood, 1 foot by 3 inches by 1½ inches, and is bolted to the planks or put on with long wire nails going clear through and clinched on the under side. The holes for the bolts and nails are bored, and each cleat has four of the bolts or nails. The roadway planks are, therefore, not fastened to each other. A cast-iron shoe is placed as a hook on the end of each plank on the under side, enabling each of the boards of the ramp to be hooked on to the edge of the car floor at the door, thus preventing slipping of the ramp when a horse is upon it. These shoes are 4 inches from the ends of the boards, so that the latter may extend well into the car. These hooks reach down at least 4 inches, so as to catch on to the door-rail of the car. There are several different kinds of these door-rails, but a hook of 4 inches will fit any kind. On the under side of each roadway plank are fastened four other cleats, two to each trestle. These are put in pairs, just far enough apart to admit of the tops of the trestles slipping between them. These cleats prevent the trestles from slipping from under the roadway. They should be far enough apart to allow the trestles to slip in and out easily. The "horse" of the trestle should be of 6-inch by 4-inch pine, and should be planed off so that the whole top surface will be in contact with the under side of the roadway. The legs nearest the car should make a smaller angle with the ground than the other legs of the trestle, to make the trestle more stable when a horse's weight comes on the ramp. The larger trestle is 3 feet high; the smaller one, 1 foot 6 inches. By sinking the legs into the ground slightly, they can readily be adjusted. In muddy weather boards or flat stones are placed under the trestles.

While it may not always be possible to carefully prepare a portable ramp similar to one of those described above, still it should be done if material is available, and if it is known a day or two beforehand that the troops are to take the train, and it generally is, time is sufficient to make one; in fact, one could be made and kept on hand by every troop to be used, when needed, without having to make one at the last minute. Many ingenious methods are open to the energetic cavalryman, and the above descriptions will give a clear idea of what is necessary. These portable ramps may, as has been said, be hung from the car for unloading. Unloading should be conducted as carefully as is the loading, with every attention to detail. Time is always saved by going at this duty in a right and sensible way, although the way may not at first appear to be the quickest; but before the last horse has been unloaded, the advantage of care will have demonstrated itself many times.

Occasionally it becomes necessary to unload the horses from the cars *en route*, for feeding, watering, and exercise; this does not happen often, but should be done every twenty-four hours if possible. The stock cars now in general use are supplied with watering- and feeding-troughs on the sides, and the stock can be attended to without being taken off. Whenever the train stops for any length of time, an inspection of all the cars should be briefly made, and all doors tried, as some may become loose and slide open.

At Sea.—In loading cavalry horses on steamships, caring for them on board, and unloading them at the end of the journey, greater care is required than is necessary when transporting them on railroad cars. To the greater difficulties encountered in the loading and unloading of the horses on horse transports is added the arduous and multitudinous duties of preserving them from injury and disease while on board, feeding, watering, policing the ship, proper ventilation, drainage, etc. To these must be added caring for the inevitable cases of sickness that occur and the efforts constantly necessary to prevent contagion.

In loading horses on stock cars, both the ramp and the car are stationary; while in loading them upon steamships, it is generally necessary to lift the animal bodily high into the air, swing him through space, and set him down on a deck often rolling more or less. The danger of accident to the horse and all concerned is very considerable. Frequently when the horse feels himself lifted up into the air, he becomes panic-stricken and struggles desperately. All this requires that every care be exercised and that strong, substantial methods and materials be used.

LOADING ON TRANSPORT BY RAMP.

Occasionally it is practicable to use a ramp similar to the ones described above, simply leading the horses aboard one at a time, taking them to their stalls, and tying them in. Generally, however, either a sling of heavy canvas or a portable "box" must be used to lift the horse up to the deck and lower him down through the hatches to the deck containing the stalls. This is almost always the case on large transports, and several methods of performing this work have been used so frequently as to have become

well known on account of their successful results. One
or two of these methods will serve to illustrate plainly
enough.

The Sling.—The sling is a heavy canvas strip about
3½ feet wide and 5 feet long, strongly bound along
the edges with leather to prevent tearing. It is passed
under the horse's belly as he stands on the wharf or

LOADING ON TRANSPORT BY CHUTE.

lighter beside the ship. The two ends of the canvas
are then brought together over the horse's back and
securely fastened together. Breast- and breeching-straps
of broad, heavy canvas are then buckled on snugly
to the sling. The hook on the end of the pulley-rope
from the deck engine is then securely fastened to a ring
in the top of the sling, and the horse is hoisted up by

the deck engine, care being taken that the horse is level in the sling. If the horse is frightened or stubborn, it is usual to blindfold him before the engine starts to lift him up. The horse is swung well up in the air, then swung over the hatch, being gently lowered through it to the deck upon which his stall is. Men are stationed up and down the hatchways to prevent the horse from swinging against the floors as he goes down, and on the stall-deck where he is to alight is placed a thick quantity of loose hay to break the shock of landing and save the horse's legs from injury. Several men here undo the rigging and sling from the horse; the horse is led to his stall and tied in, while the sling is drawn up for another horse. This method, which has been used in both the British and American services for both loading and unloading cavalry horses, has been found strong and satisfactory, though not so much so for loading as the portable loading-box; but the sling is better in unloading at sea, when it is necessary to lower the horse directly into the water.

The Portable Box.—This consists of a large, square, deep, wooden box without a top, the ends of the box being removable. The horse is led into the box from one end, as it rests on the wharf or lighter; the end is then closed, and a broad strip of heavy canvas is passed across the horse's back, and fastened securely to both sides of the box to prevent his jumping out or rearing up. The horse is usually tied in the box by the halter-strap, and, if nervous or stubborn, is blindfolded; then the entire box is lifted up by means of the deck engine and lowered gently down the hatchway. This method has been found most effective, where lifting the horse has been necessary. Men must be stationed up and down the hatchways to prevent the box from swinging against the sides of the hatchway. Ropes are frequently attached to the four sides of the box, their ends being held by men on the four sides of the floors to be passed on the way down to the stall-deck, and the box is thus kept in the center. Thick masses of hay must be placed at the point of landing, to break the shock.

Every horse transport should be carefully inspected, cleaned, and disinfected before a single horse is permitted to be loaded. The transport must be able to accommo-

PUTTING HORSE IN PORTABLE BOX.

date comfortably the number of horses assigned to it. The boat must be well ventilated, must be free from vermin, must have no bad smells that cannot be readily corrected, and the height between decks, from deck to beam, must be at least 7 feet. Vessels with less than 30 feet beam are not suitable for transporting horses. The hatchways for horses should be at least 10x10 feet or

LIFTING HORSE IN PORTABLE LOADING-BOX.

larger. In calculating the amount of tonnage required for the conveyance of horses, 10 tons may be put, roughly, as the "weight" of each horse. As a general rule, it may be assumed that the larger the vessel the better adapted it is for transporting horses, and the greater will be the economy. Steamers are always preferable to sailing vessels, as they make much quicker voyages, and this is an all-important consideration. In calm seasons large sailing vessels have been used for transporting horses, being towed by powerful steamships. Small ships should never be used, if the voyage is to be at all prolonged. Those with 30 feet beam will allow of a row of stalls on each side and of a passage in the center between them of 10 feet, besides 3 feet between each row of stalls and the ship's sides.

Horses should never be placed near the stoke-hole, as the heat is likely to bring on inflammation. In all horse ships ventilation is of primary importance; good port-holes or scuttles are indispensable; windsails down every hatchway to each deck are imperative. If time admits, fixed wooden air-shafts are better than the wind-sails. The safety and condition of horses on board ship mainly depends on their having plenty of fresh air. When the horses are below, care must be taken that no direct drafts bear upon them, especially in the region of the loins. Too much attention cannot be paid to the constant trimming of the windsails, which must be kept full to the wind at all times. The fore part of a ship is that in which sickness invariably occurs first among the horses, and therefore a constant current of fresh air down the forward hatchway, by means of windsails, must be secured. The lower ends of the windsails should reach within a foot of the floor of the deck for which the air is intended.

In fitting up a ship for horses, especial care must be taken to have the men's quarters distinct from the part of the ship occupied by the horses. This is indispensable on the score of health. Doors are frequently opened out between where the men and where the horses are. This is objectionable, as the effluvia of the horses should be kept from the men in every possible way. Every horse transport should have as many stalls on deck as possible, so that horses suffering below can be moved up there for a few days to recover, which they do quickly in the fresh air. There should be ample stowage-room for harness and saddlery; it should all be packed in sacks and placed in the room allotted especially for this purpose. If time allows, and a delay in unpacking the saddlery at the end of the voyage of a day or so will not be serious, it pays to pack all saddlery in boxes, strongly sealed, to prevent both loss and damage.

There are generally no water-tanks on the horses' decks; they are in the way, and the slightest movement near them frets the horses. They are placed in the hold, with a pump communicating with them from the horse-decks. A loose box about 7 feet wide is sometimes placed near a hatchway, to admit of a sick horse lying down in smooth weather. There is a dispensary, with fittings for the veterinary surgeon, and a forage-room, for issuing purposes, large enough to hold one day's allowance for the horses aboard, fitted with bins lined with tin for oats and bran.

The stalls are generally 6 feet long from inside of the padding on the breast-piece to the inside of the padding on the haunch-piece, and about 2 feet 2 inches clear width between the padding on the side-bales. Ten per cent of the stalls are generally 2 inches narrower, and about 5 per cent 6 inches longer, to accommodate the different sized horses. In each stall is a haunch-bar and a breast-bar, both padded, to prevent the horse from moving forward or backward; the haunch-bar is removable, to enable the horse to be taken out and led in whenever necessary. Both sides of the stall are padded; the padding used in the stalls is generally made of sheepskin, long in the wool, put on double. When this cannot be obtained, padding may be dispensed with on the sides, and bags of stout canvas stuffed with straw substituted for the padding on the breast- and haunch-bars, and this padding may be used also on the sides if necessary. In front of the breast-pieces are the mangers and feed-boxes. The horse's head is secured in the usual way by the halter and strap, although chains are sometimes used, as shown on page 288. The stall-pads should all be numbered with the stall number, and frequently taken out and shaken up,

THE HORSE IN STALL WITH SLING.

especially if of hay or straw, to prevent hardening and packing.

For every 50 horses on board there should be 2 horse-boxes on trucks, to enable sick horses to be easily moved about. For every 100 horses there should be the following articles

10 hand safety lamps;
15 rakes or scrapers;
15 shovels;
8 hoes;
4 peck measures;
4 half-peck measures;
100 horse hammocks, complete;
2 slings for hoisting horses or 2 portable loading-boxes;
100 halters;
6 large water-barrels;
6 small water-barrels;
10 large water-pails;
10 small water-pails;
2 forage-trucks on tracks, one on each side, between the ship's side and the feed-boxes;
15 manure-baskets;
15 stable-brooms;
A curry-comb and a horse-brush for each animal;
Extra blankets for sick horses;
Extra padding for stalls, 2 per cent if sheepskin,
15 per cent if straw or hay.

Feeding.—As regards feeding horses while on transports, experience has shown that about 5 pounds of
oats a day is ample, until within a few days of landing,
when the full ration is given to get the horses in condition. The bran ration is 5 pounds also. For the first
few days it is advisable to decrease the oats to 2 pounds
and increase the bran to 7 pounds. Vinegar and nitre
should be put on board at the rate of 1 gill and 1 ounce,
respectively, a day for each horse, to be used as needed.
One feed a day of 2½ pounds of carrots is invaluable for
sick horses. All horses should be watered three times
a day.

The following table, long used by the English Army
in their extensive voyages, is given by General Wolseley
as a well-tried daily forage ration for the cavalry horse
during sea travel:

FOR EACH HORSE DAILY.

Oats. . . . . .6 pounds.
Hay. . . . . 10 pounds.
Bran. . . . . ½ peck or 2¼ pounds.
Water. .6 gallons.*
Vinegar. . . . . 1 gill.
Nitre. . . . . .1 ounce.

For the first few days on board ship food is rather sparingly given, bran forming the larger part. After a few days, as the horse grows accustomed to the new conditions, his appetite will improve, and he is then more liberally fed. A bran mash, or oats and bran mixed, should be fed at least every other day.

The horses all in their stalls aboard the transport and the ship under way, guards are usually posted up and down the center passage-ways day and night, and lights are kept burning to avoid confusion and delay in the event of accident or a sick horse requiring quick attention. Beginning early each morning, a thorough police must be made of every part of the ship, refuse and manure thrown overboard, and all decks and stalls hosed and scrubbed out with the heavy stable-brooms. Horses require constant attention while they are on ship, and good hygienic surroundings are essential to their health. Every cavalry-man aboard has important and imperative duties to perform daily, on which depend, in fact, the means of his being usefully employed in the field when he reaches his destination. Horses should be kept cool before embarkation, and should be put on board ship rather low in flesh than in too high condition, in which latter state they are more disposed to be fractious and kick, and are, moreover, more liable to inflammation.

Long, slow, steady work is to be given to horses previously to their embarkation, if possible, and they should be kept fasting and without water for some hours before being put on board, as slinging them is more likely to

*Can be increased with advantage to 8 gallons.

prove injurious when their bellies are distended with food, and also they will sooner become reconciled to their changed surroundings and take to their food on board if they have been kept fasting a few hours previously. Before loading the horses, if time allows, the hind shoes should be removed; they are not needed on board, and removing them lessens the danger to be apprehended from kicking. The horses should, so far as possible, be stalled among their own stable companions, as they will

HORSES IN STALLS ON TRANSPORT, SHOWING FEEDING-BOXES AND METHOD OF TYING.

These feed-boxes, being of zinc, are also used for watering the horses; the boxes being filled by buckets or hose.

both stand and feed more quietly in this way than when placed among strange horses.

Spare stalls are usually left on each deck, so that the horses can be shifted and the stalls cleaned. The horse should be groomed and rubbed, and in warm weather his feet washed; hand-rubbing the legs gives great comfort. When the force of men on board permits this grooming,

washing, and rubbing to be done, it should not be neglected. The men are on board to care for the animals,
the voyage will be successful only if the horses arrive at
their destination in good condition, and they will not do
so unless much hard work is performed by all on board.

The horses are slung in their stalls by means of the
"horse hammocks" in smooth weather, and allowed to
remain on their feet when the weather is rough. When
slung in smooth weather, the horse will rest his legs by
putting his entire weight in the hammock. To sling the
horse in rough weather would only have the effect of
knocking him about the stall. Horses are not generally
placed in the hammocks until they have been at sea for
several days, as many horses would only be made uneasy.
After a few days of standing, the horse will quickly take
advantage of the hammock to rest his tired legs. The
hammock is a broad sling of canvas placed under the
horse's belly and attached to the ceiling of the stall, and
both rests him and prevents his lying down. The hammock is placed in the center of the belly, and then the
breast-band and breeching are fastened to the required
length and degree of tightness. The hammock, when
properly adjusted, should come just to the height of the
horse's belly, but no attempt should be made to raise the
animal off his feet. The horse will, after a few days of
standing, himself lower his weight into the hammock
without any urging.

When a horse between decks is very ill and the weather
is at all fine, he should be removed to a stall on the upper
deck; this will cure many ailing horses. During long
voyages it is wise to change all the horses in this way, if
possible. In very rough weather, if the vessel labors very
much, it will be found necessary to use all the men who
can be spared to stand by their horses' heads. The horses
are much quieter when men are with them.

Vinegar is essential to the comfort of the troop-horse
on shipboard, and is freely used. Chloride of lime should
be thrown on the deck floor, or, what is better still, pow-

dered alabaster or gypsum, to destroy the ammonia arising from the urine. A horse exhibiting any suspicious
sign of a contagious disease, or any nasal discharge that
may be the forerunner of something contagious, should
be at once taken to the upper deck and isolation of the
most strict description put in force. As soon as the disease is even fairly well determined, the horse should
be dropped overboard without compunction. Disease
spreading through the horses on board ship runs with
remarkable speed, and may even be communicated to the
men. Every precaution must be observed in the treatment of the sick horses. A part of the ship should have
a few stalls set apart, away from the other horses, for the
sick animals, generally on the upper deck, where there is
plenty of fresh air. Everything used about the sick-stalls
and horses should be kept away from the other horses.
The feed-boxes, mangers, etc., should be thoroughly disinfected whenever a sick horse has recovered, and before
they are used for another animal. Should the horse upon
which the articles were used prove to have a contagious
disease, the stall and all woodwork should be disinfected
thoroughly, and the loose articles at once thrown overboard.

Disembarking.—In disembarking horses, the same
precautions are necessary as when embarking them. For
some days after the completion of a long voyage they
should be led by hand at a gentle pace (not faster than a
walk), and no weight should be placed upon their backs.
This rule, of course, must give way to necessity. The
writer has ridden and been carried well by a horse just
landed from a ship, after a month's voyage from the
United States to the Philippines.

The disembarkation of horses by lowering the animals
into the water by the slings and then turning them loose
to swim ashore is often necessary. The horse instinct-
ively, in most cases, swims toward the nearest shore. He
will be greatly influenced to do this if a number of horses
are held at the edge of the shore at the landing-place, as

he will swim toward these horses invariably. Dropping horses out of slings into the water is said to injure their pluck and to make them ever afterward timid about ford- ing rivers or entering water at all. It should only be done when no other means are available; it will, how- ever, have to be done often in active service. This was especially the case in the Cuban campaign of the America Army during 1898.

When this method is used, the horse is lowered in the sling over the side of the vessel, without fastening the breast-rope or breeching. When the horse settles in the water the tackle is unhooked and the sling opens and is at once slipped from under the horse, and he is free. occasionally a horse will persist in swimming around the ship or even out to sea, but most all the animals will strike out at once for land, if not too far away. If it is impos- sible or unsafe to take the ship within a few hundred yards of the shore, the horses should, if it can be done, be loaded into smaller vessels, and not made to swim until they have been conveyed as near the shore as the boats can get. Occasionally horses are then towed ashore, but with a high surf swimming is the better way, and the horse free will go for the land and reach it.

Prior to 1898 practically no one in the American ser- vice had had experience in the transportation of cavalry horses by sea; but with the beginning of active hostilities between the United States and Spain the transporting of cavalry horses by sea became a most important mat- ter, and during the following three years, both to and from Cuba and Porto Rico in the Atlantic, and to and from the Philippine Islands and China in the Pacific, many horses were transported. A study of how this transpor- tation was actually managed will throw much valuable light on this subject and be a most excellent guide for future emergencies. At first the American service pos- sessed no horse transports at all, but within a few months several were being used, and these were later repaired and modified as circumstances and experience taught us the

lesson, and many more ships for this purpose were employed by us.   No better way can be had to learn the
methods best suited to this arduous work than the pres-
entation of some actual experiences.

The first trip from the United States to the Philippine
Islands was made by a sailing-ship, the "Tacoma" (2000
tons), which was fitted up by Captain George H. Cameron,
Fourth Cavalry.   The choice of vessels for this purpose
was at this time very limited, and this ship was taken
largely because she was clear of partitions between decks
and of good beam.   This vessel reached Honolulu, Hawa-
iian Islands, after a voyage of some nine days, and there
laid up in order to repair her distilling plant.   Although
this work was well under way and the ship would soon
have sailed for Manila, she was ordered to unload her
horses at Honolulu, because it was decided that she carried munitions of war, and therefore could not proceed.
The "Tacoma" then returned to San Francisco to procure
another cargo or to turn the ship back to her owners, as
circumstances might dictate.

It was found that the roll on the sailing-ship was
hardly perceptible except in calms; but, as the wind is
often dead astern, the suffering from lack of ventilation
is the most serious drawback, coupled with the slower
rate of speed and liability to entire stoppage when wind
is gone.   On the "Tacoma" all stanchions, haunch-,
breast-, and side-pieces were of dressed lumber with round
edges; the haunch-piece was continuous, and this was
found to work well; it was believed that this haunch-
piece should not be padded, on account of the droppings;
it should be frequently washed.   It was found that the
horses threw their weight against this haunch-piece and
slept practically sitting down.   The horses were not
slung; they were unable to lie down, on account of the
narrowness of the stall, made narrow for this reason.
The feed-boxes were of galvanized iron, easily removed
from the breast-piece, and were made to "nest."   Floor-
pieces were found essential in the stalls, to prevent the

animals from slipping when the stalls became wet with urine. The falling horse was apt to break his back. The beam of the "Tacoma" was sufficient to allow for three rows of stalls; the resulting two aisles were connected at the ends, and thus an exercising-track 340 feet in length was secured. With such an arrangement, no extra stalls were necessary, as the stalls could be cleaned while the horses were being exercised. Water was piped throughout the vessel and convenient faucets facilitated watering. As the horses loaded on the "Tacoma" had been kept standing at outdoor picket-lines day and night for several days before being loaded, 36 cases of pneumonia developed, but out of these only 4 succumbed. The medicine principally used to cure the trouble was acetanilid. The horses were placed aboard by means of the portable loading-box, previously described, and were disembarked the same way. It was found that between 15 and 20 horses could be loaded every hour, per box.

The "Conemaugh" (2000 tons) sailed from San Francisco for Manila on July 11, 1899, with 275 horses. Thirty enlisted men, under a cavalry officer, and a veterinary surgeon, composed the detail to care for the horses. It was found that regular troopers were much more satisfactory for this duty than civilians. However, so arduous was the work on board, which kept this number of men almost continuously at their duties, that it is believed the number of men was insufficient. The "Conemaugh" was a steamship. The slings were rarely used, and then only for such animals as appeared too tired to do without them. The horses were both loaded and unloaded by means of the portable loading-box, before described. The horse was tied in his stall by means of two chains, which were fastened to the side-posts, and attached to the iron ring on each side of the cheek-pieces of the halter. The horses were watered three times daily; once in the morning after general police was over, once about noon, and once in the afternoon, before evening feeding. The feed-boxes were of zinc, and these were filled by means of a

hose at each watering. As part of the horses were accidentally fed two full feeds just before being loaded, several cases of colic occurred; but these all appeared in one
troop only, the horses of which had received the two extra
feeds. The ship was policed thoroughly each morning,
and then disinfected by a solution of 1 pint of chloro-naph-
tholeum to 1 bucket of water, the fluid being liberally
sprinkled throughout the stalls and passage-ways by
means of stable-brooms. Covers were used occasionally
on the horses on deck, but the horses down below. were
found to sweat almost all the time. The animals were fed
hay three times a day, in the feed-boxes; bran was fed
daily for several days; later some oats were given, and the
bran was then given about two or three times a week.
Shortly before arriving at Manila the oat ration was somewhat increased. Vinegar was occasionally used to sponge
out the nostrils, etc., but was not given to the horses.
Grooming was not done, the force of men being too small;
for the same reason no hand-rubbing was done. The
refuse was pulled up to the deck and thrown overboard.
The evening police was not so thorough as that in the
morning, as it was found not necessary. The animals were
given water three times daily, as much as they desired.
Vacant stalls were available, thus enabling the horses to
be put into them while their own stalls were being policed.
As the water from the hosing was found to run through
the floor to the stores below, this was dispensed with, and
the stalls simply scrubbed out with the stable-brooms.
The hay was piled on the upper deck, under cover, and
the oats in the hold, only sufficient being kept up for the
day's feed. The backs were prevented from being burned
by the sun by the roof of the superstructure. The ship
having a plentiful supply of electric lights, these were kept
going day and night below, as it was often very dark there.
The bran and oats were mixed together occasionally, both
equalling about 7 pounds to the feed. Whenever bran
was given alone, it was in the form of a mash. Intestinal
disorders and pneumonia were found to be the most preva-

lent troubles, and the latter almost always fatal. Out of the 275 horses shipped, 13 died on voyage. On ships of this size this was an average percentage; on the larger ships it was less. The windsails down every hatchway were kept constantly going, but when the wind was from the rear, it was found that they sent very little down into the lower-deck stalls; this, however, was remedied by having electric fans below. In spite of all this, however, after reaching the tropics, the heat was terrific. During the work below the troopers had to work stripped to the waist, and the horses sweated profusely. The daily allowance of hay was about 14 pounds or a little more, given in the three feedings; the allowance of grain was never more than 8 pounds. The ship distilled an ample supply of water, but this was not needed. The troopers were housed aft, on the upper deck, and suffered very little, if at all. The stalls were 6 feet 6 inches by 2 feet 2 inches wide, and were simply rows of stanchions fitted with breast- and haunch-pieces, removable, and the horses stood facing inwards (or towards each other). Passage-ways of about 2 feet were left on each side of the ship, to enable the troopers to pass along in cleaning out. Cleats were nailed to the floor to prevent slipping. The breast-, haunch-, and side-pieces on this ship were not padded, but experience demonstrated that it should be done always. The piling of large quantities of baled hay on top of the superstructure caused the vessel to roll very much more than it would have done had these been placed below, and at times it seemed to be positively dangerous.

Many voyages were later made over this 7000-mile journey across the Pacific, and it was demonstrated that large vessels were much more economical than these smaller ones. Some of the large transports carried as many as 800 horses with losses of but 2 or 3 to the ship. In nearly every case the horses were given several days' rest after disembarkation; they were not required to swim ashore, as lighters and docks were available. The methods outlined were found to work very well, so far as loading, unloading, feeding, stalling, policing, ventilation, etc., were concerned, the principal objection being to the small size of the first transports used; this was remedied later on, and the ships fitted up on well-recognized principles, as outlined in the early part of this chapter. Rarely was it necessary to unload the horses directly into the sea and make them swim ashore. At Daiquiri, Cuba, it was necessary to use this method, as no lighters were available. Very few were lost, considering the size of the command. Some of the horses of the Eleventh Volunteer Cavalry were unloaded in this way in the Philippine Islands in 1899, and these were lowered into the sea by means of the portable loading-boxes mentioned, the front side of the box being withdrawn as soon as the box was in the water, and the horse dumped into the sea and towed ashore by small boats. In this disembarkation not an animal was lost. At one time, in the Philippine Islands, a squadron of the Fourth United States Cavalry was unloaded by lowering the horses into the sea with the sling and turning them loose to reach shore, and this was accomplished with the loss of but one animal. Some small boats were here used to tow many of the horses ashore. This transport was one mile from the shore. The greatest loss to which the American service was subjected in its transportation of horses occurred on board the "Aztec," which was proceeding from the United States to Manila in 1899 with 400 horses and mules on board. This vessel encountered a typhoon, and every animal aboard the ship was lost except one mule, which died shortly afterward.

The horse transport "Port Stephens" was a steamship used by the United States between Manila and America and for inter-island transportation. It was at first fitted up somewhat similar to the "Conemaugh," but later the fittings were changed, as experience taught better methods of stalling. During the voyage of this ship from

Manila to Taku, China, with American cavalry horses, the stalls were constructed with solid partitions of smooth-planed lumber; as they extended to the floor, this prevented a horse's getting down and rolling under the feet of or tripping the horse in the adjacent stall. Thus the difficulty of getting a fallen horse onto his feet was much lessened. The haunch- and breast-pieces were entirely done away with, and their places taken by slings constructed of canvas about 9 inches wide, the breast-sling being held in place by a strap over the neck similar to that for adjusting and supporting the collar of a light harness. In a similar manner the haunch-sling was held in place by straps over the flanks; the two slings were held in place by straps along the back, though this was afterward done away with as unnecessary; the ends of the canvas terminated in pieces of strong rope, which were attached to the cleats on the top of the partitions. This "harness" was easily adjusted; the ropes were slackened when the sea was smooth, and when it became rough were tightened so as to give the necessary support to the animal, which, as he rocked back and forth in his slings, was consequently not pounded against breast- and haunch-pieces as formerly provided; the backward and forward movements were greatly reduced, and consequently the chafing against the sides of the stall was reduced to a minimum, rendering padding of the stalls unnecessary. The galvanized iron feed-boxes were done away with, and the animals required to eat hay and grain off the floor of the deck; the forage was eaten up clean, and there was little or no loss due to this method of feeding, and the attendants were spared the work of having to replace the forage thrown out of the small iron feed-boxes previously used.

The "Port Stephens" carried three decks of animals, and on account of the great heat on the lower decks (when in the tropics), the following plan was adopted to give each horse his share of life on the upper decks: By means of a system of ramps, horses could be led without difficulty from one deck to another; the superstructure was sufficiently strong to support as many horses as could be conveniently placed upon it; a section of one of the lower decks was cleared, and the horses led onto the superstructure and groomed, and those on the upper deck were taken below.   In a reasonably smooth sea, these changes were made daily.

The first horse transports were sent to Alaska or to Honolulu, and the horses all unloaded for recreation; but after the work was well understood, this was not done, as it was found that the animals could stand the thirty-days voyage very well, and thus this additional delay and labor was dispensed with.

While the horse transports in the American service will generally be found already fitted up and the stalls built and all arrangements made before the horses are taken aboard, nevertheless a clear idea of what is essential as developed by experience, and the customs and methods employed in loading, unloading, and caring for the horses while aboard, will enable the new cavalry officer to do his part intelligently and successfully and to know what to expect when a sea voyage for his regiment is about to be undertaken.

CHAPTER XIV.

RIDING AND TRAINING.

Purpose of Riding Influences the Seat Used—Seats in General Use
—The Military Seat—Place of Rider—Use of Reins—Importance of Steady Seat—Balance, Friction, and Stirrups—Leaning Back—Leaning Forward—The Spurs—Bridle-wise—Leg-
wise—The Long Stirrup—The Short Stirrup—Posting—Ac-
customing the Horse to Sights and Sounds—To the Bridle,
and Saddle, and Pack—To Firearms—To Jumping—The Riding-Hall—The Single Rein—The Double Rein—The Bit and
Bridoon—The Artificial Gaits a Disadvantage—Necessity for
Patience—Aids in Training—The Cavesson—The Running
Rein—Martingales—The Dumb Jockey.

In the handling of the cavalry horse and his pack,
riding and training have a tremendous influence. Not
all men can become expert riders, and comparatively few
men possess the requisite coolness, patience, and peculiar
disposition of the successful horse-trainer. The service
of the American Cavalry on the great Western plains
and in the wild country of the Rocky Mountains has given
us vast experience in rough-riding in its truest sense, and
placed the American cavalryman ahead of any other cavalry soldier in the world as a hard, long-distance, tireless
horseman, and in such a school men in the American Cavalry surpass even the wonderful Cossack and fully equal
the American cowboy in endurance, while surpassing him
in the training of the horse. True, the writer has seen
many cowboys of the plains ride wild, savage brutes of
horses and remain in the saddle, but such riding and such
methods of training well-bred horses for our cavalry service are not only unnecessary, but would probably ruin
the best horses that enter the ranks, and it is believed
would have a beneficial effect only upon the few stubborn
brutes that occasionally appear. A fine rough-rider may

be a most indifferent horse-trainer and not at all an accomplished horseman. In the cattle country, where the
cowboy finds his work, his methods are the result of much
hard experience. Equally, the methods known in the
Cavalry for the riding and training of the man and horse
are the intelligent deductions from experience, and it is a
knowledge of these cavalry methods that is essential to
the young cavalryman. These methods are not perfectly
learned in one or two years of experience only; time and
hard work count for more than anything else in qualifying
as a cavalryman, and much careful training must be gone
through, besides the rougher but indispensable field service.

The best riders are almost invariably men who have
been accustomed to riding and handling horses nearly all
their lives. Occasionally men learn to ride well even
after they commence as late in life as twenty-five or thirty
years of age, but the seat and carriage of these men rarely
if ever equal that of the man who began riding as a boy—
who has "grown up in the saddle," as it were. The man
who learned his riding early in life and has kept at it usually possesses a remarkably light bridle-hand and has a
seat very erect and wholly lacking in pose or constraint,
while the other class of riders often use their reins more
or less as a support, frequently lean forward or backward,
turn in their heels, especially at the more rapid gaits,
stick out their toes to the front, and often exhibit absurd
ill temper and impatience if the horse does not, at all gaits
and times and places, travel as evenly as an automobile.

The purpose of the riding largely influences the style
of seat used. There are many different styles of riding, many of these styles possessing much to recommend
them as good; each style has a large following, sometimes whole nations or tribes of splendid riders using a
seat held in unjust contempt by the advocates of other
styles. Nothing is more unreasonable than to condemn
a seat adopted by a particular class of riders, without
trial. The jockey, riding well forward, his bridle-hand
low, on a saddle in which lightness is the chief virtue and

necessity, uses a seat wholly unlike the low, firm seat of the cowboy or American cavalryman in his strong saddle. The gentleman rider of the East, following to hounds, uses a light, strongly made saddle and a comparatively short stirrup, and a seat very much unlike either that of the jockey or the cavalryman. He would cut a sorry figure on a wild, bucking Western pony in his little saddle, but in his place his seat and saddle are what experience has shown to be the best. Likewise the cavalryman employs a seat found, by rough, long years of hard riding and much training, to be the best for the work he has to perform. His military seat differs in many ways from each of the others. Each class of riders adopts that seat and saddle and method of training their horses found by them in actual practice to best accord with the object of the riding, and each is largely correct in his own sphere. Toleration for the methods of riding used should not be withheld, as many points among the various styles are excellent and some exactly alike.

Among the best known styles of seats now used are a few that will illustrate how great a difference exists in styles of riding. The seats here considered are the "fork" seat, the "tongs across the wall" seat, the "hunting" seat, sometimes called the "long" or "chair" seat, and the "military" seat.

The "fork" seat may be said to be the typical cowboy seat; the legs hang straight down, the knees only slightly bent, but not stiff; stirrups long and often the toes depressed somewhat, and the rider rests in his saddle more on his "crotch" than on his buttocks, clinching the horse firmly with the flat inside part of the thigh; the rider is usually very erect, and yet wholly lacking in constraint. This seat is used by a large class of acknowledged rough-riders, and is frequently seen among cavalrymen; it is a very secure seat; its advocates claim it to be the strongest seat known and are very loyal to it, and claim that the extra clinching necessary ceases to be tiresome after the seat is once thoroughly learned and becomes natural. There would *seem* to be a tendency, in using this seat, to lean forward, but experienced riders using it for years never do so. Should the horse stumble or stop suddenly, there might be danger of the rider falling somewhat forward and injuring himself, but the advocates of the seat claim that the extra clinching is strong enough always to overcome this. As the legs hang down almost perpendicularly from the horse's sides, the feet are well away from the horse's flanks. The position of the feet

THE "FORK" SEAT.

when in close ranks would probably subject the rider to having his legs kicked in by adjacent riders, and for this faulty position of the feet, viewed from a *cavalry* standpoint, there appears no remedy except to put the man using it in the line of file-closers. For individual riding, when not crowded in among a line of troopers, this seat possesses much that is strong, secure, and suitable for long-distance rides, and, in fact, it has been so used in

the American West many years. In the cowboy saddle
this seat can more readily be assumed than in either the
English or "McClellan" saddles, as the stirrups in the
former hang from the center of the saddle instead of from
a point somewhat farther forward, as in the two latter
saddles.

THE ' TONGS ACROSS THE WALL'' SEAT.

The "tongs across the wall" seat is used largely by
inexperienced riders and rarely by good ones. Its chief
characteristic consists in keeping the knees stiff and
straight and sticking the feet out to the front. Whenever the trot is taken up, it is necessary to materially alter
the position of the legs, and in fact the entire position of
the seat changes, owing to the difficulty of clinching with

the thighs while keeping the legs stuck out stiffly.   Riders who use this seat generally manage to ride horses possessing easy gaits, especially at the trot.   When using this seat,

FRONT VIEW, "TONGS ACROSS THE WALL" SEAT.

there is a tendency to lean back, thus boring the cantle of the saddle into the horse's back—in fact, it is next to impossible to ride at an increased gait and lean any other way in this seat. Among even good riders this seat is occasionally seen on parade and at reviews, it being especially a "pose" seat. Some men in a troop learn this seat and they hold to it persistently, despite constant

THE "HUNTING" SEAT.

efforts to teach them its inadaptability for cavalry riding. The seat, like the "fork" seat, though to a much greater extent, is not only uncomfortable to the rider when in line, but is very exasperating to the adjacent men, who, before the drill is over, generally manage to kick the man's legs and feet repeatedly, to break him of it. It may be taken for individual riding out of ranks, but the rider who attempts to use it in a cavalry troop will suffer many hard kicks and jolts and be the recipient of much hard swearing from his comrades.

The "hunting" seat, known also as the "long" or "chair" seat, is the typical cross-country seat when riding after hounds or in park-riding, and, in its place, is found to be very excellent, especially where jumping of four-barred country fences forms such a particular part of the riding. In this seat it is customary for the rider to hold the reins, together, with both hands. This is impossible in the "military" seat, where the trooper needs one hand for his weapons at all times. The stirrup used with the saddle usually employed by these riders is of steel and open. The hooded stirrup of the American cavalryman would be unwieldy and unnecessarily bulky on this saddle, while it has always been one of the parts of our military saddle especially held to; and for keeping the trooper's feet dry and shielded from the cold and wet of his long rides, as well as for the safety to the rider, the hood is an important part of the military saddle, and affects the seat in a way, by defining the length of foot that can enter the stirrup, while with the open steel stirrup of the hunting saddle the foot usually goes in clear to the heel of the riding-boot. In the "hunting" seat the rider rests well down on his buttocks, the thigh is extended forward, generally at an angle somewhat more obtuse than that of the horse's shoulder; the leg from the knee to the ankle is loose and straight down, and if inclining in either direction, generally somewhat forward; the stirrup is very short, and the heel of the rider's foot is considerable lower than his toe; the calf of the leg touches the sides of the horse, and it will be observed that this is the only one of the seats described in which this is the case; the calf does not *press* against the horse, but, owing to the entire seat and the short stirrup, it touches slightly, especially when jumping or galloping. In this respect

the "hunting" seat resembles the Indian seat somewhat,
except that in the Indian seat the leg from the knee down
is drawn back and the heels touch the horse's flanks when
the rider is, as the Indian generally is, riding without a
saddle.

The "military" seat in the American Cavalry (see
Frontispiece) is the result of years and years of hard riding
on the vast Western plains, and is well calculated to have

REGULATION SEAT, WITH LEG TOO STRAIGHT AND
HEEL TOO LOW.

the best effect on both horse and rider of any seat known
for long rides, singly or in column, and for all drill purposes when security of seat, closeness of legs and feet, use
of one hand, and comfort to the rider and his adjacent
trooper comrades are considered. In this seat the rider
sits evenly on his buttocks, inclining neither forward nor
backward; the elbows are reasonably close to the body
and somewhat drawn back; the reins are carried together

in the left hand, thus leaving the right hand free; the thigh is nearly parallel to the slope of the horse's shoulder; the leg from the knee down to the ankle is loose and straight down, and the heel is slightly lower than the toe, which is inserted in the hooded stirrup so that the ball of the foot rests on the stirrup tread; the rider's back is straight, head erect, and chin slightly drawn in without constraint. It is especially taught to keep the toes parallel to the sides of the horse, and thus the heels and spurs do not touch the animal's flanks except when the rider uses them intentionally. This latter position of the feet, it may be remarked, is difficult to acquire, and many men neglect it and apparently fail to appreciate its two excellent purposes—of keeping the spurs and heels out of the horse's flanks and keeping the flat of the thigh against the horse. The stirrup used with this seat is such that the rider, by standing up in them, can pass two or three fingers between his crotch and the saddle. The American cavalryman is disposed to use the long stirrup, and even in our correct regulation seat the length of the stirrup is much longer than that of any seat used in European cavalry, but experience has taught us that this length of stirrup is the most satisfactory one to use, especially on long marches.

The seats used in the various European cavalry services are more like that of the "hunting" seat, before described, than any other, and it is a general practice to use the short stirrup; the saddle used, being low and flat, with a covered seat of leather, enables the rider to assume this seat with much more comfort than can be done in the "McClellan" saddle; in fact, the correct "hunting" seat is almost an impossibility in the "McClellan" saddle, owing to the high cantle. The short stirrup is not used by any of those classes of riders who have bcome famous the world over for their hard rough-riding, excepting the Cossacks of Russia, who still adhere to it. However, as the Cossack rides in a saddle considerably above the back of his horse, this short stirrup is probably necessary. On the other hand, the use of a stirrup too long will, of necessity, subject the rider to much pounding, and though many men use it, they acknowledge that the pounding is harder; but, on the other hand, they claim that the entire seat is more secure, especially in the "fork" seat.

The best seat will be that in which balance, friction, and stirrups are combined in the right degree. To ride by balance alone would be very exhausting. To illustrate this, watch a recruit taking his first bare-backed lessons, before he has learned to use friction. Clinching the horse with the thighs, or "friction," as it is called, comes naturally and almost unconsciously as the result of training. At first requiring considerable effort, the rider gradually learns how to clinch without tiring himself, and eventually his clinching becomes very powerful without tiring him. The writer remembers a Western rider with one wooden leg who declared that he had such power of clinching with his thighs on the horse's sides that he felt satisfied that he could still ride should he lose the other leg. The leg that was gone had been amputated years before, from the knee down, and from what was seen of this man's riding, it is very likely that this rider could have done what he said. The early saddles possessed no stirrups, and the riders of those days must have been very perfect riders, using only balance and friction, judging from many authenticated accounts in military history; but gradually experience taught riders the world over that stirrups saved them much unnecessary fatigue by bearing the weight of the legs and feet, and also made the seat more secure in every way. The use of stirrups on all saddles, military or civilian, has now become universal, and their adjustment is a matter of great importance in riding and training, both as affects man and horse.

The proper length of stirrup will not be the same for any two men, as men differ in length of leg and in size too much. A man having a long, thin, flat leg will require a longer stirrup than a man having a short, fat, round leg, and no arbitrary length should be required for all troopers. A good method for securing the proper length

is to hold the bottom of the stirrup-tread under the left
arm with the right hand, snug in to the arm-pit, and then
place the left hand, fingers extended, on the "D" ring
(stirrup-loop) of the saddle, and then straightening out
the left arm until the length of the stirrup thus measured
corresponds with the length of the left arm placed as

THE "BARBER-CHAIR" SEAT.

described. When the trooper is in the saddle, he should
be able to place two fingers between his crotch and the
saddle as he stands in his stirrups. All the men in the
troop should be required to ride with a *reasonably* uniform
length of stirrup; otherwise some of them will affect a

length of stirrup both unsightly to look at and absurd as regards the particular troopers.

Both the Romans and the Greeks were ignorant of the use of stirrups, and either vaulted on their horses or used the back of a slave as a stepping-stone, or sometimes had recourse to a short ladder. The earliest time when it can be proved that the stirrup was in use was in the time of the Norman invasion of England. The incidents of this event were depicted upon the Bayeaux tapestry by the wife of William the Conqueror, and on this the stirrup was shown, according to the authority of Bérenger, as a part of the trappings of the horse.

The position of the rider in the saddle is most important, because of its quick effect on the horse. If the rider leans back, his weight bores down upon the cantle, which in turn bores down upon the horse's back under the cantle, and the result, especially on the march, is a very sore-backed animal at least; the contrary fault of leaning forward causes the additional weight to bore into the horse's back under the pommel, in the region of the withers where several large, strong muscles and tendons are located, a free action of which is absolutely necessary at all gaits. The result of this leaning forward is not only a sore-backed horse, but probably it will also stiffen the animal up for weeks, especially if this fault exists during long marches. Leaning forward also makes the seat more insecure, and any stumbling or stopping of the horse at once throws the rider forward. The rider in the Cavalry should realize that the pommel and cantle on the "McClellan" military saddle are put there for the purpose of holding the pack up off the horse's back, and not as a means of support to the rider. The rider should sit in the middle of the saddle, erect, and support himself wholly by balance, friction, and stirrups. The pommel and cantle and reins should be used for what they are intended, and the seat of the rider should not depend upon them. The reins especially should be used only to guide the horse, and never as a support for the man on the horse's back. The continual sawing on the horse's mouth is a sure way of ruining the horse and tiring the rider, who not infrequently relieves his feelings by a sharp, savage tug at the reins.

The manner of riding known as "posting," whereby the rider rises at the trot, is much used in civil life and even in some European cavalry services; but, although permitted by our Cavalry Drill Regulations as a change from our close seat when in the field, is never so used, and has never found favor with American cavalry officers or troopers. Those who have thoroughly learned it speak highly of it as a seat both easy and simple, and not by any means the hard work to use that it is generally believed. Whether or not this "posting" is easy or hard on the horse has never been satisfactorily demonstrated, because no one ever has maintained it for long-distance riding. While perhaps good in park riding for pleasure, for short distances, in English saddles, this seat does not lend itself to long, hard rides, yet much praise is bestowed upon it by some European cavalry services.

The close seat is the typical American cavalry seat. There are many men, however, who never wholly acquire this close seat, but the mistake must not be made of thinking that the man who leaves the saddle more or less at the trot is a poor rider; on the contrary, many men leave the saddle somewhat at every trotting stride of the horse, and yet are excellent hard riders of record. The slight leaving of the saddle referred to, however, is very different from the awkward "bouncing" of the inexperienced rider, which is readily recognized wherever seen. Until the rider is himself proficient, he can do little but irritate the horse, and for this reason the recruit should be given a different horse every day, to enable the horse he rode the day before to recover from the awkward handling he has received. The recruit will learn more quickly to ride if given a different horse each day, although it will be hard upon him; but to ride well one must ride many different horses, hard ones and easy ones, and not confine himself to one particular animal. The gait of every horse is different from the gait of every other horse, and thus the rider learns the various forms of movement, and understands what is meant by a "hard trotter" and an "easy trotter"; until the rider has acquired skill and confidence and has had much experience in actual riding and handling of horses, he is not capable of training a horse, and

INTERIOR OF AN AMERICAN RIDING-HALL.

should not be allowed to do so except under experienced troopers.

Training.—In training the cavalry horse for his work in the troop, care, patience, and skill must be constantly exercised. The "riding-hall" exercises, which form so large a part of the winter training in garrison to-day, do much to accustom the new horse to the sights and sounds and work in the Cavalry. To this is added the troop drill in summer on the drill-ground out-doors, and then comes target practice and "mounted pistol practice"; later on parades, reviews, etc., all are gone through, and the horse gradually grows accustomed to the fluttering of flags, the playing and passing of bands, the galloping of many horses near him, the reports of firearms around him and then from his own back. As soon as the new horse is received in the regiment, he is assigned to a troop according to color; the troop commander then assigns the horse to an experienced, well-trained rider, and so far as practicable the horse is ridden by no one but his own rider thereafter. This assigning of a horse to a trooper has two good effects—the horse and rider rapidly get to know each other, and the trooper, knowing the horse is for him alone, will exert himself in many ways to teach the horse his work; it also gives the trooper a strong sense of proprietorship in the animal, and very frequently a strong fondness springs up between the man and his horse, and all this helps in the horse's care and training. Officers cannot be too careful in taking horses away from the men who have ridden and trained them, for it does much to discourage the man and ruin the horse. It is re-markable how fond many troopers become of their partic-ular mounts. The writer has known troopers to buy their horses, when sold at auction, out of their own little pay, rather than see them go to some stranger. This sentiment is one that the young officer coming to a cavalry troop is not at first apt to fully appreciate, and he may make changes, without meaning to wound his men, that will cause men to be discontented during the remainder of their enlistment in the troop.

As soon as the new horse is assigned to a troop, he is turned loose among the other troop-horses in the troop "corral," and in a few days establishes himself among them. At first the old troop-horses, like human beings, watch the new animal, and sometimes one or two kick and bite at him; but the young healthy horse generally dis-plays sufficient fighting qualities during the first few days to compel them to refrain. A stall is assigned the new horse in the troop stable, usually so that he will have an old troop-horse for a stall-companion; the horses in American cavalry stables usually stand in double stalls in pairs. The new horse is walked around the garrison at "horse exercise," and this accustoms him gradually to the unusual sights and sounds of a military garrison. Each day he is taken to the riding-hall or "bull-ring" (an outdoor elliptical track resembling the track in the riding-hall), in company with the other new horses and a few old troop-horses, and here he is put through the "bending" lessons, the gaits, and is taught to lie down, to respond to the snaffle-bit and reins, to understand the spurs and use of the legs, etc. Gradually he reaches the stage of saddling, and is carefully put through that; then comes jumping the ditch and hurdle, with and without the saddle; and he is taught to lead. When accustomed to the snaffle-bit and reins, the curb-bit and bridle are put on and he is gradually accustomed to their use. While almost all foreign cavalry services use the double-reined bridle known as the "bit and bridoon," the American Cavalry use only a single bit and rein. While the double-reined bridle has many points of excellence to recommend it for cavalry use, nevertheless the single rein and curb-bit are very simple, the reins are easily adjusted in the hand, and the weight is less. There are some horses who will not learn to take the curb-bit without careful training, and these animals should be handled gently, that their mouths be not injured. Roughness in teaching the new horse to take the curb-bit often results in his never readily taking it, probably through anticipated pain learned in his training days. The spurs must be used sparingly, and never but at the right moment; when the reason for using them at the time has passed, they should not be allowed to touch the horse as the legs swing. The constant pricking of his flanks with the spurs only excites him and accomplishes nothing. The writer has for some time ridden a well-trained, intelligent horse accustomed to cavalry work;

which rushes forward excitedly whenever the rider's heels
approach his flanks, through fear of the spurs, probably
learned years ago, and from which the horse has never recovered. If the spurs are permitted to touch the flanks
by careless riders, the horse may gradually become callous to their touch, and when used for a proper purpose,
will not respond to them without being forced to do so by
the rider using them fiercely.

The best and most patient riders in the troop should
be used in handling the new cavalry horse, and the training should always be under the immediate and *active*
supervision of an officer; absence of the officer altogether
is better than his inactive presence; if he is careless and
indifferent, the men are very apt to be more or less so,
and some of them perhaps actually brutal at times. It
must be appreciated, in detailing troopers for this training of the new horse, that, as has been said above, the
best rough-rider in the troop may not be the best trainer,
and, in fact, may not be fit to train the new cavalry horse
at all. The system of training, as briefly outlined above,
and as contained in full in the American Cavalry Drill
Regulations, is the one used in our service, and is known
as the "Rarey" system of training; it has been used for
many years with excellent results. The originator of this
system of horse-training was an American named Rarey.
In company with a Mr. Goodenough, he developed his system and used it to such excellent advantage that he not
only made considerable money out of it, but placed a system of horse-training before the public that has been
used, especially by the Cavalry, ever since, with some
modifications. The year 1858 was a memorable one for
the horse-trainers and horsemen of England, as in that
year Rarey introduced his system into that country at a
charge of £25,000, which the English horsemen paid. The
Rarey system was founded upon three ideas: first,
that the horse is so constituted by Nature that he will
not offer resistance to any demand made of him which
he fully comprehends, if made in a way consistent

with the laws of his nature; second, that he has no consciousness of his strength beyond his experience, and can be handled according to man's will without force; third, that man can, in compliance with the laws of the horse's nature (by which he examines all things new to him), take any object, however frightful, around, over, under, or on him, that does not inflict pain, without causing him to fear. Needless to say, Rarey and his partner were required to subdue many ferocious horses before he could make horsemen believe in his ideas and methods, and some of the horses he broke from restless, fierce brutes into gentle, easily managed animals proved the worth of his system very thoroughly. A full outline of the Rarey system would require a book in itself. Most of the methods employed by Rarey are used in the American cavalry service to-day, and have been quite thoroughly tested by actual use.

As has been stated in a previous chapter, training the cavalry horse in any of the artificial gaits is not only unnecessary, but is a positive disadvantage, and should not be done. The time spent on the regular, legitimate training will fully occupy both horse and rider without attempting to teach things of no cavalry value.

As in the United States cavalry service but a few new horses are, as a rule, received in the troop at a time, it is possible in each troop to entrust their education to a few picked men, who should not be changed until the horses are sufficiently instructed to take their places in the rank. Restlessness and impatience in the horse frequently arise from an exuberance of spirits or playfulness, which must be carefully distinguished from that which arises from viciousness and timidity. When restless, the horse should be handled quietly until he becomes calm; when submissive after punishment, he should be treated kindly. The power and qualities of the horse can best be brought out by kindness and encouragement; if harsh treatment is adopted, he will become timid, then sullen, and, at length, violent and unmanageable.

The first object to be attained in training the horse is to render him gentle and tractable; this is done by slow, progressive lessons. All proper means must be employed, such as feeding, handling, patting him, taking up his feet, etc., and the practice of the longe. When the horse will allow his feet to be readily handled and lifted, the trooper should practice gently tapping them, to accustom him to the action of shoeing. In entering the stalls and moving about the new horses, the men should speak to them quietly and endeavor to inspire confidence in the animal that no harm is intended. As many of the new horses are entirely unused to the Army forage and methods of feeding, the men looking to their training must exercise care, else digestive disorders may result. By commencing with the larger part of the ration consisting of hay and bran, and gradually increasing the ration to the regulation amount, the horse will gradually be brought to the habit of eating the service ration without injury.

From the time of their arrival the new horses should be exercised at least one or two hours each day in the open air; for this purpose the new horse is equipped with the halter only and led by a trooper who is mounted upon an old troop-horse. After a few days, a snaffle-bit may be placed in the horse's mouth, with the reins tied loosely and allowed to lie on the horse's neck.

In the training of the cavalry horse there are some appliances used that are well known, easy of manufacture and adjustment, and very efficacious in their results. Among these are the "cavesson and longeing rein," the "running rein," the "dumb jockey," and throwing-straps.

The Cavesson and Longe.—The cavesson is a light halter with the brow-band, throat-latch, and cheek-pieces like the bridle head-stall, and has a nose-band that may be adjusted with a buckle. A ring in which to fasten the longeing-strap is attached to the front part of the nose-band about 2 inches in front of each cheek-piece square; there is sometimes a running ring in the chin-strap for the

longe. The longeing-strap is from 20 to 30 feet long.
The lariat may be used.

The snaffle bridle having been properly fitted, the
horse should be encouraged and the cavesson put on.
The nose-band should be placed about 3 inches above
the nostrils, so as not to affect the horse's breathing; it

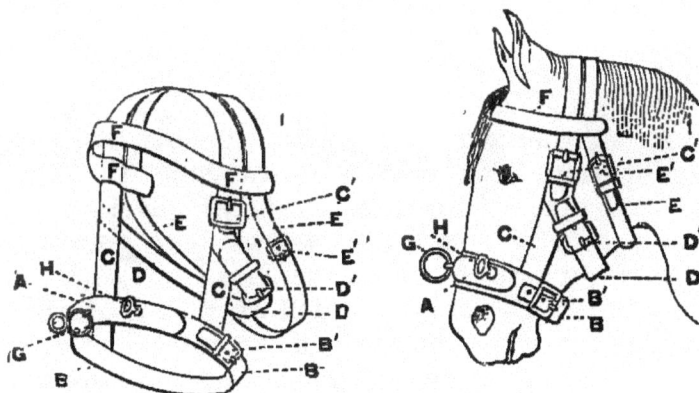

THE CAVESSON AND LONGE ON HORSE AND OFF.

A, Cavesson proper, which is a piece of iron bent to the general shape of
the horse's nose, and covered with leather, stitched to the band B, which
is tightened to the required degree by the buckle B'. In the front (center) of A is the ring G, to which the longeing-rein is buckled, and on
the sides the terrets H, H, to which reins may be attached for use by
mounted men.
B. Back strap to adjust cavesson A by buckle B'.
C, Cheek-pieces of head-stall, which can be adjusted to suit size of horse's
head by buckle C'.
D, Strap stitched to cheek-piece C of head-stall, to prevent them from work-
ing forward into the horse's eyes.
E, Throat latch.
F, Brow-band, the ends of which are turned over and stitched, so as to
allow the head-stall, cheek-pieces, strap C, and throat latch E to slip
through in adjusting them.
G, Ring in front of cavesson to which longeing-rein is attached.
H, H Terrets, ridged, for use when horse is mounted.
B', Buckle of back-strap B.
C', Buckle of head-stall to adjust same.
D', Buckle to adjust strap D.
E', Buckle to adjust throat-latch.

should act both as a nose-band and curb, and should go
over the snaffle. It must not be buckled so tightly as to
make the horse uneasy. An additional strap from cheek-
piece to cheek-piece under the jaw-bone will keep the
cavesson back from his eyes. These preparations should

be made with great care, so as not to alarm the horse.

The first lesson to teach the new horse is to go forward. Until he does this freely, nothing else should be required of him. When he obeys freely, he should occasionally be stopped and caressed.

The practice of the longe is to supple and teach the horse the free action and proper use of the legs with regard to his cavalry work; it thus aids in forming his gaits and in fitting him for the service.

This first lesson should be begun on a circle from 15 to 20 feet in diameter. As horses are usually fed, watered, saddled, and led from the near side, they are inclined to lead better from that than the off side. It will, therefore, generally be found necessary to give two lessons on the right side to one on the left.

If the horse hesitates or stands still when he is ordered to move on, he should be encouraged, as such hesitation oftener comes from fear or ignorance as to what is required than from obstinacy or vice.

The horse is first led several times around the circle at a walk. A man with a whip follows at a short distance and shows the whip occasionally, if the horse is inclined to hang back; if this does not produce the desired effect, he should strike the ground in rear of the horse and at length touch him lightly with the whip until he obeys. After he has begun to move freely at the walk, the man holding the longe should gently urge him to trot and gradually lengthen the rein, so that the horse may scarcely notice it. He should continue to go round the circle at an active pace nearly opposite the horse's shoulder, so as to keep him out and press him forward.

If the horse takes kindly to this lesson, the man holding the longe may lengthen it by degrees until he has only to turn in the same spot, the man with the whip being careful to keep the horse out to the line of the circle. Should the horse break his pace or plunge, the rein should be shaken horizontally, without jerking, until he returns to the trot. The trooper holding the longeing-rein should have a light and easy hand. For the first two or three days the horse must not be urged too much; if he goes gently, without jumping or resisting, enough is accomplished. He should be longed to the right, left, and right again, changing from the trot to the walk and back again in each case. He should be frequently halted by gently feeling the reins and speaking to him, and at the conclusion of each lesson the rein should be carefully shortened and gathered up in the hand and the horse led to the center of the circle and caressed before being dismissed.

After a few days of the above practice, the horse may be urged a little more in the trot, but the greatest care and attention and patience are requisite to teach him to use his limbs without straining them; much harm may be done in this instruction by a sudden jerk or a too forcible pull on the longe. Care must be taken that the lessons are not made so long as to fatigue or fret the horse; at first they should be short, and gradually increased in length as the instruction progresses. The man holding the longeing-rein should take it short in one hand, at the same time patting and rubbing the horse about the head and neck with the other; he should then try to bend the horse's neck a little to the right and then to the left by means of the longeing-rein; the bend should be in the very poll of the neck, and this exercise should be repeated at the end of each lesson, cautiously and by slow degrees, until the horse responds easily. This will greatly facilitate the future instruction of the animal. The longe is used to instruct new horses, especially the timid ones, to jump the bar and ditch.

The use of the "war bridle" has been known to cavalrymen for many years, and will be found of great value in training during the first few months. The illustrations show clearly how to adjust it, either in the ordinary form or in a second form; and its use will often assist materially in the training and produce gratifying results.

Bending Lessons.—Before beginning the bending lessons, it is well to give the horse a preparatory one of obedience, to make him sensible of the power man has over him. This first act of submission will prove of great service; it makes the horse quiet and gives him confidence, and gives the man such ascendency as to prevent the horse at the outset from resisting the means employed to bring him

FIRST FORM WAR BRIDLE ON HORSE.

under control. However, this lesson must be one that will not frighten or abuse him, and the following method is frequently used:

Go up to the horse, pat him on the neck and speak to him; then take the reins off the horse's neck and hold them at a few inches from the rings of the snaffle-bit with the left hand; take such a position as to offer as much resistance as possible to the horse should he attempt to break away; hold the whip in the right hand with the point down; raise the whip quietly and tap the horse on the breast. The horse naturally tries to move back to avoid the whip; follow the horse, at the same time pull-

SECOND FORM WAR BRIDLE ON HORSE, FIRST POSITION.

ing against him and continuing the use of the whip. Be careful to show no sign of anger nor any symptom of yielding. The horse, tired of trying ineffectually to avoid the whip, soon ceases to pull and moves forward; then drop the point of the whip and make much of him. This repeated once or twice usually proves sufficient.

The horse, having found how to avoid the punishment, no longer waits for the application of the whip, but anticipates it by moving up at the slightest gesture.

The "running-rein" is of great value in teaching the horse to keep his head in a proper position and affords valuable aid in his first handling; if judiciously used, it saves the rider a great deal of trouble and the horse much ill-

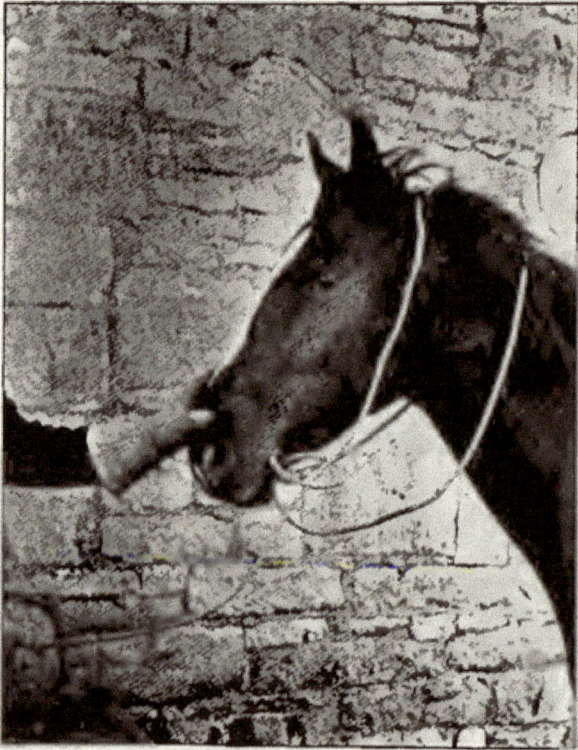

SECOND FORM WAR BRIDLE, SECOND POSITION.

usage and simplifies the subject of "bits and bitting"; it is especially useful in controlling horses that are inclined to bolt. As it can be used to advantage both before and during the "bending lessons," it is described here: It should act directly on the snaffle-bit itself and is wholly independent of reins. The running-rein consists of three parts—the chin-strap, rein, and martingale. The chin-strap, about 6 to 8 inches long, on which is suspended a loose ring, is fastened to both snaffle-bit rings. The martingale has only one ring; the loop through which the girth passes is made adjustable by a buckle. The martingale is so adjusted that when taut the ring will

SECOND FORM WAR BRIDLE, THIRD POSITION, COMPLETE AND CORRECTLY ADJUSTED.

be on a level with the points of the horse's shoulders. The running-rein is about 8½ feet long; one end is buckled into the near pommel-ring; the free end is then passed through the martingale-ring from rear to front, thence through the chin-strap-ring from left to right, thence through the martingale-ring from front to rear,

and is held in the rider's right hand.   A pull on this running-rein will act directly on the mouth-piece, drawing it
back and somewhat downward toward the horse's breast-
bone.

The "bending lessons" should be given to the horse
each day so long as the snaffle-bit is used alone; but the
exercise should be varied, so that the horse may not

BENDING HEAD TO THE RIGHT.

become fatigued or disgusted. The balance of the horse's
body and his lightness in hand depend on the proper
carriage of his head and neck. A young or new horse
usually tries to resist the bit either by bending his neck
to one side, by setting his jaw against the bit, or by carrying his nose too high or too low. The bending lessons
serve to make a horse manageable by teaching him to

conform to the movements of the reins and to yield to the pressure of the bit. During the lessons the horse must never be hurried. They should first be taught dismounted and afterwards mounted.

To Bend the Horse's Head and Neck to the Right.— Take a position on the near side of the horse, in front of his shoulder and facing toward his neck; take the off

BENDING HEAD TO THE LEFT.

rein close up to the bit in the right hand, the near rein in the same way with the left hand, the thumbs toward each other, the little fingers outward; bring the right hand toward the body and at the same time extend the left arm so as to turn the horse's head to the right. The force employed must be gradual and proportioned to the resistance met with, and care must be taken not to bring the horse's nose too close to his chest. If the horse move backward, continue the pressure until, finding it impossible to avoid the restraint imposed by the bit, he stands still and yields to it. When the bend is complete, the horse holds his head without any restraint and champs

RAISING THE HEAD.

the bit; then make much of him; and let him resume his natural position by degrees, without throwing his head around hurriedly. A horse, as a rule, champs the bit when he ceases to resist. The horse's head and neck are bent to the left in a similar manner, the man standing on the off side.

To Arch the Horse's Neck.—The trooper takes the position of "stand to horse," crosses the reins behind the horse's jaw, taking the near rein in the right hand and the off rein in the left hand, at about 6 inches from the rings, and draws them across each other till the horse gives way to the pressure and brings his nose in; prevent the horse from raising his head by lowering the hands; when the

LOWERING THE HEAD.

horse gives way to the cross-pressure of the reins, ease the hands and make much of him.

To Make the Horse Lower His Head.—The trooper now mounts the horse, and, taking the right rein in the right hand and the left rein in the left hand, lightly feels the mouth of the horse; then, holding the hands low, he plays with the bit, gently drawing in the reins as the horse drops his nose. When the horse, opening his mouth, yields the lower jaw to the bit and brings in his head so that the face is vertical to the ground, the rider releases the tension of the reins and caresses the horse for his obedience. By degrees, the horse can be taught to lower his head to any extent.

To Make the Horse Elevate His Head.— The rider induces the horse to elevate his head by holding the reins separated, as described above, and, with arms extended forward, makes slight pulls upward upon the reins. When the horse has obeyed, the rider lowers his hands, so that the horse can lower his muzzle, and he then requires the face of the animal to be brought into the vertical position.

Throwing the Horse.—Throwing the horse is a personal contest in which the horse is made to realize man's power over him, and this is most important. The horse must learn to lie down, and frequently has to be thrown at drill or when surgical operations are necessary. During each drill every horse is thrown or made to lie down three or four times and in exceptional cases oftener. The application of the system is at first confined to simply throwing the horse or making him lie down of his own accord. The horse is equipped with the watering bridle and surcingle; the surcingle is buckled securely, not tightly, around the horse's body just back of the withers. The horse is taken to an open space, preferably covered with turf, free from stones, sticks, glass, etc., to prevent injuring the horse. The trooper is provided with two stout leather straps, known as "No. 1" and "No. 2." "No. 1" is about 10 feet long, and one end of it is made into a loop or has an iron ring sewed fast. "No. 2" is about $3\frac{1}{2}$ feet long, and from $1\frac{1}{2}$ to 2 inches wide. One end of this short strap has a buckle and two keepers, one on each side of the strap; in the absence of the two straps, the halter-strap may be used for "No. 1" and the stirrup-strap for "No. 2."

In using these straps the long strap is put once around the pastern of the off fore leg, the foot being put through the loop in the end of this strap; the end of this strap is then passed up beside the horse on the off side, under the surcingle (or through a ring sewn in the surcingle so as to be on the top of the horse's back), and then carried to the near side and held in the hands of the trooper who is to do the throwing. The short strap is used to tie the horse's near fore leg up, and this should be done securely and fairly tightly, for the horse will strain with much strength to get this foot loose when he is being thrown.

THE HORSE READY TO BE THROWN.

As soon as the two straps are adjusted as described, the trooper, with the end of the long strap in his hand, takes position on the near side of the horse and somewhat in the rear, about opposite his croup. The other men then step away, and the rider urges his horse to step forward; as the horse does so the trooper pulls on the long strap, flexing the off fore leg up against the horse's belly; the animal comes down upon his knees, and may plunge sev-

eral times before taking this position for any length of
time. As soon as the horse ceases to plunge, the trooper
leans back on his long strap, and gradually the animal
will lie down upon the near side. To make the horse lie
down upon the off side, put the short strap upon the off
fore leg and the long one on the near pastern, the trooper

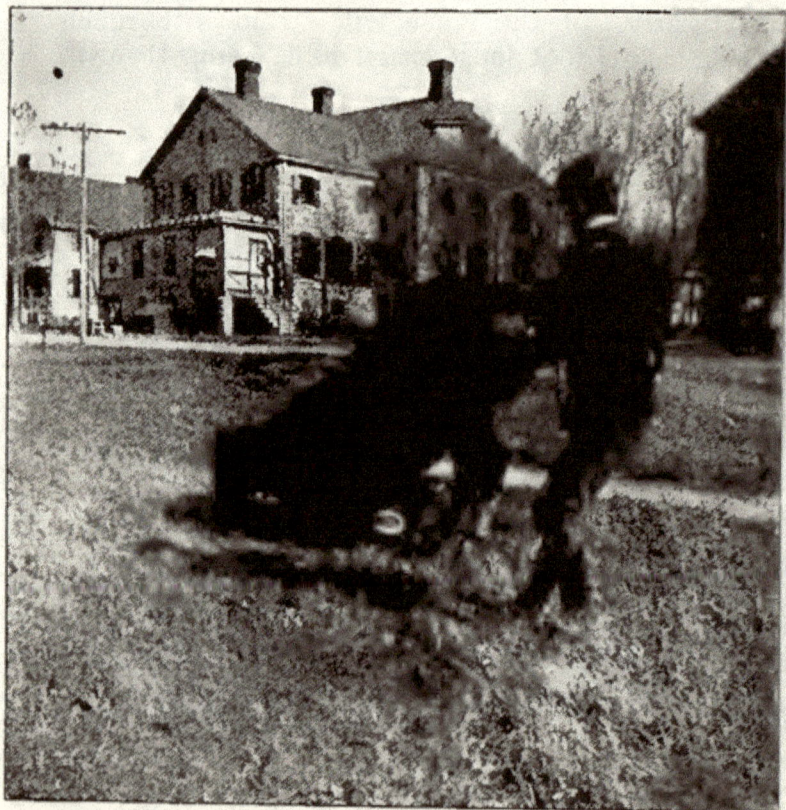

THE HORSE ON HIS KNEES.

taking his position on the off side near the horse's croup.
This method is one of the best and most successful
known, and is used in the Cavalry constantly. Before
the horse is allowed to rise, the straps should be removed
from his legs, and he should never be allowed to rise

with them on. While the horse is down, much must be
made of him. As some horses will attempt to rise as soon
as they are thrown, the following method for holding
them on the ground is successful and easy: Pass the
snaffle-reins under the surcingle, pulling the horse's head
to the right if lying upon his left side, and then carry
the reins somewhat forward and hold them in the hand.

THROWN.

The horse in this position cannot rise. While making the
horse lie down, the trooper should repeatedly command
"Down!" and as the horse gets up the trooper should
command "Up!" The horse will, after some practice,
become so accustomed to these commands that as soon
as his head is pulled to the right he will lie down. If the

horse has been well trained to lie down, he may be made to lie down by merely lifting his near fore leg up, at the same time carrying the reins of the bridle over the horse's head and together to the right and across the horse's back, thus turning his head to the right. The trooper remains on the near side in the above ways. One man can generally manage one horse. The long strap should be plenty long

METHOD OF HOLDING THE HORSE DOWN BY THE REINS.

enough, sufficiently so to allow the trooper to stand some feet away from the horse as he goes down, for the horse may plunge when his off fore leg is pulled up, and the trooper will be pulled against the horse and perhaps injured if too close to the horse. Standing *against* the horse frequently allows the horse to get his off fore leg down again, as the trooper loosens the long strap to recover his balance, and the horse, finding his struggles successful, is more apt to resist again and cause more time to be spent with him in re-training him.

There are other well-known methods of throwing the horse, but one will be sufficient; and if the above method is tried by the young officer himself, he will find it most satisfactory, and his future experience and study and observation will suggest other practical ways to him. It must always be remembered that the trooper must keep cool, never get angry at the horse, expect hard work, and take his buffeting, if he is unskillful, without retaliating upon the horse. Some horses will, of course, give more trouble than others, and thus more work and time must be patiently spent upon them, rather than abuse for their lesser intelligence and tractability.

The Dumb Jockey.—This contrivance, advocated by some very expert "practical horsemen," is well calculated to ruin the mouth of the new horse, especially if placed upon a nervous, high-spirited animal and left there too long. Used with intelligence and for a very short time, it may accomplish good when used upon those horses who persist in resisting the bit. The "dumb jockey" consists of a cross-horse of wood placed upon the center of the horse's back, the snaffle-reins being attached to the front upper ends of the crosses and a crupper attached to the rear sides of the upper cross-pieces; the reins are then adjusted so that the horse will have a slight feel of the bit in his mouth, and the crupper prevents the reins and pressure from being removed by the actions of the horse. It is customary to adjust the "dumb jockey" to the horse, then to turn him loose for half an hour or so a day with it, and let him work out the bit and pressure at his leisure. Experiments with this method have usually resulted in more or less permanent injury to the horse's mouth, and makes the bars tough and callous. It is rarely that this will have to be used, and when it is, the horse should be watched and the "jockey" taken off before he begins to fret and tear his mouth.

The Gaiting.—During all the horse's training careful attention must be paid to his gaits; these are the walk, trot, canter, and gallop. A brief discussion of these gaits, with a short analysis of each, is here given, with the preliminary caution of urging the trainer to go slow with the horse and never attempt to hurry him.

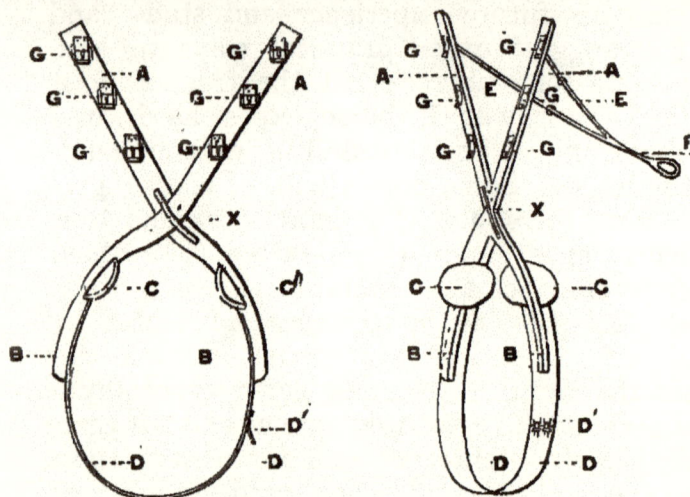

THE DUMB JOCKEY.

A, A, Upper arms of dumb jockey.
B, B, Lower arms of dumb jockey.
C, C, Panels side-bars).
D,   Surcingle or girth.
D',   Buckle of girth
E, E, Straps from top of upper arms, A, A, to a crupper, F, to prevent arms, A, A from being brought forward by the horse bearing on the reins, H, H.
F,   Crupper to steady arms, A.
G,   Buckles placed at different regular heights, to which reins, H, H, are to be attached
H. H, Reins from snaffle to arms of cross, A, A.
X,   Intersection of arms.
Y,   Blanket.

NOTE.—See page 337 also.

The walk is at the rate of 4 miles an hour, or 1 mile in 15 minutes, or 117½ yards in 1 minute. It will require much training to make the horse learn to walk this fast; most horses new to the Cavalry taking a somewhat slower gait.

The maneuvering trot is at the rate of 8 miles an hour, or 1 mile in 7½ minutes, or 234⅔ yards in a minute. It will be observed that this trot is exactly twice as fast as the walk. For purposes of individual instruction and drill the rate of the trot is sometimes diminished to 6 miles an hour, and is known in the service as the "slow trot." At the command "Trot out," the regulation 8-mile-an-hour trot is resumed.

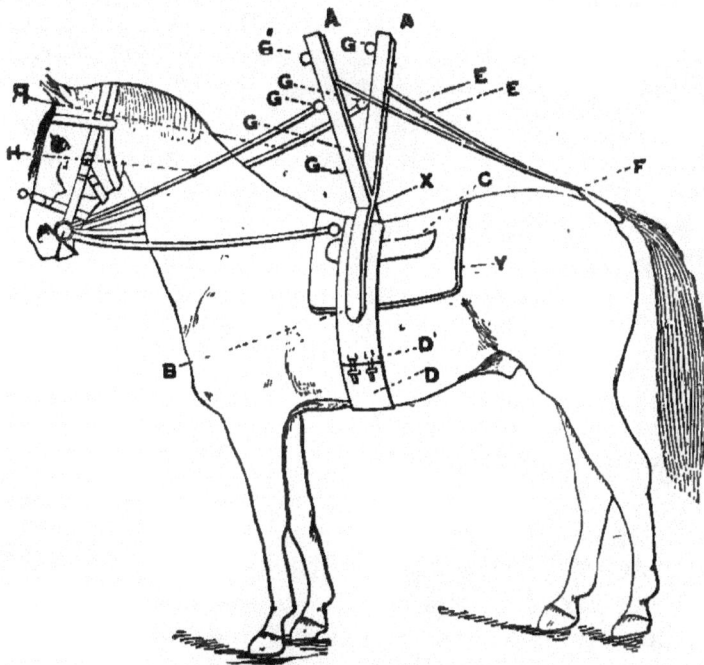

THE DUMB JOCKEY ON.

The canter is at the rate of 8 miles an hour, the same as the regulation trot, and is generally used only for individual instruction.

The maneuvering gallop is at the rate of 12 miles an hour, or 1 mile in 5 minutes, or 352 yards in 1 minute; the length of the stride is about 10 feet, as compared to a length of stride of about 8 feet in the regulation trot.

The full or extended gallop is at the rate of 16 miles an hour; this is used principally in charging, etc., at drills, and is not intended for any great length of distance, as the horses could not maintain it without exhaustion for any great distance.

The actual charge is at full speed, and is determined by the full speed of the slowest horses; to go beyond this on particular horses would only serve to scatter the command disastrously.

To instruct in the gaits, stakes are set up a certain distance apart, over a straight course, on the drill-ground. The stakes should be laid out in a straight line, the course clear of obstacles, and daily the horses should be walked, trotted at both trots, cantered, and galloped over the course once or twice. It will surprise the young officer to find how quickly the walk will fall below 4 miles an hour and how irregular will the more rapid gaits become if this practice is neglected for any length of time. The horses should be passed over the course individually and collectively; in this way the rider of each horse soon knows of what his animal is capable at the different gaits. To determine the rate of miles per hour, multiply the number of yards passed over in 1 minute by .0341, or the number of yards passed over in 1 second by 2.046, and it can easily be determined for each horse as well as for the entire troop or command when marching collectively.

A brief analysis of the gaits will help the young cavalryman in his observations of the horses in his troop; he will not be able to observe the actual motions and steps of the horse at the more rapid gaits unless he watch very closely and practice himself considerably in it.

The walk is a gait of four distinct beats, each foot being planted in a regular order of succession; that is, right fore foot, left hind foot, left fore foot, right hind foot, etc.

The trot has two distinct beats; the horse springs from one diagonally disposed pair of feet to the other pair; between the steps all the feet are in the air.

The canter has three beats, the regular order of succession being the right hind foot, left hind and right fore foot, left fore foot, and so on. From the left fore foot the horse goes into the air when cantering to the right hand.

The gallop has four beats, the regular order of succession being right hind foot, left hind foot, right fore foot, left fore foot, and so on. From the left fore foot the horse goes into the air when galloping to the right hand. In the gallop the horse is said to gallop "true" when he leads with the right fore foot when galloping to the right, and with the left fore foot when galloping to the left; when the opposite foot leads, the horse is said to gallop "false"; when the horse gallops irregularly, without rhythm, he is said to gallop "disconnectedly"; this the horse can do for but a very short distance, owing to the great jar upon his frame.

Mouths.—In the training of the cavalry horse every care must be exercised that the mouth of the animal is not injured; if it is injured much care will be necessary to cure it, and in many cases a cure will be practically impossible. When the horse responds quietly and easily to the bit, the mouth is said to be "normal"; when he resists the pressure of the bit and apparently has no feeling on the bars, the mouth is said to be "hard"; when the horse frets with a light, well-adjusted curb-bit, after accustomed to it, and evinces nervousness whenever the rein is touched, but obeys, the mouth is generally said to be "tender," and requires great care and a light hand to keep in good condition; when the horse pays practically no attention to the bit at times, while at others he frets when it is put in his mouth, the bit being carefully adjusted and the hand light, the mouth is known as a "spoiled" mouth, and perhaps no amount of work with him will ever correct this fault, which probably originated by some rider abusing the horse's mouth either by a rough hand, a cruel bit, or neglect in the nice adjustment of it in the animal's mouth.

Riding and training the light cavalry horse are so all-important to the well-being and usefulness of the horse, and to his performing the work he will surely be required to do in our service in the field, that too much stress cannot be laid upon these two things, nor can the new man in the cavalry give them too much of his careful attention and study and observation. If the points brought to the notice of the new cavalryman in these pages will help to show him what a splendid service the Cavalry is, and how much there is to keep him busy during the days and weeks of garrison service, that he may be ready for the responsibilities of field service and of commanding men and horses, it will have done a great work. The writer has set forth in this chapter on riding and training those rules and principles well established in the American cavalry service, and for a further study of the subject the student will find many books to carry him ahead.

CHAPTER XV.

The Cavalry Horse in Stable and Camp.

Necessity of Stables—American Cavalry Stables—Corrals—Sick-Stalls — Watering-Troughs — Single Stalls — Double Stalls — Swinging Separators—Feed-Boxes — Mangers—Drainage—Police of Stables—Lights—Saddle-Rooms—Picket-Lines—Grooming—Precautions Against Fire—Method of Tying in Stalls—Ventilation—The Stable Men—The Stable Sergeant—The Stable Orderly—The Farrier—The Saddler—The Blacksmith — The Wagoner — The Stable Polic e— Drafts — Windows—Grazing — Guards — In Camp— Methods of Tying Horses — Watering—Grazing and Herding—Policing—Method of Feeding—Use of Horse-Blankets—Guards—Methods of Grooming—Sick Horses—The Care of Saddle and Pack.

The necessity for cavalry stables in garrison has been recognized for centuries, and in all services the most modern, hygienic, and superior houses have been constructed as the dwelling-places for the cavalry horse. The early belief prevailed that the cavalry horse, liable at any time to have to undergo great exposure and hardship, should be "toughened" by more or less continual exposure at all seasons of the year, that he might always be in condition for active field service; and even within recent years this belief has at different times and in different services had a small following of believers, though these modern advocates have not held very extreme views upon the subject, and even they have almost all come to the rational conclusion of the present day, that the cavalry horse must be well provided for in garrison and given great care and attention if he is to perform the field service to which he is liable. While too great "coddling" of the cavalry horse would tend to make him too tender, and thus render him more liable to illness when compelled to be exposed to all sorts of weather and food in field service, at the same time exposing the horses unnecessarily to inclement weather, unhygienic surroundings, and bad food and careless treatment would be destructive of horses and consequently impair the efficiency and preparedness of the command; it must be realized that the horse is made of flesh and blood, and that his condition in garrison must be of the best and carefully looked after, that he may take the field, when the time comes, in the finest condition possible. A good knowledge of how to handle the cavalry horse in garrison and how to stable and feed him is indispensable to the cavalry officer to whose charge the horses are committed, and the manner in which he performs his duties will produce good or evil effects when the field is taken, and determine to a large extent the manner of service and its worth when called upon to perform hard campaign work.

In the construction of the cavalry troop stable, size, light, dryness, drainage, ventilation, and security all play important parts, and the neglect of any one of them brings on, sooner or later, disease and even loss among the horses. Temporarily horses may, perhaps, be placed in ill-conditioned stables and not be perceptibly hurt; but no considerable number of horses—as a troop, for instance—can be kept in unhygienic surroundings for any length of time without disease breaking out among them, and subjecting them to such exposure has often produced epidemics of contagion of the most malignant sort. There is nothing, perhaps, more difficult to control than an epidemic of sickness among the troop horses; only the most decisive and prompt measures will suffice, and even then the command will be fortunate if no great loss results before the trouble is eradicated.

In the American cavalry service each troop has its own particular stable, and whether in garrison or field, each lot of troop horses is kept together and apart from those of other troops. The stables in most of the American garrisons are modern brick or stone buildings, fitted with all the necessary appliances and conveniences. In each cavalry post possessing more than two troops one stable is usually set aside as a "hospital" for the sick horses of the garrison, and this is under the immediate charge of the veterinarian and a corps of assistants. The veterinarian makes daily visits of inspection to each troop stable, prescribes for the sick animals, and directs the most serious cases to be taken to the hospital for treatment.

AMERICAN STABLES AND PICKET-LINES IN CUBA.

Owing to the permanently warm climate in the most southerly parts of our country, the cavalry stables in the lower part of the United States, like those constructed in the Philippine Islands, are mere open sheds, possessing no walls or windows, and open throughout their entire extent; but in these warm climates even greater care is necessary that the stables be clean, dry, well ventilated, and commodious, as the danger of contagion and epidemic is vastly greater than in the cold climates of the northern portions of the United States. These open stables in warm climates are an imperative necessity, as closed ones would deny the horses that abundance of fresh air without which health is impossible. Not only is the open stable necessary to enable a sufficient supply of fresh air for the horses to breathe, but they are also made necessary because horses placed in closed stables in such

AMERICAN STABLES IN THE PHILIPPINE ISLANDS.

climates sweat profusely, especially where the number of horses is large, and thus are quickly rendered tender, and thus liable to sudden chills, colds, and even more disastrous ailments. Even in the American garrisons in the northern part of the country the horses suffer much from the closed stables in summer, unless every precaution is taken to secure ample ventilation.

Ventilation in cavalry stables is secured in several well-known ways. In our service the ventilating windows are usually placed in the ceiling of the stable, and the doors at the two ends are so arranged that the upper halves of them may be left open, the lower halves being kept closed to prevent any loose animals from escaping.

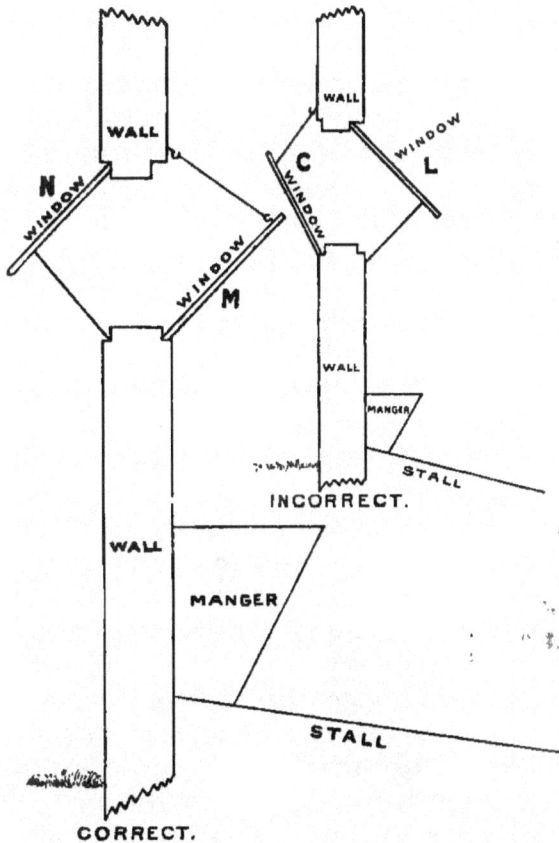

CORRECT AND INCORRECT WINDOWS.

The cubic feet of fresh air generally considered necessary for the cavalry horse is placed at 1200 feet, but a safe rule is to allow all the fresh air that is possible, due regard being had to season and weather; but it should never be *less* than 1200 cubic feet per horse. The windows provided for lighting the stables should never be used as ventilators while the horses are in the stables; and no matter what scheme is employed, care must be taken that no direct draft can blow on the horses, especially across their backs. The ventilating windows should be so constructed that any or all of them may be quickly closed or opened. The heat produced in a cavalry stable, especially at night, when all the horses are in their stalls, frequently becomes so great that it is necessary to open all the ventilating windows and the upper and lower halves of both end doors. Ropes are then stretched across the doors, or iron or wooden bars, and so arranged that no loose animal can escape. Some of our cavalry stables are ventilated by means of double walls, having windows on the outer side at frequent intervals (usually every 10 feet), placed high up, and an equal number of windows in the inner walls placed low down, and so built as to be between the outer windows and below the spaces between these outer windows. This allows excellent ventilation, and at the same time the arrangement of the two sets of windows prevents any draft from blowing upon the horses. As the end doors furnish the larger part of the fresh air, no matter what style of wall or ceiling ventilation is employed, these doors must be constantly left open when the weather permits. It is rarely necessary to close more than the upper halves of them, except in extremely cold weather. When it is necessary to use the wall windows as ventilators (see plate on page 345), the shutters on them should be so placed that they can be opened inward and downward from the top, or outward and upward from the bottom, and not the reverse. This allows the air to come in and pass upward, diverting any drafts, and also protects the horses' eyes from the glare of the sharp light, which is a prolific source of eye-trouble, in stables where the horses usually face the walls.

The modern cavalry stables recently erected at Fort Riley, Kansas, may be taken as the most improved type of cavalry stables now being constructed anywhere in the world. These stables have four rows of stalls instead of two, and the stable is made wider and shorter in consequence. The center of the stable is occupied by a double row of double stalls, facing each other, having a high wooden partition between the two rows the entire length of the two rows. On each side of the stable is another row of double stalls, facing the wall of the stable, and having one or two box-stalls or single stalls at each end. There are, consequently, two passage-ways through the stable, instead of one. The double row of stalls down the center cover about three-fourths the length of the stable, the remaining length being occupied by the saddle-room at the front end and the grain-room at the rear end. A loft is over the grain room. Outside and against the middle division of the rear wall is placed the watering-trough. The usual corral adjoins the stable. Instead of picket-posts, some of these new corrals have iron rings fastened into the outside of the wall of the stable, about four feet high, through which is run the picket-line. An outhouse on one side of the corral, near the stable, has the troop saddler shop, the troop blacksmith shop, and a room for the stable men, besides a veterinary room for the farrier.

These buildings are of native stone, and finely built, and represent the best class and style of stable for cavalry use. The feed-boxes are of the usual shape and size, and of iron, and are placed in the mangers in the usual way, and so fastened as to allow of their being easily removed for cleaning. The floors are of clay, and practically level. The windows are placed high, with shutters opening outward from the bottom, and ventilation is procured from the ventilating windows in the roof and from the end and side doors. The passage-ways in some are of stone blocks, and these, as explained above, are apt to wear slippery after a time. · The end doors and side doors slide back instead of swinging open. There is a door in each side wall, near the center of the stable, leading into the corral. Slight drainage gutters run along the rear of the stalls, emptying into underground waste-pipes.   Much time and experience and money have been used in the construction of these stables, and while they possess many of the usual features already described, the whole style and arrangement of these new troop stables are models of the most approved kind for cavalry troops.

In most American cavalry stables two rows of stalls are constructed the entire length of the stables, one down each side; a passage-way is left down the center about 20 feet wide (see plate on page 354); the stalls are usually double, each accommodating two horses; there is not generally any partition between the two horses occupying the double stall; after the horses have stood together awhile, they become accustomed to each other and stand and lie down quietly.   However, there are almost always a few ill-tempered animals in every troop, and these few horses must be kept from injuring their stall-mates.   A very effective method in such a case is to hang a "swinging separator" between the two horses (see plate on page 349); this consists of a heavy bar of wood extending the entire length of the stall, one end of which is suspended by a rope from the ceiling of the stall over the hind end, and the other end is fastened to a hinge screwed into the top of the manger at the center. This bar must be somewhat longer than the horse as he stands in the stall, and it should be on a level with the top of the manger, thus preventing either horse from getting his legs over it and perhaps casting himself.   As there are generally a few single stalls in every cavalry stable, it is still better to place the vicious horse in one of these. These single stalls, however, are for the use of sick horses and are frequently all occupied, and the use of the swinging separator is necessary.   Having stall-mates get along well and quietly together is very important, as it sometimes happens that a horse will be found in the morning so badly kicked or bitten by a savage mate as to render him totally unfit for use for several days.   The double stalls are usually constructed not less than 9 feet wide,

inside measurement. The length of the stall, whether
single or double, is from 10 to 12 feet, the latter
length being the better. Estimating the entire length of
the horse at 3 yards, this allows from 1 to 3 feet to spare.
As the stalls are sometimes made slightly higher at the
manger end than at the hind end (a very improper and
injurious proceeding), to allow for drainage, the horse will

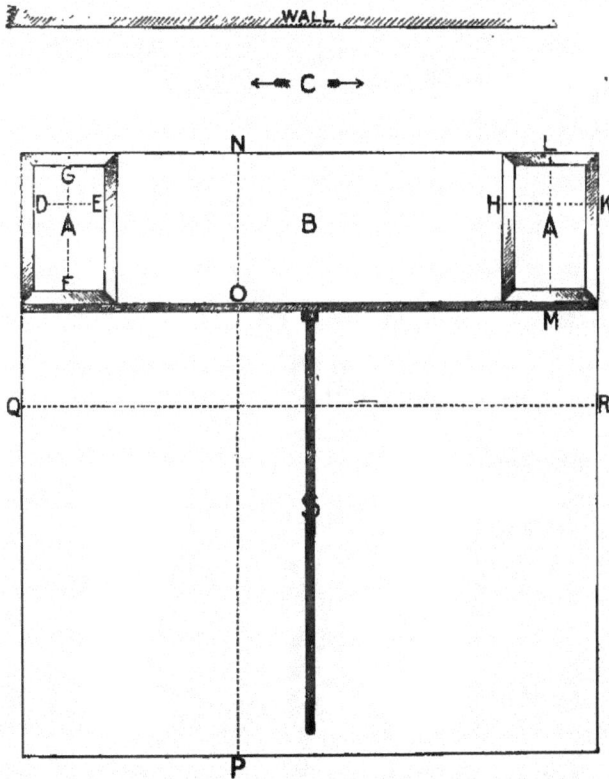

HORIZONTAL SECTION OF DOUBLE STALL.

often back out of the stall as far as his halter-strap will
permit, in an effort to get his feet all on level ground, and
in doing so his hind feet should not come into the drainage gutter, which runs along the entire line of stalls at
the hind end. The above measurements of the stall are
those usually employed in constructing our cavalry stables,

and allow ample room for the two horses to stand or lie down comfortably. The manger in each stall is a long hay-rack of wood, built from the floor of the stall, and is about 3 feet high, flaring outward at the top; if built straight, without this flaring, it is difficult for the horse to reach down to the bottom of the manger, unless the manger is made very wide, which requires much space that can be saved. The width of the manger at the top should be about 2½ feet, the bottom being about 18 inches. The manger extends across the entire width of the stall. In each stall two feed-boxes are placed, one for each horse; these are usually made of iron, but can be readily made of wood, which allows of easy and inexpensive repair when worn or broken. The feed-box should be about 8 inches deep, 18 inches wide at the top, and somewhat smaller at the bottom, and be as long as the manger is wide. One feed-box should be placed at each end of the manger, for if the two are placed together in the center, it will often happen that one of the horses in the stall will eat both feeds, especially if one of the two horses is timid. The hay in the manger should be put in liberally, and well shaken up, filling the entire manger. Both horses eat out of the same manger, thus both allowances of hay are put in together; it is more than one horse will usually eat when there is grain in his feed-box, and no harm comes even if one horse eats practically all the hay the manger will hold, no matter how hot or how wet he may be.

In every cavalry stable a few single stalls are constructed, to be used by vicious or sick animals, as circumstances require. These single stalls are built like the double stalls, the only difference being in the width. Single stalls are usually at least 5 feet wide. The partitions between stalls should be as high as the tops of the horses' heads at the manger end and slightly lower at the hind end. If these partitions are too low, it allows the horses in the adjoining stalls, if tied too long, to reach over the partition and eat the feed in the adjoining feed -

boxes, and to fight with the horse in the adjoining stall. The boards forming these partitions should have spaces between them of about 2 inches to allow for passage of air. In each stable two or three "box" stalls should be constructed, for the accommodation of the sickest horses in the troop; only one animal should be placed in a "box" stall at a time, and the sick horse in the stall should never be tied, but allowed entire freedom in the stall. These "box" stalls should be at least 12x12 feet square, and should be boarded up on all four sides, with a door at the hind end. In making the board sides, spaces of 2 or 3 inches should be left between the boards, to allow for full and complete ventilation; if the boards forming the sides are placed close together, the stall, having no circulation of air, becomes very close and hot. The ceilings of the stables should be about 12 or 15 feet high. The name of each horse and that of his rider are printed on a board or tin and placed above the end of the stall; the name borne by the horse is never changed, and follows the animal throughout his service. The horses are usually named by the troop commander, who occasionally permits the man to whom a horse is assigned to do the naming. It is customary in some squadrons to name all the horses in Troop A with names commencing with "A," all the horses in Troop B with names commencing with "B," etc.

The flooring in the stable is a most important matter. There are three materials commonly used in making the flooring—heavy wooden boards, Belgian stone blocking, and clay, and each has its advantages and disadvantages, all possessing many points of excellence. In modern cavalry stables the first two materials are largely used, but dirt flooring has been used for many years with great satisfaction. Owing to the inexpensiveness of this flooring and its easiness upon the horses' feet, it perhaps surpasses either of the other two materials, though it requires some attention to keep its surface filled in. The clay is both a disinfectant and a deodorizer. It can be dampened in hot weather to keep the horses' feet cool, and will never produce stiffness or stockiness. Boards and brick or stone pavements are objectionable because they not only make horses stiff, but they prevent the horse's putting himself in the most natural and comfortable position by pawing a hole for his front feet to rest in, and so take the strain off the tendons of the hind legs. It is to accomplish this same object that the horse backs out of his stall into the gutter, when possible for him to do so. When the board flooring is used, it covers the entire stable, both center passage-way and stalls; it is easily cleaned and gives a fair foot-hold to the horses, but it is expensive and in time absorbs much urine, which rots the boards, and the pounding of the horses' iron-shod hoofs upon it causes some splintering, which is more or less apt to injure the animals' feet. This splintering also sends into the air of the stables fine, flaky particles of wood, which, being breathed by the horses, will cause disorders of an annoying sort. The drainage afforded by the wooden flooring is very good, but the wet boards become slippery and retain more or less dampness in time. When the Belgian block flooring is used, it covers only the center passage-way of the stable, the flooring of the stalls being then made of either dirt or boards. To place the stone flooring in the stalls would cause much injury to the horses' feet, being too hard. This Belgian block flooring, while also easily cleaned and giving good drainage, is very expensive, and as it wears very slippery in time (especially is this so when wet), danger to the horses from falling is considerable. The writer has seen many horses fall violently while being led over this sort of flooring. This flooring not only wears slippery itself, but the iron shoes of the horses also become slippery after short wear, thus doubling this danger. The dirt flooring, when used, covers both the center passage-way and the stalls; it is easily pawed up by the horses, and it is necessary to keep filling in both stalls and passage-way, to keep the even surface required. If this is neglected, holes both in the

stalls and passage-way gradually appear, and danger to the
horses of wrenching and spraining their knees and pastern-
joints is to be feared. However, the dirt flooring is very
cheap, costing only the manual labor of the stable-men and
troopers, and, if proper material is used, furnishes excellent flooring, easy on the horses' feet, affording fairly good
drainage, and because of the ease with which this material
can be procured, will be found in most stables. The dirt
flooring should be of clay, clean and free from rocks,
glass, or other sharp particles, and without lumps. In
fitting the stall for the floor, the entire floor of the stall

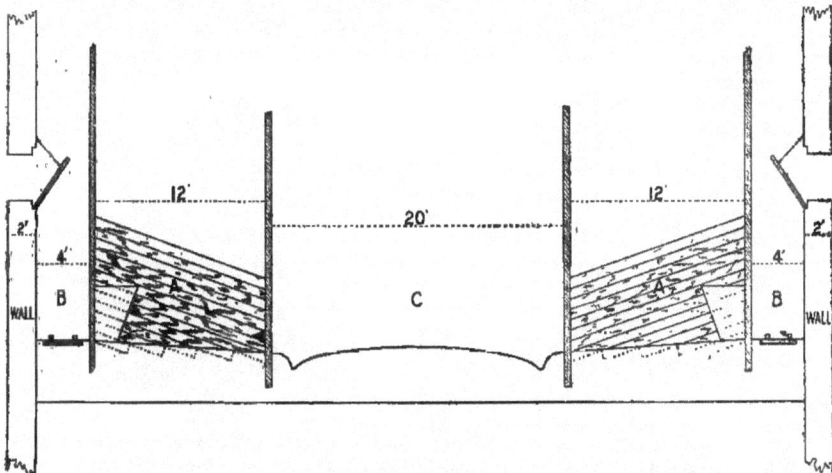

INTERIOR ARRANGEMENT, SHOWING DRAINAGE.

should be picked loose to a depth of 1 foot at least, and
all soiled or soaked dirt should be removed altogether;
the loose dirt should be then well tamped down, and the
new clay placed on top to a depth of about 1 foot, the
stall level. The entire floor should then be pounded
down until it is hard and firm. If slightly wet, the
clay will pack much better than if dry. Abounding in
mountain-sides there exists a sort of hard dirt, known
as "marl," well known to cavalrymen. This makes one
of the very best and most endurable dirt floors, and is
found near almost any cavalry garrison. Gravelly or

sandy earth should not be used; it wears away rapidly and too quickly to justify the labor. However, at times this is all that is available, and it must then be used. In the Philippine Islands the writer constructed a flooring of sand, built upon layers of crushed brick taken from an old ruin, and it made a very satisfactory flooring, especially as nothing better was to be had. The flooring required weekly filling in, however, more or less, but the surrounding country was flooded and marshy, the soil soaked into slimy mud, and the sand from the nearby river was all that could be used. It gave good drainage, this being aided by the base of crushed brick.

In constructing the stable for the cavalry horse, drainage is an all-important consideration. No matter how well lighted, policed, and ventilated, health cannot be expected if poor drainage exists. In constructing the flooring, this consideration enters in most materially. Some of the urine will soak into the flooring, no matter how well managed the drainage is. This must be hosed and scrubbed out. Any inclination of the flooring compels the horse to stand somewhat up-hill, and this is very tiresome to him. To relieve himself of this slanting surface, the horse will either paw out the front end of his stall floor, if of dirt, or else he will back out as far as his halter-strap will allow, to get his hind feet on ground level with his front feet. It must be appreciated what slope of the stall floor does to the horse, and in laying the floor make no slope. The slope recommended by some men, from manger to hind end, is believed to be wrong.

In actual fact, many of the stalls and center passageways of cavalry stables are made perfectly level, with no slope for drainage at all. In many cavalry stables even the drainage-gutters in rear of the stalls are lacking. It cannot but be admitted that horses placed in these stables are found to stand much more naturally and with more comfort. Horses will paw out a hole for their front feet, even if the floor of the stall be perfectly level. As this is true, the effect of sloping the stall from front to rear can be quickly understood—a torture to the horse as long as he is in the stall. This sloping of the stall is an old set idea which many find hard to give up, but it is even useless, considering drainage alone, regardless of the fatigue and strain on the horse. As a matter of fact, the sloping stall of dirt doesn't drain. The horse invariably urinates in his stall in the same place, and that place is near the center of the stall; this is true from the simple fact that the stall has only so much width and the horse occupies the center of it if it be a single stall, or the center of his half if it be a double stall. The wisest plan, therefore, is to make the floor of the entire stable, stalls and passageways, *level*, and every few weeks dig out the central spot in each stall where the urine has soaked in, removing all the soiled clay entirely, and fill up the hole with new, fresh clay. Fresh clay, as remarked above, acts as both a deodorizer and a disinfectant, and its renewal when soiled keeps the stall fresh and clean and healthy. The new clay put in these holes should be slightly dampened and lightly tamped down,—not puddled or packed hard. The spot needing to be renewed is comparatively small, rarely over a foot and a half or so in diameter, and nearly circular.

Furthermore, the stall, when the bedding is down, will not drain, even if it has a slope, as what does not soak into the clay floor will be absorbed in the hay or straw used as bedding. As the cavalry horse is rarely in his stall except when it is bedded down, this is generally what really happens. Consequently sloping the stall at all may be regarded as an obsolete idea, and an inspection of most of our cavalry stables will show that it is now rarely practiced.

Paragraph 1117 of our Cavalry Drill Regulations, speaking of drainage for the picket-line, states that "there should be shallow trenches behind the horses to carry off the rain, the ground on which they stand having just enough slope to let water run into the trenches, or there may be a single drain in the center along the line of posts. Constant attention must be given to keeping the ground about the picket-line in good order," and Paragraph 1118 of these Regulations states that "except at night, when the horses are bedded down, no manure or urine is to remain in the stalls; the stable police remove it as it accumulates;" and further, "Clay is the best for earthern floors; gravel or sandy soil is not suitable. The sloping of the floor of stalls from manager to heel-post is injurious and uncomfortable for the animal, making him stand in an unnatural position, with the fore legs higher than the hind ones; when the earthern floors are level, the horse will paw a hollow for his fore feet, unless he can elevate his hind quarters by backing out of the stall."

The above shows plainly what the opinion of the cavalry officer is, based upon actual experience, and the slope in stalls has been proven a mistake and is now abandoned in favor of the level flooring for both stalls and passage-ways.

In most permanent cavalry garrisons a regular system of underground sewerage exists, connecting with each stable, and the drainage-canals empty into the main waste-pipe; but if this arrangement does not exist, as it did not in the temporary garrisons in the Philippine Islands, the drainage-canals in the stable should be run out of the stables at one end, and there, forming one main canal, provide for the drainage to a considerable distance away. Stalls must not be allowed to remain in a urine-soaked condition, but should be picked-up all over the stall, the soaked soil carried away, new soil filled in after the stall has dried out, and then the whole dampened and well tamped down, being allowed to dry and harden, if possible, before the horse is allowed to re-enter the stall. As this is often necessary, there should be in every cavalry stable a few extra stalls, to allow for the repairing of soiled ones. When the wooden floors are used, round holes are sometimes bored here and there in the stall flooring, to allow the filth to run through and thence into the drainage-gutters and to the outlet; but this method weakens the boards forming the floors, and also soaks the ground underneath the stall, causing a vile odor. Usually with the board flooring the drainage is secured by *very slightly* sloping the floor of the stall, as explained, and hosing and scrubbing the flooring frequently, but this slope is alway bad.

The police of the troop stables is performed daily, twice, once in the morning and again in the afternoon, by the troopers on duty in the stable. These men, usually six in number, are assisted by a daily detail from the troop of two men, known as stable police. Shortly before "reveille" the horses are fed by these men, and then turned out into the "corral" or paddock adjoining the stable. Whenever circumstances permit, the horses should be turned loose in the paddock during the day-time, if no herding is done. When this is impracticable, they should, except in very cold, windy weather, or in very hot weather where there is no shade, stand most of the day at the picket-line, as they have better air and are less confined, while the stables become drier and more healthful. The stable-men, as soon as they turn out the horses, clean out the stalls and center passage-way, and thoroughly police the entire stables and immediate vicinity. The manure and refuse is hauled away in the troop wagon and dumped at a designated place, where it is later burned up. In cleaning out the bedding, the soiled part is carried away, while that which is still sufficiently clean to be used once more is separated from it and either left in the stall or spread out in the sun to dry. The allowance of bedding in the American cavalry service is 100 pounds of hay or straw a month for each animal, and it is sufficient, if due economy is exercised, to provide good, fresh beds in the stalls. After policing the stables and stalls in the morning, all doors and windows are left wide open and the stalls and center allowed to dry and air. Occasionally inclement weather may prevent this, but it should never be allowed to be dispensed with if it can be avoided. Just before afternoon "stables" the stable-men haul in the

new bedding and hay, bed-down the stalls, fill the mangers
with hay, fill the feed-boxes in each stall with grain, and
sweep out the entire stable. Once or twice each week
the entire stable should be scrubbed out with water and
stable-brooms. This scrubbing is especially necessary
if the flooring is of wood or stone, as much manure will
adhere to these floors and ordinary sweeping will not
remove it. Once or twice each week disinfectants should
be sprinkled in each stall and in the center passage-way.
About once in every three months the entire stable should
have its interior whitewashed. Stalls that have been
used by sick animals should be disinfected as soon as the
sick horses are removed from them, and until this is done
no other animal, sick or well, should be allowed to enter
them. There is considerable danger of contagion if carelessness exists in these matters. Slight, hardly noticeable discharges from sick animals lodge on the woodwork
and other parts of the stalls, and disease is easily carried
to other horses. As horses often gnaw the woodwork of
the stalls in which they are standing, the disease is carried into the system with little difficulty. As this gnawing mars and injures the woodwork and causes splinters,
it is well to coat all woodwork in the stalls of the horses
with a thick coat of coal tar or other ill-tasting but harmless mixture. The same precaution may be followed with
regard to troughs, picket-posts, and picket-lines. This
coating should be thoroughly dry before putting horses
near it.

During the night lights should be hung in the center
passage-way; these lights should be regular stable lanterns, securely hung, and so placed that no loose animal
can reach them. No other lights should be permitted in
or about the stables, and under no circumstances should
smoking or fires be allowed anywhere about the stables,
nor should any rubbish be burned in their vicinity,
whether the horses be in them or not. Horses are easily
frightened by fire, and it is difficult to control them.
Accustomed to absolute safety while in their own stables,

they are only gotten away from them during a fire with much difficulty, and if taken out and turned loose, are very apt to re-enter their stables and perish. It has been said that horses are attracted by fire, but this is not believed to be so; the horse tries to remain in his burning stable simply because it is his home, wherein he has been accustomed to feeding and sleeping and being well cared for. The horses, in case of fire occurring at the stables, should be removed to a safe distance and *securely tied up.* Every cavalry stable should be generously supplied with axes and water-buckets, kept constantly at hand, always in the same place, and always filled and ready for immediate use, and these should never be used for the work about the stables or for anything else other than fire. On one occasion an inspector appeared at a troop, and, in examining the precautions at hand in case of fire, found that one or two of the axes had been used by the stable-men and were not in their racks, and the water in the fire-buckets (it being winter), not having been changed in the morning, was frozen in every bucket into solid masses of ice, and nearly all the buckets, as a result, had been burst by the pressure to such an extent that even after the ice was with difficulty removed, hardly a single bucket would hold water. Fortunate for the cavalry horse, indeed, that no fire had occurred.

As it is absolutely necessary that all the horses except the very sick ones be removed from the stables during the day, to allow for policing and drying and airing out the stables, a paddock, or "corral," as it is called in in the American service, is attached to each stable, with a side-door leading from the stable into it. This corral should be of sufficient size to accommodate all the troop horses with comfort, so that they may be turned loose in it and move about. This corral has only ordinary dirt surface In the corral is placed a picket-line of sufficient length to tie all the horses to it when necessary; the line should be of stout, 2-inch rope, stretched taut and run through stout posts; the line should be

about 7 feet above the ground. The picket-line floor
should be raised somewhat above the surrounding part
of the corral, in order that it may be kept well drained
and dry, and should have a *very slight* slope from center outward. Occasionally the flooring of the picket-
line is filled in with stones, but this has been found unsatisfactory, owing to the fact that the horses often
have to be tied to the picket-line for hours at a time,
and standing upon the uneven, rocky flooring wears
away the hoofs too much, and particles of jagged stone,
sticking up here and there, are apt to injure the soles
of the feet Experiments with these stone floorings
on picket-lines have, at various times, been made in our
service, and while some officers have contended for them,
it has generally been considered unsatisfactory, even if
not positively injurious. The corral and picket-line should
be kept clean, and should be policed at least once a week
thoroughly, as much rubbish is blown in and much dirt
accumulates from the horses, from which dry, unhealthy
secretions and flakes arise. At one end of the corral
should be placed a watering-trough, constantly kept
filled and cleaned, and the horses should have free access
to the water at all times; a cover for the trough should
be kept at hand, in order that horses coming in warm
cannot drink until cooled off; if no cover is at hand, care
must be taken that the trough is emptied before the horses
are turned loose if warm. As much sediment is depos-
ited in the trough by the water itself, by the drinking and
slobbering of the horses, and by the wind and dust, the
trough should be emptied and thoroughly cleaned at least
twice weekly. Splinters occasionally break off on the
inside of the trough, and care must be taken that these
are all promptly removed, to prevent their being swallowed
by the horses.

The American cavalry horse in garrison is groomed
twice daily at the stables. The troopers of each troop
march to their stables for this purpose shortly after
breakfast and again in the late afternoon. Each horse

is groomed about twenty minutes, the morning grooming being somewhat shorter, owing to the early morning drills. In some posts the morning grooming is held after the troop returns from the morning drill, and this is considered the best time for the morning grooming; however, even when this is done, the troopers must brush off their horses before saddling, as much dirt gets on the animals during the night, and if saddled up without their backs being cleaned, soreness and abrasion may occur. Whenever the weather permits, the horses at both the morning and afternoon grooming are groomed in the open air, at the picket-line in the corral. This is done in order that the dust and loose hair from the animals may not remain in the stables. Especially at afternoon "stables" should the horses be groomed at the picket-line, as their being groomed inside would cause this dust and hair to settle in the feed, and in addition, the horse, being in the stables all night, would be compelled to breathe in much of this floating hair and dust. In inclement weather only should the horses be groomed in the stables. When groomed inside, they should be first all led in and tied in their proper stalls, and then groomed. When the horse is led into his stall, he is tied to the manger by the halter-strap; this strap should be tied only so long as to enable the horse to feed and lie down comfortably; a strap too long may become entangled in the legs and throw him; it also allows the horse, if ill-tempered, to reach over and bite his stall-mate. Occasionally, in place of this halter-strap is a steel chain; but, owing to the necessity of quickly untying the horses in case of fire or any disorder, the chain is very unsatisfactory; it frequently becomes knotted so much as to make untying it impossible without considerable delay, and in time of emergency the only way to untie the horse is to slip the halter off and turn him loose, which must be avoided, especially in case of much noise or excitement.

The importance of having a careful, well-trained lot of stable-men about the stables, to care for the horses, stables, and property and handle the feeding, is such that it is the custom in the American service to permanently detail six men in each troop to live at the stables and take charge of the work there.   These men are known as the stable sergeant, who is in direct charge, subject only to the orders of his troop commander; the stable orderly, who acts in the absence of the stable sergeant; the farrier, whose duty it is to care for and administer to the sick animals under the daily supervision of the troop commander and veterinary surgeon; the saddler, who repairs the troop saddlery; the blacksmith, and the wagoner.   One of these men, at least, is required to be always present in the stables; he is responsible for everything in and about the stables.   These six men form the troop stable crew, and are exempt from guard, kitchen police, post fatigue, etc., attending only certain drills, muster, and inspections.   As their duties about the stables are numerous and imperative, they should be spared all outside work that separates them from their stable work. These stable-men, however, must be required to attend a sufficient number of daily drills and weekly inspections to be kept abreast of their fellow troopers in all cavalry work. The stable sergeant especially should be carefully chosen, and should be an old soldier if possible, skilled in the care of troop-horses and fond of animals, and he should have a stern attention to duty, both as regards his own duties and those of the stable-men; upon his careful attention to the duties in the stables depends the health of the horses to a large extent.

In the American service the morning feed is placed in the feed-boxes shortly before "reveille," and consists of half of the daily allowance of grain, 6 pounds; the entire daily allowance of grain is 12 pounds of oats, corn, barley, or bran.   No hay is fed in the morning. A wheeled cart is supplied to each stable, holding sufficient grain for one feed; this is pushed down the center passage-way, while two of the stable-men, one working on each side, fill the feed-boxes from wooden or tin feed-pails capable of holding the required amount of grain for one feed for one horse. In modern stables, where there is a passage-way on each side of the stables between the mangers and the stable walls, tracks have been laid for the cart to run, and this much expedites the work; by using wooden rails, this scheme is practicable wherever there exists these passage-ways in the stables, and should be constructed. The afternoon feed of grain is placed in the feed-boxes in the mangers shortly before afternoon "stables" in the same way. The entire daily allowance of hay is also fed in the afternoon at the same time, consisting of 14 pounds for each horse. As soon as the afternoon "stables" are finished, the troopers lead in their horses to their stalls and tie them in, watering them just before taking them in to their stalls.

A commissioned officer from each troop superintends the morning and afternoon "stables" in each troop, superintends the grooming, the watering, and inspects the stalls and stable of the troop throughout; at afternoon "stables" this officer also inspects the entire police of the stable, and satisfies himself that the stalls are fresh and clean and properly bedded down for the night, and that the proper allowance of grain and hay of good quality is in each stall for each animal; he inspects the stable lanterns and ascertains that they are ready for lighting, inspects the sick horses and inquires as to their treatment, being accompanied at the time by the farrier and stable sergeant; examines the shoeing with the troop blacksmith; inspects the saddle-rooms and grain-room; and investigates anything reported to him by the stable-men regarding the horses. The new officer inspecting the stables should keep himself from perfunctorily walking up and down the picket-line as the men are grooming, receiving the first sergeant's report, and leaving. While he will see many older cavalry officers apparently do this, he must realize that these officers are all men of experience, who can quickly see by a glance whether or not all is as it should be; but the young man new to the cavalry will find "taking stables" is a very important matter, and he will learn much by observing everything pertaining to the management of the troop stable when he is there, if he does all there is for him to do; he will also, by his interest, encourage the stable-men to renewed efforts to have their particular stable in fine condition and the horses looking well. The work of these men is hard and important, and he can learn much from them regarding the cavalry horse and his pack, by getting all there is out of "stables."

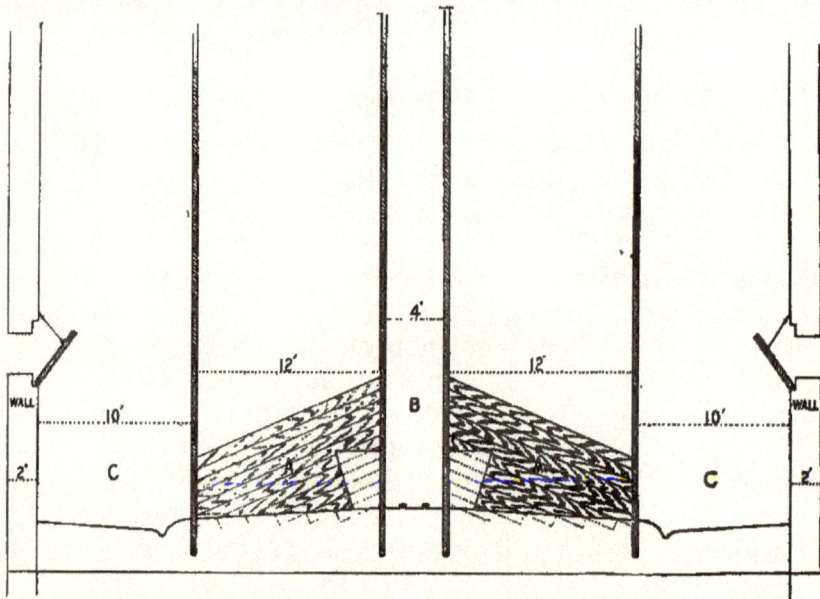

VERTICAL SECTION OF INTERIOR OF CAVALRY STABLES, SHOWING PREFERABLE ARRANGEMENT.

In each cavalry stable there is a grain-room at one end, and this should be of sufficient size to hold ten days' feed of grain for all the horses in the stable. The allowance of hay is usually drawn by the stable-men daily. Hay is furnished either baled or loose; if baled, care must be taken that the wire from the bales is carried away at once, and not allowed to lie around the stables, near the horses, which may be severely cut by it. In the grain-room there should be kept two or three mouse-traps always set, as mice are very plentiful here. The grain itself should be piled off the ground (when the flooring is of dirt), and occasionally repiled, as the under bales and sacks will mould and become wormy if left there too long; if the flooring is of dirt, the under sacks should be raised off the ground by means of poles placed parallel to hold them, as these under sacks of grain will quickly mould from the dampness.

In one end of the stable is the saddle-room; along the walls are placed rows of saddle-pegs, each capable of holding one saddle and the horse equipments belonging to it. Each trooper should be assigned a peg, which should be numbered, and the arrangement of the saddle and horse equipments on each peg should be prescribed in orders posted up in the saddle-room. Troopers are careless of their equipments in this way, and frequently lose small parts of their equipments. Every part of the saddle and horse equipments belonging to each trooper should be plainly marked or stamped with the trooper's troop number, to prevent loss, and each trooper must be made to understand he will be held to strict accountability regarding his own equipments, and under no circumstances should he be allowed to borrow the equipments of any other trooper—least of all without permission. The men should be required to keep all the horse equipments on their pegs; in this way the troop, if turned out suddenly, has everything at hand and easily found.

Each troop has its own blacksmith shop near its stable, and the horse-shoer selects the horses needing shoeing in the morning, and, taking them to the blacksmith shop, attends to them. The work of the troop blacksmith is of the greatest importance, and is hard. He is carefully inspected, and not permitted to experiment with any horse unless authorized to do so by the troop commander. As the horse-shoeing of the troop is very hard physical work, a man should be detailed whenever necessary to assist the blacksmith. In hot weather, when the insects are bad, this is very necessary. It must always be appreciated that a good troop blacksmith is a treasure indeed, and not to be worn out by hard work, when a little consideration will save him so much and result in better shoeing of the horses.

In garrison, when the weather permits, all the troop horses are taken out to graze after morning drill; they are kept out until shortly before afternoon "stables," and brought in quietly to the picket-line. Each troop herd is kept apart from the other troop herds, and should be far enough away so that any excitement in one herd will not be communicated to the others. This herding of the troop horses is most important; not only do the animals have a chance to eat the fresh, luxuriant grass, but the troop horses are thus taught to leave the stables and return to them quietly. This is a great advantage when in the field, and requires much training before it can be well done. When the horses are herded, each troop furnishes its own herd-guard of 4 or 5 men, 1 of whom should always be a non-commissioned officer. These men should be mounted upon good, well-trained horses, and it is their duty to take the herd to a good grazing-place, let it graze during the day, and bring it in in the afternoon quietly. The herding-ground should, if possible, be near good water, and the horses should be permitted to have free access to it at all times while grazing. No halters or straps should be left on any of the horses.

Light is an all-important consideration in the cavalry stable; however, the windows should be so placed that the glare will not shine directly into the horses' eyes as they stand in their stalls. Too strong a light shining directly into the eyes of the horses is injurious, and perhaps even more so than too much gloom. If the windows are so placed that opening them will throw the light into the horses' eyes, shutters should be so arranged that they will open inwards and from the top; this will cause the light to be deflected upwards and away from the horses, and at the same time will furnish ample light for the interior. The windows should never be used as ventiilators, as the drafts blow across the horses' backs. The walls directly facing the horses should be left dark; whitewashing them brings a deflection of strong light into the animals' faces, and is injurious.

Horses coming to the stable in a warm or wet condition should be turned loose in the corral, care being taken that the watering-trough is either covered or emptied, to prevent their drinking while hot. The horses will cool off without harm if allowed to walk about in the corral if the weather is fine. Stables are frequently more or less chilly, and bad results may come from tying the horse in his stall while heated or wet; when necessary to tie the horse inside, either a horse-blanket should be thrown over him until he is cooled off, or, better still, one of the troopers should wisp him dry with hay or straw.

In discussing the questions connected with the size, form, and arrangements of cavalry stables, it must not be forgotten that we have to deal with an animal generally high in spirits, condition, and strength. This cavalry horse, like the athlete, cannot be housed and denied exercise without injury. If a horse is to be kept for pleasure only, and is not regularly exercised on those days when he is not wanted, he will in time get out of health, no matter how clean and hygienic the interior of his stable may be, or how good the management indoors. A common complaint among amateur horsemen is that their horses, well housed, are often not so free from disease as those of some cab or express company in the same neighborhood, which are often kept in dark, close stables, often underground (as in large cities). The reason is obvious enough. The over-fed and under-worked horse, stimulated by his food to a great extent, is apt to have some organ become inflamed, and if the lungs or bowels do not show disease, the heels crack or the joints enlarge, and after a single day's work the horse exhibits lameness of a more or less serious character. On the other hand, the hard-worked horse of the express company is in the fresh air a large part of the time, exercising, and thus the injury done to his blood inside the close stable is remedied when he is out; but even he will become sick if the unhygienic surroundings continue to be his home at night. The food of the hard-worked horse is expended in nourishing and repairing his muscular system, and there is no surplus to form the foundation of disease. If this is so with the pleasure horse and the express company animal, how much more important are exercise and good surroundings for our cavalry horse.

In considering the cavalry stable, its situation and aspect are two important points to be considered; upon these depend, first, the power of excluding damp; and secondly, the best means of keeping up a tolerably even temperature in winter and summer. It must not be forgotten that the horse is a native of a dry country, and cannot be kept in health in a damp situation unless he is especially well cared for. Either in-doors or out, for any prolonged period of time, the horse cannot be subjected to damp without disease showing itself. Nothing except starvation tells injuriously upon horses so soon as damp when exposed to it. The horse loses all spirit, work soon tires him, his coat is staring, he will finally scarcely touch his feed, and as time goes on he becomes emaciated, and severe disease, often in the form of an epidemic, more or less fatal, shows itself. If a change is not made, many deaths will result. Grease, cracked heels, swelled legs, hidebound, inflamed eyes, coughs, and colds are diseases which attend damp, and if present even in a slight degree, any of these diseases are sufficient to interfere with the use of the horse. It must be realized that the horse is peculiarly helpless—tied, watered, fed, etc., as he is by man; he can do little for himself, and must accept whatever is given him as food or abode.

In choosing the situation, therefore, a spot should be chosen which will be high enough to allow perfect drainage at all seasons of the year; hence, low or marshy ground is unsuitable. No periodically overflowing stream should ever be allowed to discharge its contents into the foundations or under the stable, for even if the floor of the stable itself is kept dry and above water, yet the soil underneath will be saturated, and, acting like a sponge, will allow the damp to creep up the walls incessantly. Care should be taken that the site chosen is such that the rainfall of the surrounding country cannot find its way under or around the stables. While canals and ditches will do something to meet this, it is better to avoid it altogether by choosing a site out of the way of all floodwater, and with a good fall.

As to the aspect, there is some difference of opinion as to whether it should be northerly or southerly, all being adverse to a direction either east or west, the former being too cold and the latter too hot. Generally a southern exposure is best; however, one reason given adverse to a southern exposure is undeniable in the main and grounded upon fact: this is, that a more even temperature can be maintained if the situation is sufficiently sheltered from the stroke of the wind. A southern exposure allows the sun to enter with great power in the summer. Animal life is always benefited by the direct rays of the sun, although when the heat from it is intense, the mischief done is so great as to counteract the advantage. The more sun that can shine into the stable the more quickly will it be dried and freshened and bad odors and moisture expelled, but this applies only when the horses are out of it. The proper temperature in the cavalry stable should be maintained as evenly as possible while the horses are in it. Some officers contend for an amount of heat which would raise the thermometer to 60 or 65 degrees Fahrenheit, while others would never have the stables above 45 degrees. To obtain a regular temperature is difficult. In ordinary climates, cavalry stables must be kept as cool as possible. If the horses do not stand directly in the draft, the colder the stables the less will they suffer if suddenly called to take the field. This regulating the temperature daily in troop stables is often not possible beyond a certain point. In extreme cold weather it is customary to keep the horses warm by means of heavy canvas, blanket-lined horse-covers buckled over the horses with surcingles attached to the covers; these blankets, however, should never be used unless the weather is especially and unusually cold, and they should be removed from the horses whenever they are exercised, and always when the temperature has risen to a reasonable height. Some of the horse-covers are without the blanket-lining, and these should be used occasionally, especially in hot southern climates, to protect the horses' backs from the fierce rays of the sun, which are apt to cause blisters. These light blankets are sometimes used also to keep the snow off the backs, but this is not done often.

In Camp.—What has been said in regard to caring for the cavalry horse and his pack in garrison applies in general to the care to be given him when in camp, and, owing to the greater exposure, even more thoroughness and exertion must be taken to keep the horse in condition. As it is rarely practicable to erect even temporary stables in camp, the horse must of necessity be exposed to all conditions of weather, damp food, muddy picket-lines, etc. By knowing what is necessary and customary in garrison, precautions may be taken in the camp and field that will largely save the horse from disease, cure him of his minor ills, and make the exposure less dangerous.

In camp the horses of each troop are tied to elevated picket-lines tightly stretched between stout posts, similar to the picket-lines for the corral. Occasionally the picket-lines in camp are stretched along the ground, being held in place by long iron or wooden pins at intervals and at each end. This latter method should not be used if the camp is to be occupied for any length of time, as there is considerable danger of the horses getting tangled up in it, by their restless moving across it, back and forth. The horses are tied to the elevated picket-line by their halter-straps, and each horse should be tied sufficiently long to enable him to reach his head down to the ground, to enable him to eat the hay, and to allow him to lie down. Guards must be immediately placed over the troop horses when they are tied to the picket-line; the horses often tangle their feet in the straps and picket-rope when it is stretched along the ground, and often several horses will, by circling around each other, become so badly tangled up as to injure one or more of them. If the ground picket-line be used, the guards must be especially watchful and quickly free any horse which may get caught. Occasionally a horse will catch the picket-line (when it is stretched along the ground) in one of his hind fetlock-joints, and, by plunging to get free, so badly burn and cut this joint as to totally unfit him for duty for weeks. Horses caught in this way have been known to be seriously burned and cut their pastern-joints to the bone before the men could free them. The elevated line prevents this danger, saves the rope and halter-straps from being cut and worn by the horses' sharp hoofs, and lessens the liability to injuries more or less serious. Horses tied to the picket-line in camp should have more room than when tied to the corral picket-line; in camp they must stand all day and night, and they must have room to lie down comfortably. In the American cavalry service each troop often carries a complete 2-inch picket-rope about 100 feet long or more, with the necessary long pins. In the absence of this, a most successful picket-line may be made, either elevated or along the ground, by utilizing the lariats and picket-pins of the troopers. When elevated, this lariat picket-line is stretched double and tied between trees, wagons, or posts; when it is stretched along the ground, the iron picket-pins of the troopers hold it in place, as well as convenient bushes, etc.; if the ground is devoid of firm soil or bushes, the picket-pins should be sunk in the ground, horizontally, about 1 foot or more. This is a very strong method of preventing the horses from pulling

TYPICAL AMERICAN CAVALRY CAMP.

the pins up. The picket-line, whether along the ground or elevated, should be in one continuous line, straight, and half the horses tied on one side of it and half on the other side; when ground is not available for the one straight line, the line should not be made either curved or angular, but two or more short lines are preferable.

The place chosen for the picket-lines should first be carefully inspected, and the ground should be on clear, hard soil, free from broken glass, stones, brush, boggy land, etc., and should have a slight slope for drainage. If time permits, the center should be slightly elevated down the entire length of the line, and ditches a foot deep dug on each side the entire length, and far enough back of the line on each side to prevent the horses from backing into the ditches in their efforts to get on level ground. As picket-lines that are used get muddy rapidly, this drainage must be early provided for and maintained, else scratches, quittor, thrush, and many other foot diseases will occur among the animals, and are often hard to cure, especially if the muddy condition continues. The slope of the picket-line to each side should be no more than enough to afford good drainage. Holes pawed out by the animals should be promptly filled in. As the troop picket-line soon becomes untenable in muddy weather, each troop should have two, near each other, in order that one may dry while the horses use the other. This is very necessary in a permanent camp. While suitable ground for two picket-lines for each troop is not always available, the second line should be prepared and ready for use whenever it is possible. Even such serious, contagious diseases as farcy and glanders result from the use of muddy picket-lines soaked with filth.

If the camp is to be occupied for any length of time, it is necessary to have the picket-line thoroughly policed daily, and this should be done morning and evening by the stable-men, assisted by the stable police, as in garrison. All refuse should be hauled away from the camp to a considerable distance, and dumped in a designated place, and later burned up.

In the camp the same routine stable duty is performed as in garrison. There are two groomings daily, morning and evening, and two feedings. The grain is fed in nose-bags and the hay scattered along the center of the picket-line. Hay is only fed in the afternoon, as in garrison. If the horses are to be kept on the picket-line all day, feeding a little hay about noon is a good practice. Half the grain is fed in the morning and the other half in the afternoon. The entire troop attends to this feeding, each man feeding his own horse. The horses in camp are watered twice daily; the morning watering is done about two hours after morning feeding, and the afternoon watering just before afternoon "stables"; after the afternoon "stables," the horses are fed the grain and then the hay; sometimes the feed is given at the same time as the grooming. The troop watering should be superintended by a commissioned officer in the troop, and this officer also superintends the grooming and feeding. No horse should be hurried while drinking, and all those drinking together at one time should be held until all in the bunch have finished. Horses will rarely finish drinking if other near-by horses are led away from the watering-place. The watering-place for the horses in camp should be below the drinking-places of the men, and above the places set aside as bathing-places for the men, for the washing of clothing, the dumping of rubbish or slops or other unclean purposes. Lanterns should be kept ready at the picket-line, to be used by the stable-men or guards in case of need at night. When there is sufficient transportation with the command, each trooper is provided with a horse-cover similar to those used in garrison; these should only be used in very cold weather. When there are no horse-covers with the troop, the saddle-blanket may be used.

The saddles and packs of the troopers are usually kept by them in their tents in temporary camps, or in permanent camps on improvised saddle-racks off the ground, either in front or rear of the tents to which they belong or along the picket-line. The saddles, saddle-blankets, and packs should never be left on the ground, as it rots the leather and rusts the equipments, and the saddle-blankets, becoming filthy, are certain to injure the horses' backs when used.

When grazing is practicable, each troop turns its horses loose under guard. The horses are kept out until shortly before afternoon "stables." If this herding has been practiced in garrison, the horses are easily brought in to the picket-lines quietly, and this should be insisted upon. All the troopers in each troop should be at the picket-line before the horses come in, with their halters, ready to catch up and tie the horses as they arrive. Herding may often be necessary at night. As this is both dangerous and extremely fatiguing to the men, it should be done only when absolutely necessary, but the men must not be saved if the forage in camp is poor; then grazing is of the utmost importance, and in field service often furnishes the chief source of forage for the animals. Better to have tired troopers than dead horses. Care should be taken, when night herding is to be done, that the grazing-grounds of each troop during the day are sufficiently far out to preserve the grazing near the camp for use during the night. When herding at night is necessary, the guards should be doubled, especially if the night is stormy or any sudden alarm is to be feared. Usually, for day herding, with a troop, 4 or 5 men and 1 non-commissioned officer are sufficient. The strength of this herd-guard must, of course, be increased according to the danger to be feared. In the Philippine Islands this guard was never less than 8 armed men, mounted, as the danger of attack from insurgents was always great. After the horses have learned to herd well, they rarely separate, and in case of alarm, if they can be headed toward camp, they will generally all remain together and go there. Occasionally there are a few horses in the troop known to leave the herd at every alarm. If there is any danger of an attack, or the weather is bad, it will be wise to keep these few horses lariated out near the

camp, or even tied to the picket-line, as, in case of a sudden
fright, these few horses, starting off in the wrong direction, may influence the entire herd to follow them, and
all efforts to turn them back may prove unavailing without hard riding and much fierce work.

When herding is not possible and the supply of oats
and hay is limited, the horses are picketed out by means
of the troopers' lariats and picket-pins. The halters in
this case are left on the horses, and the halter-straps tied
securely around the horses' necks; one end of the lariat
is snapped into the halter-ring and the other end is attached to the picket-pin of iron, which is then driven
into the ground. As the lariat is about 20 feet long,
this gives each horse a grazing circle of 40 feet diameter.
This method requires considerable room, as the horses
must be tied well apart, in order to prevent them from
becoming tangled up with each other. This method
has been found satisfactory in some respects, but unsatisfactory in others. As some horses frequently catch
their hind legs in the rope and struggle to free themselves, the fetlock-joints of the hind legs are sometimes
badly burned and the horse disabled for several weeks. In
soft ground the iron picket-pin does not hold well, and a
loose horse running among men or the other horses is a
dangerous thing, as the lariat goes flying through the air,
with the heavy picket-pin whizzing at the loose end. In
such ground it is better to sink the picket-pin, horizontally, at least a foot in the ground. This method (lariat-
ing) is the one used by the American Cavalry, under the
conditions mentioned, after many experiments in the field.
When the horses are out on the lariats, they should never
be left to themselves; several mounted men should be
at hand, on guard, watching the horses, and should be on
the alert to prevent any injury.

A method of securing the troop horses in camp and
field for grazing, so that they may be grazed without being
herded or held, and at the same time kept together and
ready for immediate use, has been one occupying much

attention from cavalry officers for years. Various experiments have been tried, none, however, giving entire satisfaction. The lariat and picket-pin, described above, seem to come nearer to success than any other means known, and yet are still not wholly satisfactory. At one time hobbles were issued to the American troopers; these consisted of two circular leather cuffs connected with a short steel chain about a foot long. The cuffs were clamped around the horse's two front fetlock-joints. It was found, however, that after the horse became accustomed to the hobbles, he could travel miles. Side-lines were also tried, and for years were issued in our service; they consisted of a rope and two cuffs, and were clamped around the horse's front and hind fetlock-joints (the front and hind feet on the same side), the rope being pulled up until only about a foot or so in length. The horse, after getting used to these side-lines, also learned to travel more or less rapidly.

Frequently it is an absolute, imperative necessity in camp and field service to graze the troop horses as much as possible. Hay and grain are oftentimes wholly lacking, or so scarce as to be kept for the sickest and weakest animals in the troop. Herding the troop horses loosely, as described in the first method above, seems the safest way known, and even this can be satisfactorily accomplished only after the troop horses are well trained to it. Even then the danger of stampeding exists, and this may be brought about by only one restless, nervous horse becoming frightened, a vicious clap of thunder, a severe flash of lightning, or the mere striking of a match at night. The writer has seen a herd of thousands of cattle on the Western plains stampeded by such simple frights, more than once, and rush madly at a thundering pace across the vast prairies at a frenzied rate for miles. Life on the vast steppes of Russia has taught the Cossack many methods of overcoming difficulties in the field, and he has for years tethered his horse in camp by means of a short rope about 6 feet long, one end of which has a leather cuff (on the inside of which the hair is left); this cuff is buckled around the horse's near front fetlock-joint, and the other end of the rope is hooked to a long wooden pin with an iron point, somewhat resembling our picket-pin, which is driven into the ground. By this method the horse has a circle in which to graze of about 6 feet, and as the pull on the rope is horizontal, the pin is less apt to be dragged out of the ground. As the shortness of the rope prevents the horse from turning around, he is not liable to injure his hind legs by entangling the rope in his fetlock-joints. The horse has to be moved to a new place frequently to get good grazing. However, the horse has to be watched at any rate when on a rope among other horses more or less nervous. The writer has used this Cossack method in the Philippine Islands, where the ground was often soft, and by burying the pin the scheme has worked better than any of the others described above for the grazing of troop horses. The British Cavalry have used in its colonial campaigns a method which is said to work well so far as the grazing and security of the horses are concerned, but it keeps the troopers awake practically all night. This method consisted in driving one picket-pin into the ground and then tying four or five horses to it, the pin in the center. Between the ropes the troopers placed their saddles near the pin, and then lay down with their heads together near the pin, using their saddles as pillows. Any movement of the horses awoke the men, and thus the danger of a horse escaping was small, but the men got very little sleep, and ran the risk of being injured should the horses become frightened or tangled up. The writer has often known cowboys in the cattle country to tie one end of their reins to their own wrists and, lying down with their saddles for pillows, let their horses graze around them. The horse will almost never step upon the man, and any unusual occurrence at once awakes the sleeping cowboy. This method is hardly to be considered as practicable for a troop of cavalry; it is cited only to illustrate a little more fully some of the various methods that are employed for the accomplishment of the purpose.

In camp it is of the utmost importance that the sick horses be given every care. Almost wholly exposed to the elements, and facilities for caring for them being very limited, the horses that are ill are far more liable to remain so, or get worse, than when housed in garrison stables. As soon as a horse becomes ill, he should be separated from the other horses, and if the camp is to remain in one place for any length of time, rough sheds of the branches of trees, or of shelter tents, or other available material, as protection against weather and sun, should be constructed some distance away from the picket-lines, and the sick horses each placed under one of them; this not only protects the sick animal from much exposure, but it gives him a somewhat dry place to stand upon, which is important when the horse is unwell. Every precaution should be taken to prevent contagion, as in the stables; disinfectants, if at hand, should be freely used; at all events, the ground under and about the sick-sheds should be policed and the refuse taken away and burned, so that no other animal can nose in it and thus suffer. The other horses should be kept away at all times from these sheds and sick animals. Often diseases which appear simple may in reality be very catching. The danger of disease spreading when in camp is too great to be careless in observing every precaution. As in garrison, nose-bags, buckets, cloths, curry-combs, brushes, etc., that have been used about the sick horses should either be destroyed or thoroughly disinfected before being permitted to be used around the other horses. In camp a tent should be placed at one end of the picket-line of each troop, and some of the troop stable-men should be required to sleep here, in order that the guard may be able to get quick and efficient assistance, and the stable-men, who know the animals well, be ready for any emergency.

What has been said in this chapter outlines in sufficient detail the importance of careful study and observation of cavalry management in stables and camp. Much more might be added, but what has been presented will give a good general idea of how the cavalry horse is handled under the conditions of garrison and field; more than this, and the practical working described, must come from actual personal experience and time. It is a large subject, and its appreciation will go a long way towards keeping the cavalry horse and his pack in that perfect condition of health and efficiency required to accomplish all that the service demands. It occasionally happens, especially since colonial service has come into existence in the American service, that the young officer will be given a troop of cavalry in remote places. Here he must construct his own stables, and depend upon his own knowledge to protect his horses from suffering more than the occasion demands. By knowing what is done in garrison and camp, he is enabled to overcome difficulties as they present themselves, and to provide by his own ingenuity substitutes for the regulation methods wherever they are lacking.

CHAPTER XVI.

GROOMING, WATERING, AND FEEDING.

The cavalry horse must not only be well cared for b
means of good ventilation, fresh air, liberal exercise,
drainage, light, even temperature, dryness, etc., but in
his watering, feeding, and grooming constant care must
be taken that the water and food are good, wholesome,
and sufficient, fed at the right times, and varied occasionally to produce the best results, and externally he must
be kept clean and fresh bodily Good stables and clean
picket-lines and surroundings will do much for the horse,
but these preautions are of little value if the watering
and feeding are ignorantly or carelessly attended to, or
the animal himself allowed to go dirty.

Grooming.—The fact that the cavalry horse is kept
in stables and in confinement is not the real reason, or
the most important, why he should be well groomed and
kept bodily clean; for this, and the chief reason, you
must look at his work, and the highly nutritious and
nitrogenous food he must of necessity take, in order to
build him up and strengthen him for his work. It is the

amount of work and the difference in food which are the causes for artificial cleanliness in the horse in confinement, rather than the confinement and shelter themselves. Work of any kind, but hard and fast work especially, increases nervous impulse, muscular energy, and consequently increased secretions of the skin, as exemplified by the profuse perspiration of a horse doing violent exercise, particularly if he is not in the very best condition. It is simply another example of the safety-valve in the boiler. The greater the action of the skin the greater must be the attention paid to the sweat- and oil-glands and pores, which are in reality the safety-valves in this particular. Attention to bodily cleanliness is of far greater importance to the animal in confinement than it is to the creature in a state of nature. Animals at large take only the exercise that is necessary for them to discover and secure the food and water they require, and the horse, living as he does upon grass which he finds almost everywhere, the exercise or work which he does in procuring his daily food is gentle in the extreme. Apart from this, his food—grass—is laxative in its nature, and the waste material and refuse of digestion in such a diet and such a life are carried off mainly through the action of the bowels and kidneys. The harder and faster the work a horse has to do, the more nutritious, the stronger, the more liberal must be his food; consequently, greater must be the care and attention paid to his skin in order to keep the pores open, clean, and free, and, therefore, this scavenger of the body in such a condition of perfection as to meet the constant demands which hard and fast work requires of it.

It is almost inconceivable and very hard to believe, but nevertheless it is a fact, that a horse in robust health, good condition, and doing hard work gives off in twenty-four hours through the pores of the skin an amount of refuse and effete material equal to that excreted by the bowels; so it will be readily understood how necessary must be the attention paid to this investing membrane to insure its constant and unimpeded action. Perspiration goes on constantly in an insensible and imperceptible way, but of course greatly augmented under the strain of violent exercise, when it issues as a wet and moist discharge known as "sudor," or sweat. It will follow, therefore, that the sweat-glands in the horse in a state of nature, where his exercise is gentle and constant, except when in a state of repose, his food light, green, and laxative, are, although always acting as required of them, not put to the violent exertion of those in a horse that is highly fed and doing great exercise. The sweat-glands, therefore, are not in such a perfect state of development in the former animal as they are in the latter, nor is it necessary that they should be so. The horse in confinement consequently requires the greatest attention to his skin and coat; artificial cleanliness, therefore—grooming, rubbing, etc.—is of the utmost consequence and greatest importance to the horse in captivity. Grooming and cleaning not only keep the pores open and free, but they develop them in the same way that exercise and work develop muscle, and consequently keep them in a better condition to stand the strain that is put upon them by hard work. This strain is very considerable, and, if they are not in condition, they will not stand the strain, and the cavalry horse will not be able to keep in the excellent health and condition required, will not be fit for the work he is called upon to perform, and will not bring success to the troop. Grooming the horse not only keeps the sweat- and oil-glands open and working steadily, but it serves as well as a brace to the nerves of the surface by the friction of the brush or wisp. It will be appreciated from the above that the grooming must be done regularly and frequently, else it is more or less useless, as the pores will quickly work more or less irregularly and unsatisfactorily if the horse is allowed to go for any length of time without grooming, and the entire animal will exhibit lack of that mettle and coat that is necessary and indispensable to fine health for his work. Grooming, therefore, should be at least daily, and in the American cavalry service is given twice daily, morning and evening. The manner of grooming will vary somewhat according to the state the horse is in at the time; that is, depending upon whether he has been sweated and is cool again, or if he is still wet from rain, snow, or sweat, or if he has been ridden through dirty roads or over deep country; each of these conditions will therefore require some difference in treatment to get the best results.

AMERICAN CAVALRY TROOP AT STABLES.

The usual morning grooming lasts about twenty minutes on each horse; for this purpose each trooper is furnished with a curry-comb and horse-brush, and should, in addition, have a hoof-pick and a grooming-cloth. As the horses are always groomed at the stables, it is necessary that the horse-cleaning articles be handy, and for this purpose there is a rack placed at one end of the stable,.

containing as many pigeon-holes as there are animals or men, and each trooper is assigned one of the holes. Each hole should be numbered with the trooper's number, and the troopers should be required to keep their grooming materials at all times in their right holes. In the field each trooper should keep his horse-cleaning articles in his saddle-bags, to prevent delay and loss. The curry-comb is intended to remove the scurf or scales of the scarf-skin which are constantly produced from the true skin, and if allowed to remain at the roots of the hair, these have a tendency to confine sweat, and thus interfere with the relief to the circulation which is afforded by that natural process. When a horse's skin is once put in good order, it may be kept clean with very little use of the curry-comb; but a dirty coat cannot well be got right by any other means. The body brush does not penetrate deeply enough unless the coat of the horse is very thin and short; and no amount of wisping will be of any use. The curry-comb, therefore, must be used; it is also especially required to clean the loose hair and dirt from the horse-brush after every few strokes of the brush. There must be some skill displayed in the use of the curry-comb; some troopers sweep it lightly over the horse's neck, back, flanks, croup, and legs as far down as the knees and hocks, without actually scratching the surface of the skin, while others bear down on it with considerable weight, and thus punish the horse to such an extent as often to cause even a naturally good-tempered animal to use his teeth or heels most savagely. A light, thin-coated horse, even when very dirty and full of scurf, does not require the curry-comb to be pressed down hard upon the skin, while a thick-coated animal may require somewhat more pressure to clean away the fœtid matter in and about the pores. The pressure should be no more than is necessary to cleanse the skin, and it should never be used below the knees except, perhaps, to lightly scrape away thick accumulations of mud or dirt. In using the curry-comb, the trooper should begin at the neck on the near side of the horse, curry-comb in the right hand, and should proceed over the shoulders, withers, breast and chest, fore legs to the knees, the back, barrel, flanks, and lightly on the stomach (abdomen), avoiding striking the penis or tender skin of the inner sides of the upper legs, thence to the croup, buttocks, and hind legs to the hocks. The trooper should then change to the off side, taking the curry-comb in his left hand, and proceed as before. After every few scrapes, it will be necessary to knock the curry-comb lightly against the woodwork, to jar off the loose scurf and loose hair, which soon fills the comb and its teeth. In cold weather, when the horse is half chilled, the curry-comb must be used very lightly, as the horse's skin is very sensitive; when the horse is wet, the curry-comb can do little, if any, good.

The horse-brush is made of hog's bristles, is of an oval shape, about 9 inches long by 3 or 4 inches wide, with a strap of webbing or leather across the top for the insertion of the hand. The horse-brush is necessary at all times, unless the horse be very wet or wet and chilled. Using the horse-brush on the wet horse merely packs the damp, soggy hair down tightly, delays the drying of the hair, and is apt to cause the horse to chill by leaving the hair in this plastered condition; it does not clean the skin, and at such a time merely rubs the wet dirt into the pores and hair, and thus tends to prevent the pores from working freely. During the change of coat in the horse the brush should be used lightly, as its heavy use tends to bring off the old hair too rapidly, is apt to thin the coat, and brings the new coat out coarser than it would naturally be. To produce a beautiful coat, the old one should be left on as long as possible, just as we find in the sheep which is not shorn, but allowed to shed its wool, the next growth will be much shorter and more beautiful. It must be remembered, however, that beauty of coat is second in importance to cleanliness of hair and free action of the skin and pores in it. In using the horse-brush, the trooper should begin at the neck on the near side, curry-comb in right hand and brush in the left, after the curry-comb has been used as described; the brush should be used thence all over the neck, shoulders and withers, breast, chest, barrel, etc., following the course of the curry-comb and the direction of the hair; after finishing the near side, the trooper should repeat the work on the off side; after every one or two strokes of the brush, it should be scraped clean with the curry-comb, as it quickly fills with dust, scurf, and loose hair. The brush should be used lightly on the tender skin of the inside of the horse's legs and thighs, and should be used to clean the legs from the knees or hocks down to the hoofs.

The hoof-pick should now be used. It consists merely of an iron or steel hook made in the form of a right angle, one side of the angle long enough to hold the hook steady in the hand and the other side of the angel somewhat shorter and rather pointed at the end. The horse's feet should be picked up, one at a time, and the hook used to scrape away any dirt or small bits of gravel or stone that may have become packed between the shoe and the sole of the foot or around the frog. The pick must be used carefully, and never dug into the openings on the sides of the frog, which may cause injury to the foot. As the horse frequently picks up small particles of stone or wood or other more or less solid substances, these must be removed without delay, to prevent injury from treading upon them; for this reason it is wise to have plenty of hooks hanging near the stalls in the stables and to carry a few when in the field. Occasionally these hoof-picks are attached to the tops of the curry-combs by rivets; this is a good way of keeping them always at hand. The troop blacksmith can make all that are needed, however, with little trouble. The pick should not be too sharp at the point, for many troopers have a heavy hand, and in cleaning out the foot may run the point too far in and cause lameness.

After the horse has been curry-combed, brushed, and his feet cleaned, the trooper should use the grooming-cloth all over the horse. This cloth is easily made from old blankets or other woolen material; the cloth should be about 2 feet square, and kept fresh and clean by washing. In using the cloth, the horse's eyes, nostrils, head, sheath, lips, and dock should be carefully wiped out. It is very refreshing to the horse to have the cloth slightly dampened when this is done, if the weather is not cold. The cloth should be carried all over the horse and frequently dusted off while being used, to prevent carrying dirt or dust back into the hair. The cloth, like the curry-comb and brush, is of no use when the horse is wet, and should not be used.

In grooming the horse, the curry-comb should never be used to clean the mane or tail; its teeth easily pull out many hairs, and so injure these parts. The trooper should use his brush and hands to clean out dirt or mud from the mane and tail, and should use the brush and his hands when cleaning out the fetlocks. The skin in the fetlock joints is tender and easily injured, and nothing rough or harsh should be used here. The trooper can, by taking the mane or tail in his hands and separating it into two parts, rub the two divisions together and easily clean off the caked dirt or mud, after which a brisk brushing with the horse-brush will make it glossy and fresh. The grooming-cloth can be used in the fetlock joints and clean them out fully.

Whenever the horse returns to the stable or picket-line in a wet condition, he should not be groomed with the curry-comb or brush; this applies when the horse is soaked with rain or snow; when only more or less wet from sweat from exercise, ordinary grooming is sufficient. However, to groom the horse with the curry-comb and brush when his coat and skin are soaked from external moisture will do no good, and, as explained above, will simply pack down the wet hair and probably chill the animal, and never clean him. The horse should be wisped dry with hay; the trooper wisping the animal must work hard, and sweep the wisp backward and forward until the coat and skin are fairly dry; to absolutely dry out the horse's hair would consume more time than is ordinarily available to the trooper at stable-time. The wisp consists simply of a handful of dry, fresh hay or straw. If the horse can be exercised until cooled off, so much the better, but this also is not always practicable in cavalry. The trooper using the wisp should rub hard and quickly, backward and forward, beginning at the neck and working over the horse as he does with the ordinary horse brush, except that the horse-brush should never be rubbed against the direction of the hair, except to remove caked dirt or mud. After the wisping is finished, the hair may be lightly rubbed down and smoothed a little, but it is better to leave it as it is after finishing the wisping, as in this way the hair dries more quickly, there is less danger of chilling the horse, and the skin is freer to throw off the internal moisture and waste material.

Hand-rubbing the horse is invaluable, especially if the animal is wet or tired; it acts much like the rubbing-down of the athlete. In hand-rubbing the legs, the trooper should place his two hands, palms flat, around the horse's legs, below the knee or hock and rub downward repeatedly. This rubbing should not be too rapid, and the trooper should use a firm hand, but no clinching pressure around the leg. The legs should be cleaned before being rubbed.

The coat of the horse is changed twice a year, the long hair of winter coming off in April and May, or sometimes earlier, when the stables are warm and there is no exposure to severe cold. A slight sweat hastens this shedding. The long hair on the legs is about a month later in coming off, and indeed it will not fall till midsummer unless some more violent means than are used in ordinary grooming are adopted. With some breeds the winter coat is not very much longer or coarser than that of the summer, while others have most shaggy coats in the winter months.   About the middle of October or early in November the summer coat is thrown off, but some of the hair appears to remain as a sort of under-coat, among which the long, coarse hairs of winter make their appearance.   These long winter hairs continue to grow for a month or six weeks, and even after Christmas, if the weather is very cold, there will be an evident increase in length of the hair.   In accordance with this growth of hair on the body is that on the legs, which become feathered all the way down the backs of the fore legs below the knees, and half way down the backs of the hind-legs below the hocks.   Low-bred horses have more hair on these parts than thoroughbreds, but even these latter exhibit a great deal of hair on their legs.   Grooming the horse tends somewhat to shorten the growth of hair, and to slightly thin it, but not enough to produce ill effects, and the grooming is necessary to remove the mass of loose short hairs which should come off. The long coat is Nature's protection against the cold of winter; but being long, and so more liable to catch and retain dust and dirt and parasites, it needs grooming to keep the skin underneath fresh and clean and the hair itself free from filth.   In civil life clipping and singeing are often practiced, sometimes even in winter, and much has been written to defend the practice, but while the long coat absorbs a deal of moisture, and therefore is difficult to dry, at the same time it protects the horse from the chill winds of the winter months, and must be left as Nature makes it, only keeping it clean and fresh.   In the cavalry service clipping and singeing are not permitted and should never be done.   Occasionally the clipping of the long hair on the fetlock-joints is allowed, and if the weather is dry, this may do no harm; but, as the skin here is tender and easily injured, this should not be allowed if the weather is either cold, damp, or wet.   Scratches are very liable to break out after the fetlocks are clipped, should the weather turn cold or raw.

In the American cavalry service the manes and tails are never cut short, but allowed to grow long and fine. In some European services the mane is cut off an inch or two to give it an even edge, and the tail is cut off more or less after the manner of "docking," so common in civil life. In our service one or two regiments have made a practice of cutting off the tail so that its end is even with the hocks, and this practice has many advocates. The cruel practice, however, of cutting off any of the tail at all is injurious and exhausting to the horse, especially in the hot season, when he is surrounded with insects and requires his complete tail to protect himself. The long, flowing tail is very handsome in a troop, and, as the troopers keep the manes and tails in fine condition, it adds much to the appearance of the command and is the rational way.

An exhausted horse is vastly benefited by wisping, grooming, and hand-rubbing, and, if carefully worked over, many a horse thought to be too exhausted to recover may be saved and freshened up by an hour's steady work when occasion demands. Many cavalry officers are disposed to favor the abolition of morning "stables" in the service, believing that little is accomplished that benefits either trooper or horse by such early-morning grooming; others favor having the morning grooming take place immediately after morning drill; this, indeed, seems to be the rational time, for the horse has, by exercise, warmed up and the pores have opened and discharged considerable waste material which should be removed, and not allowed to remain in the hair and on the skin all day. Many cavalry officers believe that two groomings of the horse in winter are unnecessary and even harmful. These officers contend that the excessive grooming of a horse in winter shortens the hair and thins the coat to such an extent as to render the horse very liable to chills and cold; that it keeps the pores of the skin too open and in too active condition at a time when the sweating of the horse is very slight. There is much to consider regarding this theory. All men accustomed to horses realize, however, that the amount of grooming necessary in the hot season is considerably more than what is required in cold weather, just as less clothing is required by man when the season is warm than when it is cold. However, in the American cavalry service the grooming in winter and summer is conducted just the same. This is a necessity in a cavalry service where there is much to be done, and it is wise to do all things as regularly and systematically as possible, with as few variations as circumstances require.

As the necessity for grooming the cavalry horse is well appreciated in all services and is systematically and very similarly done by them all, in order to keep the horse healthy, clean, and fine in appearance, the grooming should be done well at both morning and evening stables. The trooper in grooming should assist the action of the brush and cloth by throwing his weight against it somewhat; this makes the effort expended less and accomplishes what is required. Using the arm alone, without adding the weight of the trooper's body in right proportion, becomes very tiresome before the horse is thoroughly groomed and ready for the officer's inspection. Recruits are very apt to fail to appreciate that skill in grooming will save them much expenditure of muscle, and they either tire themselves out or (what is more natural and human) they idle before the grooming is done, and thus the horse suffers. There are some parts of the horse's body somewhat difficult to reach and clean, and these are often neglected; as they are the parts where friction is considerable when the horse moves, it is especially necessary that these parts be not neglected; these places are found between the horse's thighs and under the breast and at the tops of the inner sides of the fore legs, and between the buttocks, and in the fetlock-joints. Dirt in these places soon causes sores and more or less disagreeable discharges, and they should not be allowed to be neglected. Some horses, especially new ones in the troop, do not take kindly at first to the grooming; these are apt to be neglected also. When these animals are groomed, one man should hold the head or lift up one of the fore legs, while another man does the grooming.

As horses like to roll in dry, dusty places, and also in wet places in warm weather, and as many horses come into the stable or picket-lines in very muddy condition, their coats and skin become coated with thick mud, which must be wholly gotten off. As many of the places where the horses roll may have been used by cattle or other dirty animals, there is liability of the horse, in rolling, getting parasites in the hair and skin; these may cause mange or other disorders of the skin and mane and tail, and therefore the horses require careful cleaning; this especially happens wherever the troop horses are being herded during the day. As this mud sticks fast, it is necessary to use the curry-comb to loosen it, and afterward use the brush and cloth and hands. The practice, however, sometimes prevails of washing the horse. In the Philippine Islands washing the horse all over (among the native inhabitants) was practiced as a regular thing. The little native horses there were taken to a nearby river or lake, led in up to their stomachs or deeper, and then water was splashed all over them until clean; they were then taken out and allowed to dry in the shade. In those islands the climate was so warm that little or no harm came from this practice to these wiry little native animals, but it was never practiced by the American Army there. In many fine private stables in America and Europe and England the washing of "hunters" is very frequent, but these horses are carefully dressed afterward, and not allowed to cool off exposed to sun, wind, or cold. In the treatment and cleaning of the cavalry horse this entire washing should never be permitted. In the first place, it is rarely warm enough to do so; and, in the second, carelessness in attending to the horse afterward would cause him to become ill after a little such treatment. When the horse is in this muddy condition, he should be groomed as usual, although more carefully, and only his legs from the knees and hocks down allowed to be washed. Even this should be done rarely, and never in damp or cold weather. When this is permitted, the horse's wet legs should be hand-rubbed afterward until warm. Washing the legs in cold or damp weather is apt to result unsatisfactorily at least, and it frequently causes "stocking"—swelling of the legs. Washing any part of the cavalry horse is rarely necessary; it is usually a lazy trooper's method of grooming, and such a man is not apt to hand-rub his mount afterward or pay much attention to the horse's comfort and warmth.

The cavalry horse is groomed twice a day in the British service—morning and midday—but when the troops do not come in from work before the dinner hour, the horses are groomed in the afternoon. At the evening stable hour but little grooming is done, the horses being merely generally rubbed down and wisped. In Germany the cavalry horse is groomed three times daily—morning, noon, and evening. In France the cavalry horse while at the remount dépôt is groomed, but not very thoroughly, owing to the small number of men and the large number of horses to care for; the stallions are groomed once daily, and where salt water is available, they are given a salt-water bath, in place of the grooming, every two or three days. This grooming, when done, occurs in the evening. These stallions are, however, rubbed down both before and after exercise. The regular regimental cavalry horses are groomed twice a day, once between half past 8 and 10 in the morning and again about 3 in the afternoon. In the Austrian service the horses are carefully groomed three times a day—morning, noon, and evening.

Watering.—Were the cavalry horse loose and able to go to water at his own convenience and as Nature urged him, there would be little left for us to consider in the watering of horses; but this is not so. In confinement, under the control of men, the horse must take his water when it is given him, must then, if thirsty, drink all he can to avoid the physical inconvenience or suffering of going a long number of hours without any more, and if the horse is an old cavalry horse, he has learned to make the most of his opportunities of drinking. All these considerations and many more teach us that the watering of our horses must be carefully done, its effects on the horse studied, and caution observed that he does not injure himself by overdrinking, drinking when heated, or drinking bad water, etc. Horses must be watered quietly and without confusion; the manner in which this duty is performed will bring good or bad results, according to its wisdom. In leading horses to and from the watering-trough in garrison, or to and from the watering-places in the field, the gait should never be faster than a walk, and the horses should never be watered unless cool and quiet. While the horse is actually drinking, his head should never be jerked up, nor should the horse be harshly spoken to or punished near the watering-place. In the field or on the march, the watering-place is from the most convenient running water; in garrison, it is from the watering-troughs in the various troop "corrals," and these troughs should be cleaned frequently, at least twice each week. In warm weather water drawn from a well should be allowed to stand awhile before being given to the horse, in order that the chill may pass off of it. Cavalry horses in each troop should be watered under the immediate supervision of the stable sergeant and the officer attending "stables," and in the field or camp an officer should always be present. Ordinarily horses should be watered twice daily; in warm weather this should, if possible, be increased to three times. When in the "corral" or herding, the troop horses should have free access to water at all times, care being taken that the animals are all cool. When on the march, troop horses not too warm may be allowed to drink whenever good water is passed; those too hot should not be allowed to do so until cooled off sufficiently. The horses in the rear of the troop, often compelled to close up when distance has been lost by slight increases of the gait, are generally the warmest in the command, and these should be looked out for. The water given to the horse to drink should never be taken from stagnant pools or low, marshy ground if it can be avoided. Giving the horse good, clean, fresh, sparkling water to drink is as necessary for him as for man. The impression that any water is good enough for the horse is one based upon inexperience only, and many ills result from carelessness in this regard. The quality of water for the horse is one moderately soft, but it should not be rain-water collected in tanks, which soon becomes full of decomposing vegetable matter. The health of a whole stableful of horses may be seriously injured by using rain-water that has been kept too long. Water not suitable for horses to drink may be made fairly good, if it be necessary to use the supply stored up, by filtration through charcoal, gravel, and sand. The use of very hard water often produces what is known as ''hide-bound,'' and sometimes affects the bowels in the form of serious diarrhœa; but in the course of time most horses become used to drinking hard water, and then a change to soft water may cause some slight trouble. This change of water is of such importance to trainers of race-horses that in traveling to their races they frequently carry the water with them which the horse is accustomed to, despite the risk of the water being poisoned. Hard water, if it contains large quantities of carbonate of lime, may be made to deposit it to some extent by boiling, but the sulphate of lime (or gypsum), which is a far more common ingredient, is as soluble in hot water as in cold. This watering the horse with good, pure water is very important. As the horse drops seeds of grain from his mouth into the water-trough at times, these often decay and gradually form a green slime in the watering-trough, which must be cleaned out. It is generally felt that live vegetable matter in a lake or pond is not in itself cause for fear as to the healthfulness of the water, but dead vegetable matter in the water at once renders it dangerous for drinking purposes, either for man or beast. In the field and camp it will often be necessary for the horses to drink water that is anything but good, but whenever a selection is possible, it should be made, and the horses given as good as can be secured, as a serious matter of health, if not for the greater kindness it is to the horses.

In very cold weather watering the cavalry horse but once, about noon, is sufficient; this must not be set down, however, as a hard-and-fast-rule, for if the animal wants water more frequently, he should be allowed to have it. It is absurd to decide to water horses once or twice and no more daily. Let the horse drink naturally and as frequently as he desires, taking care only that the water is fit and that the animal himself is not too warm. Some horses will rarely drink very early in the morning, and these should be given an opportunity of drinking after they have traveled or exercised awhile. If a command has to march a long distance without water, so that it will be necessary to encamp *en route*, the horses should all be fed, but denied water until just before starting, when they are permitted to drink freely; better still, water the horses twice before starting, as some of them will not drink even at the last moment, while, if two attempts will make them drink, the horses will be saved great suffering. On severe marching frequent watering is of great benefit. When horses are somewhat warm in marching, it is not harmful to water them all, if the march is to be immediately resumed. If very warm, a few mouthfuls will do no harm and will be a great relief, whenever the chance offers, but the horse must not be allowed to gorge himself; three or four mouthfuls, under such conditions, are all he should be allowed to take.

The daily allowance of water for the cavalry horse varies greatly with season, climate, the amount of work he is performing, etc. No hard-and-fast-rule can be given. A horse should be allowed to drink what Nature demands. Care should be taken that the horse is not allowed to fill himself with water, as he will do if he has been denied it

for so long that he is craving it; the horse is unreasonable
in this, especially when in confinement, and he must be
watched.   A loose horse rarely injures himself by drinking
too much water, but again it must be added that he must
not be turned loose when very hot.   When the horse is at
rest, he will ordinarily consume about 6 gallons or so of
water daily; when at work, he requires from 8 to 12 gallons.   This all varies, of course, with circumstances, but
is a fair average.   The trooper will use about 1 gallon a
day for all purposes.   A gallon of fresh water weighs 8⅓
pounds, approximately, or a pint to a pound.

The cavalry horse should be watered immediately
before feeding, or not until at least two hours after eating.
Watering the horse immediately after he has eaten floods
the stomach and drives much of the food, especially the
grain, into the intestines undigested, and causes much
trouble and may ruin the horse.   The animal also loses
the nutrition in the food thus expelled from the stomach.
By observing the fæces of a horse that has been watered
immediately after feeding, there may be seen whole
grains of the feed which have passed entirely through the
horse without being digested.   This is injurious to the
delicate lining of the internal organs of the horse, and
many instances are known where horses have died from
this ill-timed watering.   The stomach of the horse is very
small, and should not be distended by large draughts of
water at one time.   Better several small waterings than
one large one.   What is remarkable about the stomach
of the horse is this very small size; that of a large
horse will not contain more than 3 or 4 gallons, whereas
the first division of the ox's stomach, the "rumen," will
alone hold about 60 gallons.   Another remarkable feature is, that the stomach is so curved on itself that its
two extremities—the œsophageal and intestinal portions
—are quite near each other.   This fact, the acute angle
at which the œsophagus joins the stomach, the folds of
membrane inside this junction, and which form a kind
of valve, the special arrangement of muscular fibers

around this junction, together with the small size of the organ itself, are held to be the reasons why the horse can not vomit unless under very special conditions, one of which is the rupture of the stomach. When the horse does vomit, the discharge issues out through the nostrils.

Experiments with the stomach of the horse have demonstrated that this organ must fill and empty itself two or three times for each feed given. One experiment by a celebrated veterinary surgeon, made to determine just what occurred when the horse was fully watered on a full stomach, showed that 3 quarts of oats (out of 4 fed) had been carried into the intestines undigested. The grain of the ration, being full of protein, should remain in the stomach as long as possible, for the digestion of this nutrient. Sanborn, the celebrated veterinary expert, studying the effects of watering just before and also after feeding, concludes as follows:

"Horses watered before feeding grain retained their weight better than when watered after feeding grain. Horses watered before feeding had the better appetite and ate the most. Horses watered after feeding grain, in ratio to the food eaten, seemed to digest it as well as those watered before feeding. In a prior trial there was a small advantage in favor of feeding after watering, on digestion. Result: It seems advisable to water both before and after feeding."

The above will show that even the most learned veterinarians differ as to the proper order of watering and feeding. In the experiments cited above, made by Sanborn, the watering after feeding was about two hours after feeding. In general, we may say that horses should have their regular and largest supply of water previous to feeding, and it may also be well to supply a limited quantity some time after feeding. This, however, because of the other many duties in the cavalry service, cannot well be done, and the watering before feeding usually is all that is given, unless chance later on offers another opportunity to water. When the horses come to the stable or picket-line heated or fatigued, a little water, fresh, may be given with beneficial effects, but not too much—say 4 or 5 quarts. Then, when cooled off and rested, what they still require should be supplied.

Feeding.—The horse in cavalry service receives two kinds of feed—grain and hay. The allowance of grain in the Cavalry of the United States is 12 pounds daily and of hay 14 pounds daily. There are some three thousand varieties of hay known, and these will be discussed later on. Of the grains, there are four generally used in the cavalry service—oats, corn, bran, and sometimes barley. This latter was used considerably years ago in the far Southwest, but, as it is not often used, one of the other grains mentioned usually takes its place. The allowance of grain and hay, as fed in cavalry services, differs very much from the allowance given to the horses of large express and cab companies in civil life. These latter horses usually are fed three times daily, as is the civil practice, while the cavalry horse receives only two daily feeds. This cavalry practice has been found to answer all purposes, to economize work, to keep the horse in excellent shape, and to allow, in field service, of long marches between the two feeds with no ill effects. Oats and hay are the ideal foods for the horse. However, variety is essential to him, and thus bran takes the place of the oats once or twice a week. As bran acts as a gentle laxative, it not only furnishes variety to the animal, but keeps the bowels open as much as is required. In field service bran is often lacking, but the rich, green grasses of the prairies and valleys then take its place as a regulator of the horse's bowels. For this reason the feeding of grasses must be watched carefully, and a change made back to oats and hay in the feed of any horse whose bowels appear too loose. While change of feed for the horse is essential to good health and appetite, nevertheless great care must be taken that these changes are not too sudden and are composed of the proper grains and grasses, or the horse will suffer. The cavalry allowance given above is believed to be all-sufficient, and where grazing is indulged in, the grain allowance may be, and frequently is, somewhat reduced; when the troop horses are not exercising much, the grain allowance need not be so large, and may often, as in winter, when there is much bad weather, preventing out-door work and drills, be reduced 2 pounds or so with beneficial results. The hay allowance is rarely reduced when hay is plenty.

Race-horses in large stables are fed from 6 to 8 pounds of hay daily and from 15 to 20 pounds of the best oats daily; if needed, a bran mash once a week is given; one-third of the hay is given after the morning exercise and the balance at night, and the oats are fed at four feeds. In feeding the "hunter" more hay is given, up to 10 pounds daily, 6 pounds loose and 4 pounds cut and mixed with the oats, which run from 16 to 18 pounds a day. In Scotland a favorite feed is cut oat sheaves, and the horses do hard work upon it. When horses are in the stable much of the time, the feeding must be carefully managed. In many parts of Canada roots are a favorite winter food. Swede turnips are relished by horses, and seem better food for them than carrots, which, however, are known for their fine effect as food upon the horse. Elaborate and careful experiments made years ago showed that horses do better on raw food. Crushed or ground oats are much used in civil life, though the American Cavalry has never so fed it. Some horses have a tendency to bolt their food, half chewed, and some of the grain is voided, because of this, whole. Grinding helps to remedy such evil.

In England some of the large companies which work a great many horses give mixed food, and use considerable quantities of American corn. The following table will illustrate what constitutes a day's ration in several of these great company stables:

The North Metropolitan Company, London: corn,
13 pounds; oats, 3 pounds; peas, 1 pound;
beans, 1 pound; hay, 7 pounds; cut straw, 3
pounds; total, 22 pounds daily.

The South London Tramway Company: corn, 7
pounds; oats, 7 pounds; beans, 1 pound; hay,
11 pounds; straw, 3 pounds; total, 29 pounds
daily.

What needs special attention in feeding is the desir-
ability of a quantity of hay and a small quantity of straw
in the ration for these large companies. These rations
are divided into from three to five feeds daily.

The allowance of grain in the British cavalry service
is 10 pounds of oats daily and 12 pounds of hay on
ordinary feed; if out on active service, the oats are
increased to 15 pounds.

The forage allowance in the Russian cavalry service
is 9 pounds 5½ ounces of oats daily, 9 pounds 1 ounce
of hay daily, 3 pounds 10 ounces of straw daily. One
month of grazing is given all cavalry horses per year and
this is in lieu of all forage rations. If necessary, hay may
be substituted for oats at the rate of 4 pounds 8½ ounces
of hay for 3 pounds 1⅘ ounces of oats. In time of war
the ration is 12 pounds 15½ ounces of oats and 13 pounds
9½ ounces of hay daily.

The forage allowance in the German Cavalry is distinguished, according to the nature of the service which
the horses are performing, into garrison, march, and field
ration; again, it is classified, according to the breed of
the horse for which it is intended, into heavy, middle,
and light cavalry of the guard ration. In order to compare it with the American forage allowance, the following
is the middle allowance for German cavalry horses, daily:

Garrison: oats, 10.37 pounds; hay, 5.58 pounds;
straw, 7.81 pounds.
March: oats, 11.5 pounds; hay, 3.34 pounds;
straw, 3.9 pounds.

Field: oats, 12.61 pounds; hay, 3.34 pounds; straw, 3.9 pounds.

This is also the light cavalry allowance, nearly.

The following is the forage allowance of the Austro-Hungarian Cavalry, daily:

> In time of peace: 4.2 kgs.* of oats; 3.4 kgs. of hay; 1.7 kgs. of straw for litter.
> In time of war: 5.8 kgs. of oats; 2.8 kgs. of hay; no straw is allowed.

For one-half ration of oats may be substituted an equal weight of corn, rye, barley, lentils, or vetch.

For one-half ration of hay may be substituted one and one-half weight of barley or oat straw.

The following is the French forage ration, on peace footing, for horses belonging to the troops:

> Heavy cavalry: hay, 3.5 kgs.; straw, 4.25 kgs.; oats, 5.0 kgs.
> Medium cavalry: hay, 2.5 kgs.; straw, 3.5 kgs.; oats, 5.0 kgs.
> Light cavalry: hay, 2.5 kgs.; straw, 3.5 kgs.; oats, 4.5 kgs.

The French forage allowance varies in many ways, according to the duty and according to whether the horses are also on grass or not. In the hot countries of Algeria and Tunis the following is the regular ration for horses belonging to the troops:

> In time of peace: hay, 2.5 kgs.; straw, 3.5 kgs.; barley, 4.5 kgs.
> In time of war: hay, 2.5 kgs.; straw, 2.0 kgs.; barley, 4.5 kgs.

Indian corn, buckwheat, wheat, and horse beans are substituted in the above forage allowances under certain conditions; carrots, barley meal, and bran are occa-

---

*Note.—1 kilogram (kg.) is equal to 2.2046 pounds.

sionally given; the horses are also occasionally allowed mashes or green food.

Oats.—Good oats should be sound and whole, with the covers on, and should have the beards on; they should be rather milky, and, when dented with the thumb-nail, not be found brittle; they should have a sweet, fresh odor, be dry and clean and free from dust; the oats may be either white or black, color not affecting their value as a food. Old oats are readily told after a little experience; they are very brittle, have a metallic luster, the beards are broken off and gone, and the covers of the oats are often lacking. These covers and beards, breaking off, gradually become so much dust in the oats and make them dirty and musty. Horses nurtured on oats show mettle which cannot be reached by the use of any other feeding-stuff; there is no other grain so safe for horses. The horse may be seriously injured, however, if by accident he receives and eats an oversupply, although an oversupply of any grain is a risk, especially if the horse be hot. The comparative safety in oats is due in no small measure to the oat hull or "cover," which causes a given weight of grain to possess considerable volume, and because of this there is less liability of mistake in measuring out the ration to the horse. The horse, if left to himself, will often eat too much oats and will even cause himself pain by overloading his stomach, if not actual injury. Unless the horse is hard-pressed for time or has poor teeth, oats should be fed in the whole condition. Musty oats should be avoided. Horsemen very generally agree that very new oats should not be used; however, Boussingault, the veterinary scientist, conducting extensive experiments with army horses, arrived at the conclusion that very new oats do not possess the injurious qualities attributed to them. Oats should be kept off the ground and dry, as they quickly mould and become sour if exposed to damp or wet, and may become full of bugs or worms. Good oats should weigh about 40 pounds to the bushel.

Corn.—Corn is the common grain for horses in America, and indeed, it might be said, throughout the world.

Corn is not the equal of oats as a grain for the horse, but, because of its low price and the high feeding qualities it possesses, this grain will be extensively used wherever large numbers of horses must be economically maintained. Corn may be fed whole to horses, and in cavalry usually is, but in civil life it is often made fine by grinding, and is often mixed with various other concentrates. Ground corn alone is a sodden substance in the horse's stomach, and should be diluted or extended with something of light character; bran serves well for this purpose, because of its lightness and cooling effect, as well as for the protein and mineral matter it furnishes. Corn is best suited for animals doing plain, steady work; it is lacking in ash and protein; this makes it undesirable for feeding growing horses. Wolff quotes the celebrated Lehman in the following statement:

"Corn contains a high proportion of digestible carbohydrates, and tends to make horses fat and liable to sweat; while it improves their appearance, it detracts from their physical energy."

Corn should never be fed in hot weather or permanently warm climates, for this reason. Good corn should be whole, free from dust or dirt, either light yellow or yellowish white, free from mould and vermin, and of a fresh, sweet odor. Corn weighs about 56 pounds to the bushel.

Barley.—On the Pacific coast and in the far Southwest barley is extensively used for feeding horses in civil life. It is purchased by the cavalry service only when oats are not available. In civil life it is given to horses doing all kinds of work, from the light buggy horse to the express animal. When the horse's teeth are good and the labor not severe, barley may be fed whole. Ground barley, when mixed with the saliva, forms, like wheat, a pasty mass in the mouth, and is therefore unpleasant to the horse while eating it; if, instead of grinding, the grains are crushed to flattened discs between iron rollers, they are more palatable and acceptable to the horse.

Good barley should weigh between 45 and 48 pounds to the bushel.

Bran.—Bran is used as a change from the oat forage of the cavalry horse, and should be given twice each week as a mash in lieu of other grain. One feed in the afternoon is the best way to feed it to the horses. It should be mixed with water and thus formed into a mash, but may be fed dry. Feeding bran dry is unsatisfactory, because the horse in eating breathes strongly through his nose, thus scattering the bran out of the feed-box, whereby much loss occurs; it also is inhaled up the horse's nostrils, causing much sneezing and discomfort, and in the mouth it is not agreeable unless wet. The horse takes to it as an occasional change very readily. As it acts as a laxative, is should not be fed too often, twice a week being generally sufficient, with an occasional extra feed to the sick horse, if needed. Good bran should weigh about 20 pounds to the bushel. In appearance, the bran, if good, should be a brownish yellow, with small white specks of the interior of the crushed seed, free from mould and vermin, and free from lumps; should be dry and sweet, clean in smell, and free from dust or dirt, and altogether light and flaky. As bran will sour very quickly if damp or wet, care should be taken to keep it thoroughly dry until fed. The uneaten part, if any, should never be left in the feed-boxes after the feeding is over, as it will sour there and spoil the new grain placed in the box for the next feed.

The following table shows the properties contained in the various grains used in the cavalry services:

	Woody Fiber.	Starch and Sugar.	Fibrine and Albumen.	Fatty Matter.	Saline Matter.	Water.
Oats.........	20.	53.	11.4	.6	2.5	12.5
Corn.........	6.	62.	12.	.5	1.	14.
Barley.......	14.	52.	13.5	2.5	3.	15.
Bran.........	54.	2.	20.	4.	7.	13.
Hay..........	30.	40.	7.	2.	7.	14.
Straw........	55.	27.	.5	0.0	5.5	12.

The hay and straw may vary somewhat. The above is old hay and wheat straw. Straw is not fed in the American service. It is used only as bedding. The allowance is 100 pounds per horse per month.

The peculiarities of each horse must be studied before it can be known whether the average quantity and quality of food which will suit the majority of horses doing the same kind of work will be enough or too much for him. Some animals pass their food through them so quickly that they do not absorb from one-half of the nutritive elements contained in it. However, in a large cavalry stable an average can be struck very quickly, much depending on the stable-men getting to know the animals in the troop, which they soon do.

The blood of the horse fed on highly nitrogenized food does not differ on analysis from that of another which has been kept on the opposite kind of diet. Physiological research, however, tells us that muscle is composed of fibers and that every time a bundle of them contracts a certain expenditure of nitrogen is made, calling for a corresponding supply from the blood, which cannot be afforded unless the food contains it. Hence, the badly fed horse, if worked, soon loses his flesh, and not only becomes free from fat, but also presents a contracted condition of the muscles. And thus science is confirmed by every-day experience; and the fact is generally admitted that to increase the muscular powers of the horse he must have a sufficient supply of nitrogenized food. The nutrition of muscle requires nitrogen But in addition to this, the brain and nerves must be supplied with fatty matter, phosphorus and albumen. The bones demand gelatine and earthy salts, and the maintenance of heat cannot be effected without carbon in some shape or other. However, it is chiefly with nitrogenized food that we have to deal, there being plenty of the other substances mentioned in all the varieties of food which are not largely composed of fibrine. It may, therefore, be taken for granted that the cavalry horse requires oats or beans or both mixed up together in varying proportions, together with such an amount of hay as will supply him with starch, gum, sugar, fat, and saline matters, which his sys-

INDIAN GRASS

tem requires. While, on the other hand, it may be added, the inactive horse does not use his muscular system to any extent, and therefore does not require much oats or beans.

Hay.—Hay or grass is indispensable; upon either one horses have kept up strong and well and performed their regular work for some time, when grain was not to be procured. By reference to table on page 406 it will be seen

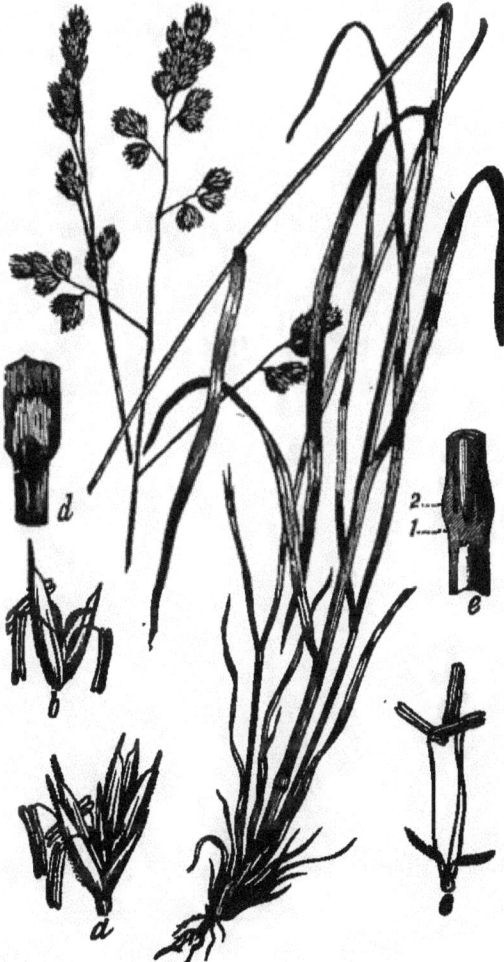

Courtesy of Hon. F. D. Coburn.

ORCHARD GRASS.

of what hay is composed within itself. There are some three thousand varieties of grasses, wild and cultivated, from which hay is made for food for horses, and a few will be mentioned here. In general, hay is known as upland,

lowland, and wet meadow hay. These names in themselves describe their location. The upland is considered

Courtesy of Hon. F. D. Coburn.

TIMOTHY GRASS.

the best, then the lowland, and the wet meadow last.
These three classes are generally distinguished from

each other by the fine, slender stalks of the upland, the
rather wider and somewhat coarser stalks of the lowland,

THE LITTLE BLUE-STEM OF THE WEST.

and the broad, wide, and very coarse stalks of the wet
meadow hay. Chief among the grasses out of which hay

is made are timothy, considered the best, red-top, Bermuda, orchard, Kentucky blue, and clover, red or white;

RED-TOP GRASS.

all of which are largely raised in the Eastern United States, while in the Western part are the alfalfa, gramma,

gietta, bunch buffalo, Western blue-stem. There are
many others, both East and West. To distinguish the
several varieties and classes of hay is not to be learned

Courtesy of Hon. F. D. Coburn.

KENTUCKY BLUE GRASS.

BIG BLUE-STEM.

from books, but must be studied personally before it will
be possible to classify with any assurance of certainty.*

*The Agricultural Reports of the United States or of any of the
States can always be easily procured and furnish the most authoritative information upon these matters.

However, there are several things concerning the hay that
are easily learned, and while it may not be possible to
feel sure which hay it is that is being fed in the troop,

SHORT GRAMMA GRASS.

nevertheless the officer can tell whether it is good and fit
for horses or not; these indications are rather plain.

Good hay should be rather sweet-smelling, should
always have the tops on, and the narrow, delicate cover-

ings of the stalks should be present.   A little herbage in
hay does not matter, and, in fact, is, by some horsemen,
considered an advantage; but no weeds should be present.
Good hay weighs about 11 pounds to the cubic foot
when pressed into bales, and much lighter when loose.

Courtesy of Hon. F. D. Coburn.

RED CLOVER.

Hay that has been cut too soon or which has been baled
or stacked before drying generally becomes "mow-burnt."
This condition may be told by observing the heat in the
bale or stack, by the more or less complete absence of the
sweet smell characteristic of good, fresh hay, and by the

color changing on the inside to a dark brownish or black tinge, especially if the mow-burn has existed some time. "Dust in hay" is frequently observed—hay that has been handled too much gradually loses its fine coverings of the stalks, and these, becoming dry and brittle, break up and by the moving of the hay are ground into fine dust,

Courtesy of Hon. F. D. Coburn.

ALFALFA GRASS.

sometimes so filling the hay with the light, flaky substance as to be readily mistaken for dirt. "Mow-burnt" hay or "dust in hay" are both signs of its being unsuitable for feeding the troop horses, and should not be purchased or used if it can be avoided. Good hay is never

brittle, and rarely thoroughly dry. There should be in it
some slight natural moisture, but no external damp should
enter, else the hay spoils. Hay that has heated in the
stack is worthless, and, if fed to the horses, will cause much
sickness and digestive troubles. An almost infallible

Courtesy of Hon. F. D. Coburn.

BUNCH BUFFALO GRASS.

sign of dust in hay is the continual coughing of the horses
in their stalls at the afternoon feed, or very early in the
morning, after they have stood all night in their stalls,
and before they are taken out; this often, when the hay

is dusty, becomes so noticeable as to cause much serious consideration. The fine, flaky particles of the hay mentioned above float about the stable and are inhaled by the horses and cause this coughing. The color of good hay should be neither bright green nor a dark brown, an intermediate shade of brownish green being its characteristic color. By the green cast it will be evident that the hay has not been lying out in the rain, and by the absence of any deep blackish brown tint that it has not been put together too soon and thereby become heated. After hay has been baled and exposed to the weather on stock-cars or transports, it will generally show a dark shade of brown on the outside, from the exposure; but this should not be the case on the inside, else the hay is spoiled. It can be only its natural color on the inside if good.

The order of administering water, grain, and hay to the horse is a matter of the greatest importance. To feed the hay, the grain, and then the water would be to almost reverse the natural way as learned through many years of experience. First the water should be given, then the grain, and finally the hay. To give the hay before the grain has been found not to work well, as the horse, demanding the grain, will hardly eat the hay until the grain has been devoured. The horse will invariably eat all his grain before he even touches his hay. The hay should be placed in the manger and the grain in the feed-box, and then the horse tied in the stall, after being watered. In the cavalry services the concentrates are always given after watering and before the hay is fed. No one can review the literature of horse-feeding or personally observe the practices in various stables in civil life and in the Cavalry, as the writer has done, located at widely separated points, without realizing that there are many successful ways of feeding and managing the horse. The uses to which this animal is put are so varied, and the varieties of hay and grain at command so diverse, for different localities, that any hard-and-fast rules as to kind of feed and quantity to be supplied are out of the question.　However, one thing is certain: whatever feeding-stuffs are employed and whatever order of feeding is adopted, regularity and uniformity should prevail at all times.　The horse of the Cavalry, during his work in garrison or field, anticipates the feeding hour; to observe this, and how the regularity of cavalry feeding is learned by the horses in troops, let the young officer approach the troop stables while the "stable call" is sounding, and he will observe nearly every horse prick up his ears, walk toward the stable door, and stand there with a bunch of his fellows, whinnying and calling to the troopers to come and feed him.　The digestive system, and indeed the whole organization of the body, becomes accustomed to this certain order, and thrift and health are the natural concomitants, while irregularity and uncertainty always produce unsatisfactory results.

In America and England the horse is fed generally on hay, grass, roots, oats, corn, wheat, rye, bran, and barley, and many horsemen believe that the horse can be fed successfully on nothing else.　However, Stewart, in his "Stable Book," gives the following extract from Loudon's "Encyclopedia of Agriculture," which will show what is done in out-of-the-way parts of the world:

"In some sterile countries horses are forced to subsist on dried fish and even on vegetable mould; in Arabia, on milk, flesh-balls, eggs, and broth.　In India horses are variously fed, the native grasses being adjudged very nutritious.　In Bengal something like the tare is used. On the western side of India a sort of pigeon-pea, called gram, forms the ordinary food, with grass while in season, and hay all the year round.　Indian corn or rice is seldom given.　In the West Indies maize, Guinea corn, sugar-tops, and sometimes molasses are given.　In the Mahratta country salt, pepper, and other spices are made into balls with flour and butter, and these are supposed to produce animation and to fine the coat.　Broth made from sheep's head is sometimes given there.　In France, Spain, and Italy, besides the grasses, the leaves of limes, vines, the tops of acacia, and the seeds of the carob tree are given to horses."

To the above may be added the fact that the American cavalry horses in the Philippine Islands at times ate both hulled and unhulled rice, dried thatch from the fallen roofs of the native houses, green rice as it stood in the fields soaked with water, and sugar-cane as it stood in the fields; but while this was at times necessary because it was all there was for them to eat during the actual campaigning, nevertheless the greatest care was necessary to prevent sickness, and even with constant care some horses suffered much and were difficult to get back into condition even after the regular oats and hay forage was at hand, and some died, though not many, considering the terrific work and exposure.

In feeding in civil life hot feeds are frequently given, but no cavalry service ever does so, except so far as the sick horses in the veterinary hospital are concerned; these, of course, under the care of the veterinary surgeon, are treated as the nature of their ailments require, but hot feeding is neither practicable nor desirable in cavalry troops, and is not done. Few of the stable-men understand the giving of hot feeds, and unless carefully prepared and fed they are more liable to cause trouble than satisfaction. In civil practice cooked foods are sometimes given; but these have a tendency to soften the flesh, are difficult to prepare, and could not be done where large numbers of horses are together to be cared for. A feed of cooked food once or twice a week is said to have a cooling effect upon the horse; but, as the bran mash fed in the Cavalry has the same effect, cooked food is never given. Another method in civil practice in feeding horses which are required to do hard work is to grind all the grain and feed it to the horse upon moistened, chaffed hay. Food thus prepared is more rapidly masticated and consequently remains a longer time in the stomach; a little long hay is then supplied the animal, to be consumed at leisure after the stomach is well filled.

Idle horses may be maintained wholly, or almost wholly, upon hay, straw, or corn-fodder,* fed uncut. Horses eating hay alone have been so fed for considerable periods and performed more or less work, but it should never be allowed to go on when grain is to be had. The component parts of necessary material contained in the oats have already been shown, and will illustrate why the concentrates are necessary to the horse. Ground grain and chaffed hay are fed in mixed form, that the animal may masticate his food and pass it into his stomach more quickly than is possible with the material whole and dry. When fed thus, a fair allowance of long hay should be placed in the manger, for the animal to finish on after the stomach is replenished and while the horse is resting, but still requiring more food. The morning meal, either in cavalry or civil life, should be comparatively light, consisting mostly of grain; in the cavalry service it consists entirely of grain, while civilians generally also feed some chaffed hay. This morning feed should not possess very much bulk, as the horse in cavalry is usually required to perform quick, hard drill work in the early morning after this feed has been consumed, or to take up the march under a heavy pack when in the field. The heavy feeding should come at the evening meal, after the day's work is over and when the animal has time for masticating and digesting his food. In the Cavalry the morning feed consists of 6 pounds of oats or other grain (though oats are invariably fed), and the evening meal consists of the remaining allowance of the day's grain, 6 pounds also, and all of the hay allowance, 14 pounds. When the horses are to stand all day at the picket-line in camp, it is well to feed a little of the hay about noon.

Salt is the only kind of "seasoning" which has stood the test of experience in the various cavalry services, and some of it is always given during the month. There are several well-known ways of feeding it to the horse,

---

*Dry corn-stalks minus the ears of corn; also known commonly as "roughness."

which may be mentioned. Some horsemen give an ounce of common salt daily in the water, others give it by sprinkling it upon the grain in the feed-boxes, while others leave a lump of rock-salt constantly in the manger for the horse to lick. The last is the only really satisfactory and useful way of using this article, as horses will thrive on it better if they are allowed a lump of rock-salt constantly within their reach. The quantity which is thus taken is by no means large, for rock-salt does not easily dissolve by the mere contact of the moist tongue. Rock-salt is only to be procured in certain localities, where it is found in the earth in large quantities. In feeding this rock-salt to the cavalry horse, a lump weighing about $\frac{1}{4}$ of a pound is placed in the manger, and 1 pound will often last a horse for a whole month, but there is great variation in the quantity consumed by different horses.* Occasionally in the cavalry service this rock-salt is placed on the ground of the "corral," several large lumps of it being left there, and the loose animals help themselves by licking, a few horses even trying to eat it. It is still a better way to place wooden boxes, each about one foot square and about six inches deep, on short wooden posts about two feet high, in the corral, and put the rocks of salt in them. From $2\frac{1}{2}$ to 3 ounces of salt a week is sufficient for the cavalry horse, and it should be fed about once a week.

When the troop is in the field, the horse is watered, fed his grain and then the hay, as in garrison. When herding for grazing purposes or feeding green grasses, care must be taken to watch the animals closely, as the change to green forage is apt to cause diarrhœa and colic. It often becomes necessary to feed the cavalry horse whatever grasses and grains are at hand. In the Philippine Islands the cavalry horse was fed sun-dried rice-heads with six-inch stems, known as *palay*, for the grain, and a short, curly, somewhat wiry native grass, known as *sacati*, and after a time they thrived upon it

---

*The maximum Regulation Allowance of coarse salt is 1 pound per horse per month, in our service.

under all conditions. It was found that the *palay* was rather heavier in the stomach than oats or corn, and thus had to be fed somewhat lighter, though issued in the same weights as oats. Overfeed of this *palay* produced serious disorders in the horses, and more than once one or two troop-horses will be found in the morning too stiffened up in front by an overfeed of this *palay* to walk a yard, and it will require ten days or two weeks to get the horse back in shape, if he ever is. The *sacati* grows very close to the ground and is cut by hand. As the natives bring it in in large, loose bales, still wet, no more than one day's supply should be taken at a time, as it will quickly mould and spoil if piled up in this wet condition for a few days, as any wet grasses will do. During the campaigns in the Philippine Islands in 1899 the troopers, after arriving in camp for the night, would proceed to the rice fields near by and cut the long, green rice-stalks with heavy clusters of rice at the end, and, bringing this to camp, feed it to the horses morning and evening. It was absolutely all there was to use, but there was an abundance of it in most parts of the islands. The horses thrived very well on it and performed very hard field service. During these same campaigns hulled rice was often captured from the insurgents in large quantities, and this also was fed to the horses as grain, herding providing the grass necessary when time allowed. At one time a large quantity of this white hulled rice was captured by General Lawton's Division in the northern part of Luzon, and was fed to the horses and mules. It had been stored a long time and was alive with maggots, and it seemed deadly to feed to animals, and was used as sparingly as possible. However, many of the horses ate it daily for nearly two weeks, and while some suffered, the majority stood it very well until something else could be procured. This will show how necessary and difficult it is in field service that the cavalry horse be fed good forage, and what he has had to put up with in past service, and how he has stood it. When pushed to it, the thatch from the roofs of the native houses in the Philippines was utilized as feed, and the horses lived to tell the tale. This same thing was done by the British Cavalry in their Indian campaigns. General Wolseley refers to the experience, and states that the horses did very well on it, under the circumstances.

As the grain usually arrives at a garrison in sacks averaging 100 pounds or so, all that is necessary is to store it off the ground, in a clean, dry location, and occasionally repile it to prevent the under sacks from spoiling by heat and the damp that always rises from the ground underneath. The hay, if it arrives in bales, can be handled the same way, but it frequently comes loose, and must be then placed in stacks. These stacks should be built not over 8 feet in diameter and 16 feet in height, neatly topped, and the top layer raked down toward the outside, in order that the stack may shed the rain that falls upon it. If possible, iron or wooden sheds should be placed over the stacks; but, as this is not often possible, a few sheets of corrugated iron, zinc, or wooden boards should be laid upon the top of the stack, to save, as far as possible, any rain from entering the stack and spoiling it. If the stack is made much larger in diameter than 8 feet, ventilation of the stack becomes impossible, owing to the packing of the hay, and the interior of the stack is apt to mould and spoil. The stack must not be too high, else heavy winds will pull it over. If the hay, when taken from the stack for feeding, shows a little too much dust, this can be settled, when placed in the mangers, by sprinkling with water.*

So many excellent Agricultural Reports on the various grasses used for hay are already available to the student that no attempt has been made here to go into detail in considering these various grasses; the attempt rather has been made to help the young cavalryman to know the

---

*The hay, whether baled or loose, should be well shaken up with the pitch-fork before being placed in the mangers or on the picket-line, to get as much dust out as possible.

practical handling of the feeding of the cavalry horse, to know good grain and good hay when he sees it, to be able to tell whether or not it is fit and sufficient for the horses, how to administer the horse's food, how to vary it, etc. The great number of grasses grown for feeding purposes enables the cavalry to vary its kind of hay occasionally. Most of the well-known hay grasses are perennial, and vary considerably as to the number of tons to the acre; alfalfa furnishes about 4 tons to the acre and has gone even beyond 6 tons; clover gives from 3 to 4 tons, but, if fed too much, is apt to bloat; timothy yields as high as 4 tons.

As the care of considerable quantities of hay will frequently devolve upon the men in the Cavalry, it should be known what is done in caring for it beforehand. Hay cures quickly; it should remain in the sun only long enough to assure it against mould; after it is well wilted, it must be raked into windrows and afterwards made into small cocks 4 feet in diameter at the base and about 5 feet high, well pointed, and rounded off at the top. Within a day or two the hay will be cured sufficiently to put into permanent stacks or to be baled up. If a rain should unfortunately fall while the hay lies in the windrows or in cocks, wetting it to a considerable depth, it must be immediately opened to the sunlight until it is dried out. It is best for the quality of the hay that not a single drop of water fall upon it and that it be cured, as far as possible, with the least amount of sunshine. This method will make sweet, fragrant, and nutritious hay of prime quality with an excellent odor. Hay should be mowed at the time when the nutritive elements—those which give strength and produce flesh—are at their maximum. The art in curing hay is to retain as many of the life-giving constituents in it as possible, or to preserve it as nearly as practicable in the same condition in which it is cut, with the water only abstracted. Care should be taken not to allow heavy dew to fall upon the hay before it is cured, as it tends to destroy its worth.

If the hay is mowed too early, before it is ripe, the seeds and nutritive qualities are not fully developed, and part of the value of the hay is lost. If the hay is let stand in the field too long before cutting, much of the seed becomes over-ripe and falls off, while part of the nutritive qualities passes back into the roots, and the hay will lack strength and value accordingly.

The work required to keep the grain and hay in good condition, to feed it properly, and to understand what the cavalry horse needs, cannot be learned quickly. Upon the careful attention given to these matters, however, depends the welfare of the cavalry horse, and consequently the efficiency of the command, at all times, whether in garrison, camp, or field. Observation daily will do wonders to prepare the cavalryman for bestowing that careful attention upon his horses which is required.

CHAPTER XVII.

THE PACK-TRAIN.

It has been said in a previous chapter that the best
known way to relieve the cavalry horse of the weight of
his heavy pack and to carry the necessary field outfit of
rations, equipments, etc., is to have a troop pack-train of
mules. As these trains are old institutions in the American cavalry service, and as it may suddenly fall to the
lot of the young cavalry officer to take charge of the
pack-train, he should be familiar not only with methods
of actual packing, but especially with the methods employed to keep the "riggings" in perfect shape and condition. Without this care, no pack-train can expect
to be of continued service to the troop. Carelessness or
ignorance in packing, or in promptly readjusting loosened
packs when on the march, will do much serious injury,
but perhaps not more than neglect in fitting and shaping the "rigging" to the mule's back, ignorance in carefully adjusting it when in use, or carleessness in caring
for the "rigging" when off the mule's back.

Many times the troop will be called upon to traverse territory over and through which wheeled transportation cannot pass. The illustration below shows the wheeled transportation in the American Army; the capacity, etc., of these wagons is important to know, in order that loads may be made up suitable to the wagons used. The ordinary two- and four-mule wagon weighs about 1,550 pounds and is known as an "escort wagon." This wagon

WHEELED TRANSPORTATION, U. S. ARMY.

is of the following dimensions: Body, 3 feet 4 inches wide; 9 feet 6 inches long; 1 foot 9 inches high. Capacity of body, about 57 cubic feet. Cover, 3 feet 4 inches wide; 8 feet long; 3 feet 6 inches high. Total capacity, about 144 cubic feet. The six-mule "jerk-line" wagon weighs about 1,950 pounds, and is of the following dimensions: Body, 3 feet 6 inches wide; 10 feet long; 2 feet high. Capacity of body, about 72 cubic feet. Cover, 3 feet 5 inches wide; 10 feet long; 3 feet high. Total capacity, about 176 cubic feet.

The following are the estimated weights, ordinary, that should be considered as loads for wagons used upon marches:

Two-mule wagon, in addition to its weight, 1,000 to 1,200 pounds.

Four-mule wagon, in addition to its weight, 2,000 to 2,400 pounds.

Six-mule wagon, in addition to its weight, 3,000 to 3,300 pounds.

While it is remarkable to the inexperienced cavalryman in the field to observe over what terrible country the American wheeled transportation can and does go, nevertheless there are times when it is imperative that all wagons, etc., be left behind and only pack-animals used with the troop. The pack-train, if well handled and trained, should be able to accompany a troop of cavalry anywhere the horses of the troop can go, and except on forced marches, where the gait is unusually rapid and long sustained, the train should be able to keep up with its troop. To appreciate the use of the mule pack-train, let us look somewhat into its past history.

The system of using pack-animals for the conveyance of supplies, etc., is of Spanish origin, both in the United States and in Mexico. The Spaniards excelled the rest of the world in this, and their descendants in Mexico improved upon the system greatly, as pack-animal transportation in many mountainous parts of that country forced upon the Mexicans the almost exclusive use of the mule pack-train. From Mexico the mule pack-train gradually crept into use in the far Southwest of the United States, and eventually, about the time of the discovery of gold in California in 1848, it was the principal means of transportation through the interior of the great West, and by the use of these hardy pack-animals thousands of daring scouts, miners, cavalrymen, and cowboys were enabled to cross almost impassable mountain ranges and vast plains, and to penetrate the innermost portions of our great Western frontier. It may be said that hundreds of frontier towns owe their very existence to the mule pack-train. Although the railroad and wagon largely super-seded the pack outfit as time passed on, it is still indis-pensable in many parts of America, and in war service it furnishes the cavalry with rapid, sure-footed, hardy means of penetrating into any country in which it may have to operate. During the many Indian campaigns of the American Cavalry these pack-trains were invaluable, and in the more recent campaigns in Cuba, the Philippine Islands, and in China their extensive use made cam-paigning comparatively easy, and enabled the Cavalry to maintain its high reputation for rapid prolonged marches independent of outside help, at all seasons of the year, across arid Western plains, through almost impenetrable jungles and across the most difficult mountain ranges, and proved its enormous value beyond question.

The American pack-train of the United States Army is organized as follows:

> 1 pack-master;
> 1 *cargador,* or assistant pack-master;
> 1 cook;
> 1 blacksmith;
> 10 packers;
> 1 bell-mare;
> 14 saddle-mules;
> 50 pack-mules.

This makes the pack-train comprise 14 men and 50 pack-mules and 14 saddle-mules for the packers to ride. There are in the American Army 8 of these permanent pack-trains in the United States and several in the Philip-pine Islands and Alaska. The number of trains in the colonies varies with circumstances; oftentimes they are broken up, divided, etc., as scouting, reconnoitering, etc., require. Each pack-train is supplied with the following outfit:

14 cowboy saddles, Texas pattern;
50 *aparejos*, complete with cruppers, canvas *cinchas*, saddle-blankets, *coronas*, and *sobre-jalmas.*
100 lair-ropes, each 30 feet long, ⅜-inch;*
50 sling-ropes, 28 feet long, ⅜-inch;*
50 lash-ropes, 46 feet long, ⅜-inch, with *cincha;**
10 blinds (1 for every 5 mules).
100 *mantas;*
14 riding-bridles, curb, single-reined;
14 saddle-blankets for the riding-saddles;
1 picket-rope, 125 feet long, 2-inch. *

The pack-master has immediate charge of his train of men and animals, and is responsible for the welfare of his train, its instruction and efficiency, and for the equipments, etc.

The *cargador* acts as assistant to the pack-master, and also acts as the train-saddler and repairer.

The packers employed with these American pack-trains must be large men, weighing from 175 pounds up, and able to lift up on the mule's back and tie there a side-pack equal to their own weight—175 pounds. These men are all civilians and usually Western men—ex-cowboys, miners, etc.—and peculiarly well fitted for the work required. The importance of having large, strong, experienced men in the train soon becomes evident when their work is inquired into. On slippery mountain-sides, often knee-deep in snow and slush, the pack-mule must be stood sideways and the load readjusted; this requires one man to stand on the down-hill side to load that side, and only tall, strong men can successfully do such work well.† Oftentimes the pack-mule, loaded, becomes mired down on the march, when it requires some of the packers to go in and get him out, and this will require men used

---

*The size of the above ropes is the diameter.

†Nevertheless the writer has known many medium-sized men who were expert packers in every sense of the word. Practice is everything.

to such work and inured to it by long practice and much natural skill. It is held by the packers themselves that a strong, healthy, bright man can become well acquainted with packing, etc., in one month, but that it takes at least one year to make the new packer fairly expert and inured to his work in the train. There are two classes of packers, first and second. The first class comprises those packers that have shown the greatest expertness in all that pertains to the train service; excelling in several things about the train, and only indifferent in one or two other duties, will debar the second-class packer from being rated a first-class packer: to gain the first class, he must excel in every individual part of his work, riding, etc., and the standard of efficiency maintained is very remarkable for its thoroughness.

The pack-mule in the American service must be from four to nine years of age, either male or female, from 13½ to 16 hands high and from 850 to 1200 pounds in weight. The mule considered most thoroughly satisfactory is about 14 hands in height and about 850 pounds in weight. This small, blocky animal is preferred to a tall, rangy one. The pack-mule should not be broken to harness, should have perfect health, especially perfect feet, clear vision, etc., as pertains to the cavalry horse. The new mule is trained to lead, to herd, to keep with his own train, to stand quiet when being loaded or unloaded, to come quietly in to the picket-line, and even to take his own place at the picket-line between his own mates, to follow the bell-mare everywhere, to allow himself to be caught whenever necessary, etc.; and the thorough training in the American pack-trains is a revelation to those not familiar with packing. To train the mule well depends a good deal on the mule and a good deal on the patience and kindness of his trainer. Brutality is no more successful with the mule than with the cavalry horse.

The daily allowance of forage for the pack-mule is 9 pounds of oats, corn, bran, or barley, and 14 pounds of hay. He is fed twice daily at the picket-line, the feed being placed on the ground or on canvas feed-covers, shelter-halves, or gunny-sacks. The morning feeding should be light if the train is to march, and the balance of the grain and all of the hay given at the evening feed, after camp is reached.

The pack-mule should be liberally watered just before starting on the march and allowed to drink whenever opportunity offers during the march, care being taken that he is not too warm at the time, and especial care should be observed if the mule has been going at a rapid gait. What has been said about good water for the cavalry horse applies equally well to the mule in the pack-train. In camp the mule should be watered twice daily, if kept at the picket-line, and three times daily in hot weather. As the train is usually herded daily as long as work will allow, the herding-ground should be near good, running water, and the mules allowed free access to it at all times while out grazing.

The pack-mule should be groomed at least once daily, and this thorough grooming should be given in the afternoon, after the work of the day is finished. In addition to this, the mule's back should be carefully brushed off in the morning, before putting on the "rigging," so as to avoid sores from dirt on the sides or back. The pack-mule, like the cavalry horse, should never be washed.

The pack-mule must at all times be shod all around. The shoes should be changed at least once a month, as with the cavalry horse, and the methods of shoeing are practically as laid down for the cavalry horse.

Herding the pack-mules and allowing them to graze is practiced daily, for the purpose of giving the animals plenty of good, green grass and, if possible, good, running water, and also for the purpose of training them to keep together, to follow the bell-mare, and to come into and go out of the camp quietly and "in herd." Herding is one of the most important parts of the training as well as one of the most imperative parts of the feeding of the pack-animals, and should be done daily whenever possible. This is also absolutely necessary for the pack-mule, in order to keep the picket-line clean and dry and fresh.

When it becomes necessary on the march to cross rivers by swimming, the pack should be removed and sent across by other means—boats, rafts, foot-bridges, etc. Only under the most imperative and unavoidable circumstances should an attempt ever be made to swim the pack-mule with his load on. As the load is very top-heavy, the mule is apt to turn on his side and get drowned. The "rigging" may be left on when swimming the pack-mule; but if there be a good way to cross the "riggings" also, and time allows, these too should be removed and sent across, leaving the mules free to swim their best and saving the packing in the pads of the *aparejo* from getting wet. Pack-mules loaded should never be made to ford unknown or uncertain rivers until the ford has been carefully examined (by sending several packers or troopers, mounted, entirely across the stream first); these men should then remain in plain sight at the landing-place until all the mules have crossed. Never should the train be pushed into a river to ford it if the depth be greater than $3\frac{1}{2}$ feet, and if the current is swift, this depth must be reduced to insure a successful pass-age of the train. As the mule, heavily loaded, is very liable to slip and drown if the bottom of the ford be rocky and slimy or too soft, the loads should be removed before they are sent into the water, and the loads after-wards sent over by other means. Whenever crossing a river, either by swimming or fording, the bell-mare should first be sent across in front of the mules, as they will then follow her across with little difficulty if the ford is good.

The bell-mare is a female horse, unsaddled, led by one of the packers mounted on his riding-mule, at the head of the train. The mare has a large metal bell sus-pended around her neck by a strap, and the mules soon learn to follow her everywhere. This training is most important, as it often happens that the bell-mare, during

dark nights or blinding blizzards, is out of sight for several minutes at a time, and the train must follow the tinkle
of the bell, and thus keep together. The pack-mules soon
learn to follow the bell, and after practice little trouble is
experienced in having the mules follow anywhere. For
this reason the packer leading the bell-mare must be careful always to choose the best places, both across country
or mountains and through timber or streams. The bell-
mare should be specially chosen for her nerve, sense, and
strength, as an obstinate, easily frightened, or physically
weak one will prove of little or no value, and will confuse
the herd, often at the very worst places.

All the packers are mounted on saddle-mules, and
these animals also must be well trained for their work.
They must be bridle-wise, tractable, strong, and intelligent; agility is a prime requisite. They should be
trained to stand still whenever the rider dismounts to
readjust a loosened pack. By throwing the reins over
the mule's head and allowing them to trail on the ground
many saddle-mules are taught to stand wherever left;
others, however, are not so satisfactory, and if turned
loose when the rider dismounts during the march, these
will follow the pack-mules up ahead, and leave the rider
to follow on foot. One method employed to make these
mules stand wherever they are left is to bend the mule's
head around toward his flank, usually the left one, and,
passing the reins over the mule's head, tie them together
to the large "horn" or pommel of the saddle, so as to
keep the head thus turned. The mule, in endeavoring to
go forward, can only walk around and around on a small
circle, and can be easily caught up again. Another way
is simply to tie the mule to any convenient bush or tree
by the reins. As the packer has frequently to dismount
on the march, to readjust loosened packs, to unpack a
mule which has lain down with his pack on and cannot
get up, and repack him after up, it is essential that his
saddle-mule be well trained. These saddle-mules average about 14 hands in height and about 850 pounds in

weight, and are required to fulfill the usual requirements for pack-mules.

On the march the train moves a short distance in
rear of the troop to which attached. Troop pack-trains
are generally smaller than the regulation pack-train,
and usually have twelve pack-mules and two or three
packers on saddle-mules. The train should not be so
close as to crowd the rear horses of the troop at a halt
or when temporarily delayed for a few moments, and yet
should never be so far behind as to compel the troop to
halt for it to catch up. Occasionally, however, it becomes
impossible for the train to keep thus closed up on its
troop, as at the more rapid gaits and when crossing
especially bad country. At such times a sufficient guard
from the troop should always be left to guard the train.
Although the packers are frontiersmen, generally, and
well armed, they are very busy readjusting the packs and
looking after their mules, and sudden surprise may over-
whelm them. When marching, the pack-master should
lead the entire train, and the bell-mare should be led by
another packer immediately behind the pack-master;
the remainder of the packers should ride on the near side
of the train, and when the country is bad or the trail narrow, the packers riding on the side should distribute
themselves *in* the train, each about five mules ahead or
behind the nearest packer; at the rear of the train should
ride the blacksmith and one other packer. These men
should keep the pack-animals closed up reasonably on the
train, drive ahead any mule that may attempt to wander
too far off the line of march, and be ready quickly to dismount and readjust any pack that needs it.* During the
first few hours of marching almost every pack will require
readjustment, but after they have all been readjusted,
they will generally remain secure for the balance of the
march, unless some specially difficult country is encoun-

*Under ordinary circumstances no effort should be made to
keep the animals "bunched"; they soon acquire the habit on the
march of travelling in single file, and this should be allowed, as it is
the most satisfactory way.

tered or the gait unusually rapid. No time should be lost in dismounting and readjusting packs whenever necessary. One mile of travel with a loosened, sagging pack will do more to ruin a pack-mule than ten additional miles added on to the journey. The blinds should be distributed among the packers, and should be used whenever a mule is being attended to. The pack-train must, except under extraordinary circumstances, be required to keep up with its troop; and this it will generally be able to do, and for average daily marches of from twenty-five to thirty miles, over fair country, no trouble will be experienced in keeping the train near the troop. It is wisest for the troop to regulate somewhat on its train as to gait, so as to make it possible for the train to keep up without unduly tiring the mules. Leaving the train to come on by itself is always a bad practice. The march should not be made so long that the camp is reached after dark, if it can be avoided; camp should be made early enough to allow the unloading of the mules quietly, and allow for grazing for an hour or two before dark, and for the grooming, etc. Getting into camp with the troop after dark, and then having to wait several hours for the train to come up, will be found so disagreeable an experience, after once tried, that whenever it *can* be done, the train should be brought in at the same time. Thus supper is not delayed, time is allowed for arranging the packs, and the "riggings" may be left on the mules' backs for fifteen or twenty minutes to allow for the gradual cooling of the backs, an essential point to remember.

It is important that every cavalryman, whether officer or soldier, be reasonably expert in all that pertains to packing. Many times in field service the troopers will be needed to assist the packers in crossing the train over bad country or rivers, or packers may be wholly lacking, when the troop will have to do its own, and if it is not well understood and carefully done, the mules will soon be ruined. This training should be not merely in "throwing the diamond hitch," but, to be good, must embrace the "setting up" of the *aparejo* and "rigging," keeping it in shape, knowing what to do in emergencies, how to put the "rigging" on, how to take it off, etc. This all requires much training and practice, but its value will be

THE "RIGGING" AND NAMES OF PARTS.

1, *Corona.* 2, Saddle Blanket. 3. *Sobre-jalma* (folded back to show lacing).
4, *Aparejo* proper. 5, Crupper. 6, Lacing.

quickly demonstrated when the troop is given a train and told to pack it and take the field.

By the "rigging" is meant everything that goes on the mule's back, except the pack; in other words, the entire "harness" and saddle which go on for the recep-

tion of the pack.   This "rigging" consists of the following
parts:

The Aparejo.—This consists of two large leather pads,
square, usually stuffed with hay or straw, joined together
at the top by the leather being continuous the entire length
of the top.   The *aparejo* possesses a pommel arch, and
the center (spinal) elevation is so made as to leave the
entire spine untouched.   The *aparejo* has two circular
holes, each about 5 inches in diameter, cut in the pads
on the center of the inner sides, and these holes, if not
present (and they sometimes are not in the newly issued
aparejo), must be cut in; care must be taken not to cut
them too low, else the large, flat bar of wood which must
be placed across the inner bottom of the pads cannot be
gotten in it.   To "set up" the *aparejo* requires skill and
care, for upon its being well done depends the fit of the
whole "rigging," as well as the condition of the mule's
back.   To set up the *aparejo*, first spread it out in clean
water and let it soak for about twenty minutes; then take
it out and lay it on the ground, inner sides of the pads up,
and drain it thoroughly.   Now take a piece of stout wood
(the width of the inner measurement of the pad from
front to rear in length, 3 inches wide, and 1 inch thick),
and introduce this stick into the pad through the circular hole in the center of the pad, and press this stick
down into the pad, so that it is in the bottom of it; this
stick is known as the "boot-piece."   Now, cut a slit
2 inches long in the middle of the pad, at the center
of the upper inner side of the pad, at the center seam,
above the large center hole; through this hole introduce
green sticks about ¾ of an inch in diameter into the
pad, perpendicular to the "boot-piece," and place them,
one at a time, from front to rear, in the pad.   These
sticks should be nearly as long as the pad is high, and at
the bottom should rest on end on the "boot-piece."   When
the large center hole is reached, begin again and introduce
similar sticks, of about ¼ to ⅜ inch in diameter, into the
back part of the pad, in the same way, and work toward

the center again, thus wholly lining the pad with these sticks; these are known as the "ribs." Now fill the pad up with dry hay, first filling the lower corners and tamping with a stick until the corners are hard. Make the hay fairly snug between the pads of hay at these corners, and slightly lower, in a curve, downward; then fill up the rest of the pad with the hay, making the upper forward part of the pad (the pommel) slightly thicker than the upper rear part; leave the center of the pad fairly loose, as this part must form well on the back; do the same with the other pad; have no lumps at all in the pads. The sticks must be green and the hay dry. This padding must be done carefully, and the center of the pad must curve slightly inward to fit the mule's back.

The Crupper.—Stand the *aparejo* up on the ground, so that it rests on its lower edges. Lace the ends of the crupper, one on each side, to the flaps formed on the rear of the leather bindings on the forward part of the pads, on the outer side as shown in illustration on page 439; make the length of the crupper, by shortening or lengthening the laces, so that the crupper when on the mule's back will allow its tail end to come snugly under the mule's tail without chafing it; tie the upper edges of the crupper to the holes in the double welt of leather that stands out on each side of the rear of the pads, so that the crupper will sit well up on the mule's flanks, and not down on his sides.

The Sobre-Jalma.—This consists of a broad piece of heavy canvas, bound at the edges with leather, and having a stout curved stick at each end. The width of the *sobre-jalma* is the same as the width of the *aparejo*, and the length is the same as that of the entire *aparejo*. While the *aparejo* stands on the ground as before, lay the *sobre-jalma* over it, width with width and length with length. Bore two holes through the pommel of the *aparejo* near the edge, and two through the cantle near the edge, and bore two corresponding holes through the *sobre-jalma* over the holes bored in the *aparejo*, and tie

with buckskin the *sobre-jalma* to the *aparejo* through
these holes.   The lower ends of the *sobre-jalma* on each
side (the sticks outward) should be even with the lower
edges of the *aparejo*.

The Saddle-Blanket.—This blanket is similar to the
cavalry saddle-blanket; it is folded in *six folds*. To
fold the blanket, hold the blanket by the corners, the
short way up and down; fold across the longer edges,
right hand holding corners, left holding folded edge at
corner; shake the blanket and spread it on the ground,
the hands still holding the corners; carry the upper
edge to the front, so as to leave a portion of the blanket,
22 inches wide, on the ground; then fold back so as to
leave the blanket in three equal folds, 22 inches wide and
22 inches long; fold once more, bringing the ends together,
and it is now ready for use.

The Corona.—This is a woolen pad for the mule's
back.   A strip of canvas equal in width and length to the
corona is issued with the "rigging," and this should be
sewn all around at the edges to the under side of the *corona;* the upper side of the *corona* has the number of the
"rigging" on it.

The Canvas Cincha.—This is 10 inches wide, double,
edges sewn together, and has at one end the "latigo-strap"
and at the other the cincha-ring; this *cincha* is about 10
inches longer than the *aparejo* with which it is to go.

The above completes what is commonly called the
"rigging."   It requires care and skill to set it up properly, but the above will show how to put it together when
received from the Quartermaster's Department and make
it ready for use.   By experienced packers there are many
tricks employed to prepare it properly, but these cannot be given here, and must be learned by experience.

Now come the various ropes used with the *aparejo*
for loading the mule.   These are known as the "lair-
ropes," the "sling-rope," and the "lash-rope," and are
described below:

The Lair-Ropes.—These are two to each *aparejo*,
and have at one end a permanent loop about 3 inches in

diameter; the length of this rope is about 30 feet. The lair-ropes are used to tie up the side-packs, before putting them on the mule, and are of ⅜-inch rope.

The Sling-Rope.—There is one sling-rope to each *aparejo;* this rope is about 30 feet long. Both the lair-ropes and the sling rope are of ⅜-inch rope. The use of the sling-rope is to tie the side-packs together, after they are on the mule's *aparejo.*

The Lash-Rope.—This is about 46 feet in length, and of ⅜-inch rope; there is one to each *aparejo.* The lash-rope has at one end a short, narrow, canvas *cincha,* with an iron rope-hook in the end of the *cincha.* The use of the lash-rope is to tie the side-packs to the *aparejo* by means of the "diamond hitch."

The Manta.—This is a piece of heavy canvas, 6 feet square, about the size of the saddle-blanket; it is used to wrap around each side-pack, before tying up the side-pack with the lair-rope. It prevents the contents of the side-pack from being injured by rain, snow, etc.

Now comes the placing of the "rigging" on the mule's back; this must be done carefully and slowly until thoroughly learned. It is on the fitting of the entire "rigging" that the welfare of the mule's back and the satisfactory carrying of the load depend.

To Put on the "Rigging."—Place the *aparejo* on the ground, standing it up on the lower edges of the two pads; on top of the *aparejo* bend over the crupper; on top of the crupper place the folded saddle-blanket; on top of the saddle-blanket place the *corona,* so placed that when lifted up and placed on the back the number on the *corona* will come on the off side and on the outside. Stand the mule beside the *aparejo,* facing to the rear of the *aparejo;* have one man hold the mule's halter-strap; put on the blind so as to cover both of the mule's eyes; have two men do the loading; let one man stand on the off-side, facing the mule's back, and the other man on the near side, abreast of the mule's shoulder, and thus between the mule and the *aparejo;* the man on the near side is designated as

No. 1, and the man on the off side as No. 2.   No. 1 now
lifts the *corona* and places it on the mule's back, canvas
side down, the number on the *corona* coming on the off
side.   No. 1 now lifts the saddle-blanket and places it
on the mule's back, on top of the *corona*, both of these
being placed as the cavalry saddle-blanket would be

READY TO PUT ON THE "RIGGING."

placed, but about 2 inches farther forward.   No. 1 now
lifts the *aparejo*, crupper still bent back over the top
of it, and assisted by No. 2 places it on the mule's back,
on top of the saddle-blanket, pommel about 2 inches
farther forward on the back than the cavalry saddle would
be placed.   Both men now slightly raise the *aparejo* and

place it several inches to the rear of its proper position;
they now bend the crupper back and place it under the
mule's tail and then raise the *aparejo* and place it in its
proper place. No. 1 lets down the big canvas *cincha*, the
latigo-strap on the near side and the cincha-ring on the
off-side. No. 1 passes the latigo-strap through the lower

CINCHING THE "RIGGING."

cincha-ring, from rear to front, and carries it up and
through the upper cincha-ring, from front to rear, and
carries it down again through the lower cincha-ring, from
rear to front; No. 1 now places his left foot against the
heavy wooden bar on the lower edge of the *sobre-jalma*,
and No. 2 his right knee, as shown in above illustration,

and they pull together on the latigo-strap and tightly cinch the mule, being careful to keep the *cinchu* in the center of the *aparejo*; if properly cinched, the lower cincha-ring of the canvas *cinchu* should be against the boot stick of the *sobre-jalma* (near side); then No. 1 carries the end of the latigo-strap up on top of the *cincha* to the small leather loop on the *cincha* canvas, and passes the end of

"MANTAING UP" THE SIDE-PACKS

the strap through this loop, from top inward and down-ward; bring the end of the strap down beside the other part of the strap, pull downward on the end of the strap slightly, lightly pound down on the latigo-strap where it was passed through the little loop, and leave. The "rigging" is now all on and ready for the side-packs. (See illustration on page 447.)

Before putting on the "rigging," the side-packs should be made ready and laid near at hand, where they may be quickly reached when needed. The preparation of the side-packs is very important; there are two of them, and each is prepared as follows:

To Prepare the Side-Packs.— Spread out the *manta* on the ground; place the side-pack in the middle of the

THE "RIGGING" CORRECTLY ON AND CINCHED.

manta, diagonally; fold over the two side corners of the *manta* about 10 inches (according to the size of the bundle to be covered); carry one of these folded sides of the *manta* over the side-pack; then turn the other folded side of the *manta* over the first side snugly, so that the edge of the last fold will come near the center of the side-pack throughout its entire length; now fold over one of the other two ends of the *manta* about 6 inches, and carry this end over the side-pack; now fold over the remaining end of the *manta* about 6 inches, and carry this end over the side-pack, over the previous fold, and draw snugly. The side-pack is now ready for the "lair-rope."

To Tie the Lair-Rope About the Side-Pack.—Pass the end of the lair-rope through the loop in the other end of itself, and pass the loop thus formed around the side-pack, about 1 foot from one end, and draw the loop tight; now face the other end of the side-pack, and, standing astride of it, form a loop in the remaining portion of the lair-rope and make one additional turn in this loop, and pass the loop around this end of the side-pack and draw this loop tight; if the rope is long enough, make one of these loops in the remaining part of the rope and pass this loop around the center of the side-pack before making the second loop; draw the rope tight and carry the end of it tightly around the end of the pack, then turn the pack over, and carry the rope along this upper side to the other end, taking a turn with it around each of the ropes passed, drawing the rope tight each time; then pass the remaining rope around the near end, turn over the pack and fasten the end of the rope by taking half-hitches around the part of the rope forming the first loop. Do the same with the other side-pack. The side-packs are now ready to be loaded.

In loading the two side-packs, care must be taken that both are even in weight and size, and as similar in shape as possible. When placing the side-packs on the *aparejo*, see that they are evenly placed, so that even weight comes on each side of the *aparejo*; otherwise the mule's back will suffer badly and the pack will not "ride" well. Now comes the loading of the mule; first, the two side-packs are tied together by the sling-rope.

To Tie the Side-Packs on with the Sling-Rope.—No. 1 takes the sling-rope in both hands, holding it so that a large single loop is formed between the hands; No. 1 now tosses this loop over the *aparejo*, so that by stooping down he can just see the end of the loop hanging down on the off side, under the belly. No. 1 should make the front end of the rope several feet longer than the hind end. No. 1 and No. 2 now each takes up his side-pack and places it on the upper side of the *aparejo*, so that the two packs come together over the top of the *aparejo*, their long edges touching throughout their entire extent; No. 2 now throws the loop of the sling-rope over the top of the packs to No. 1, spreading the sides of the loop out so as to cover the side-pack on his side well, and No. 1 passes the front end of his rope through this loop, from top to bottom, and draws it tight, both men lifting somewhat on their packs at the time. No. 1 now holds this front end in his left hand, and brings the rear rope up with his right hand and passes it into the left hand, to the rear of the rope already in that hand; No. 1 leaves the end of the rear rope falling downward, thus forming a small loop; now with the right hand pass the front rope through the rear rope and pull *down* with the right hand and *up* with the left, forming a simple knot; then turn the left hand slightly to the right, towards the body, bring up the middle of the front rope with the right hand and pass the loop through the loop of the rear rope held in the left hand, grasp this loop that is passed through with the thumb of the left hand, and with the right hand grasp the end of the rear rope and pull it downward tightly; this ties the sling-rope; place the ends of the sling-rope between the tops of the packs. Now comes the "settling" of the side-packs.

To Settle the Side-Packs.—No. 2 holds steady to the top corners of his side-pack the lower corners of his pack pressing against his upper arms near the elbows; No. 1 takes hold of his pack the same way and lifts up on the lower corners of his pack, and slightly outward; the side-packs now settle snugly down together, if the sling-rope has been tied sufficiently tight; No. 1 then walks to the rear of

the mule and sees if the two side-packs are evenly balanced on the *aparejo;* if not, the side-packs are again
settled until they do. The side-packs are now ready for
the lash-rope and the "diamond hitch," which holds the
load on the *aparejo.* It must be studied with care, as it is

FIRST POSITION OF THE "DIAMOND HITCH," NEAR SIDE.

difficult, though never forgotten when once thoroughly
learned.
. }*The "Diamond Hitch."*—Near packer: The near
packer (No. 1) takes the coiled lash-rope in right hand
and throws the rope to the rear of the mule, passing the
end of the rope over the mule's croup to No. 2. No. 1
holds *cincha* in left hand and with right hand he grasps

rope about 4 feet from lacing, and with left hand passes
cincha under mule to off packer; then, standing near
mule's shoulder, facing to the rear, the near packer with
left hand takes hold of rope near the *cincha*, palm up; the
right hand slips forward on rope about 3 feet, palm up
as in illustration on page 450; he then draws the right
hand well back, and with a quick swing causes the rope

SECOND POSITION, NEAR SIDE.

to pass over the mule's haunches and to settle between the
packs; this brings the right hand to the front of the load;
draw down with the right to the full reach of the arm,
causing the rope to slip between the packs, the rope riding in front between the packs; grasping this rope with

right hand, palm down, draw down to full extent of right
arm; keep the left, still grasping the rope, about 3 feet
from *cincha*, which is kept near center of pack; No. 1 lets
the loop thus formed fall to his right and changes hands,
keeping the loop outside, over right fore-arm, as in illustration on page 451; then raise both hands to the position

FIG. 152. THIRD POSITION, OFF SIDE.

shown in figure on page 451; now give a swing to rope
with both hands, causing the loop to pass over load, the
right hand guiding to center of pack; as the ropes pass
over bring the left hand down on mule's neck; this separates the running rope (A) in left hand from standing
rope (B) in right hand.

Off packer: While the near packer is doing this, the off packer, with left hand, grasps rope about 6 inches from its end, picks up the hook of *cincha* with right hand, and with left hand grasps *cincha* at its corner, mouth of hook to the front; he then stands beside the *aparejo*, facing to front, holding left hand about 10 inches below edge of boot, and waits for rope. While near packer is taking sufficient slack on rope, by drawing it to front between packs, the off packer may guide rope with right hand. When near packer throws loop over the top of load, the off packer grasps it, and, holding the end of *cincha* with left hand well under mule's belly, draws rope down with right hand and engages standing rope (B) in hook, from within outward. He then slides the right hand up the running rope from the hook; with both hands he passes the end of the rope which he has in his left hand under running rope and well up on top of pack, draws it forward about 3 feet, and lets the end fall over about 12 inches on near side of mule's neck; and, with assistance of near packer, raises running rope from animal's neck up to top of pack.

Near packer: While off packer is engaged in passing the rope into cincha-hook, etc., near packer, having passed the loop over load, grasps the running rope where it lies on the mule's neck against the front of the *aparejo* with right hand; he draws down so as to pull rope through between packs, thus gaining slack, and carries or swings this part of rope to rear over the pack, so that it lies as shown at E, Figure 153, page 454; this rope, called the "rear rope," pulls the standing rope (A) to the rear when the hitch is tightened, thus forming rear portion of the "diamond"; the near packer then assists the off packer in raising the running rope off the mule's neck, bringing it to center of the load, so as to lie near and in rear and against the standing rope; he then takes hold of running rope with right hand, and passes it in, from right to left, behind standing rope, as shown at F; receives this rope with left hand, and pulls through enough slack so that, using both hands, he can pass the rope down between the *cinchas*, as shown at G; the hitch is now formed, ready for tightening.   Fig. 152 shows the arrangement of rope on off side, and Fig. 153 on near side.   The near packer now takes hold of the running rope at F with right hand; places left hand, palm down, on center

FIG. 153.   THIRD POSITION, NEAR SIDE.

of pack, and brings rope held in right hand so as to rest in this hand; he bears against load with left hand as hard as he pulls with right, and calls out, "Cinch."

Off packer: At the word "Cinch," off packer raises the left knee, placing it against the boot, in rear of rope as shown in illustration on page 455; grasps the running rope (B, Fig. 152) close to cincha-hook with both hands, takes a good, steady pull straight out in line with cincha-hook, and gives slack quickly to near packer, calling "Take" as he releases slack; in giving slack, do not let go of rope; takes another similar pull, rendering slack likewise; if needed, he takes a third pull, and then calls,

CINCHING PACK.

"Break"; he then takes the rope that passes between the running and standing ropes and carries or swings it forward so that it will drop in front of off pack (or this may be done before beginning to tighten the lashing); this, called the "front rope" (C, Fig. 152), draws the running rope (A) to the front when hitch is tightened, and so forms the front part of the "diamond"; the off packer then steps to the rear of *aparejo*, facing to front, and takes hold of rear rope near rear end of his pack.

Near packer: The near packer, as slack is being rendered by off packer, takes it in with right hand and holds it with left; at the word "Break" from off packer he

TRAVELING THE ROPE.

passes the running rope, held in right hand, between the standing rope and side of pack, receiving it with left hand; with both hands he draws the rope well up so as to bind it between standing rope and pack (this is called "breaking the rope"); he then, with left hand, brings this rope around and under front corner of boot; the right hand in rear of

cincha takes the slack from left and passes the rope under
rear corner of boot and upwards (this is called "traveling the rope"); the left hand now grasps the rope
below the right, and, carrying it up over the corner of
pack, holds it there taut until the slack is taken by off
packer; the appearance of the near packer's hand on top
of load is the indication to off packer to take in slack on
the rear rope; slack being taken by off packer, the near
packer grasps the rear rope above boot, as shown in illustration on page 456; he may place his left foot against
the rear of the *aparejo;* then with both hands he draws out
all slack to the rear; he holds until he sees off packer sitting on rope, when he lets go quickly and calls, "Take,"
repeating the pull and command until all slack has been
taken up by off packer, and then calls, "Good," and steps
to animal's shoulder, facing to rear.

Off packer: The off packer, noticing the left hand
of near packer on corner of pack, takes in slack, hand over
hand, quickly; takes a wrap of rope around right hand,
inclines body forward, placing the left foot against the
rear of the *aparejo*, and sits back on rope each time the
near packer calls. "Take." The rear rope on both sides of
the mule passes over the rear ends of the side-packs.
Packers should never pull on rope standing well out from
side of mule, as they are more apt to cause the animal to
step on their feet. The off packer holds slack with left
hand and with right passes rope under boot of *aparejo* to
front, swinging the body to the front as he does so, and
facing to the rear; the right hand having brought the rope
up above the front corner of boot, the left hand grasps it
below the right, and, sliding upward, holds the rope taut
near the top of the corner of the pack, thus indicating to
near packer to take in slack.

Near packer: The near packer takes hold of end of
rope on near side of mule's neck and draws in slack; coils
hand over hand enough to pass the end over the center of
load to off-side; throws this coil over with right hand,
takes in all remaining slack, hand over hand, and then

wrapping rope around right hand, grasps with both hands, inclines body forward, and places left foot against the front of the *aparejo*, as in the position of off packer when previously pulling in slack to the rear, and sits back on rope.

THE COMPLETED "DIAMOND," NEAR SIDE.

Off packer: The off packer takes hold of rope above boot with both hands, his left foot against the front of the *aparejo*, and pulls taut, as explained for the near packer; seeing the near packer in the act of sitting on the rope, he lets go quickly, calling "Take" each time he releases slack, and "Good" when all slack has been taken up by near packer, and then steps to center of *aparejo*, grasping the end of the rope.

Near packer: The near packer, having sat on rope, holds slack with left hand and with right passes the rope under boot from front to rear, and then up toward top of pack, near center, holding it there, palm outward, gives one good pull upward on the rope, and calls, ''Tie.''

THE COMPLETED ''DIAMOND,'' SHOWING KNOT, OFF SIDE.

Off packer· The off packer meanwhile takes up the end of the rope and coils hand over hand, being careful to leave sufficient rope to near packer to get around the rear corner of boot; if the near packer sees he can give more slack, he calls out, ''Take slack,'' and, bracing with left knee against boot, hauls the rope taut and gives slack to off packer; the off packer holds coil in right hand, places left hand against pack, and takes slack with right; at the word "Tie" from near packer, he holds taut with left hand, raising this (called the "top rope") clear of the pack; with right hand he passes the coils up under the top rope and lays them between the packs, leaving enough of the bight hanging down for fastening;

POSITION OF SLING-ROPE FOR A TOP-PACK.

then with left hand he brings the bight down over the coils and fastens the bight by taking a turn from right to left, first under both standing and running ropes and jamming between ropes and load, and then between the standing and running ropes, and again drawing upward snugly. The "diamond hitch" is now complete, as shown in illustrations on page 458 and 459.

In the formation of the "diamond hitch," though only one rope is used (the lash-rope), five portions of this rope are, for convenience, given special designations as follows: the standing rope, the running rope, the rear rope, the front rope, and the top rope. The hitch has a single knot in its formation; this is undone, when taking off the

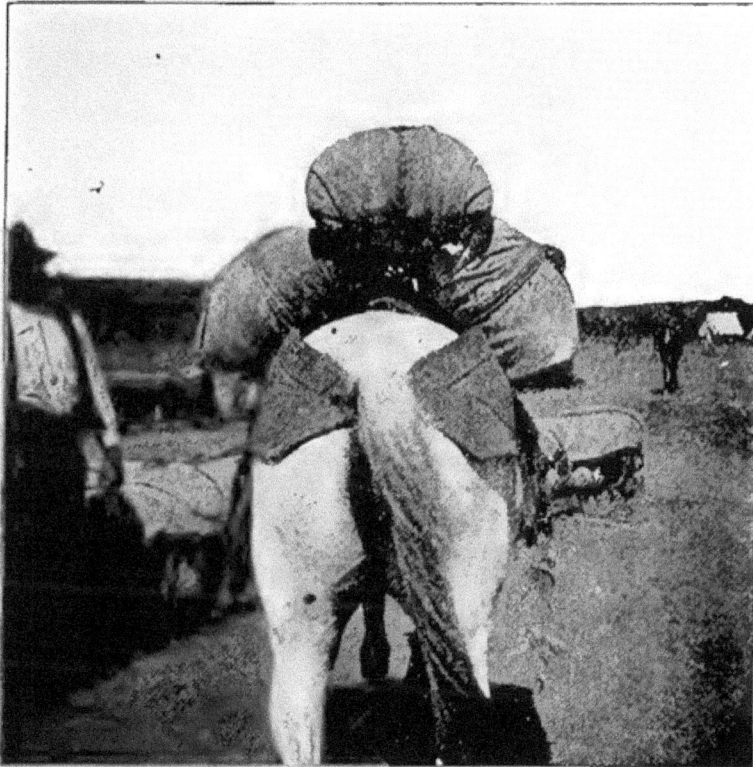

REAR VIEW OF PACK WITH TOP-PACK ON.

lash-rope, by pulling out the front rope on the off-side, from between the standing and running rope, and this should always be done in taking off the "diamond."

This method of forming the "diamond hitch" is the regulation one, and is the one that the writer has used many times on the Western ranges and in the cavalry service. Though difficult to understand at first, once learned, it is equally difficult to forget, and is the securest method known for lashing on the load to the *aparejo*. The time consumed in putting on the "diamond" is about one minute, when well understood. The record in the American service for putting on the entire "rigging" and

SIDE-PADS FOR LOADING BALE OF HAY.

load (two side-packs), complete, is held by Pack-train No. 24, and is 47 seconds. This entire method of loading can be done by one man. The writer has seen Assistant Chief Packer Thomas Mooney, United States Army, put it all on in less than 2 minutes.

It frequently becomes necessary to put on a top-pack between the two side-packs; this is not difficult, but, as it happens so often, it should be known how to do it. The only difference in the entire arrangement is in the tying of the side-packs with the sling-rope; this is as follows:

. *Tying Sling-Rope for Top-Pack.*—Place sling-rope on top of *aparejo*, the loop falling on near side and the two ends on off side, front rope several feet longer than rear

SIDE-BLOCKS FOR LOADING LARGE BOXES.

rope; now put up off side-pack; off packer throws both ends of rope over pack to near packer, who spreads them out outside of loop; near packer then throws loop over to off packer, over the off pack, as shown in illustration on page 460; near packer now puts up near side-pack, and, taking front end of rope, passes it through loop, from top to bottom, bringing the end down and pulling tight; then tie the two ends of rope, as previously explained for tying sling-rope when only two side-packs are used; No. 2 now places top-pack between the two side-packs. The "diamond hitch" is then put on as usual; it reaches entirely up and over the packs. (See illustration on page 461.)

It also frequently is necessary to load one large box on the mule; this must be loaded carefully; if extra canvas is available, it should be rolled from both ends until two pads are formed and these placed over the center, so that the unrolled part comes across the top edge of the *aparejo*, and the box then set on top of these pads; gunny-sacks or shelter-halves, stuffed with hay, grass, or straw, will answer. The sling-rope is not used. The "diamond hitch" is thrown just the same as before. The illustration of packing the bale of hay will show how the pads are placed, *under the canvas cincha*, and how the box is set on. Blocks of round wood are often used instead of these pads, the blocks being placed outside of the *cincha* and hobbled together with the sling- or lair-ropes at both ends; these blocks of wood give more satisfaction than the canvas pads, but either may be used. This is the proper way to pack any large, single box, as a field desk.

In packing side-packs, three packs, or the one box, care must be taken that they ride squarely, equal weight coming on each side of the mule's back, and that the packs do not sag down either forward or backward; if they do, they must be at once readjusted tightly.

Potatoes, onions, bacon, sugar, coffee, beans, salt, etc., should be done up in double gunny-sacks before being placed in the *manta*, and each sack should not exceed 100 or 125 pounds in weight. Bacon should have clean hay (about 5 or 6 pounds per 100 pounds of bacon), packed around it before being sacked; breakable articles, such as tin cans, glass, tin plates, etc., should be snugly packed in hay or grass in light, strong, wooden boxes about the size of the gunny-sack, and these boxes should be about the length of the *aparejo* from front to rear, about 18 inches wide and about 14 inches thick; axes, spades, shovels, etc., should be done up in gunny-sacks, the necks tied, and the pack placed as a top-pack, care being taken that the ends do not touch the mule's withers, neck, head, or croup as he travels. Ammunition may be used as side-packs, in the original boxes, one box being used on each side. Hard bread comes in light, strong 50-pound boxes, which make very good side-packs. Side-packs must be even in weight.

Whenever the pack-mule is loaded, the blind should be put on over his eyes. The mule is taught to stand still whenever the blind is put on, and it should be kept in place by the men·packing the mule. The blind is of leather, about 5 inches deep, and formed somewhat like a huge cuff with depressions for the eyes. At the two ends of the cuff are buckskin strings; around both of these is a small leather loop, which may be pushed up so that the blind fits the head and covers the eyes. Some blinds have throat latches, but these are rarely necessary.

Under favorable circumstances and conditions of travel and country, the good pack-mule should be able to carry about 30 per cent of his own weight. The load should not be much in excess of 200 pounds when long or hard marches are to be made. The following table of some actual marches made by pack-trains in the American service, taken from Chief Packer Daly's excellent book on "Packing," will show what the American pack-train has accomplished under good management:

WEIGHT OF LOAD.	Maximum Rate of Travel per Hour.	Number of Miles per Day.	Number of Days Continuous Travel.
200 pounds	8	25	7
200 pounds	7	40	10
200 pounds	6	50	7
200 pounds	6	100	3
250 pounds	8	25	3
250 pounds	6	100	1
250 pounds	6	20	60
250 pounds	5	50	10
300 pounds	5	75	1
300 pounds	5	50	7
300 pounds	5	25	30
300 pounds	5	20	60
350 pounds	4	20	30
400 pounds	4	15	30

Among the California, Oregon, and Idaho pack-trains no mule carries less than 300 pounds, some of them 400 pounds, and at one time a pack-mule was seen on the Klamath River, California, loaded with an iron casting weighing over 500 pounds. However, these animals travel from 12 or 15 to 18 or 20 miles per day over good trails, and are well cared for under a perfect system. The writer has many times seen cowboys and prospectors on the frontier put loads of over 300 pounds on their pack-mules and make very long, hard journeys over difficult country at various seasons of the year. The gait of the pack-train is usually a walk, but as the rate of travel is increased a trained pack-mule instead of quickening the walk, falls into an amble or fox-trot; at this ambling gait he is able to go at the rate of 5 or 6 miles per hour without undue fatigue. This is about as rapid as the cavalry troop will ordinarily travel.

The actual working of the troop pack-train, which generally consists of about 12 pack-animals and 2 or 3 packers on saddle-mules, is well explained by giving the methods employed in one of the troop pack-trains some time ago used in one of the troops of the Fourth Cavalry.

Troop B, Fourth United States Cavalry, possessed a troop pack-train when serving in Arizona, and the use and management of this train will illustrate what advantage it is to a troop of cavalry, and also how it was kept up in efficiency, etc. This troop pack-train consisted of 12 mules, 2 of which were reserved for saddle purposes in conjunction with the train. The mules were quartered in the troop stables, forage and other allowance being drawn for them, shod by the troop blacksmith, and turned out daily with the troop horses on herd, thus soon becoming attached to them and indifferent to others; therefore easy to herd. They were looked after by the wagoner, farrier, and stable orderly; these men were taught to pack, and frequently practiced, as were the other troopers. The *aparejos* were kept in the stable. The troop quartermaster sergeant had charge of the train, etc. It was required at all times to have on hand in the troop ten days' rations, liberally estimated, with other articles necessary for taking the field; namely:

Flour, 500 pounds;
Hard bread, 50 pounds;
Bacon, 350 pounds;
Sugar, 75 pounds;
Coffee, 60 pounds;
Beans, 50 pounds;
Salt, 25 pounds;
Baking powder, 20 pounds;
Box of ammunition (carbine), 110 pounds;
Box of mule-shoes and nails (two shoes and nails per mule), 25 pounds;*
Six camp-kettles, (about) 40 pounds;
Two mess-boxes, (about) 15 pounds;

*The extra horse-shoes were carried by the troopers in their saddle-bags, with sufficient nails to put them on when needed. As the packs diminished these were carried on the pack-mules.

Twenty mess-pans, (about) 10 pounds;

An axe, spade, small coffee-mill, two butcher knives, two long forks, two long spoons, three or four tin plates, three frying-pans, a few farrier's medicines, a few blacksmith's tools, soap, pepper, and matches, all told, about 25 pounds.

An excess over the ration of about 100 pounds of flour and bread, 50 pounds of bacon, 15 pounds of sugar, and 20 pounds of coffee, allowing for the contingency of guides and couriers being attached for rations, of any necessity for "making the ration hold out a little longer," and for the tendency of men, in the absence of vegetables, to consume an over-allowance of the above-named "components." The troop mess-boxes were of light wood, about 2½ feet long, 1½ feet wide, and 2 feet deep; these were strengthened and made water-tight by rawhide covers. Six camp-kettles were necessary, because water was sometimes found in places inacessible to live stock, whence it had to be drawn by lariats and kettles. Some of the mess-boxes then served as a watering-trough, and the animals were watered without interrupting the work of the cook and baker. The coffee was roasted and placed in a rubber-blanket bag. The total weight of the above, including an officer's bundle of some 30 pounds and 20 pounds of fresh bread always taken upon starting out, was about 1400 pounds, or an average of 140 pounds per mule, which the necessary protecting covers brought up to 145 pounds. Everything was weighed and divided into 10 loads of 20 side-packs, allowance being made and places left for the officer's bundle and the fresh bread referred to. The camp-kettles, being of three sizes, were telescoped together into two sacks, ready for slinging over a pack. The usual ropes pertaining to the "riggings" were kept with all of this near the *aparejos.*

Upon notification at night of an order to move out, the stable men began putting on the *aparejos*, being soon joined by 2 or 3 men from the troop; the party then saddled, mounted, took the train to the store-room, lashed on the packs, and joined the troop, usually in less time than if ordered out during the day, there being no herd to be brought in, nor men dispersed about the garrison on various duties to be sent for. On the march, the train followed at a sufficient distance to prevent the mules crowding in among the rearmost horses when the troop halted or was crossing bad ground. The cook and baker rode ahead to keep the mules together during halts or to halt them when necessary, while 4 other troopers rode in rear of the train, where the packs could be over-looked. The "mess-boxes" containing the first things the cooks would need upon arrival in camps were borne by the "kitchen mule," an animal selected for its good behavior, steady habits, and easy gaits—shaking its rather miscellaneous load as little as possible—which always kept the trail, and could be easily caught when its pack needed adjusting. Upon reaching camp, the mules were turned out with the horses or picketed, according to circumstances. The 20 pounds of fresh bread were taken for the first meal after reaching camp; the hard bread was reserved for emergencies. The baker was required to keep the troop at least one day's supply of fresh bread ahead. He baked in the 20 mess-pans mentioned; these pans were of sheet iron, circular, and made in two sets, one about 12 inches in diameter across the top and 9 inches across the bottom, and the other about 11 inches across the top and 8 inches across the bottom; all had the same depth, about 5 or 6 inches. Every evening the packs were rearranged, the weight fairly distributed, the ropes put in place, and such changes as were necessary made in the "riggings," shifting the side-stuffing, lengthening or shortening the cruppers, etc.

The above pack-train gives a typical American troop pack-outfit, perhaps somewhat more lightly loaded than might ordinarily be possible. This train was found able to keep up with its troop at the walk, trot, and gallop for 12 or 15 hours daily for several consecutive days over rough country. While the troop horses were favored by the occasional dismounting of their riders, the mules at all times had to carry their packs; besides, the horses carried live weights, while the loads on the mules were dead weight. On one occasion this troop, while scouting in the Sierra Madre Mountains, was compelled to travel, the troopers leading their horses, for three days, owing to the roughness of the country, yet the train kept up; showing the remarkable powers and sure-footedness of these little pack-mules. This train once made 140 miles in the first three days, just after having renewed the rations, and though some of the pack-mules suffered very much, the train kept up with the troop.

In camp it becomes important to care for the mules and packs and "riggings," and the efficiency of the train will depend on the thoroughness with which this is done. Upon arriving in camp, the side-packs are at once removed from all of the mules and piled together and covered, if possible, with canvas; the extra *mantas* may be used for this, gunny-sacks, shelter tents, or brush. The "rigging" is allowed to remain on the mule for a quarter of an hour or so after taking off the side-packs, so that the backs may cool off gradually; then the "rigging" is taken off, the process of removal being the reverse of putting it on. The *aparejo* should never be dragged off, but should be *lifted* off, the crupper first being taken from under the tail and bent forward over the *aparejo*. The *aparejo* should be set up straight, resting upon the lower edges of the pads, and never thrown down or spread out. No one should be permitted to sit on or lean against the *aparejo*, as it will alter the shape and necessitate re-setting up. On top of the *aparejo* is placed the blanket, folded; on top of the blanket, the *corona*, canvas in, number on top, so that it can be quickly seen. Each mule is numbered with the number of his "rigging," so that the "rigging" fitted to him may be always used; as the "riggings" are each fitted to particular mules, other "riggings" must not be used on the mule until refitted for him. The number of the mule is fastened to the near side of the halter by means of a leather tag. The *aparejos* should be placed one beside the other, lower edges of adjacent pads touching. The whole number of "riggings" should then be covered with canvas or gunny-sacks or brush. It is customary in the American service to run the picket-line parallel to the line of *aparejos* and about 18 feet from them. The picket-line is either stretched along the ground or elevated on posts similar to the one for the troop horses. The mules are tied to the picket-line, each opposite his own "rigging," by the halter-strap; they soon learn their right places, and will take them without being led.

All ropes must be carefully coiled up, fastened, and *hung up*, or put under cover—never left on the ground. The riding-saddles should be hung up over improvised saddle-racks near the *aparejos*—never laid on top of them. About once in two weeks every *aparejo* should be well oiled with neatsfoot oil to keep the leather in good condition. The blanket should be cleaned, dried, and never placed on the mule's back dirty. The *corona* should be cleaned frequently, and the canvas scraped clean every time it is taken off the back. The picket-line must be chosen carefully and be free from stones, rocky ground, broken glass, brush, etc., and kept well policed at all times.

The above outlines the usual methods pertaining to the troop pack-train. Only by experience can efficiency be attained. There are many special knots used by experienced packers, but it is not possible to give them all here. In the setting up of the *aparejo*, in its careful fitting to the back, in the cleaning of the entire "rigging," etc., there is much to learn to secure satisfactory results, but space does not permit all of these to be entered in this book. By practice much can be learned, special methods understood, and the train kept up to a standard of efficiency that will enable it to perform its arduous work when the time comes.

It will often happen in field service that there are no pack-mules present with the troop, and that there are supplies, etc., which must be carried along; even the "riggings" may not be present. It then becomes necessary to utilize the extra horses, with their ordinary cavalry saddles, as pack-animals; this, however, should be done only when no better means are at hand to carry the impedimenta, and only temporarily employed, as

ONE METHOD OF PACKING THE CAVALRY SADDLE.

danger to the horse's back is very great. One way of packing the cavalry saddle is to place the side-packs well up against the saddle and lash them together with an improvised sling-rope (the lariat can be so used), and then securely tying the two packs to the pommel and cantle with additional lariats. Care must be taken that the two side-packs do not injure the spine or sides, that they are even in weight, and do not touch the croup or withers. The stirrup-straps may be used, by crossing them over the top and fastening them one into the other by means of their buckles; this forms a middle loop to sustain the side-packs. Another method is to place but one pack on the saddle, stretching this one across the

PACKING TWO SIDE-PACKS ON THE CAVALRY SADDLE, USING LARIATS.

seat of the saddle and lashing it on with lariats and the coat-straps as shown on page 472. The surcingle is used as a breast-strap, to overcome the tendency of the pack to work the saddle back. Even two side-packs can be so placed, putting one on top of the other, when they are small, the whole being lashed to pommel and cantle. Nothing should ever be placed either in front or behind the saddle, as the croup, spine, and withers are sure to be injured.

Another method of packing the cavalry saddle when used as a pack-saddle is to bind shelter-tent poles or

THE "SAW-BUCK" ON THE CAVALRY SADDLE.

similar stout sticks to the pommel and cantle on each side, so that the two at the pommel and the two at the cantle form two crosses, similar to the old "saw-buck"* pack-saddle used years ago on the frontier. These poles must be tightly bound, so as not to touch the horse's

*The "saw-buck" is principally good as a one-man arrangement, and it was the necessity of having such a pack-saddle that brought it into existence.

back or sides, and from them the side-packs may be
slung, using a lariat as a common sling-rope and another as a sort of lash-rope, binding the packs to the
cross-trees.   The side-packs must be up snugly against
the cross-trees, and not allowed to sag at either end, and

THE "SAW-BUCK" PACKED WITH THREE PACKS.

must be even on the back.   This arrangement allows more
to be packed on one horse, as a middle-pack can be
placed in the crotches of the two crosses and be well off
the back. The coat-straps are used to fasten the two crosses
to the pommel and cantle; the point of intersection of
each cross must be firmly bound by a center coat-strap.*

*The coat-straps must be left attached in the usual way to the
saddle.

This method was used by the writer in campaigning in the Philippine Islands, and for short distances, temporarily, it served very well, and there was not a back injured, although considerable mountain-climbing was necessary.

The packing of the troop horse, equipped with but the ordinary cavalry saddle, may at times be necessary, and should be understood by all cavalrymen; it is open, however, to many objections, the chief among these being the liability of ruining the back; when it is used, the side-packs must be fastened firmly and great care taken to keep them evenly balanced, frequently readjusting the entire pack whenever necessary. When the number of horses is limited, and it is absolutely imperative that the supplies should be taken, the *travois* may be used, either alone or in conjunction with the above-described method of packing the saddle.* The *travois* consists of two long poles, about 18 feet long each, having an improved sack or "body" attached to them about 5 feet from the two heavy ends, which rest on the ground; this "body" may be made by utilizing a shelter-half, a blanket, or by laying short sticks across the tops of the two long poles and binding these short sticks to the long poles firmly. The diameter of the two long poles should be about 4 inches at the base ends, gradually tapering down to about 2 inches at the far ends, and must be straight. To adjust the *travois* to the horse, pass the slender ends of the *travois* through the stirrup-straps near the buckles, and bind them there firmly with lariats or coat-straps. The width of the *travois* must be such that the long poles do not chafe the horse; the sack, or "body" should be no nearer the horse's hocks than 3 feet, and must not be so deep as to cause it to scrape along the ground. As the strain on the saddle is great, it is liable to slip backwards, and this may be prevented by the use of a breast-strap;

*The *travois* has been frequently used in transporting wounded men, where other means were lacking.

a surcingle passed around the horse's breast and fastened into the spider-straps can be made to answer for a breast-strap, or three halter-straps may be formed into a rough breast-strap for this purpose.

The importance of understanding packing is so great that every young officer should be an adept in it, so far as relates to the formation of the train, the regulation

BRITISH INDIAN PACK-MULE.

"rigging," the throwing of the lair-ropes, the sling-rope, and the "diamond hitch," for either two or three packs or one large one, etc. Under stress of field conditions, when pack-mules are conspicuous by their absence, many ingenious methods are open to the energetic cavalryman. Those improvised methods explained above for packing the cavalry saddle are not new ones, but have been used for years; they have been used by our cavalry in the West, in the campaigning in the Philippine Islands, and in teaching packing to the troopers of different troops, with much success as *temporary* packs, the only purpose for which they are intended.

In the Philippine Islands, where for months at a time the mud was belly deep on the horses, it was very discouraging to scout through that land of blistering plain and seemingly impenetrable jungle, or through miles upon miles of oozy, black, and apparently bottom-

BRITISH PACK-MULE CARRYING TWO 80-POUND BOXES.

less mud in the rainy season, lacking pack-mule transportation. For awhile the only available transportation consisted of the rough, small, native "bull-carts," hauled by great, slow-moving, powerful carabaos. The cart had two solid wooden wheels and a solid wooden axle about 12 inches in diameter, with a rude box of bamboo on the axle; the body was held on the axle by means of long wooden spikes, two of which passed behind and two in front of the axle on each side, from the bottom of the body. The carabao, so long as there was water to drink and flounder in at least hourly, was a power in its massive, slow strength; but without water it soon became exhausted. The average gait was about 2 miles an hour, if one's luck was good and nothing broke, and the cavalry troop, unable to leave the wagons, was forced to travel at that pace many times. As it was very often necessary to push on ahead, leaving a guard from the troop to bring along the carts, the troop was often depleted in numbers at just the wrong time, and when the last view of those carts was taken, everyone wondered if we would ever see them again, and many times we did not. Even the strong regulation army wagon with its six mules was helpless at times to pass through the many bottomless stretches of mud we encountered, and it was not until later on, when the pack-trains came, that the troops could maintain their record for rapidity in service. The little native pony made a sort of pack-animal, and enabled us to pass mud, bad bridges, and mountains, where the heat was beyond description, but it required almost as many of them as horses in the troop, and besides, these ponies were not always to be had, or. if available, were dangerous around our horses, because of their more or less diseased condition.

Later, when the pack-mule came, the Cavalry once more surpassed even itself in its field service. The mule was found to be able to live on the native grasses, *palay*, etc., as well as the troop-horse, and was invaluable, as will ever be the case.

CHAPTER XVIII.

DISEASES AND MEDICINES.

Necessity for Study and Observation—What to Do with the Sick Horse—Methods of Administering Medicines—The Healthy Horse—Pulse—Temperature—Cold Applications—Hot Applications—Sponging—Supply of Veterinary Medicines for Cavalry Troop—Instruments—Various Diseases—Treatment.

No matter how hygienic the surroundings, how excellent the management, or how careful the feeding may be, the horse, being composed of flesh and blood, will occasionally become ill. The cavalry horse, frequently exposed to the greatest hardships and exposure, must then, at times, suffer from physical ailments of various kinds, and only observation and study and careful attention will effect a cure.

The sick horse should be separated from the other animals whenever rest and quiet are necessary; for this purpose the separate stalls, or the box-stalls, should be used. If the horse is apt to be ill for any length of time, all the shoes should be removed to ease his feet and legs. The horse must be attended to regularly, and at each treatment the care bestowed upon the animal should be thorough. The horse should be kept in a well-ventilated stall, free from draughts. His stall should always be kept fresh and clean and be liberally bedded down; as he will very often lie down, he should have a good bed, and not be required to lie on the floor or ground. A bucket of water should be left within reach at all times, as the sick horse will drink at odd times and needs this refreshment. As the appetite of the sick horse is often very capricious, he should be fed several times a day with fresh, clean food in small quantities. No food left over from a previous feed should be allowed to remain in the feed-box; it will only become nosed and stale by the horse's slobbering, and is apt to sour and ferment. All woodwork in the stalls should be kept clean, and the stalls should be aired at least once daily and kept dry, the horse being removed from it when this is done, if he can walk. His food must be varied somewhat, as he will often refuse the regular ration. His bowels should be watched, and an occasional feed of bran mash given whenever he appears costive. He should be handled quietly and slowly and as little as possible, and the light should be modified so as not to tire his eyes.

It must be constantly remembered in dealing with the sick horse that good nursing is far more effective than much medicine. Frequently an entire cure can be obtained by the use of care and skill in handling the sick horse without the aid of drugs. It is impossible to lay down any exact rules for good nursing, but the general rules given above will be found useful. Gentle hand-rubbing of the skin is very refreshing to sick animals, and this should not be neglected. Cold applications are very invaluable, as they tend to harden and brace up the parts and steady the nerves; hot fomentations are also of great utility, but must be used with care, and should be continued for one or two hours to obtain best results. In the hot or cold application the water should be allowed to trickle slowly and continuously over the part. Bandages are of great use in keeping the extremities warm; they should not be put on too tight; they are especially good after hot or cold applications, as they prevent chill.

It must be remembered that the prevention of disease is far more important than its cure; but when it actually exists, it must also be realized that it does not occur without a cause. As a general rule, the cause of any disease may be found out, and if ascertained, a more speedy cure may be effected, and the disease may be prevented in future. Accidents will occur; the nature of cavalry work entails such a liability, but they will be much less likely to occur when the horse is in good condition, when he is fit to go without being unduly fresh, and when the shoeing, etc., are good, than when these favorable conditions are reversed. Good hygienic surroundings are very important; so much so, in fact, that very few cases of disease under good sanitary arrangements are ever transmitted by infection or contagion. Fresh air, plentifully and frequently renewed, is the great antidote to all contagion or infection.

Medicine may enter the body of the horse through any of the following designated channels: first, by the mouth; second, by the lungs and upper air-passages; third, by the skin; fourth, under the skin, by hypodermic methods; fifth, by the rectum.

(1) BY THE MOUTH.—Medicines can be given by the mouth in the form of powders, balls, drenches, and electuaries.

Powders.—These should be as finely pulverized as possible in order to secure a rapid solution and absorption. Their action is in this way facilitated. Powders must be free from irritant or caustic action upon the mouth. Those that are without any disagreeable taste or smell are readily eaten on the food or taken in the drinking-water. When placed on the feed, they should first be dissolved or suspended in water, and then sprinkled on the feed. If mixed dry, the horse will often leave the medicine in the bottom of his manger. The practice of blowing an impalpable powder up the horse's nose is occasionally indulged in, but does more harm than good.

Balls.—When properly made, these are cylindrical in shape, about 2 inches in length, and about ¾ inch in diameter. They should be fresh, but if necessary to keep them some time, they should be made up with glycerine or some such agent to prevent them from becoming too hard. Very old, hard balls are sometimes passed whole with the manure without being acted upon at all. Paper is to be wrapped around balls when given; it should be thin, but firm; toilet paper is the best. Balls are preferred to drenches when the med-

icine is extremely disagreeable or nauseating, when the
dose is not too large, when the horse is ugly to drench,
and when the medicine is intended to act slowly. Certain medicines cannot or should not be made into balls—
medicines required to be given in large doses, oils, caustic
substances, unless diluted and thoroughly mixed with a
vehicle, deliquescent or efflorescent salts; substances suitable for balls can be made up by the addition of honey,
syrup, soap, etc., when required for immediate use. Gelatine capsules of different sizes are now obtainable and
are a convenient means of giving medicines in ball form.
The ball should be soft enough to be easily compressed
by the fingers. Always loosen the horse before attempting to give him a ball. The tongue should be firmly
grasped with the left hand and gently pulled forward;
the ball, slightly moistened, is then placed with the tips
of the fingers of the right hand as far back in the mouth
as possible; as the tongue is loosened it is drawn back
into the mouth and carries the ball with it. The mouth
should be closed for a minute or two. We should always
have a pail of water or two to offer the horse after balling;
this will often prevent him from coughing out the ball or
its becoming lodged in the gullet.

Drenches.—Drenches are to be given when the medicine is liquid, when the dose is large, and when we desire
speedy action. They should never be given through the
nose, as they are liable to strangle the animal or irritate
the nose and windpipe, and sometimes even the lungs.
Enough water or oil must be used to thoroughly dissolve
or dilute the medicine; more than this makes the drench
bulky and is unnecessary. The bottle used for drenching
purposes should be clean, strong, and smooth about its
neck; it should be without shoulders, tapering, and of a
size to suit the amount to be given; a tin bottle is better,
as it is not easily broken by the teeth. The bottle should
be well shaken immediately before giving the drench.
If the dose is a small one, the horse's head may be held
up by the left hand while the medicine is poured into the

mouth by the right. Should the dose be large, the horse ugly, or the attendant unable to support the head with his hand, the head should be held up by passing the halter-strap over a beam and pulling the horse's head upward; this elevation of the head need only be carried far enough to have the horse's face in a horizontal position. In case the horse coughs, his head should be immediately lowered. The bottle should be introduced into the mouth from the side, in front of the molar teeth. Do not rub, pinch, or pound the throat, nor draw out the tongue when giving a drench.

Electuaries.—These are medicines mixed mostly with licorice-root powder, molasses, or syrup to the consistency of honey, or a soft solid. They are intended chiefly to act locally upon the mouth and throat. They are given with a wooden paddle or strong, long-handled spoon.

(2) BY THE LUNGS AND UPPER AIR-PASSAGES.—Insufflation, inhalation, and nasal douche are the methods employed. Insufflation consists of blowing the powder directly into the nose, and is rarely resorted to. Gaseous and volatile medicines are given by inhalation. These are inhaled by placing a bucket containing hot water, vinegar and water, scalded hay or bran, to which carbolic acid, iodine, or other medicines have been added, in the bottom of a long grain-bag; the horse's nose is then inserted into the top of the bag, and he thus inhales the vapor. Care must be taken not to have this hot enough to scald the animal. Scalding bran or hay is often thus inhaled to favor discharges in sore throat or distemper. The nasal douche is employed only by the veterinarian in treating some local disease of the nasal chambers. Special appliances and professional knowledge are necessary when using liquid medicines by this method; it is not often resorted to even by veterinary surgeons, as the horse objects to it very strongly.

(3) BY THE SKIN.—Medicines are often administered to horses by the skin, yet care must be taken in applying

some of these medicines, as carbolic acid solutions, etc., over the entire body may poison the animal, and death follow by absorption through the skin. Care must be exercised also not to apply poisonous medicines over very large raw or abraded surfaces for the same reason. These medicines are only applied to the skin for local purposes or diseases.

(4) UNDER THE SKIN; HYPODERMIC METHOD.—Medicines are frequently given by the hypodermic syringe under the skin; it is not safe for any but a veterinary surgeon to use this method, as the medicines thus given are a powerful poison.

(5) BY THE RECTUM.—Medicines may be given by the rectum when they cannot be given through or retained by the mouth; when we want a local action, to destroy small worms infesting the large bowels, to cause evacuation of the bowels, and to nourish the body. Medicines are given by the rectum in the form of liquid injections (enemas).

Enemas.—These, when given for absorption, should be small in quantity, neutral or slightly acid in reaction, and of a temperature of from 90° to 100° Fahr. Like foods given by the rectum, they should only be introduced after the last bowel has been emptied by the hand or by copious enemas of tepid water. When given to aid the action of physics, an enema should be sufficient in quantity to distend the bowel and cause the animal to eject it. Simple water, salt and water, or soap and water, in quantities of a gallon or more, may be given every hour. The horse should be made to retain it for some little time, as the liquid serves to moisten the dung in favor of passage. Before giving stimulating enemas (turpentine 2 oz. in linseed oil 6 oz.) the bowels should be emptied by a simple enema of warm, soapy water. Liquids may be thrown into the rectum by means of a large syringe. A very good injection-pipe can be made by any one at a trifling cost, and should be constantly on hand in every troop stable. It consists of a funnel about 6 inches deep and 7 inches in diameter, which is to be attached to a piece of ordinary garden hose about 2 feet in length. Introduce this hose about 1 foot into the horse's rectum, first thoroughly oiling it, and pour the liquid into the funnel rapidly. For all ordinary purposes this instrument is very good, and passes the fluid into the rectum by means of the force of gravity. Ordinary cold water or even ice-cold water is highly recommended as a rectal injection for horses overcome by excessive heat in summer, and in febrile diseases to reduce high temperature, and may be given by this simple contrivance.

The healthy horse can generally be readily distinguished from the sick one by his manner and actions, his high spirits, clear eyes, and general physical exuberance; but even these signs at times are present in the horse that is not wholly well, when it becomes necessary to examine the pulse and temperature.

PULSE.—By the pulse is meant the beating of the arteries which follows each contraction of the heart; in the healthy horse the average number of beats in a minute is about 40; but in different horses the number may vary from 35 to 45 and still be consistent with health. The breed and temperament of an animal have much to do with the number of pulsations. In a thorough-bred the number of beats in a given time is generally greater than in a coarse-bred horse. The pulse should be taken when the animal is quiet and at rest; work, exercise, and excitement increase the number of pulsations. The artery usually selected in the horse for taking the pulse is the sub-maxillary where it winds around the lower jaw-bone; on the inner side of the jaw-bone the artery may be readily felt when pressed against the bone; it may also be taken by pressing the ear against the left side of the horse just behind the elbow.

The number of pulsations per minute under different circumstances in disease varies from 20 to 120 or even more. The pulse may differ slightly on the two sides of the horse, and when it is impossible to find the pulse on one side, it may be found on the other. A strong, full pulse is indicative of good health, and is rarely present if the animal is in a morbid condition; a weak pulse is indicative of great debility, especially if the pulse is easily extinguished by pressure; an imperceptible pulse indicates approaching death.

TEMPERATURE.—The temperature of the healthy horse ranges from about 99½° to 101½° Fahr.; the average may be placed at about 100°. The temperature is subject to slight alterations by certain influences. A high surrounding temperature increases the animal temperature, and cold the reverse; exercise increases it; mares have a higher temperature than males; drinking cold water lowers the animal temperature; it is higher in the young than in the old horse; the process of digestion increases the temperature.

The only accurate method of taking the temperature is by introducing a small clinical thermometer into the rectum; the thermometer should be self-registering; it should remain in the rectum for about 3 or 4 minutes; before inserting it, care should be taken that the mercury is below the minimum temperature (down to about 95°) by shaking it; the end of the thermometer should be pushed in gently, leaving only sufficient outside to take hold of when about to withdraw it.

Temperature has been known to rise as high as 108° Fahr. in disease. A dropping of one or two degrees in temperature is indicative of great danger.

There are several contrivances used in handling sick horses which should be present in every cavalry stable; these are very easily made and inexpensive, and will do much to facilitate administering medicines and treatment to the horses needing them.

THE TWITCH.—The twitch consists of a stout stick about 2 feet long with a hole near one end through which a loop of cord of about the thickness of clothes-line is fastened; the left hand should be passed through the loop and grasp the horse's upper lip, on which the loop is then placed; by twisting the stick with the right hand the loop of rope is drawn tight. The upper lip of the horse is very sensitive, and he soon realizes that it hurts him more to resist than to yield. By some practical horsemen the twitch is at times applied to the ear instead of to the nose; but this is not only a more brutal way of managing the horse, but it is apt to injure the horse's hearing if he struggles much.

THE HALTER TWITCH.—The ordinary halter and strap can be used; this is put on in the usual way, and there must be no knot or check in the halter strap, which is made into a half-hitch, passed over the head, and the loop carried under the horse's upper lip. Jerking the loose end inflicts pain, and to avoid it the animal will generally stand steady. A simpler way to use the halter twitch is to put on the halter and then make a half-hitch around the lower jaw with the halter-strap.

SIDE-LINES.—An ordinary rope should be passed around the horse's neck like a collar and then between his hind legs and picked up again in such a manner as to bring it round the pastern; it is then turned once around itself, so as to make a loop nearer the fetlock, and the end pulled through the collar-loop which was first formed. The loose end of the rope should then be pulled and the horse's hind leg drawn up sufficiently to compel him to stand on three feet; it is a useful contrivance when a torn quarter has to be sewn up and there are reasons for not casting.

DOUBLE SIDE-LINES.—The double side-line is adjusted in much the same way as the single, only that the rope is first folded in the middle and a knot made, so that when put over the horse's head it will be about the same size as his collar; the free ends are carried between the hind legs and passed through in exactly the same way as the single line; allow the knot to fall on the chest, and pass the lines between all the legs; more power for throwing, however, is obtained by keeping the knot on top of the withers and the lines outside the fore leg. With nothing more than this 36-foot rope very difficult operations have been performed for ages. The men handling the rope, when about to throw the horse, should pull well together and behind the horse.

HOBBLES.—Casting the horse by means of leather hobbles is a very excellent method. Place one set of hobbles around the front pasterns and one set around the hind pasterns and pass a long rope through the rings in them all; tie one end of the rope to the ring in the hobble on the near front pastern, so that this end of the rope cannot pull out of the hobble, and then pull the other end steadily, and the horse will usually go down on his side as soon as he feels his legs going from under him. Care must be taken in using this method that the rope does not burn the pastern-joints. One man should slightly back the horse up at the same time.

STRAPPING UP A FORE LEG.—This can be done with a stirrup-strap or the halter-shank, and frequently is all that is required. The fore leg is strapped up in the same way as described in the chapter on throwing the horse.

BLINDFOLDING—Is an efficient means of control with the majority of horses, although it sometimes excites the horse too much; it can be used whenever necessary in combination with any of the above methods. .

No attempt is made in this book to describe the various instruments used by the veterinary surgeons; these instruments are constantly being changed, and there are very few of them that would be safe to be used in the hands of anyone not thoroughly experienced. The best way to learn these instruments and how to use them is to have the veterinary surgeon show them to the student, and for him to be present when the surgeon is performing veterinary operations. Each troop of cavalry is given an emergency or field equipment of veterinary instruments in the American Cavalry, and these are as follows:

1 farrier's case, leather folding, containing the following instruments.
1 bistoury, curved, probe-pointed;
1 bistoury, curved, sharp-pointed;
1 director, grooved;
1 forceps, artery;
1 forceps, dressing;
1 hoof-knife, searcher;
½ dozen needles, suture, half-curved;
1 probe, silver;
1 scissors, curved on flat;
⅛ ounce silk, suture, heavy;
1 thermometer, clinical;
1 glass graduate, 4-ounce;
1 rectal douche;
1 syringe, hard rubber, 1-ounce;
1 syringe, hard rubber, 2-ounce;
1 pair saddle-bags, farrier's, for use in the field.

The above emergency equipment is not furnished to the troop until it takes the field. In garrison the veterinary surgeon has charge of all the instruments, and they are all used by him alone or by his assistants.

The medicines supplied for veterinary purposes in the United States Army are furnished by the Quartermaster's Department and are only issued to troops as needed, and usually for short periods of time. By reference to Appendix III. the complete list of medicines on the veterinary supply table, United States Army, can be seen.

While all serious diseases among the horses of the troop will generally be treated by the veterinary surgeon, at the same time the cavalry horse has many ailments, more or less severe, which must be treated in the troop; this especially applies when the troop is in the field. A discussion of these common diseases with their causes and treatments, is given below:

LAMPAS.—This is a swelling of the mucous membrane covering the hard palate and projecting in a more or less prominent ridge immediately behind the upper incisors;

it occasionally becomes so prominent as to interfere with the horse's closing his incisors, and is painful during feeding; it is a very minor trouble.

Causes.—In young animals, from irritation set up by the growth of or changes in the teeth; may also occur in

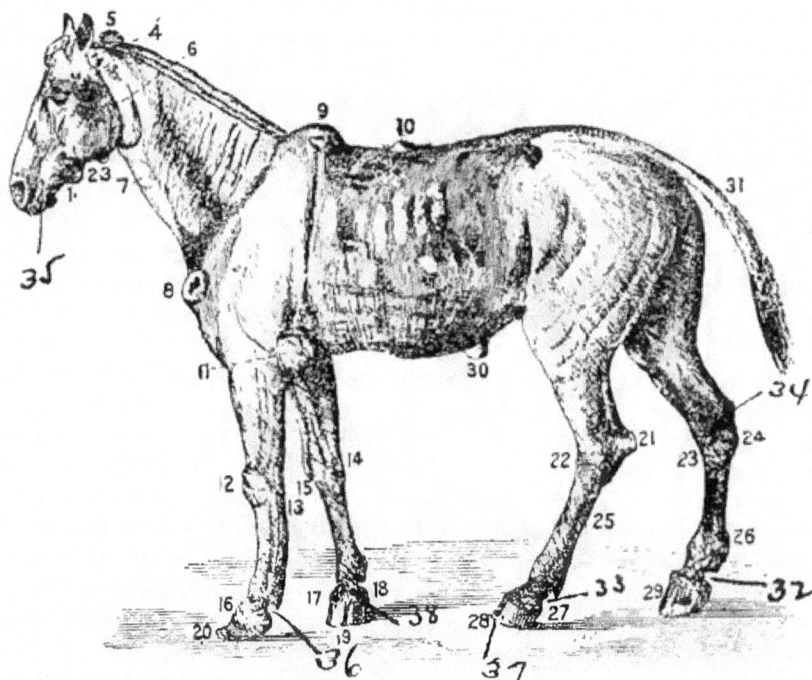

DISEASED HORSE, WITH NAMES AND LOCATION OF DISEASES.

1, Caries of the lower jaw.
2, Fistula of the parotid duct.
3, Bony excrescence or exostasis of the lower jaw.
4, Swelling by pressure of the bridle.
5, Poll evil.
6, Inflamed parotid gland.
7, Inflamed jugular vein.
8, Fungous tumor, produced by pressure of the collar.
9, Fistula in the withers.
10, Saddle gall.
11, Tumor of the elbow.
12, Induration of the knee.
13, Clap of the back sinews.
14, Malanders.
15, Splint.
16, Ringbone.
17, A tread upon the coronet.
18, Quittor.
19, Sand crack.
20, Contracted or ring-foot of a foundered horse.
21, Capped hock.
22, Malanders.
23, Spavin.
24, Curb.
25, Swelled sinews.
26, Thick leg.
27, Grease
28, A crack in front of the foot, called cow crack.
29, Quarter crack.
30, Ventral hernia.
31, Rat-tail.
32, Wind galls.
33, Scratches.
34, Thoroughpin.
35, Lampas.
36, Scratches.
37, Seedy toe.
38, Side bone.

older horses from inflammation set up by bit injuries, and in old horses from irregularity of the teeth.

Treatment.—Feed bran mash and use an astringent wash of alum-water several times daily; scarifying the palate should never be done if it can be avoided, and never should it go back of the second bar; when this is done, the cutting should never be deep. This will generally subside in a few days by the above treatment. Burning the palate with a hot iron is brutal and worse than the disease.

STRANGLES.—An infectious disease of the horse, seen most frequently in young animals, and usually protects the animal from a future attack; appears as a fever, lasting for a few days, with formation of one or more abscesses; usually leaves the animal perfectly healthy after recovery, but sometimes the abscesses prove fatal.

Causes.—Infection by direct contact with an animal suffering from the disease; indirect infection through contact with the discharge from an infected animal; frequently contracted by being placed in infected railway cars.

Symptoms.—The horse at first is a little sluggish and dejected; appetite poor; very thirsty; coat dry; occasional chills in the legs; in severe cases chills of the whole body; eyes and mouth turned bright rosy color; pulse quickened; breathing slightly accelerated, followed by cough and discharge from nostrils; this discharge is at first watery, then becomes thicker and somewhat bluish in color and sticky; finally a yellowish color and very profuse; swelling under the jaw shortly after discharge begins from nose; this swelling develops into an abscess, which breaks and discharges the pus; this abscess may form anywhere along the track of the windpipe, but will usually form under the lower jaw.

Treatment.—Ordinary light cases require but little treatment beyond fresh air, diet, warm mashes, steaming, moistened hay, and protection from cold; this latter is imperative; bran mash for a day or two should be given.

If the horse be suffering, give three times daily, either as a drench or in the feed if the animal will eat, 2 drachms of nitre and also 1 drachm of quinine as a ball, wrapped in tissue paper, three times a day. Open the abscess as soon as it comes to a head, for if it opens of itself, it will generally leave a permanent blemish. Keep the opened abscess clean and fresh by washing it out frequently with a 2% creolin solution.

CATARRH, OR SIMPLE COLD.—This is an acute inflammation of the mucous membrane which lines the nasal cavities, very similar to cold in the head in the human subject.

Causes.—Exposure to draughts or sudden alterations of temperature, as from a hot stable to a cold corral; dampness; swimming rivers when hot, etc.

Symptoms.—The animal is dull, frequently has a cough; a few days after the attack begins the discharge from the nostrils changes from a watery to that of a thick mucilaginous state of a yellowish white color, and may be more or less profuse; poor appetite and more or less debility; tears from the eyes at times; some slight fever.

Treatment.—A few days of rest, pure air, and good food, no excitement, no draughts, and reasonably warm temperature; steaming. The steaming should be given four or five times a day, about fifteen or twenty minutes each time; bran mashes, linseed gruel, and grass if in season; enemas of warm water into the rectum, if constipated, two or three times a day if necessary, but no purgative medicines.

Give the following as a drench, three times daily:

Aromatic spirits of ammonia, 1 ounce;
Nitrate of potassium, powdered, 1 drachm;
Water, 1 pint.

If the animal has difficulty in swallowing (indicative of sore throat), do not drench, but give the following in the drinking water, several times daily:

Nitrate of potassium (saltpeter), 1 drachm.

Blanket the animal according to season and keep him in a comfortable stall, and when inflammatory symptoms subside, if appetite is not regained, give three times a day for several days, as a ball, the following:

Gentian root, ½ ounce, in tissue paper.

If, after ten days or two weeks, the discharge from the nostrils continues, give 1 drachm of powdered sulphate of iron three times a day, either as a drench dissolved in a pint of water or mixed with the feed.

INFLUENZA.—This is a contagious and infectious fever, with alterations of the blood, stupefaction of the brain and nervous system, great depression of the vital forces, and inflammatory complications, especially in the lungs, intestines, brain, and laminæ of the feet. One attack usually protects the animal from future attacks of the same disease for about two years. Influenza usually prevails as an epizoötic, and danger of an epidemic is considerable.

Causes.—Bad ventilation, dirty stables, insufficient supply of nutritious food, bad forage, or an excess of food, even though the quality be good, combined with an insufficient amount of exercise; wet, muddy picket-lines in cold weather, etc.; due to a germ.

Symptoms.—A rapidly developing fever; the animal dejected and inattentive; head down; coat becomes dry and rough; temperature increases as high as 105° Fahr., or even 108° in severe cases, within the first twelve or eighteen hours; stupor becomes rapidly more marked; often eyes puffy, swollen, and full of tears; respiration accelerated at times to 25 or 30 a minute; pulse runs up to 70, 80, or even 100; great muscular depression; animal stands limp, as if excessively fatigued; the horse staggers when moved; the mouth, especially the gums, become violet-red in color, a condition not found in any other disease; loss of appetite and excessive thirst. Specific course of disease about seven days. Fever abates almost as rapidly, the swelling of the legs diminishes, appetite returns; strength is rapidly regained, and the animal soon regains ordinary health and weight. During the course of the disease the loss of flesh is very rapid and noticeable. For the first three days of the high temperature there is great tendency to constipation, which, if not corrected, may turn into diarrhœa. In severe cases death frequently results.

Treatment.—While appetite remains, feed moderate quantity of hay, oats, and bran, the latter as mash. Never bleed the horse. The animal should be blanketed and kept warm, and the legs warmly bandaged, but not too tightly; this blanketing must be regulated according to season.

Give a ball of the following, if appetite is poor:

Gentian, ½ ounce, two or three times daily.

And as a stimulant, if the heart-action appears weak, give the following as a drench once or twice daily:

Alcohol, 2 ounces;

Water, 1 pint.

If bowels are affected, as manifested by colicky pains, give the following drench, repeated several times daily, until these colic pains disappear:

Bicarbonate of soda, 1 drachm;

Water, 1 pint.

If the eyes are affected, bathing with warm water and the introduction into the eyes of a few drops of a saturated solution of boracic acid* will alleviate the soreness in them. If fever is very high, with great destruction of tissue, rectal injections of cold water will reduce the temperature for several hours. The horse should be kept from all draughts and cold, and by good nursing, and his food frequently changed as the appetite changes, he can frequently be carried through the disease without injury, as influenza is a disease which must run a specific course. If possible, the horse should not be used after he has recovered for several weeks, for, if used too soon, his wind

*A saturated solution means water and as much boracic acid as the water will wholly dissolve.

may be affected. From the sixth to the fourteenth day is considered the most dangerous time.

PNEUMONIA; LUNG FEVER.—Inflammation of the lung structure; very similar to that in the human being and may attack both lungs, but, as a general rule, one lung only is affected, and in the great majority of cases it is the right lung.

Causes.—Result of common cold or sore throat, if neglected; bad quarters, such as badly ventilated stables, where the foul air is shut in; draughts of cold air. An animal is predisposed to pneumonia when debilitated by any constitutional disease, such as influenza, strangles, glanders, etc.; most common during cold, damp weather, being tied on cold, damp picket-lines in severe weather.

Symptoms.—Ushered in by chill more or less prolonged, breathing becomes accelerated; head hangs low; general dull appearance; mouth hot and sticky; temperature increased as high as 103° or higher; pulse from 70 or 80 to 100, and more or less irregular; dry cough from the beginning, gradually becoming moist; whitish yellow discharge from nostrils, sometimes tinged with blood; poor appetite and excessive thirst; membrane in nostrils at first dry, but later may become moist; legs cold; more or less constipated, and dung usually covered with slimy mucus; little urine passed, and of a dark color; horse does not lie down; if severe, may lie down for a few moments, but soon rises or dies from suffocation; breathing very rapid; in severe cases usually dies from suffocation attended with considerable pain, death coming in from ten to twenty days. Favorable signs are improved spirits, better appetite, lying down and resting easy, and more interest in his surroundings.

Treatment.—Blanketing and bandaging the legs according to the season; freedom from draughts or colds; dry surroundings and lots of pure air; bandages should be removed once or twice daily, the legs rubbed and the bandages reapplied; a woolen blanket should be wrapped around the chest; it must fit closely to the skin; do not let it sag; the blanket should be left on the chest until well. Never bleed the horse. Do not give purgatives; if constipation exists, overcome it by an allowance of laxative diet, such as scalded oats,* bran and linseed mashes, and grass, if in season. Hay-tea, made by pouring boiling water over good hay in a large bucket and allowing it to stand until cool, then straining off the liquid and letting the horse drink it, will frequently create a desire for food. Allow the animal as much water as he desires.

The following powder, made into a ball with tissue paper, should be given three times a day:

Gentian root, ½ ounce;

Quinine sulphate, 1 drachm.

If the horse becomes very much debilitated, give the following drench every four or five hours:

Alcohol, 2 ounces;

Water, 1 pint.

If this is not available, give 6 ounces of good whisky, diluted with 1 pint of water, as often.

GLANDERS.—Glanders is a contagious disease, readily communicable to men, sheep, goats, dogs, cats, etc. It runs a variable course until it produces the death of the animal affcted with it. Glanders and farcy are one and the same disease, differing only in that the first term is applied to the disease when the local symptoms predominate in the internal organs, especially in the air-tubes, and that the second term is applied to it when the principal manifestation is an outbreak of ulcers on the exterior or skin of the animal, usually in the region of the inner side of the thighs of the hind leg, but may extend all over the animal. In the case of farcy it may be always assumed that interal lesions exist, although they may not be evident. A horse known to have glanders should be isolated and killed at once. It is one of the earliest dis-

---

*To scald oats, place the oats in a bucket and pour a moderate amount of boiling water over them, and then cover the bucket so as to retain the heat and steam. The oats should be so left for at least one hour.

eases of which we have a knowledge in the history of medicine.

Causes.—The reception into a healthy animal of the specific virus or poison from a glandered animal. Watering-troughs and feed-boxes are among the most common recipients for the virus of glanders, and it has been known that animals have contracted glanders by feeding from the box or standing in the stall used by a glandered animal more than a year before; overcrowded stables, where the air is very vitiated, frequently conveys the disease readily. Bad ventilation, imperfect drainage, insufficient and unsuitable food, dirt, and general neglect in the stable management are prime factors in rendering animals more susceptible.

Symptoms.—In acute glanders there is a rapid outbreak of ulcers in one or both nostrils. This ulcer is a small sore with serrated edges, from the size of a shot to that of a small pea, or larger. It may be just inside of the wings of the nostril or higher up; these break and form pit-like depressions, which later run together, and from which considerable discharge issues; the discharge is oily, greenish yellow, and very sticky, and the irritation of the discharge often ulcerates the entire lining of the nose, causing serpentine gutters with bottoms resembling those of the chancres themselves. The discharge is at first without odor, but often throws off a vile smell, due to an accumulation of pus in the sinuses, or it may be due to the ulcer attacking the bones; sometimes a cough, more or less severe; body swellings over the surface of the horse, which later break into ulcers, and then known as "farcy"; bleeding from the nose; sudden swelling of one or both of the hind legs; difficult respiration; heaving flanks; quickened pulse; fever not always present, but may run as high as 105°; a marked symptom is the painful swelling of the gland between the horse's jaws; it becomes hard and firmly adherent to the bone, and ceases to be painful on the application of pressure. This peculiarity distinguishes it from the soft, diffuse swellings of the glands often found in diseases of the air-passages. Before ulceration the nostril lining assumes a dull leaden or slate-colored hue, but the ultimate symptom, the ulcer, leaves no doubt. Weakness and emaciation increase. Chronic glanders may exist in an animal for a long time, but it is as dangerous to the other horses as acute glanders. This disease in the mule runs a very much more rapid course.

Treatment.—As soon as there is no doubt that glanders actually exists in the horse, he should be killed and the body burned, and everything that has been used about the horse should be destroyed or repeatedly disinfected; as the slightest carelessness in this disinfection may cause glanders or farcy even after months have elapsed; the safest way is to destroy everything. From the moment the horse shows any symptoms touching on glanders he should be completely isolated. What has been said about glanders also applies to farcy, which, as remarked above, is glanders manifested by swellings of lymphatic glands over the body.

SURRA.—A specific and continuous infectious febrile disease, capable of being transmitted, by inoculation, to other animals. Chiefly met with in an epidemic form, during the wet seasons in tropical countries; common in India, among both cavalry and native horses, and common in the Philippine Islands in the same way; sometimes breaks out just *after* the close of the wet season. The disease is invariably fatal, death being generally due to exhaustion or complications. Surra has been known in India for several generations; whether or not this be also true in the Philippine Islands has not yet been well established. In India, the Philippines, and other tropical countries considerable loss of horses has been due to this disease; it is one of the most difficult which cavalry in tropical service has to contend with.

Causes.—Due to a flagellate protozoan in the blood. All authors agree that surra is a disease which coincides with moist tropical conditions, occuring during or imme-

diately after the heavy rainfalls in tropical climates, although it has been known to appear at other seasons, as,
for instance, the hottest.   Most common in the vicinity of
canals, rivers, flooded or inundated lands, etc.

Opinions differ as to source of infection.   While the
drinking-water and herbage and grain containing feces of
rats and bandicoots have been viewed with suspicion by
prominent authorities, other authorities suspect that flies
act as transmitters of the disease.   This latter belief is
strongly supported by analogy, for "tsetse disease," which
some authorities look upon as nearly identical with surra,
is known to be carried by flies; also, lice are believed to
disseminate this disease.   Lingard assumes that "animals
acquire surra by the entrance of the germ into their systems in one of four ways:

1. From eating grass and vegetation grown upon
   land subject to inundation.
2. From drinking stagnant water during certain
   months of the year.
3. From the bite of certain species of flies, probably as carriers of the virus.
4. From the ingestion of corn (or oats) soiled
   with the excrement of the rat or bandicoot.

Of these four ways, it is believed the insect theory is
by far the most plausible.   It is a fact that the disease
does spread mostly at those posts where horses are closely
packed and the flies are in greatest numbers, but those
are the posts also where the drinking-water is the worst.
Experiments in India and the Philippines have shown that
all four of the above causes cited by Lingard as causing
surra are actually concerned in the spread of the disease,
and probably in its first infection.

Symptoms.—Fever; progressive anemia; rapid emaciation; capricious appetite and extreme thirst; more or
less paralysis; temperature of 103° to 107° F.; pulse at
first full and frequent (56 to 64 per minute), gradually
growing erratic and more rapid and weak as animal becomes worse; some cases last for a long time, being in

hospital two or three months; swelling of belly, sheath, and legs; as animal grows weak he weaves from side to side, and hind quarters particularly seem weak. Horse finally goes down and may be unable to rise. No marked constipation or diarrhœa; feces are normal; urine slightly increased, but usual color; tendency to relapse even when apparently convalescent; these relapses are invariably fatal. Records of the British cavalry in India show that no cases ever recover; some cases are alternately better or worse for a year or more, but they all eventually succumb. Animal very dull; an early symptom of great importance in determining the disease is the presence of a general or localized urticarial eruption. The visible mucous membranes may appear clean, but the conjunctival membranes are usually the seat of dark red patches, varying in size. Slight catarrhal symptoms and a little mucous discharge from the nostrils, slightly tinged with yellow, increasing as disease runs on. No rigors. Coat staring. Watery eyes, increasing until profuse as disease runs on. Tongue and membranes of the mouth extremely pale and later assume a yellow tinge. Death sometimes comes suddenly, animal dropping dead even while eating; ordinarily animal eventually lies down and slowly dies from exhaustion. Gurgling a marked symptom. Breath smells very bad.

Treatment.—Nothing very encouraging can be said on this subject. The disease is invariably fatal. Immediate isolation is imperative for the safety of the other horses; the most thorough disinfecting of every part of the stall, as well as of all cloths, nosebags, horse-brushes, etc., used about the horse, must be done without delay. The danger of epidemic is great.

Experiments have been exhaustively made with a change of food and water, using large quantities of quinine, iodine, iodide of potassium, arsenic, and many other drugs, without material success. Once the disease is known to exist, the horse should be taken away, killed, and buried. It is almost as dangerous as glanders. Of all medicines used, arsenic has given the most satisfactory results.   It was given by Lingard in the form of "Fowler's solution" (arsenious acid in powder form, 87 grains; carbonate of potassium, 87 grains), to which was added ½ pint of distilled water, in a flask, and the whole heated until dissolved, then cooled and 5 drams of compound tincture of lavender added, then enough distilled water to make 1 pint.   In most cases of surra in horses, a dose of 5 grains may be commenced with and given twice daily for 48 hours, the quantity being increased by ½ grain after every four doses have been administered, until 7 grains are reached.   The latter amount should be continued twice daily for about seven days; the dose should then be reduced by ½ grain or 1 grain, according to condition of patient, until a 4-grain dose has been reached. Again, if possible, after a period of two days, repeat the treatment, increasing and decreasing the arsenic dose as above described.   The fact, however, must not be lost sight of, that continued doses of arsenic will produce gastric irritation.   It has been found that by giving the surra horse the following, morning and evening, directly after the medicine, these gastric symptoms have not appeared:

Linseed, ½ pound;

Rice, ½ pound;

Water enough to mix well.

Boil for ¾ of an hour and give when cool.

Most animals will take "Fowler's solution" in 1 or 2 pints of water, from a bucket, without any trouble, or the arsenic can be mixed with a bran mash.   In obstinate cases, the medicine may have to be given as a drench.   As arsenic poisoning can result from this treatment of surra, it must be used guardedly, and, whenever it is possible, only by a veterinary surgeon.   If no veterinary surgeon is available and the symptoms are plainly those of surra isolate, kill, and bury the horse immediately, and disinfect everything that was anywhere near the horse—thus running no risk and saving your other horses.   The treatment for glanders—immediate killing—is the best the officer can administer to any horse which develops surra when on the march or in station, where veterinarians are lacking.

The following official circular will be instructive:

CIRCULAR { HEADQUARTERS, DIVISION OF THE PHILIPPINES,
No. 4.   }   *Manila, P. I., January* 11, 1902.

The board ordered to inquire into and investigate a disease called "surra" have found that "Fowler's solution" of arsenic, given intravenously, destroys parasites in nearly every case, and animals so treated are doing well; but such treatment is as yet not conclusive as to cure. Such treatment may be tried at all points where animals are infected.

The board also reports that common flies taken on sick animals have been found full of parasites, and it is therefore ordered that all abrasions or wounds be kept covered to prevent possibility of infection from this source.

BY COMMAND OF MAJOR-GENERAL CHAFFEE:
(Signed)   W. P. HALL,
Assistant Adjutant-General.

Undoubtedly the intravenous injection of arsenic will be found much more satisfactory than Lingard's method. The fly referred to is the stable-fly—the common house-fly does not bite.

Prevention.—All valuable. If the horse is to be kept for treatment, not only isolate him completely, but protect him from flies, especially if he has wounds or open sores of any kind. A coating of tar and linseed oil or any similar substance over a cut will protect it from flies. Flies biting the sores of an infected horse will readily communicate the disease to other animals in the troop. So far as possible, avoid camping in moist and marshy localities when in tropical countries. So far as possible, prevent flies from breeding; since the biting stable-fly breeds in manure, the fly pest may be greatly lessened by a proper handling of the dung. The manure must not be allowed to lie around at all, nor piled in heaps within the vicinity of the stables or picket-line. Haul it away entirely, at least a half-mile or so, and there sprinkle it with a shovelful of chloride of lime, and later burn it up. If possible to use them with safety, smudges will be found a great protection to the horses, and in some tropical countries are much used.

Keep all native ponies and carabaos away, as many of them are chronically diseased.

As surra is the principal disease of animals in the Philippine Islands, it will be of advantage to the cavalryman to read the "Emergency Report on Surra," 1902, from the United States Department of Agriculture, wherein this and kindred tropical diseases are exhaustively considered.

FOUNDER; LAMINITIS. — Inflammation of sensitive laminæ of the feet; original attack always acute; recurrence probable.

Causes.—Overexertion, exhaustion; rapid changes in temperature, indigestion; too much purgative.

Symptoms.—Attack is very sudden; horse can hardly move; comes in both feet, either hind or fore, sometimes in all; heat in the affected feet; intensely painful; accelerated pulse, caused by pain; the two well feet usually drawn well under the horse to sustain the weight.

Treatment.—A mild purgative if constipated; shoes should be removed; cooling diet, as bran mashes or green grass; fresh water within reach, with ½-ounce of nitre dissolved in it; stand the horse on soft ground in cold water for several hours daily to reduce the inflammation in the feet; stall well littered with straw; ordinary shoes may be applied in the course of a few days.

Give:

> Saltpeter,* 2 to 3 ounces, dissolved;
> Water, 1 pint.

Give as a drench every 6 hours; continue three or four days.

COLIC.—Contraction or spasm of a portion of the small intestine.

Causes.—Indigestible food; large drinks of cold water when the animal is warm; taking heated horse through deep streams; cold rains; draughts of cold air, etc.

---

*Nitrate of potassium.

Symptoms.—Invariably begins suddenly; horse evinces acute pain; pawing; suddenly lying down, rolling and getting up; then an interval of ease and animal will appear entirely well; pains return in a little while, are somewhat more severe, and again pass off; animal acts frightened, whirls around, and difficult to handle; favorable sign is passage of urine and evacuation of the bowels.

Treatment.—Enema of hot water and soap-suds through the rectum, and give the following drench every one or two hours until relieved:

Tincture opium, 1 ounce;
Sulphuric ether, 1 ounce;
Powdered ginger, 1 drachm.;
Water, enough to make drench.*

Or give a drench every hour until relieved, if necessary, as follows:

Aromatic spirits of ammonia, $\frac{1}{2}$ ounce;
Sulphuric ether, 2 ounces;
Fluid extract of belladonna, 2 drachms;
Water, 1 pint.

SPRAINS, BURNS, BRUISES.—Burns rarely occur except from ropes. Wash the parts with warm water, cover with vaseline and keep clean, and they will probably readily get well. The use of oxide of zinc ointment in place of vaseline has been found very beneficial; the parts should first be bathed with a 2% solution of creolin, dried, and the ointment then freely applied. The formula for making oxide ointment is as follows: oxide of zinc, 1 part; cosmoline, 10 parts. In sprains, hand-rubbing or bandaging the leg, hot or cold applications, are all that is required. Bruises can usually be managed by means of hot or cold applications, repeated several times a day, and kept up for about half an hour each time; in case the skin is

*This prescription, while a well-known colic mixture, has been found not so good as the prescription which follows it above, owing to the constipating effect of the opium. This may be overcome by substituting 2 drachms of cannabis Indica for the opium.

broken, the part should be thoroughly washed with warm water, adding about 5 parts of carbolic acid or 2 parts of creolin to 100 parts of water, and repeating this treatment until the wound heals. Severe bruises or cuts may require several stitches to be taken. The silk thread used should first be disinfected in a mild carbolic solution, and also the needle. Care must be taken in these open cuts or bruises to protect the parts from insects.

DIARRHŒA.—Excessive evacuation of the bowels.

Cause.—Due to eating mouldy or musty food; drinking stagnant water; diseased conditions of the teeth; eating irritating substances; grazing on low, marshy pastures; change from dry to green food; exposure during cold nights; low, damp stables.

Symptoms.—Frequent evacuations of liquid stools, with or without pain; loss of appetite; emaciation, etc.

Treatment.—If due to faulty food or water, it is sufficient to change these; if it results from some irritant in the intestines, this is best gotten rid of by the administration of an enema of hot water and soap-suds. Give:

Powdered opium, 2 drachms;
Water, 1 pint.

Give as a drench three times a day, or, without water, as a ball.

Regulate the feed in any case; the majority of cases will yield to change of food and water. The body should be warmly clothed. Small and often repeated physics are to be avoided, as they are apt to cause the animal to become predisposed to this disorder. A good, practical remedy, almost always available, is brandy, in doses of from 2 to 4 ounces, mixed with milk and eggs, given as a drench four or five times daily.

CONSTIPATION.—The symptoms in this disease are the retention of the fæces, or those passed being few and dry and hard; the abdomen is full and more or less distended with gas. This trouble frequently comes from feeding too much dry food and also from failing to vary the food with an occasional bran mash. The passage of air is a good sign.

Treatment.—A rectal injection of warm water and soap-suds will often bring about proper passages, and a change to green food will also often effect a cure. When green food is not available, give bran mashes. When physic is given, it is essential that a full dose be administered, and it is better to do this than to give small and repeated doses. The horse requires about twenty-four hours in which to respond to a physic. Allow the horse all the water he will drink. In giving physic, give as a drench the following, once only:

> Water, 1 pint; .
> Powdered Barbadoes aloes, 1 ounce;
> Calomel, 1 drachm;
> Powdered nux vomica, 1 drachm.

Or give:

> Raw linseed oil, 1 quart, as a drench.

THRUSH.—An excessive secretion of unhealthy matter from the cleft of the frog; very common among work horses and among horses in wet, marshy districts.

Causes.—Filthy condition of stables or picket-lines. Mares are more liable to contract the disease in the hind feet when the cause is due to filth, while the gelding and stallion are more likely to develop it in the fore feet; hard work on rough and stony road, change from dry soil to excessive moisture, muddy roads and trails; contracted heels, scratches, and navicular disease predispose to thrush.

Symptoms.—At first there is simply an increased moisture in the cleft of the frog, accompanied by an offensive smell; after a time a considerable discharge takes place, thin, watery, and highly offensive, changing gradually to a thicker matter, which rapidly destroys the horn of the frog; only in old and severe cases is the horse lame and the foot feverish, as in cases where the whole frog is involved in the diseased process.

Treatment.—Dryness and cleanliness are the essential things in the treatment of this disease; removal of exciting causes, such as damp, muddy ground, filthy stables, etc. The diseased and ragged portions of horn should be pared away; foot poulticed for a day or two with boiled turnip, to which may be added a few drops of carbolic acid or a handful of powdered charcoal to destroy the offensive smell; clean out the cleft of the frog and the grooves on the edges and fill with dry calomel, and dress foot with oakum and a bandage of gunny-sack or cloth to keep the foot off the ground; if discharge is profuse, change dressing daily; otherwise, it may be left on for two or three days at a time. A leather boot put over the hoof after it starts to recover will do much to keep it clean. Thrush is hard to cure, and if but a sequel to other diseases, a permanent cure may not be possible.

QUITTOR.—A term applied to various affections of the foot, wherein the tissues which are involved undergo a process of degeneration that results in the formation of a slough, followed by the elimination of the diseased structure by means of a more or less extensive suppuration. It is an extremely painful disease; may be in either the fore or hind feet; while any part of the coronet may become the seat of the attack, the heels and quarters are most liable.

Causes.—Often develops without any known or traceable cause; bruises and other wounds of the coronet often bring it on; cold and mud may produce it; however, often seen in Colorado, Wyoming, and Montana in the fall and winter seasons when the weather is the dryest. Horses well groomed and cared for in stables are less liable to the disease than those running at large or those on field service.

Symptoms.—Lameness, lasting from one to three or four days; the appearance of a small tumor or swelling, which opens at the top of the coronary band on the side, which may involve the lateral cartilage, and a small discharge of pus issues from the opening. If only a single abscess forms, recovery under proper treatment may be effected in from two to three weeks' time, but severe cases are very stubborn and may last months.

Treatment.—Remove all exciting causes. Dry watering-places. Carefully clean the foot and leg with warm water, and dry the parts thoroughly; a constant stream of cold water in the very earlier stages will do much good. As soon as the tumor breaks, wash out with carbolic solution consisting of 5 drops of carbolic acid to 100 drops of warm water; then poultice with linseed meal or boiled turnip. If tumor is of rapid growth, free incision of it does much good; after opening the tumor and cleaning it out, place the foot in a warm water bath for half an hour or longer and then poultice with linseed meal; use plenty of small balls or pledgets of oakum carefully packed into the wound and held in place by bandages; keep the foot bandaged so that it cannot become dirty or muddy. To stimulate the healing process, inject the following, two or three times daily, with a syringe, into the abscess:

> Bichloride of mercury, 1 part;
> Water, 500 parts.

A ball of oakum soaked with this solution and placed in the abscess is easily applied and is as effective or even more effective than the injection; or apply to abscess:

> Sulphate of copper, iron, or zinc, 5 grains;
> Water, 1 ounce.

Or apply:

> Carbolic acid, 20 drops;
> Glycerine, 20 drops;
> Water, 1 ounce.

These solutions should be placed in the tumor either by injection or soaked oakum. The only real way to cure quittor is by an operation performed by a competent veterinarian.

BEANS.—These are accumulations of a natural oily secretion which are not thrown off in the channel of the penis, and may be so large in size or number as to prevent urination.

Symptoms.—Frequent ineffectual strainings to pass urine; more or less indications of pain; horse frequently bends around and looks at his flank.

Treatment.—The sheath and penis should be freely washed with warm water and soapsuds and the finger run in the cavity of the penis and the beans extracted if near the mouth; this will remove the beans. After the beans have been removed, the sheath and penis should again be washed with warm water.

THOROUGHPIN—This is the name given to a bursal enlargement which occurs at the upper and back part of the hock; the swelling appears sometimes on one side only, but more frequently on both sides. They are quite common among cavalry horses. They may be so small as to be scarcely perceptible, or of enormous size.

Cause.—From sprains, or may accompany certain other diseases of the hock-joint. The swelling appears movable and by moderate pressure may be forced from one side to the other by the fingers; hence is derived its name of "thoroughpin," or running through from side to side.

Treatment.—Rest is a primary requisite and will allay the irritation in the part affected, and with the cessation of the inflammatory action which produced it the increased secretion will soon cease; friction and pressure will also assist Nature to take up the extra secretion; brisk hand-rubbing, a sweating bandage, or repeated applications of tincture of iodine, or a blister may be applied. In any case it is not at all a severe trouble, and while a blemish, is not considered a defect by many horsemen.

WIND-GALLS.—This name is given to the enlarged bursæ found at a little above the side of the posterior part of the fetlock-joint; they are common among old cavalry horses, and not much treatment is ever given them.

Cause.—Wind-galls may be attributed to external causes, such as severe labor or strains resulting from jumping or hard riding, or they may be the sequelæ of internal disorders and appear as a result of a pleuritic or pneumonic attack.

Treatment.—Pressure by bandages, slight alcoholic frictions, sweating, or the use of liniment, or even a stiff blister of the ordinary kind, will accomplish all that will be desired. Rest should always be given; if possible, as it will do more good than anything else. This trouble is apt to return at any time when the horse is subjected to work again.

NAVICULAR DISEASE.—An inflammation of the soft structures of the navicular joint, and may be complicated by inflammation and caries of the navicular bone. A Thoroughbred is more commonly affected with the disease than any other horse, probably owing to the nature of the work he is made to perform; the mule rarely has it. The hind feet are rarely affected; as a general rule, but one fore foot suffers from the disease, but both may be attacked.

Causes.—Repeated bruising or laceration of the part; hard riding over hard roads; heredity predisposes the animal to this disease; dry stables, bad shoeing, etc., all have their influence in developing this disease.

Symptoms.—In the early stages, pointing the affected foot while at rest; gradually becomes lame in one or both affected feet; this lameness occasionally disappears as suddenly as it came, and at varying intervals reappears; may last a whole day and be gone the next morning. Occasionally these lame attacks extend over a week or more, when a remission takes place, and it may be months before another attack occurs; finally he becomes constantly lame, and the more used the greater the lameness. Constant stumbling; shoulders stiff, and profuse sweating from intense pain while being used; the whole foot gradually becomes hot to the touch; foot very sensitive, the horse flinching when the shoeing nippers or hammer are lightly applied to the frog or heel; later on the foot is found to be shrunken in its diameter and apparently lengthened; horn dry and brittle; circular ridges cover the upper part of the hoof.

Treatment.—But few cases of navicular disease recover. In the early stages the wall of the heel should be rasped away until the horn is quite thin; blister the coronet with Spanish fly ointment; turn the horse out to grass in a damp field; repeat blister after three or four weeks' time; this treatment to be continued for two or three months. Plain shoes are to be put on when the horse is to be used.

CRACKED HEELS, SCRATCHES.—Usually sets in with swelling, heat, and tenderness of the hollow of the heel, and stiffness and lameness, which may be extreme in irritable horses; similar to chapped hands in the human being to a certain extent; slight cracks appear transversely, and may gain in depth and width, and even suppurate; frequently these cracks become covered at the edges or throughout by firm encrustations resulting from the drying of the liquids thrown out, and the skin becomes thick in ridges; a watery discharge exudes from these cracks.

Causes.—Unwholesome bedding; close, hot, dirty stables; constant contact with dung and urine and their emanations; working in deep, irritant mud; sandy dust in dry weather on dirt roads; cold draughts, snow, and freezing mud; washing the legs may cause it; clipping the long hair from the fetlock will produce it, especially if the weather turns cold or damp; overfeeding and lack of exercise.

Treatment.—Ascertain and remove the cause whenever possible. Reduce the feed somewhat; give bran mashes several times weekly; wash the parts with weak carbolic solution, and keep dry and clean; witch hazel may be applied and the parts subsequently hand-rubbed and bandaged. After the cracks appear, wash the parts several times daily with the following:

Sulphate of zinc, 1 ounce;
Acetate of lead, 1 ounce.
Water, 1 pint.
Applied with cotton.*

*The above prescription is known as the "white lotion"

In case this should not bring about a cure, the part may be painted about twice daily with tincture of iodine.

HOOF-CRACKS—These are, as the name implies, simply cracks in the hoof, and are known as sand-cracks, quarter-cracks, etc.

Cause.—Hard riding on hard roads or over rocky country, especially after the horse has been living in surroundings possessing soft or damp soil.

Symptoms.—The crack is through the wall of the hoof; it may be an inch or more in height, and in depth may penetrate even to the sensitive interior; lameness is apt to appear, and if the horse is used, the crack will continue to increase in size.

Treatment.—Rest; burn the top of the crack with a hot iron; if the crack pinches the sensitive laminæ, manifested by bleeding, cut the edges of the crack away so the pressure will be removed; Nature will itself close the opening and heal the crack if these methods are used. Recovery is almost always secured, but is slow. If the crack causes any suppuration, it should be washed out two or three times daily with a weak carbolic solution, or afterwards filling in the crack with powdered charcoal with an application of subiodide of bismuth or iodoform.

CORNS.—This is an injury to the living horn of the foot, involving at the same time the soft tissues beneath; they always appear in that part of the sole included in the angle between the bar and the outside wall of the hoof; the fore feet are almost exclusively the subjects of the disease; corns are either dry or suppurating.

Causes.—Heavy work on rough roads and streets; high heels on shoes; contracted heels; long feet, which, by removing the frog and heels too far from the ground, reduce the elastic properties of the horn; weak feet, or those in which the horn of the wall is too thin to resist the tendency to spread; bad shoeing; a shoe so set as to press upon the sole, or one that has been on so long that the hoof has overgrown it until the heels of the shoe rest upon the sole, becomes a direct cause of corns; small stones, hard or dry earth, or other objects collected between the sole and the shoe in marching.

Symptoms.—Ordinarily a corn induces sufficient pain to cause lameness. With a suppurative corn a small amount of blood escapes and stains the neighboring tissue a dark color. Restlessness; the lameness varies with the degree of pain; at rest, the foot is so advanced that it is relieved of all weight; when much inflammation exists, the foot is hot and tender to pressure. In looking for the corns, remove the shoe, as the shoe almost always conceals the corn.

Treatment.—Tapping the heel of the shoe with a hammer and grasping the wall and bar between the jaws of a pair of pincers with moderate pressure will cause more or less flinching if the disease is present, and thereby locate the corn; remove the shoe and slightly cut away the heel. If any pus collects, it must be allowed to escape by opening the corn, and the opening then kept clean and dry; poultice the foot for a day or two, and cut out the discolored horn, care being taken not to injure the soft tissues; if necessary, the foot may be shod with a bar-shoe to relieve the pressure from the affected part. Oakum balls saturated with tar should be applied in the corn after it has been opened, and the whole foot covered with a bandage to keep it clean; change the dressing every two or three days until a firm, healthy layer of new horn covers the wound, when the shoe may be put on and the horse returned to work.

SEEDY TOE.—This consists in a separation of the crust from the laminæ; the disease always commences in the lower portion of the laminæ and extends upward and laterally; it may even extend to the quarters.

Causes.—Often a result of laminitis, but more often caused by the pressure of the clip of the shoe; sometimes due to constitutional causes; bad shoeing; naturally weak feet.

Symptoms.—Lameness is not usually present until the disease has run to a very considerable extent upward;

but the blacksmith, when shoeing the horse, ought to de-
tect it in its very earliest stages.

Treatment.—Dirt or gravel getting into the hollow
easily aggravates this trouble, and, as in all other diseases,
the parts must be kept thoroughly clean and fresh. All
that portion of the crust which has become detached
from the laminæ must be cut away with the knife. If
the disease shows signs of extending, such further portions as may be necessary must be cut away. Blistering
the coronet is frequently done. A long rest without
shoes will generally effect a cure.

SPEEDY CUT.—An injury caused by collision of one
foot with the leg immediately below the knee of the opposite leg; it is due to peculiarity of action in the horse;
common in impetuous horses.

Causes.—Riding the horse at rapid gaits when very
tired, or making quick turns, faulty shoeing, etc.

Treatment.—A few days' rest is all that will generally
be required. If any pus forms, it should be allowed to
eseape, and the part kept thoroughly cleaned and washed
with a mild carbolic solution.* If the shoeing is defective,
it should be corrected.

CONTRACTED HEELS.—A very common disease, especially among horses kept on hard flooring in dry stables
and in such as are subject to much saddle work; it consists
in atrophy or shrinking of the tissues of the foot, whereby the lateral diameter of the heels in particular is diminished; affects the fore feet principally, but occasionally
seen in the hind feet; usually but one foot is affected at
a time; occasionally but one heel, and that the inner one,
is contracted.

Causes.—Animals used on hard roads, during heavy
marching, after being kept on wet or soft soil, are apt to
suffer much with this; hard, dry, stony picket-lines or
stable floors; faulty shoeing, such as rasping the wall,
cutting away the frog, heels, and bars; high calks, and
the use of nails too near the heels; may also be one of the

---

*A 5% solution is fully strong enough.

results of other diseases of the foot, as thrush, side-bones, corns, navicular disease, etc.

Symptoms.—The foot has lost its circular shape, and the walls from the quarters backward approach to a straight line; ground surface of the foot may become even smaller than the coronary circumference; the frog is pinched between the enclosing heels, is much shrunken, and at times is affected with thrush; the sole is more concave, heels are higher, and bars are long and nearly perpendicular; the whole hoof is dry and so hard it can scarcely be cut; parts toward the heels scaly, often ridged; fissures more or less deep may be seen at the quarters and heels; later on, considerable lameness; stumbling, especially on hard roads.

Treatment.—Remove the shoe; keep the foot moist, and prevent the horn from drying out by the use of moist sawdust or other damp bedding; occasional poultices of boiled turnip, linseed meal, etc., and the use of greasy hoof ointment to both the soles and walls of the foot; do not rasp the wall of the foot; the frog, heels, and *bars* must not be touched with the knife; shoes should be re-set at least once a month; daily exercise must be insisted on; the shoes, when replaced, must be wide at the heel, so as not to compress the frog. Lightly blister the coronet to stimulate new growth of horn.

SPAVIN.—Divided into two classes: bone spavin and bog spavin. When spavin alone is spoken of, bone spavin is always meant. Bog spavin is a distension of the capsular ligament at the hock, and bone spavin of the bone. Bone spavin, which is the most important, is a bony enlargement in the region of the hock, and usually involves two or more of the weight-bearing bones. Bone spavin may be so bad as to absolutely prevent the moving of the hock-joint, and it is almost impossible to cure it. If bone spavin is suspected, flex the hock-joint very severely; after a few moments, let the leg down and lead the animal off at a trot. If spavin is there, lameness will show.

Causes.—Undue concussion, pressure, strain, or such like causes; defects either in conformation, structure, or position of the hock; speaking generally, it may be described as situated in the inner and lower side of the hock-joint, and a sprain of the ligaments or such like causes may induce pressure or concussion to such an extent as to cause it.

Treatment.—Rest is the great essential; cold applications or fomentations are also useful in reducing the inflammation; the greatest ease and relief is gained by removing the shoes altogether; sometimes the rear of the bed is raised with a view of throwing the weight off the hind and onto the fore quarters, but it is best to keep the bed perfectly level. The slight exercise taken by a horse in the sick-stall will prevent the horse becoming stiffened; blisters, setons, and firing are also resorted to, but firing should never be done except by a veterinary surgeon. A spavin, once fully formed, cannot be removed, though it generally becomes less as age advances. Spavins which, when fully formed, do not cause lameness, should never be subjected to active treatment.

MANGE.—This results directly from the attack of a parasitical insect, which burrows beneath the epidermis or scarf skin. The insects are so small they cannot be seen with the eye. The attacks of these animalculæ cause irritation and itching of the skin, and as the result the hair falls off in patches.

Cause.—Injudicious feeding, want of grooming, or poverty of the blood or system invite attack.

Treatment.—Clip the horse if possible. Thoroughly wash the entire horse with soft water and soap; when fully dried, dress with the following liniments:

> Oil of tar, 4 ounces;
> Linseed or olive oil, 1 pint;
> Sulphur, powdered, 4 ounces.
> Mix and apply to every part of the skin with a soft brush; repeat every day for three or four days, then thoroughly wash off.

Thoroughly washing the affected parts with a 10 or 15% solution of creolin is very good.

Any slight inflammation that may remain can be allayed by bathing the parts with a lotion composed of the following:

Sulphuric acid, 2 drachms;

Water, 1 pint.

If the skin is inclined to crack or become rough, it should be lubricated with a little vaseline or glycerine.

Many practitioners advocate a strong infusion of tobacco with the addition of glycerine as a mange dressing, while others recommend a lotion composed of 1 part of carbolic acid to 20 parts of water. The animal's head must be tied up to prevent his biting himself when the disease lasts, and be prevented from rubbing himself against ropes, boards, etc., which he will do if left to himself, until he is half raw. As the disease is highly contagious, everything about the horse and the horse himself should be strictly isolated. Horses are often a long time before they recover their condition. There is no need to destroy the clothing or equipments of the horses; it is generally sufficient to bake or boil everything thoroughly. Horses, especially in hot countries, are frequently subject to mange. A change of diet is always desirable. Mange is one of the most pernicious troubles known.

SIDE-BONES.—On each side of the bone of the foot known as the coffin-bone there are two organs, which are called the lateral cartilages of the foot; they are soft and in a degree elastic, yet somewhat resisting, and are implanted on the lateral wing of the coffin-bone. Their office is to assist in the elastic expansion and contraction of the foot. These organs are liable to disease, which results in an entire change in shape and they become hard, and are then known as side-bones; they are unyielding under pressure, and may come on one or both sides of the leg, bulging above the superior border of the foot in the form of two hard bodies.

Causes.—Side-bones often grow without any apparent injury; they are most common in heavy horses, and their development has been attributed to the over-expansion of the cartilages caused by the great weight of the animal; blows may cause them; high-heeled shoes, high calks, and long feet are causes; often seen in connection with contracted heels, ringbone, navicular disease, punctured wounds of the foot, hoof-cracks, and occasionally as a sequel of founder.

Symptoms.—In the earlier stages of the disease the only evidence of the trouble is a little inflammation over the seat of the affected cartilage and a slight lameness. The toe of the foot first strikes the ground, and the step is shorter than usual; the horse comes out of the stable stiff and sore, but the gait is more free after exercise. The diseased process may exist for some time before the bony growth can be seen or felt; later on, however, it can be felt, and by standing in front of the animal can be plainly seen; they may become so bad as to render the animal entirely useless for cavalry purposes.

Treatment.—As soon as the disease is known, active treatment should be adopted; cold-water bandages for a few days, to relieve the inflammation and soreness; rest is essential; the use of blisters will do much good; little treatment will arrest the growth of these side-bones, as they are very stubborn. A predisposition to develop side-bones may be inherited. An animal suffering from this disease, while he may be used, is of little value if the disease is severe. A bar-shoe, so made as to take the pressure off the inside, or off both heels, according to the particular case, is sometimes beneficial; shoeing on the Charlier system, where the feet will allow it, is sometimes good. Side-bones, once formed, are quite incurable.

RINGBONE.—This is a growth of a bony tumor on the pastern, and is the result of an inflammatory action set up in the large and small pastern-bones.

Causes.—Injuries, such as blows, sprains, over-work, fast work on hard roads, jumping, etc., are prime causes;

improper shoeing, such as the use of high calks, a too great shortening of the toe and correspondingly high heels, predispose to this disease by increasing the concussion to the feet.

Symptoms.—Lameness, more or less severe; the pastern of the affected limb presents more or less heat; the pastern is kept as rigid as possible, and in walking the toe strikes the ground first; appearance of the bony tumor on the pastern, which is readily seen.

Treatment.—It may come in any one of the feet, and if the bony growth has not commenced, the disease may be cut short by cold baths and wet bandages, followed by one or more blisters; if the bony deposits have begun, the firing-iron should be used by the veterinary surgeon. Recovery is hardly to be expected, but by proper shoeing the animal may be kept serviceable; rest is absolutely essential; if the toe touches the ground first, the horse should have his foot carefully leveled; occasionally it will be found, especially when this disease is in a hind leg, that the heel comes to the ground first, and consequently a thick-toed and thin-heeled shoe must be worn. There is an hereditary predisposition to ringbone.

CURB.—This is an enlargement on the lower and back part of the hock, while in the normal state there should be a straight line extending from the upper end of the point of the hock down to the fetlock; this may sometimes be so prominent as to take on the appearance of an egg under the skin.

Causes.—Heavy pulling, high jumping, slipping, violent effort; as the result of habitually being suddenly halted from rapid gaits. A horse with weak hind legs is predisposed to this disease.

Treatment.—A curb constitutes an unsoundness; it often yields to treatment, or at least the lameness it occasions may generally be relieved, though the loss of contour caused by the bulging may be permanent. Warm fomentations do good; blisters of cantharides often help; frictions with ointments of iodine are good; firing may be required, but should never be done except by a veterinary surgeon. The lameness usually subsides as soon as inflammation is reduced. The strain of the ligament will be lessened by the application of a high-heeled shoe; rest for at least ten days should be at once given.

STOCKING, SWELLED LEG.—This is a swelling of the legs, either of the front ones or hind ones, and is not serious.

Causes.—Washing the legs with cold water in cold weather; fording cold streams in cold weather; lack of exercise; especially apt to occur in horses being transported on ships at sea; due also to some debilitating diseases.

Symptoms.—These are explained by the name itself, stocking, or swelled leg; the swellings usually occur from the knee or hock down.

Treatment.—Removal of cause; plenty of exercise, hand-rubbing the legs, and rubbing them dry briskly when wet, will usually be all that is necessary. A teaspoonful of saltpeter (nitrate of potassium), given twice a day in the drinking-water or feed, is beneficial.

CALKING.—The fore feet are more liable than the hind ones, and the seat of injury is usually on the quarter; it is in the form of a bruise or wound of the coronary region; they are not serious, but require attention, or may become so.

Causes.—Either from the horse tramping on himself or being tramped upon by other horses; especially apt to occur where horses are herded loose; the wound sometimes results from the animal resting with the heel of one foot set directly over the front of the other; the symptoms are contained in the definition of the disease.

Treatment.—Changing the shoes to correct any tendency there may be to repeated calking; if the wound is not deep and the soreness slight, cold-water bandages and a light protective dressing, such as carbolized cosmoline, will be all that is needed; where the injury is deep, followed by inflammation and suppuration, cold astringent baths, made by adding 2 ounces of sulphate of iron to a gallon of water, should be used, followed by poultices if necessary to hasten the cleansing of the wound; where the wound is deep between the horn and skin, the horn should be cut away, to allow for perfect drainage; thorough cleanliness is necessary; the foot should be bandaged to keep out dust.

SORE BACKS.—These are sloughs of limited portions of the skin on the back, and may be anything from a mere slight chafing to a deep-seated, pus-discharging sore of considerable dimensions. The sitfast, as these chronic sore backs are sometimes called, is a piece of dead tissue which would be thrown off but that it has formed firm connections with the fibrous skin beneath, or may even extend down into the muscles as far as the bone, and is thus bound in its place as a persistent source of irritation.

Causes.—Bad riding, badly fitting saddles, careless saddling, dirty saddle-blankets, wet saddle-blankets, etc.

Treatment.—The wounds should be washed with carbolic solution composed of 1 part of carbolic acid to 0 parts of water, and the wound then covered with subiodide of bismuth, and the horse allowed complete rest for a few days. If it is necessary to use the horse, the saddle may be changed for a better fitting one, or a hole may be cut in the saddle-blanket over the sore, thus removing pressure from it. Whatever is done, the sore must be kept clean and soft. The white of an egg mixed with alcohol makes a very good dressing after the sore has been washed. If the sore has developed into a sitfast, it may be necessary to remove the dead irritant by dissecting it off with a sharp knife, after which the sore may be treated with simple wet cloths or a weak carbolic lotion like a common wound. As these sore backs will frequently appear to be trifling, they are apt to be neglected, and may become very serious and take months to heal. If it is the fault of the rider, he should be made to suffer for it, and given a tough old troop-horse which he cannot hurt.

PUNCTURES OF THE SOLE.—These may be caused by pricking the interior of the foot by a misdirected nail in shoeing, or by picking up a nail along the road, or by picking up a small stone or stepping on anything sharp.

Treatment.—When the sensitive sole is injured by any such cause, inflammation sets up, and, unless very slight, this causes a secretion of pus. The pus which forms in the internal structure—that is, the sensitive sole—must have an exit. Nature must be provided with one, or else the pus will work its way upward to the soft parts of the interior of the foot, and probably ruin the foot. Pare out freely, not merely the seat of the puncture, but the whole of the surrounding insensitive sole for a slight distance, to allow the pus to escape; bathe the foot in hot water for about an hour; complete rest is essential; open up the wound, cleanse thoroughly with a solution of creolin (1 part to 30 parts water). The wound should not be allowed to close until all pus has ceased to appear. In most cases the horse will be fit for work in a few days. A bandage must be put around the entire foot, to keep the wound from becoming filthy. The wound must be kept thoroughly clean and dressed at least once a day, and should be washed out with warm water containing carbolic acid in quantities of 5 to 100 parts of water or the creolin solution given above.

PUNCTURES OF THE FROG.—These are similar in nature and require similar treatment to those of the sole. When taken in time, they are not serious, and yield even more readily to treatment than injuries of the sole. The frog should not be pared; when there is raggedness or unpleasant smell, remove the ragged parts and keep the frog clean but dry; but do not pare down the frog, as it will do more harm than good.

THE TEETH.—The horse rarely has the toothache, and little treatment is required for his teeth; they are best let alone; but with time they wear down and often unevenly; this frequently causes the outer edges to become sharp and lacerate the inside linings of the cheeks, and the inner edges of the teeth sometimes become sharp and lacerate the tongue in the same way; these lacerations may become so painful to the horse as to make him bolt his food without mastication, and this in turn will result in internal disorders, a loss of flesh, poor appetite, etc., and it will be difficult to know what is the matter with the horse unless his mouth be carefully examined. The teeth should be examined occasionally to see if they are level in bearing and smooth on the edges, and if not, they must be rasped down until they are. When a tooth requires to come out, it is extracted by means of the powerful horse-forceps used by a veterinary surgeon. As the extracting of a tooth from a horse's mouth requires considerable strength, an inexperienced operator is very apt to injure the jaw, but the rasping down of the teeth to keep them level is not difficult.

The diseases mentioned above and the modes of treatment are those most commonly existent in a cavalry command. Other serious diseases and complications will occasionally appear, but it is not likely that they can be satisfactorily handled by anyone but a veterinary surgeon, and to give them would be an idle waste of time and space. By daily observation, reasonable study, and occasionally witnessing the methods adopted by the post veterinarian in the treatment of sick animals, much can be accomplished in the way of recognizing diseases in the horse and how to treat them. In measuring out medicines, use the glass graduate contained in the farrier's veterinary kit; this graduate has the drachms and ounces marked upon it plainly. There should always be a graduate in the troop.

APPENDIX I.

GENERAL ORDERS,   HEADQUARTERS OF THE ARMY,
                         ADJUTANT-GENERAL'S OFFICE,

No. 20.   *Washington, February 26, 1902.*

The proceedings of the board of officers convened by paragraph 10, Special Orders, No. 197, Adjutant-General's Office, August 23, 1901, and paragraph 2, Special Orders, No. 255, Adjutant-General's Office, November 4, 1901, to consider the subject of the Veterinary Supply Table and cognate matters, having been submitted to the Secretary of War, he directs that the accompanying supply table be adopted and published for the information and guidance of the Army.

While approval for the issue of some of the medicines recommended by the board is withheld, it is believed that the list will amply meet the ordinary requirements of the service.

The emergency equipment for troops of cavalry and batteries of field artillery will be provided by the Quartermaster's Department after a uniform pattern, as recommended by the board. A model equipment will be prepared and submitted to the board before final adoption.

A supply of medicines just sufficient for the needs of a command is much more desirable than the accumulation of a large stock apt to deteriorate by age. Requisitions should, therefore, be prepared with great care. Issues should be controlled by the actual necessities of each command, and the quantities authorized by the supply table should in no case be considered merely as expendable allowances. The hypodermic tablets will be issued only for use by veterinarians.

The veterinary instruments for each post will, for the present, be supplied only to those posts at which veterinarians are stationed. At the smaller posts the emergency field equipment of veterinary instruments in the hands of troops of cavalry and batteries of field artillery will be availed of. In case of epidemics or other necessity arising at posts at which no veterinarian is present, instruments and supplies from neighboring posts will be utilized by the veterinarians detailed for temporary duty where the emergency exists, so that accumulations of expensive instruments and supplies may be avoided at small posts. At posts not provided with veterinarians estimates for veterinary supplies will be confined to such articles as may be safely intrusted to non-professional hands.

By command of Lieutenant-General Miles:

THOMAS WARD,

Acting Adjutant-General.

VETERINARY SUPPLY TABLE.

Allowance of Medicines for Three Months.

Articles.		Quantities.		
		For 100 Animals.	For 200 Animals.	For 300 Animals.
MEDICINES.				
Acetanilid....................pounds		1	1½	2
Acid:				
Arsenious ....ounces		1	1	2
Boracic ....ounces		4	6	8
Carbolic, pure ....ounces		16	18	24
Salicylic ....ounces		4	6	8
Tannic ....ounces		2	4	6
Aconite, fluid extract of....................ounces		1	2	3
Alcohol ....gallons		1	2	3
Aloes, Barbadoes, in original gourds ... .ounces		20	24	32
Alum ....pounds		½	½	1
Ammonia:				
Aromatic spirits of, in glass-stoppered bottles ....pounds		1	2	3
Aqua (solution of), in glass-stoppered bottles ....quarts		1	2	3
Chloride of, granulated, in glass-stoppered bottles ....pounds		2	3	4
Belladonna, fluid extract of ......ounces		4	6	8
Camphor, gum ....pounds		1	1½	2
Cannabis Indica ....pounds		1	2	3
Cantharides, powdered....................ounces		1	2	3
Capsicum ....ounces		4	6	8
Charcoal, willow, powdered ....pounds		½	1	1½
Copper, sulphate of ....pounds		½	1	1
Collodion, flexible, glass-stoppered 1-ounce bottles ....ounces		4	6	8
Chloroform.................... pounds		1	1	2
Cosmoline, 1-pound cans....................pounds		4	8	12
Creolin ....pounds		2	4	6
Digitalis, fluid extract of ....ounces		4	6	6
Ether, nitrous, in glass-stoppered bottles....pounds		2	3	4
Ether, sulphuric. ....pounds		1	2	3
Fenugreek, seeds, powdcred ....pounds		1	2	3

Articles.	Quantities.		
	For 100 Animals.	For 200 Animals.	For 300 Animals.
MEDICINES—Continued.			
Flaxseed, meal .. ..pounds	25	30	40
Gentian ....pounds	1	2	3
Ginger, powdered ...., ...pounds	1	2	3
Glycerine ....ounces	8	12	16
Iodine, crystals ....ounces	4	6	8
Iodoform ....ounces	4	6	8
Iron:			
Tincture of chloride of ....ounces	8	12	16
Sulphate of, desiccated .. ..ounces	8	12	16
Lanolin ....ounces	8	16	24
Lead, acetate of ....pounds	1	2	3
Lime, chloride of ....pounds	25	30	40
Lunar caustic ....ounces	1	1	2
Mercury:			
Bichloride of (corrosive sublimate tablets)..ounces	8	12	16
Mild chloride (calomel) ....ounces	2	4	6
Biniodide ....ounces	1	2	3
Nux vomica, powdered............pounds	$\frac{1}{2}$	1	$1\frac{1}{2}$
Oil:			
Linseed ....gallons	2	3	4
Olive ....gallons	$\frac{1}{2}$	1	$1\frac{1}{2}$
Oil of tar ....pounds	$\frac{1}{2}$	1	1
Oil of turpentine ....gallons	1	$1\frac{1}{2}$	2
Opium:			
Tincture of ....pounds	2	3	4
Powdered ....ounces	2	4	6
Potassium:			
Bromide ....pounds	2	3	4
Nitrate ....pounds	3	4	6
Iodide ....pounds	$\frac{1}{2}$	1	1
Permanganate ....pounds	1	1	1
Quinine, sulphate of ....ounces	4	6	8
Salol ....ounces	4	6	8
Sodium, bicarbonate ....pounds	2	3	4
Sulphur ....pounds	1	1	2
Strychnine ....drachms	1	2	3
Tar, pine ....pounds	1	2	3

Articles.	Quantities		
	For 100 Animals.	For 200 Animals.	For 800 Animals.
MEDICINES—Continued.			
Witch hazel, distilled .... quarts	2	4	6
Zinc:			
Sulphate of .... pounds	1	2	3
Oxide of .. .. ounces	8	12	16
Chloride of......................... ounces	2	4	6
HYPODERMIC TABLETS.			
Atropine sulphate of, in ½-grain tablets, 20 tablets in each tube .... tubes	1	1	2
Cocaine, muriate of, in 4½-grain tablets, 10 tablets in each tube. .... tubes	1	1	2
Digitaline, in ¼-grain tablets, 10 tablets in each tube, ... tubes	1	1	2
Ergotine, in 2-grain tablets, 10 tablets in each tube, ... tubes	1	1	2
Eserine, sulphate of, in 1-grain tablets, 10 tablets in each tube .... tubes	1	1	2
Morphine, sulphate of, in 3-grain tablets, 10 tablets in each tube....................... tubes	2	2	3
Pilocarpine, muriate of, in 1-grain tablets, 10 tablets in each tube . ... tubes	4	4	6
Strychnine, sulphate of, in ½-grain tablets, 10 tablets in each tube . ... tubes	2	2	3
Allowance of Veterinary Dressings for Three Months.			
DRESSINGS.			
Absorbent cotton, ½-pound packages ...... pounds	2	3	4
Antiseptic gauze, carbolated, carton packages (5 yards) .. . . packages	2	2	3
Bandages:			
Red flannel, 4 inches wide and 4 yards long, heavy .... dozen	2	3	4
White cotton, 4 inches wide and 4 yards long, ... dozen	4	6	8
Oakum, pound packages. .... pounds	10	15	20

Articles.	Quantities.		
	For 100 Animals.	For 200 Animals.	For 300 Animals.
DRESSINGS—Continued.			
Plaster, adhesive, 2 inches wide and 10 yards long, ... rolls	1	1	2
Rubber tubing, red, ¼ inch inside diameter . . . . . feet	15	20	30
Silk for ligatures:			
Ordinary size . . . . ounces	½	½	¾
Heavy braided . . . . ounces	1	2	3
Soap, white Castile . . . . pounds	10	15	20
Sponges, surgeon's, extra heavy . . . . . pounds	1	2	3
Allowance of Dispensary Supplies for Three Months			
Bottles:			
1-ounce . . . . dozen	1	2	3
4-ounce . . . . dozen	2	4	6
8-ounce . . . . dozen	4	6	8
Boxes:			
Tin, ointment, 2-ounce . . . . dozen	1	2	3
Tin, ointment, 4-ounce . . . . dozen	2	3	4
Capsules, 1-ounce capacity . . . . dozen	2	3	4
Corks, for bottles, four times the allowance of bottles			
Labels, blank . . . . gross	1	2	3
Stationery: A 2-quire blank book for record of cases, and such pens, pencils, ink, and paper as may be necessary			

Emergency or Field Equipment of Veterinary Instruments.

For each troop of cavalry and each battery of field artillery:
1 farrier's case, leather, folding, containing the following instruments: 1 bistoury, curved, probe pointed; 1 bistoury, curved, sharp pointed; 1 director, grooved; 1 forceps, artery; 1 forceps, dressing; 1 hoof knife, searcher; needles, suture, half curved, ½ dozen; 1 probe, silver; 1 scissors, curved on flat; silk, suture heavy, ⅛-ounce; 1 thermometer, clinical.
1 graduate, glass, 4-ounce.
1 rectal douche.
1 syringe, hard rubber, 1-ounce.
1 syringe, hard rubber, 2-ounce.
1 saddle-bags, farrier's, for use in the field.

Equipment of Veterinary Dispensary

1 funnel, small size, enamel ware.
1 funnel, medium size, enamel ware.
1 graduate, glass, 2-ounce.
1 graduate, glass, 4-ounce.
1 minim measure.
1 mortar and pestle (Wedgewood), $3\frac{3}{4}$ inches inside diameter.
1 mortar and pestle (Wedgewood), $6\frac{1}{2}$ inches inside diameter.
1 mortar and pestle, glass, 4 ounces.
1 pill tile, 10 inches square.
1 scales and weights (Troemer's new dispensing scale).
3 spatulas, being 1 with 3-inch, 1 with 6-inch, and 1 with 8-inch blade.

Veterinary Instruments, etc., for Each Post.

The following veterinary instruments recommended by the board to be kept at each post will ordinarily be in the immediate charge of the veterinarian, who will keep them in the dispensary or in his office. He will be held accountable for the articles and responsible for their condition.

Articles.	Quantities.		
	For 100 Animals.	For 200 Animals.	For 300 Animals.
Ball forceps	2	2	2
Case, dental	1	1	1
Case, hypodermic, containing bottles, capacity of barrel of syringe $\frac{1}{2}$ ounce	1	1	1
Case, hypodermic antitoxine	1	1	1
Case, post-mortem	1	1	1
Case, surgical, to contain the following instruments: 1 bistoury, probe pointed; 1 bistoury, sharp pointed; 1 caustic holder; 1 director, grooved; 2 forceps, artery (French snap); 1 forceps, dressing; 1 fleam, three-bladed; 1 needle, seton, three sections; 12 needles, suture, half curved, spring eye, assorted sizes; 1 probe, silver, jointed; 3 scalpels; 1 scissors, curved on the flat; 1 scissors, straight; 1 tenaculum; 1 trocar and canula, cæcum (horse)	1	1	1
Casting harness, with side ropes	2	2	2
Catheter, male, with stylet	2	2	2

Articles.	Quantities.		
	For 100 Animals.	For 200 Animals.	For 300 Animals.
VETERINARY INSTRUMENTS—Continued.			
Clippers, hand	2	3	4
Forceps:			
Bone	1	1	1
Dressing, with catch straight and long	2	2	2
Hones, oil	2	2	2
Medicine droppers . . . . dozen	1	1	1
Ophthalmoscope	1	1	1
Powder-shaker, for medicine	2	3	4
Probang, celluloid, jointed	2	2	2
Rectal douche.	1	1	1
Reflector, with head band, 4-inch	1	1	1
Seton needles, 8-inch	1	1	1
Slings, suspending, complete.	2	2	2
Speculum:			
Bilateral	1	1	1
Eye.	1	1	1
Nasal	1	1	1
Syringes, hard rubber:			
2-ounce	2	3	4
4-ounce	2	2	3
Thermo-cautery, Paquelin's	1	1	1
Thermometer, clinical	2	2	2
Tracheotomy, tube	1	1	1
Urine, test case, complete	1	1	1

APPENDIX II.

*Number and Average Value of Horses on Farms and Ranges in the United States June 1, 1903.—Official Census.**

	States and Territories.	Total Number.	Avg. Value.
1	The United States†	18,280,007	$49.07
2	North Atlantic States..	1,699,139	72.60
3	South Atlantic States	1,071,070	55.93
4	North Central States	9,794,262	52.69
5	South Central States	3,424,763	38.29
5	Western States	2,277,786	29.01
7	Alabama	152,643	51.79
8	Alaska	5	93.00
9	Arizona	125,063	13.61
10	Arkansas	253,590	40.08
11	California	421,293	42.36
12	Colorado	236,546	30.90
13	Connecticut	52,576	72.54
14	Delaware	29,722	59.47
15	District of Columbia	854	67.17
16	Florida	42,811	53.49
17	Georgia	127,407	55.67
18	Hawaii	12,982	34.02
19	Idaho	170,120	24.24
20	Illinois	1,350,219	51.62
21	Indiana	751,715	54.07
22	Indian Territory	217,699	28.59
23	Iowa	1,392,573	55.81
24	Kansas	979,695	44.67
25	Kentucky	451,697	54.35
26	Louisiana	194,372	34.08
27	Maine	106,299	66.41
28	Maryland	148,994	62.77
29	Massachusetts	75,034	77.65
30	Michigan	586,559	61.22
31	Minnesota	696,469	60.67
32	Mississippi	229,311	47.46
33	Missouri	967,037	43.53
34	Montana	329,972	23.60
35	Nebraska	795,318	46.10

*Compiled from the latest reports of the United States Department of Agriculture.

†Data for Alaska and Hawaii included in totals for United States, but not in those for five geographical divisions.

	States and Territories.	Total Number.	Avg. Value.
36	Nevada	80,295	$15.85
37	New Hampshire	54,866	70.00
38	New Jersey	94,024	80.64
39	New Mexico	131,153	16.93
40	New York	628,438	76.34
41	North Carolina	159,153	55.27
42	North Dakota	359,948	63.14
43	Ohio	878,205	57.12
44	Oklahoma	303,631	34.96
45	Oregon	287,932	30.05
46	Pennsylvania	590,981	69.29
47	Rhode Island	11,390	86.12
48	South Carolina	78,419	61.81
49	South Dakota	480,768	41.78
50	Tennessee	352,388	55.85
51	Texas	1,269,432	27.18
52	Utah	115,884	29.31
53	Vermont	85,531	62.19
54	Virginia	298,522	51.34
55	Washington	243,985	35.04
56	West Virginia	185,188	56.03
57	Wisconsin	555,756	61.75
58	Wyoming	135,543	23.79

APPENDIX III.

The common expression, "standard-bred," is so often applied to the horse that it is believed the following correspondence will be of much interest to all cavalrymen:

FORT RILEY, KANSAS, Nov. 15, 1902.
The Hon. F. D. Coburn, Secretary State Board of Agriculture, Topeka, Kansas:
MY DEAR SIR,—Will you please send me a clear definition of "standard-bred," as applied to the horse?
Very cordially, JNO. J. BONIFACE,
First Lieutenant, Fourth Cavalry.

KANSAS STATE BOARD OF AGRICULTURE,
TOPEKA, KANSAS, Nov. 22, 1902.
First Lieutenant Jno. J. Boniface, Fourth Cavalry, Fort Riley, Kansas:
MY DEAR SIR,—Here are two definitions of a "standard-bred" horse by as competent authorities as there are.
Yours, F. D. COBURN.

KANSAS STATE BOARD OF AGRICULTURE,
TOPEKA, KANSAS, Nov. 22, 1902.
Hon. F. D. Coburn, Secretary Kansas State Board of Agriculture, Topeka, Kansas:
MY DEAR SIR,—The term "standard-bred," as applied to the horse tribe, technically applies only to trotting- and pacing-bred families.

Primarily, performance at the trot or pace, 2.30 trotting or 2.25 pacing, either by the animal itself or by its immediate progeny, constituted an introduction to the class, and after that all descendants from matings with a certain number of trotting or pacing crosses were entitled to standard rank. Earlier, a single registered cross on

535

each side was all the rules required; now the requirement is advanced :ill the fourth cross is exacted.

Registration in the books of the American Trotting Register Association, under the rules in force at the time of application for registration, is an essential condition to being accredited as standard.

There are now two departments of the Register—trotting and pacing, each with distinctive rules determining qnalification. There are two classes recorded in the books: the class admitted as "standard," embracing animals meeting all the requirements; and the "non-standard" class, including animals with one or more standard blood-crosses, but not sufficient to entitle to standard rank. These latter become standard when the fourth cross is reached.

The rules, as adopted by the Association, at present in force, are as given in the form of application herewith enclosed.

Yours truly, J. W. THOMPSON, D. D.
("*Winfield James.*")

OFFICE OF THE
AMERICAN TROTTING REGISTER ASSOCIATION,
355 Dearborn St., Ellsworth Building,
CHICAGO, ILL.

APPLICATION FOR REGISTRATION.

Sex........ Under what rule eligible...... Name............
Color......foaled......day of....,1... Record, if any.........
Where and when made ...... Marks...... Bred by.........
P. O. and State...... Name of sire............Reg. No.......
Son of...... Certificate of owner of sire at time dam was bred must be furnished. Name of dam......Reg. Vol......Page......
When registered dam is reached, give page and volume. Bred by ......P. O. and State...... Furnish a certificate from breeder of unregistered dam. Got by......Reg. No......Son of..........
Name of second dam.....Reg. Vol......Page...... Information about names of dams must be positive. Bred by......P. O. and State......Got by......Reg. No.....Son of...... Name of third dam......Reg. Vol......Page...... Attach list of produce of all mares sent for entry, if possible, on separate sheet. Bred by......P. O. and State...... Got by......Reg. No......Son of...... Name of fourth dam......Reg Vol......Page......

If dam is thoroughbred, give volume and page in Bruce's American Stud Book where recorded. ·Bred by......P. O. and State......
Got by...... Succeeding dam and sires.....................
Give address of all successive owners.........................
.Present owner......P. O. address..............

I hereby certify that the foregoing pedigree is correct.
Signature of breeder or legal representatives or reason for not giving it ....
Signature of Applicant.................
P. O. address................Dated.....................

THE TROTTING STANDARD.

When an animal meets these requiremements and is duly registered, it shall be accepted as a standard-bred trotter:

1—The progeny of a registered standard trotting horse and a registered standard trotting mare.

2—A stallion sired by a registered standard trotting horse, provided his dam and grandam were sired by registered standard trotting horses, and he himself has a trotting record of 2.30 and is the sire of three trotters with records of 2.30, from different mares.

3—A mare whose sire is a registered standard trotting horse, and whose dam and grandam were sired by registered standard trotting horses, provided she herself has a trotting record of 2.30 or is the dam of one trotter with a record of 2.30.

4—A mare sired by a registered standard trotting horse, provided she is the dam of two trotters with records of 2.30.

5—A mare sired by a registered standard trotting horse, provided her first, second, and third dams are each sired by a registered standard trotting horse.

THE PACING STANDARD.

When an animal meets these requirements and is duly registered, it shall be accepted as a standard-bred pacer:

1—The progeny of a registered standard pacing horse and a registered standard pacing mare.

2—A stallion sired by a registered standard pacing horse, provided his dam and grandam were sired by registered standard pacing horses, and he himself has a pacing record of 2.25 and is the sire of three pacers with records of 2.25, from different mares.

3—A mare whose sire is a registered standard pacing horse and whose dam and grandam were sired by registered standard pacing horses, provided she herself has a pacing record of 2.25, or is the dam of one pacer with a record of 2.25.

4—A mare sired by a registered standard pacing horse, provided she is the dam of two pacers with records of 2.25.

5—A mare sired by a registered standard pacing horse, provided her first, second, and third dams are each sired by a registered standard pacing horse.

6—The progeny of a registered standard trotting horse out of a registered standard pacing mare, or of a registered standard pacing horse out of a registered standard trotting mare.

RIVERSIDE STOCK FARM,
TOPEKA, KANSAS, Nov. 26, 1902.

Hon. F. D. Coburn, Secretary State Board of Agriculture, Topeka, Kansas:

DEAR SIR,—Another absence has delayed the answer to your request for my understanding of the words *standard-bred*. This term is only (or should be) applied to *gaited horses*, either trotters or pacers, that are bred in lines that conform to the arbitrary rules laid down by the American Trotting Register Association, and when, by *breeding* or *performance*, or both, they fill the requirements of *either of these rules*, they are "standard-bred" and entitled to registry, though a horse does not have to be registered to be a standard-bred trotter or a standard-bred pacer. The enclosed are the rules referred to, which, I trust, will fully explain.* In horse lore, the words *standard-bred* and *thorough-bred* are often confounded; the latter word applies only to *running* horses, while the former, as above, to *gaited* horses.

Truly yours,   O. P. UPDEGRAFF.

---

*These rules are the same as those previously given.—J. J. B.

www.ingramcontent.com/pod-product-compliance
Lightning Source LLC
Chambersburg PA
CBHW031558110426
42742CB00036B/106